# HISTORY OF WORLD ARCHITECTURE

Pier Luigi Nervi, *General Editor*

# PRIMITIVE ARCHITECTURE

*Enrico Guidoni*

*Translated by Robert Erich Wolf*

*Harry N. Abrams, Inc., Publishers, New York*

Series Coordinator: Giuseppe Positano de Vincentiis

*Produced under the supervision of Carlo Pirovano,
editorial director of Electa Editrice*

*Design: Diego Birelli, art director of Electa Editrice*
*Drawings: Studio of Enzo Di Grazia*

Editor: Ellyn Childs Allison

Library of Congress Cataloging in Publication Data

Guidoni, Enrico, 1939–
   Primitive architecture.

   (History of world architecture series)
   Translation of Architettura primitiva.
   Bibliography: p.
   Includes index.
   1. Architecture, Primitive.   I. Title.
NA205.G8513        720'.9        77-21788
ISBN 0-8109-1026-8

Library of Congress Catalogue Card Number: 77-21788
International Standard Book Number: 0-8109-1026-8
Copyright © 1975 in Italy by Electa Editrice, Milan
Published in 1978 by Harry N. Abrams, Incorporated, New York
All rights reserved. No part of the contents of this book may be
reproduced without the written permission of the publishers
Printed and bound in Japan

*Architectural criticism has nearly always been concerned with the visible aspect of individual buildings, taking this to be the decisive factor in the formulation of value judgments and in the classification of those "styles" which appear in textbooks, and which have thus become common knowledge. But once it is recognized that every building is, by definition, a work subject to the limitations imposed by the materials and building techniques at hand, and that every building must prove its stability, as well as its capacity to endure and serve the needs it was built for, it becomes clear that the aesthetic aspect alone is inadequate when we come to appraise a creative activity, difficult enough to judge in the past, rapidly becoming more complex in our own day, and destined to become more so in the foreseeable future.*

*Nevertheless, what has struck me most, on studying the architecture of the past and present, is the fact that the works which are generally regarded by the critics and the general public as examples of pure beauty are also the fruit of exemplary building techniques, once one has taken into account the quality of the materials and the technical knowledge available. And it is natural to suspect that such a coincidence is not entirely casual.*

*Building in the past was wholly a matter of following static intuitions, which were, in turn, the result of meditation, experience, and above all of an understanding of the capacity of certain structures and materials to resist external forces. Meditation upon structural patterns and the characteristics of various materials, together with the appraisal of one's own experiences and those of others, is an act of love toward the process of construction for its own sake, both on the part of the architect and his collaborators and assistants. Indeed, we may wonder whether this is not the hidden bond which unites the appearance and substance of the finest buildings of the past, distant though that past may be, into a single "thing of beauty."*

*One might even think that the quality of the materials available not only determined architectural patterns but also the decorative detail with which the first simple construction was gradually enriched.*

*One might find a justification for the difference in refinement and elegance between Greek architecture, with its basic use of marble—a highly resistant material, upon which the most delicate carvings can be carried out—and the majestic concrete structures of Roman architecture, built out of a mixture of lime and pozzolana, and supported by massive walls, to compensate for their intrinsic weaknesses.*

*Would it be too rash to connect these objective architectural characteristics with the different artistic sensibilities of the two peoples?*

*One must recognize, therefore, the importance of completing the description of the examples illustrated with an interpretation of their constructional and aesthetic characteristics, so that the connection between the twin aspects of building emerges as a natural, logical consequence.*

*This consequence, if understood and accepted in good faith by certain avant-garde circles, could put an end to the disastrous haste with which our architecture is rushing toward an empty, costly, and at times impractical formalism. It might also recall architects and men of culture to a more serene appraisal of the objective elements of building and to the respect that is due to a morality of architecture. For this is just as important for the future of our cities as is morality, understood as a rule of life, for an orderly civil existence.*

PIER LUIGI NERVI

# TABLE OF CONTENTS

There is no real precedent for this book, whose subject is primitive architecture considered as a global phenomenon. Since the field itself awaits coherent scientific codification, a book about it can neither pretend nor even aim to sum up everything known, described, and interpreted that has a bearing on the architecture of the populations that are the traditional concern of ethnology. What such a book as this can do is offer a selection of materials that cast light on the role of architecture in societies that, almost until the present day, have remained outside the large, highly organized political entities into which the modern world is organized. For this reason, we have drawn examples from about two hundred architectural traditions within specific geographical regions and presented them not as piecemeal data but in a synthesis both technical and descriptive in character. The book should not—cannot—be read without constantly referring to the wealth of photographs and diagrams, which are an integral part of the documentation and form a basis for the conclusions drawn. The books recommended in the bibliography should also be closely consulted. In short, what you are about to read is a pioneering exploration of a body of knowledge that, it is hoped, will expand greatly in years to come as regards both theory and fact.

Publisher and author are both aware that this book introduces a very new subject into the domain of the history of architecture which has so far been treated at length only by specialists in another discipline, who have only relatively recently begun to realize that architecture plays a central role in the economic, social, and cultural life of populations we think of as primitive.

The fact that there has as yet been no systematic analysis of this vast body of material by no means exempts us from dealing with current methodologies, tentative approaches, and also fundamental conclusions arrived at in certain specific sectors. On the contrary, it obliges us to clarify our own particular positions and to select the terminology that, in our judgment, best defines the field of primitive architecture and distinguishes it from that of popular architecture, while establishing a basis for those critical approaches most serviceable in tracing historical changes and reciprocal influences between different sociocultural units and complexes.

The story of the discovery by modern artists and architects of "exotic" and "savage" architecture and its influence on their work has often been told.[1] They justifiably admired its solutions to problems posed by climate and available material and the originality and thrift of its formal solutions; but, however sincere their praise of the architecture they lauded as ingenuous, sincere, and genuinely responsive to the needs of society,[2] their understanding of it has been superficial and exterior (that of an outsider looking in) and, moreover,

frankly simplistic as regards products and systems of relationships that certainly must be thought of in the context of a specific history and economy. Too much attention has been given to collecting geographical and historical examples that have nothing in common except, to some extent, their forms. When one is trying to comprehend the function of architecture within the social system, this is somewhat less than helpful: Architecture is never a literal translation of whatever it is we mean by "society," nor do partial analogies justify assuming a common significance for buildings belonging to different historical contexts.

The positivist school mapped out the worldwide distribution of the basic forms of dwelling in order to demonstrate how types of construction become localized in accordance with climate, natural resources, availability of materials, and the like. This proved enlightening. Profounder analysis, however, must reckon with cultural currents, social and economic structures, and ritual and mythic complexes. At this level it becomes quite clear that the influence of environment on architecture tends to be more negative—preventing, for example, the use of certain materials and types of building—than positive. It is despite, not because of, environmental limitations that architecture develops and becomes differentiated as an aspect of social life. While architecture reflects the environment, on the whole it tends to be only minimally affected by its restrictions.[3] This is so because architecture is, in fact, more a historical than a geographical product, the outcome of a multitude of cultural factors acting diachronically and in reciprocal relationship. On the other hand, the fact that particular types of buildings exist at the same time in very different places almost never reveals any important information that can be used in explaining differentiations within a given area. What is more, that same fact has been used to prove (for reasons that are not always clear) the somewhat doubtful necessity of those types.

One must always keep in mind the rapid mutation in typologies, materials, and, often, inherent meanings that architecture has undergone in recent centuries (and particularly in recent decades) wherever there has been extensive contact between primitive communities and Western colonizers. Myths, community organization, and language are all somewhat change-resistant, but architecture has often proved highly sensitive. With the first pressures, important materials and building techniques brought in from outside are promptly adopted. Indeed, an architectural tradition seems to be modified even more hastily than the sociocultural context in which it exists. There are two possible explanations as to why architecture should be the Achilles' heel of primitive societies: Either primitive architecture is not defined exclusively by constructed material objects but also reflects a specific attitude toward physical space and its transformation and interpretation; or else it is a marginal activity (an aspect of what used to be subsumed under the heading of "material culture," as distinguished from "true culture," the immaterial system of myths, language, religion, and social regulations), and thus subject to all of the climatic, technological, or political accidents that affect a population.

Architecture, we claim, is more than the totality of the transformations man effects on his physical environment. Broad as that definition is, it fails to consider a crucial point: With regard to the constructed object, its use, and its significance in relation to all the societies in contact with it, every culture—every class—furnishes its own *interpretation*, attitude, associations, and explanations of why it is what it is. Such interpretations are not merely *a posteriori*. They reflect a complex of attitudes toward architecture, which, as values only partially put into use, each culture develops for its own particular social and economic needs. These attitudes permit the rapid assimilation and transformation of architectural types and materials without necessarily implying a total mutation in the social context. On the contrary, the social context often reinforces itself in its traditional structures precisely by means of a "new" architecture.[4]

In every social context, architecture, therefore, plays a relative role, one that changes during the course of history. To consider it as an aspect of technology without regard to its relationship with all the problems that are bound up with it produces only a sketch of the history of building materials and of types of buildings and their local variants.[5] Nowadays, however, it is firmly accepted that the architecture of a particular historical and cultural complex comprises a variety of diverse solutions that derive from the specific historical relationships of the group; but within the group, these solutions are meaningful only in relation to the totality of the system.

Two things must be understood to be inseparable: the architecture of the dwelling, and the architecture of the territory. For both of these, we reject the overly simplistic, purely technological approach that results in overvaluing the "material" factors (particularly the "resources") in primitive societies, and reinforcing them with an idealistic dialectic of man-nature. Architecture seems, rather, to play a fundamental role as political and social instrument. From this viewpoint, architecture—and primitive architecture in particular—to be historically comprehensible must be considered in relation to the whole gamut of activities having to do with the comprehension and transformation of space and their interpretation *within* the society in question; it must also be considered in relation to other kinds of activity: economic, ritual, and so forth. The contradiction between physical, architectonic, and material structure and cultural and interpretative superstructure, then, becomes a matter internal to the society, revealing itself as a contradiction between the real organization of space and construction and the system of interpretation inherent in it. In short, the foundation of architecture is physical space; its various cultural relationships predominate over such concrete factors as form, dimensions, material, and technical solutions.

Figuring more or less implicitly in a great many anthropological studies, primitive architecture has yet to be considered a subject in its own right, with its own explicit terrain, problems of methodology, and avenues for further work. Nor is it clear whether the history of the architecture of individual ethnic and cultural groups will continue to be looked on as unique. Much will depend on whether we can resolve, in historical terms, the problems that recurrently arise from the indisputable fact that phenomena within vast geographical and cultural areas are undoubtedly comparable. Here, the concept of ethnocentrism, generally used to explain the limited point of view of the Western anthropologist faced with cultures unlike his own,[6] becomes to some extent—insofar as it recognizes the relativity of all cultural viewpoints—a positive one. Since every society not totally subjugated by another does, in fact, tend to consider itself as the center of the world, its architecture must be considered as an internal matter, viewed as if from within and as a product of the whole.

There still persist a great many ambiguities in the field due not only to marked differences in the background and training of the specialists in this subject but also to contrasting methodologies and disparate areas of investigation. In the absence of general discussion of the sort that primitive art, for example, has enjoyed for decades,[7] too much of what is being written fails to reach all those concerned, and therefore contributes little to establishing an overall view of the essential problems in the study of primitive architecture. For this reason, it seems worthwhile to compare three contributions published about the same time, in 1968 and 1969, but which are independent of each other and represent very different viewpoints. These are the brief but dense work by Fraser entitled *Village Planning in the Primitive World*, the volume of studies edited by Oliver published under the title *Shelter and Society*, and the methodological investigation by Rapoport *House Form and Culture*.[8]

Fraser states that his method is structural-functional. He refuses to draw general historical conclusions and makes use of a certain number of examples that, he says, extend from the simplest to the most complex. Furthermore, he limits himself to defining such elementary spatial concepts as centrality, linearity, and orientation, and lists a series of factors—military, religious, and political—useful in explaining the plan of so-called primitive settlements. He maintains that the predominance of social relationships over spatial order is the determining factor, separating, in fact, two terms that are of uncertain definition, as neither can be considered by itself alone. Rightly, we think, he rejects the formalistic approach, avoiding any in-depth exploration of the historical reasons for the analogies that patently exist, without sacrificing the notion of cultural and social unity. While his individual analyses are interesting and are in part based on material made public for the first time (some of which we have used here because it makes particularly clear the links between society and settlement), certain features of the book do seem unacceptable: the casual order in which the examples are presented, which makes the book seem only a haphazard collection, the omission of structures having "informal" or nongeometrical plans, and finally the postulate that a correspondence exists between the level of economic development and the complexity of the architectural schemas. Despite these defects, the choice of regions considered (including the African cities of the Yoruba area), the important place allotted to ground plans, and the treatment by ethnic units appear to be by and large correct; the author rightly confines his discussion within precise limits beyond which, to our mind, one cannot go in studying primitive architecture. It is also true that most of these features of Fraser's study also characterized Forde's *Habitat, Economy and Society* (1934), an extremely effective global treatment. In our opinion, Fraser accords too little space to the ways in which primitive men view and explain the territory they inhabit, a subject certainly deserving of more attention in a work devoted to village planning. It is only fair to say, however, that his theme, the village as such, may not have permitted an approach that could be valid as regards both the territory and architecture.[9]

The argument of Paul Oliver's preface to *Shelter and Society* is based on the supposition (characteristic of scholars involved in teaching architecture) that there is significant similarity in approach between primitive architecture, present-day "popular" architecture, and what can be called "vernacular" architecture. He rejects the formalism of scholars like Rudolfsky but groups together, under his favorite term, "vernacular" (that is, provincial and belonging to a specific locality within a geographical area), a series of examples that are so various—the Peruvian *barriada*, the walled city of old Delhi, the experimental "drop city"—as to deny any pretense at methodology. While Oliver's concern is still with architecture (though only as a minor factor), his approach is unhappily based on geographical environments rather than on specific historical complexes. The various studies making up the volume are conceived as different aspects of one and the same problem, namely, the architectural response to a given environment (even when, as in the paper by Rapoport,[10] the aim is to show the diversity of responses to a diversity of cultures). In point of fact, these studies subordinate historical-social factors to ecological-formal ones.

Nor does the book by Rapoport *House Form and Culture* escape this underlying ambiguity, oscillating between a scientific anthropological approach and one that may be described as a pulverization—an atomizing—of the system we think of as architecture-society. Rapoport is concerned with demonstrating that architecture is determined above all by sociocultural factors (a thesis accepted by every ethnologist because of the very object of his study: man within a specific social complex). By way of evidence, he offers a body of examples that, he maintains, includes almost everything built by man since he first started to build[11] and that remains generalized so that the text will not flounder about in details. Interpretations based on single factors (climate, materials, defence, economy, religion, and so on) Rapoport judges incomplete and lumps all together under the term "physical determinism." On the other hand, he does consider climate, construction, materials, and techniques as "modifying factors" of the "sociocultural factors" that he takes as fundamental.

Such an approach, even when supported by a meticulous system of classification (indeed, perhaps percisely because it is), inevitably affirms an interchangeability between very different architectural traditions by stressing the existence of general common factors or of concomitant factors in individual solutions while ignoring the relationship of architecture to territory and of primitive architecture to popular and cultivated or civilized architecture. As a result, such concepts as habitation, space, and typology seem to have no connection with each other, and, indeed, *do not*, insofar as they are dealt with as isolated from the totality of the society (or the people) whose architecture one is attempting to analyse.

Such difficulties can only be overcome by an extension, not of the concept of "primitive," but of the field implied in the term "architecture." Thus, one must consider the territory, the settlement, and the habitation as inseparable and must refuse to think of isolated technical solutions as results of environmental pressures defined *a priori* as independent. With such a broad approach, one expresses the whole as well as the specific significance of primitive architecture, defined not only by what is built but also by the interpretations—and therefore also by the intentions—of those who build and use it.[12] In an encyclopedia article on this subject[13] (which also made schematic reference to the constructional typologies, derived in the main from the syntheses of Lanternari[14]) we proposed that the point of departure should always be the prearchitectural state, the ineluctable

10

*The Compact Dwelling with Flat Roof (plates 1–9)*
1–4. *Laying a roof with palm stalks, matting, and a protective coat of mud and straw, Baluchistan (Pakistan).*

5. *Cochiti pueblo, New Mexico (USA).*

6. *Village, Magar (Nepal).*
7. *Village in the vicinity of Bojnord (Iran).*

8. *Berber village (Algeria).*
9. *Berber town, Warzazate (Morocco).*

*The Hut: Roof and Wall (plates 10–15)*
10. *Somono: hut (Niger).*
11. *Mosque, Mamu (Guinea).*

basis for any constructional activity. By bringing into the purview of architecture the problems connected with spatial conceptions and social functions, we underscore the architectonic quality of every active interpretation of the physical environment, the significance of spatial models as mediation between social structure and constructional typology, and the symbolism underlying architectural organization, which belongs to the historical-mythical patrimony of a people. The basis of the articulation of space is thus fixed in the elementary realities of the point and the line, which have the specific values of stasis and of movement that are inherent in the territory. As we put it in that article, "The spatial sign is never apart from a strong semantic charge that has to do with the link between the prevalent myths (therefore essentially historical) and natural reality . . . whose spatial interpretation is a valid instrument for establishing order at the level of architecture as inserted into the environment and at the level of the cosmological referent."[15] The role of architecture in society is thus defined inasmuch as it decisively maintains the existing social order. Our brief articles on various populations and cultural areas in that same encyclopedia suggested that the study of primitive architecture should be oriented toward specific historical and ethnic facts.

Especially since the 1960s, numerous anthropologists in their field research in various corners of the world have been making important contributions to the field of architecture, directly or indirectly. The widespread use of archaeological evidence and techniques is casting increasing light on historical connections and chronology. At the same time, a broader and more open-minded interest in social and economic matters and in political and other kinds of power system is enabling us to test and extend the theories put forward by the proponents of Structuralism.[16] A considerable number of monographs have supplied us with detailed data concerning the territorial organization, architectural aspects of the settlements, the technologies, and the art of populations not very well known previously. Unfortunately, however, given the rapid changes in research methodologies and the very different approaches of the various schools, it is simply not possible here to offer any sort of summary of those contributions. Nevertheless, we must consider, however briefly, certain studies made in Africa by a group of French investigators that, to our mind, will prove fundamental for future developments in our discipline.

West Africa and the southern Sahara still offer a very fertile field for investigation because of the genuinely primitive—that is, segmentary—societies and the types of governmental system (city-states and confederations of cities) that still exist there. Within the context

12. *Rebuilding a conical roof (Guinea).*
13. *Gamò: hut (Ethiopia).*

14. *Chipayas: roof laid over interlocked arches (Bolivia).*
15. *Frame of a vaulted roof made of interlocked arches of mud-coated wood, Tahwa (Niger).*

of every problem, the reciprocal counterinfluences between dissimilar economic and political systems help to define an extremely wide and varied gamut of situations and, at the same time, throw light on their archaeological and historical solutions. They have a particular pertinence to our theme because of the internal correlation between the various spheres of power, on the one hand, and between the types of settlement and architectural tradition, on the other. The characteristics of these primitive populations—the systems of myth and symbolism, the subdivision into classes by age, the dwelling unit based on the extended family group, and so on—have, to some extent, preserved their fundamental function throughout the course of history, even in the areas most intensely influenced by Islam. But even though such alien decorative elements as arabesques and such nonnative building types as the mosque and the urban merchant's house have been assimilated there, we cannot consider the urban architecture and way of life as a whole to be the product of importation, as are the economic and political systems; we must understand them as a compromise in which animistic religion, with all that it entails, still clearly predominates over the Islamic component.[17]

For this reason, these studies dealing with the significance and techniques of architecture in segmentary societies have proved of basic validity; they also shed considerable light on the interpretation of the stratified societies of the city-states, inasmuch as the intrusive Islamic culture not only adapted to its own purposes the economic and political nexus already existing there but also often respected the cultural superstructure as well.

The study by J.-P. Lebeuf on the Fali of the northern Cameroons is, to our mind, an unsurpassed model for the analysis of the architecture of a single segmentary population.[18] A quantity of data accumulated, sifted through, and put into systematic order culminated in a significant qualitative leap forward with respect to previous research. While some may find Lebeuf's structuralistic symmetries with regard to mythology and cosmogony somewhat excessive, his analysis offers a degree of detail that opens up perspectives for research not as yet adequately envisaged by others, precisely because it is restricted to a scientifically delimited theme. Here, for the first time, the objective evidence regarding spatial factors and materials decisively guides an investigation into architecture—with a meticulousness usually found only in linguistic literary research. In subsequent studies the focus shifted to the foundation rituals, social organization, and history of the numerous kingdoms that arose in the southern Sahara during the past thousand years. Although their viewpoints differ, V. Pâques, A. Masson-Detourbet Lebeuf, and a few others[19] have succeeded in broadening the semantic aspect of architecture—under-

stood by them as a physical and at the same time symbolic relationship between the facts of reality, myth, and history—precisely because their interest is not specifically in technical and constructional matters but in the relationship between power and what can be called the arts of space. In their studies, as in the seminal one by J.-P. Lebeuf on the Fali, it is significant that the boundary between the reality of the construction and the way it is "interpreted"—understood, explained, rationalized—by the primitive populations responsible for it is no longer an impassable one for investigators from the outside. Once the ideology is understood, it becomes possible to view the constructed product from *within* the society and, in that way, to go beyond ethnocentric classification. Such studies, with their increasing attention to economic and political aspects, can certainly provide the basis for future work in defining the historical role of architecture, in all its particulars, as a fundamental instrument of power and of the art of governing.

Finally, in the light of discussions as to whether it is feasible to apply the methodology of historical materialism to the study of primitive societies, thought is increasingly being given to the possibility of revising the basic concepts used in determining in what way primitive architecture may be, at one and the same time, the instrument and product of the modes and relations of production, of the economic structure, and of the inequality and exploitation present to some extent in most agricultural societies.[20] While more contributions to methodology and more data are needed, this point of view does offer a guiding principle that can be generally followed when questions about the connections between architecture and private ownership of land, architecture and the community (or group) involved in production, and architecture and social imbalances or stratifications are to be explored. In this context, as we have repeatedly had occasion to verify, it proves consistently possible to test the legitimacy of extending the field of primitive architecture to include its territorial and superstructural connotations.

If it is true that, in the abstract, the modes and relationships of production are able to introduce only socioeconomic parameters of a general nature (thereby encouraging the grouping of cultures into a few fundamental types), they lend themselves at the same time to defeating just that sort of generalization. First of all, they cannot be isolated except in broad outline within the cultural complex, and this means that any detailed analysis will disclose relationships with the essential aspects of the cultural superstructure, with the mythic and ritual system in the first place. What is more, since there is no such thing as a "pure" culture, one based entirely on a single method of production, the possibilities of reciprocal rapport and interference

17. *Farmhouse in castle form, Sunkarabu (Dahomey).*
18. *Ovens for smoking fish (Ivory Coast).*

*Granaries in Africa (plates 20–31)*
19. *Granary (Upper Volta).* ▷

between the various coexisting methods are not only indefinite but also favor as a parallel extremely various corresponding models of life and behavior, among them, naturally, architecture. Finally, inasmuch as the methods and relations of production are synonymous with the productive activity and the relationships between individuals and the group, they cannot be thought of as metahistorical entities. They are the conditions of the relationship, respectively, between group and territory and between individual and community; in both cases, the first term is related to the second as unit to totality.

From the theory that states that there are at least two modes of production in every culture, no matter how primitive, and that they coexist in a clearly defined relationship of interdependence, it follows logically that there exists a more or less conspicuous stratification that affects architecture as well. The dominant mode of production stamps all the other activities, which are kept alive precisely in order to reinforce the primacy of its role. In sedentary or semisedentary societies, there exists an effective line of demarcation between two or more ways of conceiving architecture, and these correspond to the different modes of production. While this observation demonstrates the meaninglessness of any purely linear interpretation of progress, it also takes into account the internal social inequalities, which, from the architectural point of view, among others, are the key to understanding the particular model of equilibrium that any society sets up for itself.

Architecture, in the broadest accepted sense of the term, acts, simultaneously, as product and instrument of social cohesion or, in other words, as spatial coordination and spatial conditioning even before construction as such. In-depth analysis of the nature of the relationship between architecture and society must take into account these two roles, which we maintain are fundamental and primary in that they clarify the historical aspect of architectural activity.[21]

For nomadic societies, architecture is essentially organization of the territory, of the land about which they move. This implies that construction as such plays a secondary role as social activity; that is, as product and instrument of relationships. By definition, nomadic societies have as their economic basis their wealth in portable possessions (utensils, luxury articles, livestock). Since there is no private ownership of the land, and since the group must be able to move about rapidly, the dwelling is, at the very most, the largest and most valuable item among their household goods, and is of value to the extent that it is prefabricated, lightweight, and easy to set up and dismantle. This is true specifically of nomadic stockbreeders. The dwellings of gatherers and hunters are built as needed, utilized, and then abandoned, so they can be said to form part of the natural territory, the

20. *Small huts and granaries, Ubangi-Shari (Central African Republic). (Engraving by Schweinfurth, 1874.)*

21. *Nyangatom: granaries for millet (Ethiopia).*

22. *Dogon: granaries of banco (shaped, beaten clay), Lower Ogol (Mali).*

23. *Granaries and poultry coop (Upper Volta).*

24. *Gurunsi: granary for sorghum and millet (Upper Volta).* ▷

29. *Granary for millet, Lebu (Senegal).*
30. *Fulakonda: granaries for millet and rice (Guinea).*
31. *Millet granary set up on a platform (Guinea).*

environment. In any case, unlike the chief economic activity (whether hunting, gathering, or stockbreeding), building such dwellings never requires the services of productive communities larger than the immediate family nucleus itself. This means that the construction is not an image of the society but of the family. Only the way such dwellings are disposed with relation to others within the campsite in any manner reflects the relations between families, whether they are of association or of consanguinity.

What can be done by an individual or by a limited family nucleus never requires more than minimal social coordination, nor is it susceptible to development. Obviously, it has its place within the cultural complex, but by no means does it constitute a conditioning element. The contrary is true of the territory. Not only do cooperation and conflicts develop within the territory between the family nuclei belonging to a clan or tribe, but there, too, the struggle between different groups for possession, control, and exploitation of the natural resources (wildlife, fruit-bearing plants, grazing land) has as background and basis a very precise architecture of the terrain and its landmarks, which acquire vitality, so to speak, insofar as they constitute boundaries, ways of access, mythical cult places, and sanctuaries. While all populations that do not develop complex constructions requiring the work of a more or less expanded community of production strike one as "poor" from the standpoint of architecture, this characterization ignores the fact that it is the territory itself that acts as architecture—as construction, utilizable object, instrument of social order—and that it is on the territory that the community concentrates its interpretative activities, attributing to the physical environment significances that other, more advanced, cultures reserve for their buildings.

A territory takes on definite structure only when it supports a historically and geographically determined group. As a consequence of the exigencies of gathering and hunting, the rights of groups or individuals tend to become localized in specific places—sometimes even in particular plants. The same exigencies are responsible for forging an economic (and thus also mythic and ritual) link between group or individual and place. While the relationship between nature and society is continuous, when man begins to interpret his territory, he also, in reality, commences on a schematization in terms of social relationships of something which is inherently formless. On a different level, one can say that the relationships of kinship in themselves express the requirements of an orderly, well-balanced economic activity involving groups and individuals. But as soon as it becomes necessary to translate those relationships into spatial terms—because the occupied place cannot be permitted to contradict the social

23

order, and vice versa—they, too, take their place within physical space and play a part in the complex field of architecture. Although from the standpoint of material production the architecture of nomad populations cannot go beyond precise technological limits, in terms of the general system architecture is already a complete social instrument in that the spatial configuration and the connotations of the landscape make it possible to distinguish, within a given historical context, one group from other conterminous groups. The complex body of mythology further underscores that difference by semanticizing—giving meaning to, interpreting—the elements of the landscape. Thus, however ephemeral a form it may take, architecture has its own place in the service of existing social institutions because it has the function of clarifying and maintaining the relationships between the group and the territory.

The architecture cannot be considered apart from the territory of those populations whose chief mode of production is hunting or gathering; for stockbreeding nomads the portable house is the most important of their utensils and the container of all their personal goods. When, however, agriculture is the predominant activity, the crucial factor becomes ownership of the land, and this exercises a very definite influence on the construction of buildings, whether collective or familial. The territory becomes divided into two parts: primeval nature and cultivated fields. The latter constitute the economic, juridical, and symbolic base for the development of the house, the village, and what we can call an artificial, manmade, world, one that is stable and capable of maintaining a particular socioeconomic state. No longer restricted by the requirements of a nomadic life, dwelling and community houses can develop in forms that become more complex and more durable the more the two determining factors—ownership of the land and social stratification—are emphasized. Construction itself becomes an institution.

The mode of production, therefore, influences architecture indirectly, through its effect on the interpretation of the ownership of land and on the development of hierarchy within the society. Thus, we find societies in which the prevailing mode of production is fishing but where the existence of an abundant surplus and the almost complete permanence of the sites occupied by the community are combined with a marked predominance of family ownership of land as opposed to ownership by the tribe or clan; such a situation favors a development of craft and building activities entirely comparable to that found in strictly agricultural societies. What encourages the parallel growth of private property and social inequalities is, basically, competition. If the restraining mechanisms of family power can no longer control the tendency to internal imbalances, then one finds

an "architecture of class" more or less clearly superimposed on an architecture that, in comparison, can be called "popular."

For preagricultural societies we are still far from being able to make even the broadest sort of scientific reconstruction of the interweaving of cultural influence and historical movements that has taken place over vast geographical areas. Even the recent history of individual peoples can be reconstructed only approximately, and then chiefly on the basis of oral tradition and of specific material elements whose diffusion in time and space has to some extent been traced. But even within quite restricted areas the cultural currents are so varied and complex that many of the fundamental relationships between peoples, whether in adjacent territories or not, cannot be easily clarified. This is true of their architecture as well. It is obvious that we simply cannot do without architectural histories, but it is equally obvious that this demand is not likely to be satisfied within a foreseeable time. In the vast majority of cases, this means that we cannot document the derivation of a particular type of building or technique or symbolic conception from any specific cultural contact. However, it is rather less difficult to discern general links between the way the territory is exploited, the general plan of the settlement, and the types of constructions. Those links are commemorated in tradition, in a population's own historical and mythical rationalization of the evolution of the group and the social order, and are transmitted in cultural "models," which may vary greatly but can be broken down analytically into their constituent parts to reveal at least partial areas of mutual agreement.

Despite the claims of the Structuralists, such analogies cannot be explained solely as universal constants in human thought. They have much to do with the structural and superstructural complexity of the societies themselves, a complexity rooted in the historical events that have given rise to the interaction of easily distinguishable elements. Thus, through the connection between architecture and society even the most original local developments can be understood as accentuations of characteristics present in other cultural contexts, though to a different degree and in a different way.[22] For this reason, the essential terms are not only form and function but also *significance*, the instrumental role an element assumes in intensifying some particular characteristic of a society.

What is actually constructed is only a small part of the system of architectonic relationships elaborated by a society. The selection operated is at the same time reductive and decisive. The most convincing proof of this is the plurality of significances that an architectonic ensemble or detail can assume not only for different populations

*Assembly Sheds in African Villages (plates 32–34)*
*32. Senufo: assembly shed, Korhogo (Ivory Coast).*

but even within the same group.[23] Differing explanations often reflect different aspects of an overall relationship of architecture to society, a relationship to which any construction whatsoever can allude, though certainly without exhausting all of its possibilities. Often a superabundance of significations is due to different interpretations of the same spatial object on the part of different subgroups or different classes. Despite their differences, however, they all form part of the same way of thinking about architecture.

The spatial language of architecture involves the territorial organization, reciprocal relations of buildings to each other, dimensions, orientation, and function of the constructions; the artistic language of architecture is primarily concerned with applied decoration. These, of course, reflect the two extreme poles of a continuum of thought about architecture, which proposes answers to the problem of how the objects constructed by man should be disposed in space and how space must be filled with them. While the language of architecture changes with history, in primitive societies it does not seem to be independent (in its increasing complexity and refinement, techniques, and materials) of the larger mythical explanation of the society. In other words, as we have already pointed out, the active, important, constructional factor is always the social context while the building type and the decorative detail are materials, so to speak, utilizable only if one wishes to give some sort of statistical account of the evolution of the technologies involved.[24] This means that the language of architecture must be part of the language as a whole, at the risk of losing its historical meaning. The associations made between architecture, human body, and natural environment in all sorts of cultures guarantee that there will be meaning in the whole and the parts, and at the same time these parallels have a role in explaining why, in the course of history, certain things have been, say, changed—perhaps given increased emphasis. In this sense, when sculptured or painted decoration is applied to a building—an extension to the architectural scale of the artistic motifs already tried out and accepted on small household objects and the like—the aim is to endow the building with more *significance*, with an ulterior linguistic and explicative charge, so as to bring out to the fullest extent the connection with the mythological superstructure of the culture as a whole.

In primitive architecture there is little leeway for personal, gratuitous interpretation, for artistic significance in and for itself. Indeed, should one wish and be able to analyze in real depth the connections revealed in different interpretations, what would emerge would be the historically differentiated roots.[25]

Even if it cannot always be demonstrated, everything in primitive architecture has a meaning and a connection. Yet this does not mean

*34. A* khoss, *oasis of Siwa (western Egypt).*

*Thatched Buildings in India; Horns as Insignia of Rank (plates 35–38)*

*35. Toda: houses with a low front wall (Deccan).*

*36. Naga-Mao: thatch-roofed houses with the horn motif (Assam).*

that everything is comprised within a static system. The divergent significances, those that are not confined within an official interpretation, may be considered traces of an inheritance from the past, of an internal social discrepancy, or of a dynamic relationship with some other, different, group. The language of primitive architecture is, thus, essentially collective. Even when an individual or family expresses initiative, the result is meaningless unless understood by everyone; that is, if it cannot take its place as one more useful element in the larger context within which the culture is conscious of its own identity.

In point of fact, there is no architecture—in the broadest sense—without inviolable rules of construction and interpretation that are formed in the course of history for every people by means of a more or less complex convergence and superposition of elements. It is, in fact, the associations between diverse elements—their similitudes—that, within the field of collective and individual expression, permit us to glimpse an attitude that aims incessantly at an all-embracing explanation of the world.

While primitive architecture must respond to social necessities, it is also subject to symbolic and cosmic interpretation. Furthermore, it is the very core of the orderly relations established between the various parts of the physical environment and the social group as a whole. From the semantic standpoint, the principal channel between architecture and society is the connection with "history" and "science" experienced in the guise of myth. Constructional activity itself always reflects a divine model that must be imitated faithfully and belongs to that body of models invented once and for all time either by the spirits presiding over building or by the ancestors. Only this explains fully why we can speak of *architecture of the territory* even when the physical transformations of the environment and the dwellings erected in it are of no particular importance in themselves.

The myths explaining how man and the world had their origin give solidity and significance to the presence of a group in some particular area by providing them with a historical and existential justification for their own presence there, for their relationship with their neighbors and with the natural resources, for the relationships between their clans, and so forth. Everything in the life of the group, however, is conditioned by the need for an exact repetition of the events of original creation. While all this may appear to be exclusively mythic, in reality it is also practical needs—the need for food, the need to live together—that make necessary what we call the architecture of the territory: Paths, sources of water, favorable hunting grounds need to be defined so they can be used again and again, and in order to forestall intrusions by and conflicts with outsider groups. Under such

conditions, the myth acquires an eminently mnemonic value, serving not only to preserve in an exact formulation the rites of reconstruction of the world and of propitiation of the vital forces but also to keep fresh in mind the activities and tasks of each season and the skills needed in hunting, in finding one's way about the territory, and in carrying out everything to do with architecture and the transformation of the territory. The re-creation of the landscape through the mediation of the myth recapitulates an all-encompassing architectonic activity involving all the aspects of physical reality; in all the societies we can call primitive, it acts, to varying degrees, as a guarantee that the group can have some active control over a given territory. Every act, no matter how unimportant, therefore tends to take its place in a system, and every intervention involving transformation of the landscape must belong to a significant whole. Here again, we cannot accept the notion that the mythic models are to be understood as an ahistorical expression of mankind in general. On the contrary, they are complexes deriving from specific historical-cultural ensembles and have a function constantly subject to variation. They are the contexts to which the individual articulations and interpretations of architecture belong. The various stratifications of the mythic models reflect the general sequence from the territory (in hunting and gathering societies) to the constructed dwelling (in agricultural societies), though it should be kept in mind that within this spectrum there are no fixed compartments.

Elsewhere we have attempted to establish the salient points in the symbolic interpretation of architecture with respect to anthropomorphic and zoomorphic models and their social utilization.[26] The degree of symbolism investing territory, village, or dwelling depends not only on individual developments within the course of a general historical stratification (in gathering, hunting, or agricultural societies) but also on that specific intensification of themes, present also in other contexts, that constitutes the basis of the historical differentiation of the languages of architecture. In other words, if the essential elements—those that are simpler and more general—make up a complex that is widely diffused and survives as substratum for later developments, the specific interpretations associated with cultural currents that are more recent and thus more limited in scope reveal anything but uniform elaborations of a basic matrix that is increasingly utilized for specific ends within particular social relationships.

Hunters and gatherers tend to visualize the territory, or some part of it, as the image of the hero-creator or first ancestor, thereby assuring it some recognizable human meaning. Sometimes it is the cosmic creator who binds together sky and earth, and the parts of his body are identified with the salient features of the landscape—hills, rivers,

*Anthropomorphism (plates 39–44)*

39. A group of springs (small numbers 1–11) identified with the female being Mnaga (large numbers 1–9), oasis of Gafsa (Tunisia).
1. head; 2. chest; 3. belly; 4. right hand; 5. left hand; 6. right thigh; 7. left thigh; 8. right leg; 9. left leg.

40. Fali: territorial organization and the relationship between the four principal groups (Cameroon).
1. Bossum (arms); 2. Kangu (head); 3. Tingelin (trunk); 4. Bori-Peské (legs).

41. Fali: granary of the ma type (Cameroon).
1. head; 2. neck; 3. arms; 4. trunk; 5. feet.

42. Fali: central area of the domestic enclosure (Cameroon). The supporting posts are marked in black.
1. head (or sex organ); 2. back; 3. right arm; 4. left arm; 5. right thigh; 6. left thigh; 7. right leg (left leg not represented).

43. Dogon: organizational principle of society, with "joints" (1–8) and connecting "stones" (Mali).
1–4. the four primordial male ancestors (pelvis and shoulders); 5–8. the four primordial female ancestors (knees and elbows); 9. territorial order (head).

44. Dogon: ground plan of a family house (Mali).
1. kitchen (head); 2. main room (trunk); 3. larders (limbs); 4. vestibule (sex organ).

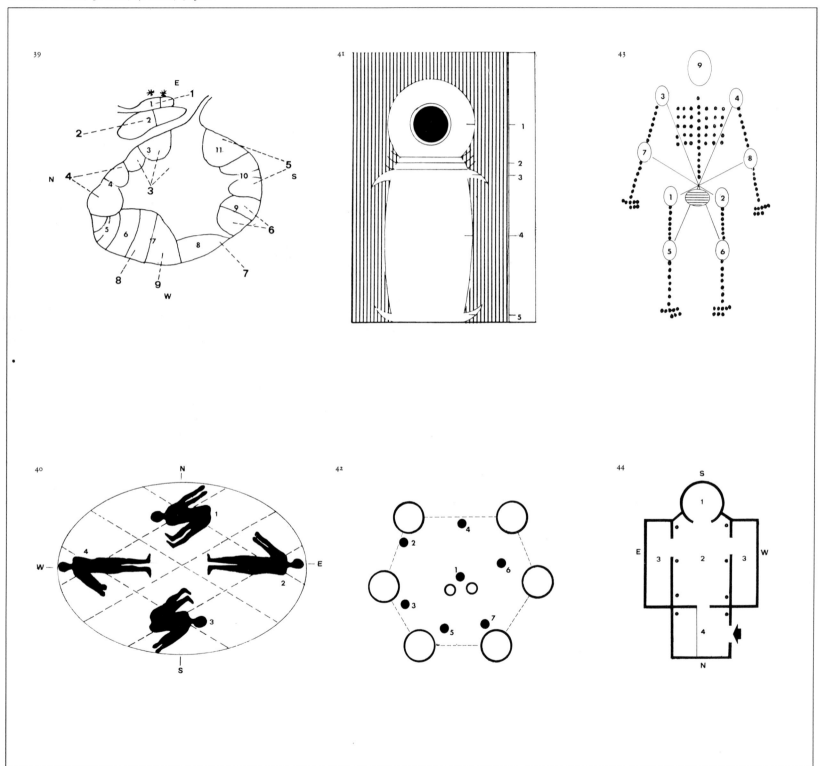

rocks, and so on—which then can be thought of by the primitive mind as interacting in a recognizable and reassuring human manner.

Such an anthropomorphic territory is architecture in the broadest sense: a symbolic construction effected by a tribe, group, or clan. In it, a social whole is represented in the guise and form of the body of the ancestor or culture hero. Thus, an archipelago is interpreted as the aggregate of the parts of the body of the primordial giant, so that an apparently casual relationship of contiguity is transformed into an organic unity believed to possess a high significance. Such conceptions survive in agricultural societies as cultural substrata and, in part, as eternally present economic and social models of the remote past, serving both to provide a harmonious explanation of the relationship between human space (cultivated, inhabited) and natural space and to correlate intimately, in symbolic terms, all the various structural components of whatever the society may build. Thus, the territory of a clan may be equated with the house of the clan (the "long house"), whose image is in turn often equated with that of a human body: an artificial manmade body, but, for that very reason, so much the more an image of the society and its environment.[27]

The family house, seat of the couple that produces children, may be divided into complementary male and female parts and be identified with the human figure or some zoomorphic model. It is the place where opposites come together, the place of complementary forces— sky and earth, man and woman, and so on. The hierarchy within society and the couple themselves is expressed through the preference given the element that coordinates and commands—the head—with respect to the other members, and this applies equally to the house, the plan of the village, and the organization of the territory. This symbolic hierarchy always reflects, and justifies, a real economic and policial hierarchy: The "head" is the head of the family, the house of the dominant line, the seat of whatever power is recognized and accepted. From this point of view, the anthropomorphic myth proves to be increasingly exploited to the benefit of the social order most likely to maintain the privileges acquired by a particular family or class; so true is this that, at the foundation of royal courts, the myth is taken over to explain the disposition of the dignitaries around the king.

But there are very numerous variants of the model. Inasmuch as it can always be specifically tailored, it is in no way an archetype. Individual parts of the body may be lacking or given special prominence in the figure that is employed to render architecture significant. The position of the body, the way it is subdivided, and other features may vary—so much so that, while the general interpretation remains

31

necessarily unchanged, there are in fact as many anthropomorphic and zoomorphic images as there are cultures.

Finally, the economic and political mainspring of these interpretations is to be sought in that figuration of authority as a person that is part of the process of attraction of the economic surplus to the centers of power and prestige. Whether in the form of "tribal being" (or the figure of the clan) or of despotic king, such an image becomes the symbol of the unity in whose name the major collective works are undertaken.

There are no clear and objective boundaries between those cultures (and architectures) that can be defined as "primitive"[28] and others characterized as "popular,"[29] and the problem has given rise to a great deal of debate because it touches on certain essential difficulties. The frequently used terms "primitive," "vernacular," and "popular" are by no means equivalent. "Primitive" refers to cultures and cultural products that are essentially different from ours and technologically less advanced than those of the Western countries and the great civilizations of the Orient. "Vernacular" is usually taken to comprise all architecture thought of as "uncultivated"—without a conscious style and unrelated to what we think of as "official" architecture—in its spectrum of regional variants. "Popular" is applied to the architecture of the lowest social classes within a highly stratified system.

It is clear that, according to the context, a given tradition can be more or less arbitrarily assigned to one or another of the categories. Passing over the term "vernacular" because of the loose, generalized sense in which it is normally used, we may profitably look further into the differences between "primitive" and "popular," if only to clarify the way in which the former is used in this book. Here, we must repeat what was said above—that what we consider as architecture comprises a body of operations and significances and is by no means restricted to things constructed. For this reason, primitive architecture can be defined as the expression of the spatial activities of a prestate society occupying a specific territory and preserving a high degree of economic and political independence with respect to the other societies with which it is in contact. By contrast, then, popular architecture would be the expression of the spatial activities of a group that occupies a territory in economic and political subordination to a dominant state complex or that exists within the limits of a system of unequal distribution of the means of production in a broader territory than its own.[30]

Not only have the majority of the elements that make up primitive architecture been historically assimilated into an original and relative-

48. *Figural decoration with warriors, Ubangi-Shari (Central African Republic).*
49. *Lunda: figural decoration with hunting scenes (Angola).*

ly self-sufficient context, but that context is perceptible in its integral significance (since it is, if not "reinvented," at least "relived" continually) without reference to external factors conditioning it. From a historical point of view, society and architecture are facts that are contemporaneous, and they are developed and undergo modification in immediate contact with each other. In popular architecture, on the contrary, what is expressed is the dependence of one society on another, in the sense that the society under consideration cannot be understood except as intermediary between a community that is semi-autonomous administratively and a center of political and cultural influence that often is located at a considerable distance from it. This is why one finds in popular architecture not only primitive types of constructions, often as yet unvaried technically, but also other types imported more or less arbitrarily, together with decorative details and techniques that are decidedly alien and exterior or that, at any rate, have been imposed by the particular relationship the culture has with the state dominating it.

This distinction can be sharpened further by taking into account the particular world view that a given group holds. There is, in fact, a clear correlation between the broad animistic program of belief and the architecture we call primitive. Popular architecture, on the other hand, thrives in that area of interface or overlapping between the animistic population and the much greater political and religious group to which it is subject. Because of this, we are not so much interested in discovering the supposedly authentic or supposedly ingenuous use of materials in popular architecture as in discovering a precise link between architecture and society that, however deformed, survives as a historical heritage from the primitive antecedents of that society. It should now be clear that, from the historical standpoint, popular architecture is situated in an area of contact between cultures that are better documented historically and others known only through external testimonies, oral tradition, and archaeological research. It is the result of the submission of one area politically and economically to a larger one, with consequent loss (or fixation in a state of latency) of the primitive characteristics genuinely native to it.

By not focusing on the outward aspects of the architecture but instead on the economic and political structure producing it, our definition has the advantage of eliminating the old ambiguity inherent in the term "primitivism," understood as applicable to an inferior cultural level, to a condition left behind by more advanced societies. Instead, we may view primitive society as existing in a historical situation, complex and self-sufficient, from which are virtually absent the most conspicuous phenomena of unification such as the territorial state, the art of writing, commercial and industrial development,

*50. Tshokive: village with decorated houses; the men's house (tshota) at the right. Annex to the Museo do Dundo, Luanda (Angola).*

and the city; or in which—even if certain of these features do exist—they are not experienced passively, as something imposed from outside, but as a relatively autonomous development of the primitive society itself.

Future research into primitive architecture can therefore expand by taking as its base two ineluctably indispensable guiding principles. One is adherence to a global historical perspective[31] that must weigh its means and arguments attentively so as not to fall back into deterministic or idealistic paths or lose sight of the unity of architecture and the social and political context. The other involves detailed and exhaustive analysis in the field, taking as evidence the architecture of each local group that can be said to hold a specific set of beliefs and a specific technology in common. Furthermore, this research must be carried through in the light of an extremely articulated conception of architecture that we have tried to clarify and to which we believe some contribution is made in the pages that follow. In choosing and presenting the most significant historical and cultural contexts we have aimed at focusing attention on the approaches we hold to be valid, methodologically, for all research in the subject, whether general or particular: the architecture of the territory, the relationship between ownership of the land and architecture, and ways in which tradition is used in its artistic and symbolic aspects by the group fostering its conservation and renewal.

The criteria reflected in the text, appendix, bibliography, and choice of illustrations call for a brief explanation. Because of the difficulty of treating together a wide range of cultures all presently at different stages of acculturation—some, in fact, no longer extant, some radically changed—all in constant flux, we have chosen to discuss them in the historical present tense, except in such cases where social change has a bearing on our argument or when a particular aspect of architectonic culture has an exclusively archaeological interest. As a matter of principle, we rejected the idea of either an approach by geographical area or region or a synthesis (obviously impossible in any case) of hundreds of histories of architecture, each pertaining to a specific culture or region, each potentially worthy of detailed and exhaustive study in itself. Even more decisive was our rejection of the over-used and abused typological method of classification, which, by its nature, cannot take into account either the internal complexity of every culture or its history.

The appendix should be read in close connection with the main body of the book. For the various populations discussed in the text or, in some cases, presented only through illustrations (certain others are included in the appendix to provide additional documentation), the brief descriptive articles offer a summary of geography, history, social and economic activities, and architectural forms and techniques. The articles are presented in broadly geographic sections according to the proximity of the various ethnic-linguistic groups to each other, and the material presented has been in part reworked from our articles in a specialized encyclopedia.

Understandably, the bibliography does not aim to be exhaustive. It concentrates on problems and fields we consider most relevant for future researchers: the connection between archaeological research and anthropological practice and between economy, society, habitat, and architecture; the geographical areas where, because of particular historical and environmental conditions, there has been in relatively recent times the most marked development of a constellation of political-economic units linked by specific cultural ties (as in Polynesia) or where the formation of a city-state over a preexisting network of agricultural communities has been most evident and most precocious (as in West Africa).

In choosing illustrations we have kept in mind the importance of not breaking down the documentation into too many isolated and fragmentary images. For that reason, we have aimed less at variety than at showing the relationship between man and what he builds, between decoration and the architecture it adorns, between settlement, habitation, and specialized forms of architecture, and between technologies and the production of the object made. This made it possible to round out the text and appendix with a comprehensive selection of documentary illustrations and, in this introductory chapter, to suggest confrontations and problems to be analyzed more fully in the body of the book.

The organization of the four chapters of the text and the sequence in which they follow each other has a historical basis that, naturally, is only relative; as far as possible, it is linked with the general problems of primitive architecture and with the broad stages of economic development and social structure among the peoples with whom we are concerned. The first chapter has no specific geographical focus; its aim is to bring out the connection between architectonic activity and the territory for a population that has no fixed home site. The second chapter, focusing on populations of the Americas, Southeast Asia, and Melanesia, deals principally with the relation between agriculture, dwelling, and village. In the third chapter, limited in scope to Polynesia and the Indians of Northwest America, the theme is the relationship between social stratification, social prestige, and the development of more advanced building techniques and elaborate decoration. The fourth chapter attempts to pinpoint, within a limited area of West Africa, the transition and differences between village and city and to do this by characterizing the means of political and social control, which, in that region, include to the highest degree architectural activity.

THE BAND OF HUNTERS AND THE CAMPSITE

Forever nomadic within a particular range of territory, hunting and gathering populations do not have an architecture of permanent constructions. Individual and group alike have as assets no more than the objects indispensable for their survival, chiefly weapons, receptacles, and tools. Their dwellings are provisional and often serve more to protect the fire than to offer any sort of effective shelter from inclement weather. The windbreaks and little huts improvised each day (*plates 51, 52*) are abandoned without any attempt to salvage the material for reuse. Yet the sites selected for these temporary camps reflect the spatial and temporal relationship between the group and the natural resources of their habitat.

Although the nomadic life by definition prevents the erection of durable structures, the connections between economic activity, social cohesion, and modification of terrain are part of a rigid program aimed at rendering the inhabited environment not only productive but also to the highest degree *significant*. Some property is held privately: Beehives, ant hills, and fruit trees, for example, lend themselves to being parceled out among the basic family units. At the same time, the territory as a whole is defended collectively as the patrimony of the band, clan, or tribe. Every activity of any sort takes its place within a context of mythic interpretations that help to preserve the particular equilibrium that functions within every group—and also between every group as a cultural entity, the neighboring groups, and its own territory. Maximum attention is concentrated on the territory because it is the source of food and the background and base for all social activities. For nomadic populations, architecture is above all an interpretation and humanization of the territory effected by means of a vast number of bonds of relationship that are believed to exist between the human world, the animal and vegetable species, and the particularities of the environment.

*The Pygmies of the Central African Forest*
The hunting and gathering bands of the forest-dwelling Mbuti Pygmies[1] number at most a few dozen individuals who are not, however, blood-relatives. The components of the band change continually, and even the function of chief is effective only during the time when the collective hunt is organized. For this reason, their camps do not reflect a hierarchical criterion or a specific structure based on kinship; instead, they reflect a particular moment in the history of social relationships between the various families occupying the campsite (*plate 60*). The camp is generally located not far from a watercourse, in a clearing whose center is left free to be used for the more formal or ceremonial functions of the whole group. This central open plaza

51. *Temporary shelter of branches and pandanus leaves, Kunggava Bay, Rennel Island, Solomon Islands (Melanesia).*

52. *Puri: lean-to shelter with hammock (eastern Brazil). (Engraving from M. von Wied-Neuwied, 1815–17.)*

53. *Tehuelce: habitation with framework of poles and covering of hides, Rio Santa Cruz, Patagonia (Argentina).*

54. *Open-sided shelter from the sun, Andaman Islands, Bay of Bengal (India).*

55. *Yahgan (Yamana): framework of a conical hut, Navarino Island (Chile).*

56. *Alakaluf: two phases in the construction of the frame of a dome-shaped hut, using bent branches to make two separate quarter-spheres, Tierra del Fuego Archipelago (Chile and Argentina).*

57. *Alakaluf: building a dome-shaped hut, Tierra del Fuego Archipelago (Chile and Argentina).*

58, 59. *Nakua (Nyangatom): dome-shaped huts made of quarter-spheres of branches and grasses, in part supported by large branches still partially attached to the tree (Ethiopia).*

confers on the encampment a definite structure, irregular but roughly ringlike. Since no hut is situated in the center, in what would be a privileged position, one may say that the open plaza respects an egalitarian principle but also constitutes a human and social definition of the territory, a space left empty within the clearing.

This open space is charged with functions so intense as to suggest that there is some conscious link here between social relationships and space. Certainly it has connections with speech, since anyone speaking in the center is heard by all and, because he is in a space not immediately adjacent to his own hut but in one that belongs to the group, he speaks in the name of the group as a whole. However, this does not so much indicate that there is parity between the family nuclei—though that does indeed exist—but more precisely that communication by speech and gesture is more important than any fixed system of relationships in a society undergoing continual modification, whose chief activities—hunting and gathering—are responsible for the fact that the smaller units, the bands, are continually brought together and broken up.

The small huts are each a simple framework of branches covered by leaves, built by the women and altered by them as necessary. The direction in which these shelters open is itself of some social significance. They face the openings of the huts those occupants are most friendly—like an open mouth, as it were. The siting of these hemispherical shelters and the alterations they continually undergo can be viewed as embodiments in architectural form of social attitudes and bonds of kinship. This same expression of feeling is found in the way single huts are combined with or set up next to others among the Pygmy groups that hunt with nets in the central Ituri River area.[2] In these group encampments one clearly sees the link between the individual and the simple sheath of branches and leaves that shelters him and at the same time indicates his social status and family ties.

### The Semang of the Malay Peninsula

The Semang depend chiefly on gathering fruits and vegetables in a forest area where hunting and fishing are practiced only exceptionally.[3] Each group is made up of, at the most, twenty to thirty individuals who are related to each other, and they never remain more than a few days in any place (though without ever covering any great distances). The territory of the group is defined only with regard to their most important foodstuff, the fruit of the durian tree. Each group has its own area where it alone may gather the fruit, whereas there are no boundaries between territories when it comes to less highly prized edibles such as roots and root vegetables.

The camp is set up in a clearing in the forest and comprises a group of varyingly complex shelters disposed in a circle or oval around an open space. The shelters consist of an inclined wall of interwoven branches and leaves held in position by lianas or forked stakes (plate 61). The angle of inclination is varied according to weather conditions, as is also the covering of leaves. When the group moves on, the simplest shelters are simply abandoned; however, more complex ones that are connected to make a single structure in the shape of a truncated cone around a central open space, are left in place to be used again. These more elaborate shelters are built in areas where the group remains for considerable periods or returns often because of the abundance or quality of the food supply; they are confined to the zone where the group has the exclusive right to gather durian fruit.

The territory reserved for gathering this fruit is considered also to contain all the fruit trees that belong by right to the various family heads and are bequeathed by them to their heirs.[4] While foods are exchanged within the group, the territorial boundaries are strictly closed to other groups as concerns the gathering of durian fruit, under threat of grave sanctions. Essentially, then, the territory as an economic and political entity is not thought of as a piece of land as such but as the totality of food resources, both common and choice, sufficient not only for the needs of a particular group but also capable of satisfying certain social needs through the existence of a surplus, however limited. In fact, the gathering of the durian fruit promotes contacts between groups and motivates their joint celebration of ritual feasts.

### The Bushmen of South Africa

The hunting bands of the Bushmen consist of a few dozen persons linked through kinship. They operate within a specific territory and are headed by a chief whose functions are primarily connected with the provision of food and water and the choice of the campsite.[5] Each camp is made up of a number of screens or windbreaks of branches for protection against sun and cold, and these are set up in a semicircle and connected with each other at the top. At the center of the encampment is the sacred fire. The settlements (werf) follow no single pattern, and the camps are oriented either in the direction of the rising sun or toward such natural features as a particular tree. Among the Kung, for instance, the camp is composed of family shelters, each with its own hearth, but the hut of the young bachelors (kao) is situated a few hundred yards to the east of these, in the direction of the sacred place set aside for initiation (plate 62). The shelters themselves often open toward the east, again because of the sacred character of that direction, which is considered to be the abode of the gods.

60. *Mbuti Pygmies: plan of an encampment showing changes in disposition of the huts that reflect personal friendships and hostilities (central Africa).*
*a. first day; b. second day; c. third day; d. fifth day.*
*1. The wife moves out and builds herself a new hut on the arrival of the son of her husband's sister; 2. the rear entrance is closed off on the twelfth day; 3. a hut built the second day and abandoned the third day, is reoccupied the fifth day; 4. the rear is closed off on the twelfth day; 5. a move is made on the eleventh day; 6. a common hearth is removed on the twelfth day; 7. a move is made to a new camp.*

61. *Semang: bamboo lean-to with pallet raised above the ground, Malacca Peninsula (western Malaysia).*

62. *Bushmen: plan of an encampment (werf) connected by a path with the site for initiation ceremonies, Kalahari Desert (South Africa).*
*1. circular plazas for dances; 2. campsite; 3. chief's hut; 4. path; 5. site of initiation ceremonies; 6. shelter for the young bachelor initiates.*

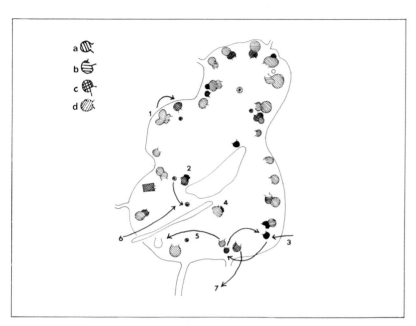

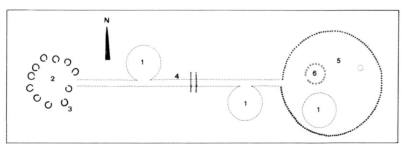

The Heikum, on the other hand, dispose their camps around a sacred tree regarded as the central point of the territory. At the foot of that tree the chief lights the sacred fire, builds his own hut, and holds his assemblies. The other shelters are erected in a semicircle on the opposite side of the tree. The youths and maidens have their huts at opposite ends of the central axis of the *werf*, and the married daughters of the chief are allotted places as far as possible from his hut. Thus, both the position of the dwellings and the distances between them are determined by the rules of kinship and by the social status of the members of the band. However, it is always the territory that commands the maximum attention in architectonic and interpretative terms alike. For the Bushmen both the tree (natural) and the fire (artificial) are centers of irradiating power as well as fixed points of reference and an indispensable sacred link between group and environment. But equally vital, perhaps even more so, given the semidesert nature of the regions the Bushmen inhabit, is the connection between the encampment and the water holes where the wild game gathers, though in order not to disturb the quarry the camp may be set up at some distance from them.

In times past, the most energetic building activity took place on the occasion of the great hunts. A large number of groups all participated in preparing the terrain by chopping down trees, erecting barriers, and digging pit-traps.[6] As in other regions rich in wild game, the herds were driven into fenced-in areas and then trapped in pits. The enclosures and other structures used in this kind of hunting were periodically repaired and improved.

THE ABORIGINAL AUSTRALIANS: HISTORY AND RE-CREATION OF THE LANDSCAPE

The ideological and artistic (that is, superstructural) aspects of the myths and art through which the tribal groups of Australian aborigines interpret the most salient features of their territory have received more attention than the decisive relationship between how they understand, represent, and give meaning to the territory and the economic and social context of which it has been, in the course of time, the instrument. The result is an incomplete picture that ignores the fact that these people do have a conscious concern with and capacity for architecture as it applies to the territory. Instead, the absence of permanent edifices has been taken as evidence of passive adaptation to the environment and inability to produce any kind of architecture.[7]

The notion that the Australian tribesmen are cultural survivors of paleolithic man has long been abandoned[8] and, with it, the supposition that in historical times the continent was entirely isolated from the outside world until the first colonists arrived; the fact is, it has been constantly swept by Indonesian and, especially, Melanesian cultural currents. While those influences had no substantial effect on an economy based almost exclusively on hunting and gathering, they nevertheless helped to consolidate the contacts between separate but neighboring groups—with relative diffusion of cultural elements over very vast areas[9] —and, as a by-product, to further a consistent mythic and historical interpretation of the territory. The relationship thus established between tribal group and territory is extremely active: The legendary civilizing heroes who "constructed" the most important places and who were first to travel the itineraries essential to the sustenance of man gradually took the place of the abstract divinities who dispensed all things to man; the latter were thenceforth relegated to the mythical "epoch of the sky," where they retired and were constrained to eternal idleness.[10] Through the heroes who replaced them—beings of the "epoch of the dream," the dreamtime—whose gestures man can imitate and repeat, man himself became capable of molding nature, of controlling what it has to give, and of introducing it into his own social system. In this way, A. Rapoport points out, the aborigine could find a place in his social system for all the species and all the things and phenomena of nature, reducing them to parts of his own organization of kinship class, clan, and so on.[11] Even comprehension of the physical features of the territory came to be considered an integral part of the activity of the group: One of the reasons why a group is rooted in a specific area is because it *knows* how that territory was given its shape and form and because it descends from the one who made it. The attitude can be called "scientific": It proceeds by way of social necessities to an examination of analogies within the natural world and goes on to appropriate them for itself, instituting a relationship of cause and effect, which, precisely because it cannot be verified, is said to have taken place in the mythical dream-time.

In a number of studies, W. Arndt has tried to show how the artistic representations of the Australians can be traced back to such natural phenomena as lightning, thunder, clouds, and the like. Thus, the figures called *wandjina* are, according to Arndt, personifications of rain clouds,[12] which may be so, although the supposition is difficult to verify. However, if one studies the relationship between the construction of the landscape by the mythical ancestor-snake and the movement of a real snake across a sandy terrain,[13] one grasps a salient point in the function of myth: It serves to explain, on the basis of experience and comparison, the origin of natural forms.

How can a snake create a landscape? The difficulty implied in the vast jump in scale is easily overcome: The mythical snake was

gigantic. Then, the similarity between the traces of a snake slithering along and a meandering watercourse is interpreted as perfectly obvious proof that the latter was the sinuous route the ancestor took in crossing the territory. It is also easy to account for the small ridges on the flat surface of the ground that are found just downstream of every bend along the Ord and Victoria rivers: They were raised up in the epoch of the dream by the snake proceeding countercurrent, exactly as the blackheaded python (*Aspidites melanocephalus*) moves when crawling across a rough terrain (*plate 64*).[14] Thus, the mythical voyage puts the reptilian progenitor and the human group on a par: The snake formed the landscape in the dream-time in the same way as the group constructs its own habitat (or, firmly considers itself able to do so) by representing the great mythical deeds in the form of art.

This active attitude toward the territory even extends to an extremely detailed classification, by complementary concepts, of its peculiarities in terms of human and, so to speak, historical geography (history taking place entirely in the epoch of the dream, of course). The basis of this classification is the dualism between the tribe's temporary halting place and the way to be traveled, an elementary but extremely conceptual expression of the hunting and gathering life, which involves preestablished itineraries and camping sites. The halting place and the way are represented on the communicative plane by the circle and the straight line; on the mythological plane by the "holes" through which the heroes of the myth appear and disappear from the surface of the earth and by the routes they take; on the plane of classificatory correspondences by the dualisms of male-female, past-present, outside-inside.

The myth of the routes taken by the ancestral heroes is prevalent throughout the vast aboriginal area. The most widely diffused word, found in local variants practically everywhere in Australia, is *ngura*, signifying camping place.[15] Moreover, a sometimes very extensive intertribal collaboration on what we can call the construction—the construing—of the mythology (in the sense that every local group or clan possesses a segment of the total mythic patrimony that concerns only the passage and exploits of the principal culture hero within its own territory) makes it impossible to consider the territories that belong to the various tribes as completely closed within themselves.[16] This means that the construing of the territory was carried through by all the groups interested in maintaining an ethnic-social equilibrium in often extremely extensive territories. It also means that the evidence of particular historical-cultural contributions that the aborigines are tempted to discern in the exploits of the heroes of the dream-time has a basis in fact, in the general warp and woof of the relationships between the groups and their natural environment.[17]

The real underpinning of tribal unity and, above all, of the unity of the clan, is the territory conceived as a network of sacred centers and of routes linking those centers (*plate 67*). The tribe is, thus, a kind of "family of places" linked by bonds similar to family ties. By analogy with the social system, the boundaries of the ambit assigned to the clan are more precise than those assigned to the tribe. But it is the individual who recognizes as his "homeland" a mythical path or sacred center[18] that links him to a vital expanse or feature of the natural world, one made vital—infused with life—in the epoch of the dream.

*Alimentary Itineraries and Itineraries of the Myth*
The exigencies of hunting and gathering oblige the groups to follow specific itineraries as the seasons change and to halt only in places where food and water are abundant. Thus, particularly in the semiarid and arid regions of central Australia, there has come to be a close association between the so-called center of the territory, the halting place (that is, the campsite), and the water hole, the latter being by antonomasia considered the point used by the mythic progenitors to issue (*wilbibari*) from the earth at the start of their peregrinations and to reenter it (*yuga*). For the Walbiri[19] those two acts synthesize the activity of the ancestors as well as of their descendants—themselves—who can, in their turn, enter (*yuga*) symbolically into the epoch of the dream through the sacred point. This implies that their actions can be considered true and right since they follow a model established aeons ago for all time.

The water hole is indicated by a circle or spiral (the whirlpool, the clearest expression of the notion of the ascent and descent on the mythical journey and of the opening on the earth's surface that communicates with the subterranean world) and is the most common among what are thought of as the sources of life. By connecting the earth's surface (*gangalani*) with the subterranean region (*ganindjara*), a vertical pathway is established that functions as local cosmic axis, as origin of space, and as point of passage and connection between the present and the epoch of the dream.

The water hole is, as we have seen, the place where normally the peregrination of the creator-hero on the territory began and ended. In his "walkabouts" the hero had as his primary function the establishment of centers of life in every halting place, vital sources that would ensure the fruitfulness of the various animal and vegetable species and of man himself. In addition, he localized all the other phenomena that might in any way concern the community of man. Thus, as halting places one finds isolated trees or rocks of value as landmarks, caves on which the hero first impressed the magical images that favor the

64. *Mythical formation of the dunes along a river: schematic representation and axial section of the river-as-serpent (Australia).*

65. *Walbiri: drawing representing a cave (center) surrounded by an oval encampment; the outer semicircles are four kangaroos that came to the campsite from different directions in the territory, as indicated by the linear tracks of their tails and their hoofprints (Australia).*

perpetuation of the living species, sites where there is rock useful for making utensils or colored earth to make pigments for painting, and the like.[20] The route traveled never directly connects two important localities. Instead, these itineraries are associated with the very slightest traces left on the terrain in the dream-time. Because these routes are fixed, the community or family group can be certain of reaching again, in orderly fashion and without confusion, all the places that for one reason or another are necessary to the perpetuation of its own existence, to its fertility, and to the maintenance of its social structure. Contiguity between groups gives rise to problems that, however, can be resolved by referring back to the myth and thereby eliminating the grounds for friction. A group can cross the territory of another group under specific conditions: following a definite route, restricted to a specific goal—a particular sacred center. When the campsite is laid out during assemblies of a number of groups, each group takes its place according to the direction from which it came.[21] Within the territory, the area allotted to each tribe or clan is clearly fixed, and, if it is changed, the myth that links the group precisely to a specific place must change accordingly.

The vital centers established by the mythic heroes are believed to be fountainheads removed from which the group cannot survive. Some tribes, in the person of the chief, carry a sacred pole along with them. Symbol of their vital center, which also indicates the direction of their march, this pole must at every halt be pointed in the direction to be taken on the next lap. It is recounted of the Achilpa that once when this sacred pole (*kauwa-auwa*) was accidentally broken, an entire group was seized with such anguish that they simply let themselves die, convinced that they had been separated forever from their vital fountainhead.[22] In the region of Lake Eyre the richly decorated poles (*toa*) are the present-day symbols of the walkabouts undertaken aeons ago by the ancestral constructors of the territory (*mura-mura*).[23]

The inclined pole unites in itself the motif of the halt and of the route. The Achilpa myth of the hero Numbakulla, who climbed to the sky on one such pole, expresses the vertical aspect of the sacred center, linking earth to sky. Analogous myths speak of sacred mountains, ropes, trees, and spears as vehicles of that connection.[24]

### The Centers of Life

In the places made sacred because the primordial heroes rested there, a large number of "vital spirits" are present, potentially always ready to incarnate themselves in individuals, both animal and human, and continually renewed by ceremonies that repeat the heroes' exploits. Conception is not associated directly with the sexual act but rather with the passage into the uterus of one of these "spirit babies" dissemi-

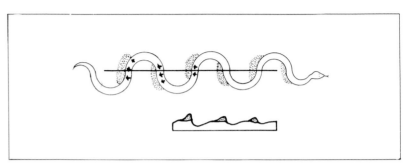

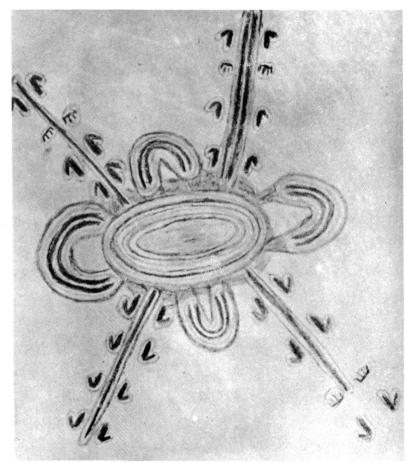

66. *Schematic representation of a river territory (Australia).*
    *1. Indian Ocean; 2. De Grey River; 3. Oakover River.*
    *a, b, c, d: bends in the river and lines of separation between the bands of the diagram indicating the locations of the various tribal groups.*

67. *Diagram of the relation between different aboriginal groups (a, b, c), the sacred centers established in the dream time (1, 2, 3), and the itinerary (x) of the culture hero (Australia).*

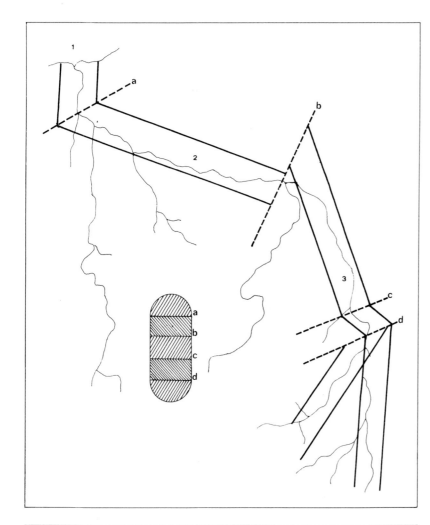

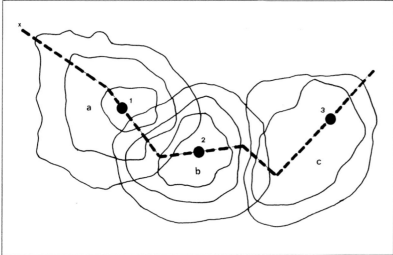

nated in specific points of the territory traversed by females. Since every individual existed prior to his birth in a specific territorial "life center," he considers himself more intimately linked to the place of his conception than to that of his birth.

The whole of living nature is the object of constant attention on the part of the group lest the vital potentialities of all the species become diminished. The rites of growth enacted in various places are the rites performed there in exactly the same way by the culture-heroes in the epoch of the dream. Those rites consist not only of propitiatory ceremonies but also of creative and artistic activities, repeated continually so as to ensure continuity. An important body of rites involves consecrating particular points of the territory, the centers of life, by painting on rock in caves and incising ritual motifs on trees.

The culture-heroes first gave visual representation to the various animal and vegetable species, and assured their multiplication in the mythic times of the epoch of the dream. By renewing the paintings, present-day man imitates that primordial act, identifying himself with the hero and thereby participating actively in maintaining the fecundity of nature and the equilibrium between the species.[25] The incisions cut in trees (*plate 63*) have a similar significance. A tree is designated as "life center" because a primordial hero halted by it, and it serves as support for sacred images intended to perpetuate access to the vital fountainheads for particular species of animals as well as man. The motivations behind these ceremonies that repeat over and over again a model established in the dream-time are not only religious but social. These rituals, which are the patrimony of the group, codify the relationship between the various members, the essentials of life and, above all, the indissoluble link with the territory. The sanctions applied to anyone who violates the taboos associated with the totemic ceremonies and the complex rules governing the interpretation and utilization of space are proof that the ritual represents the fundamental law of the tribe, a law with its roots not only in myth but in history.

The most important creative activity, in cosmological terms, is the conventionalized repetition of the exploits of the mythic heroes in a landscape that, prior to the epoch of the dream, was still amorphous, chaotic, and lacking in any meaningful landmarks. This is effected in ceremonies where dance and song are elements of considerable artistic complexity. In these ceremonial representations, artworks are created in order that the terrain used for the *corroboree*-dance may contain all the landscape elements needed to identify and reenact the myth. Although these constructions and decorations are for the most part only temporary, they are evidence that the tribe deliberately, architecturally, re-creates the landscape in its effort to understand, interpret, and make use of the territory in which it lives. A few examples showing how the dance terrain is laid out will elucidate the aboriginal Australians' essentially active interest in territorial structures.

*Ceremonial Camps and Symbolic Space*
For their initiation ceremonies, the Kamilaroi prepare a sacred terrain of obviously cosmological character.[26] Two circles are traced on the ground and linked by what is designated as a path. One circle, with a diameter of about twenty yards, has in its center a sacred pole about eight feet high, to the top of which is attached a tuft of emu feathers. Within the smaller circle are placed two shrubs with their roots in air. At the sides of the connecting pathway are disposed a series of representations, either drawn or modeled in earth. These include the supreme being Baïami in the form of a figure some fifteen feet in length, the mythical ancestral couple, the twelve companions of Baïami who dwelt with him in the primordial campground, and various sorts of animals and nests. Here then is the full ritual repetition of the first encampment where, for the first time, the creator-god initiated the ceremony of circumcision (*bora*); here, once again, the initial model is created and the living participants identified with the mythic personages of the dream-time.

Innumerable other examples of arrangements of the ceremonial terrain make use of stylized representations of natural phenomena: Heaps of sand represent rocks and hills, hollows in the ground are identified with water holes, and the sacred pole, which is almost never absent from these ceremonies, is the symbol of the contact between earth, subterranean world, and sky, as well as of the male sex.

In the course of a *banba* ceremony of the Walbiri, the "rite of the flying ant," a pole about three feet high is erected and, like the dance that follows, it is intended to increase the ant species.[27] First a hole is dug and water is poured on the ground. The moist earth is then made sacred with blood. Concentric circles are traced around the hole with tufts of down soaked in red ocher to represent blood, and the drawing is completed with white pigment similarly applied. The pole is decorated with small white spots representing ants, and at the top is fixed a tuft of leaves of the bloodroot plant considered by the Walbiri as source of life and therefore called *gudugulu*, "containing a baby." The pole is then placed in the hole. It symbolizes the anthill, while the circle and the hole represent the encampment of the ants. Dancers crawl across the symbolic campsite in imitation of the insect, coming closer and closer to the center and finally symbolically entering the hole; this is the purpose and end of the dance, being no less than a representation of the act of procreation that concludes every act of

"entering" (*yuga*) the sacred center. Although the pole is above ground, in this case it does not represent so much the link with the sky as the link with the most sacred, and therefore the deepest, part of the hole. Viewing the ceremony in terms of two-dimensional design, the center represents the hole, the sacred source, and the concentric circles stand for degrees of distance and imply increasing remoteness on the horizontal plane but also vertical movement toward the surface of the earth (hence, gradual desacralization, sloughing off of sacred qualities) and entry into the present.

The representation of the sacred hole and the path leading to it carries a great weight of associations and correspondences. According to N. D. Munn,[28] the center is the *djugurba*, the place in the territory representing the point of contact with the dream-time; the concentric circle is the primordial campsite, the earth's surface in the dream-time (*ydjaru*, symbol of the mother); the path leading to it signifies present time, the directions of descent and ascent, the sexual act, and the male organ. Since territory and tribal group are closely identified, these complementary models have the force of poles and pathways, of basic structures of the economy as well as relationship with the natural environment.

The symbolism of the complex geometrical patterns is based on connection and juxtaposition of two basic elements, the circle and the straight line. With them, the Walbiri represent in their *guruwari* designs the itinerary of the mythic heroes and, at the same time, give a summary picture of the territory. The latter includes landscape features, animal and human figures, and even the traces they leave on the ground (*plate 65*). A radial line directed toward the center of the symbolic water hole or campsite indicates access to the sacred center and participation in and attainment of the epoch of the dream. As consequence of this semanticization of the environment, almost all of the Australian tribes have developed a particular approach to territorial representations. This, as we have seen, chiefly results in geometric and planimetric syntheses of the system of sacred centers and routes peculiar to the territory of each tribe, with the addition of the specific elements of myth that concern them. Water always receives attention: One circle around another can stand for a watercourse around a hill, and a line or group of parallel lines can indicate not only a fixed itinerary but also a watercourse.

An extremely instructive example of the link between myth, natural structures, and relationships between neighboring tribes is found in the geometrical maps made by the tribes in northwestern Australia. According to C. G. von Brandenstein, who has made a broad study of the meaning of the zigzag motif (snake, watercourse),[29] the explanation for the birth of rivers is that they were formed when

68. *Central Eskimos: drawing, ground plan, and section of an igloo with a corridor of chambers (Canada).*

69, 70. *Igluligarjumiut Eskimos: building an igloo, district of Keewatin, Chester region (Canada).*

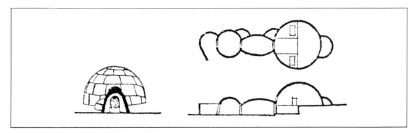

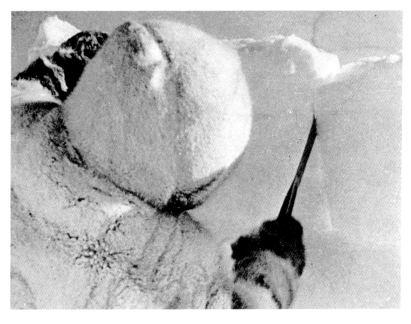

the Great Father Snake emerged from the sea and crawled across the dry land leaving his sinuous track imprinted there forever. Thus, the changes in direction of watercourses are interpreted as sinuous curves of the body of the snake, "creator of the waters," and they are made use of as reconnaissance elements in identifying terrain and showing the relative positions of the various tribes living along the rivers. Each of these tribes has what we can call a coat-of-arms of its own, consisting of connected bands incised with diagonal parallel lines inclining alternately to right and to left: The portion of the band between two of these parallel diagonals represents a particular stretch of the watercourse (which is, for diagrammatic purposes, shown without its minor twists and turns) and therefore the territory inhabited by a particular tribe. The whole course of the river is thereby synthesized into a zigzag design. The drawing (*wanparda*) that shows the course of the De Grey and Oakover rivers from the Indian Ocean to their sources (*plate 66*) is made up of five bands crossed by alternating diagonal lines. The design represents the entire course of the rivers and is the symbol of the tribe situated farthest from the sea. Since the origin of the rivers is thought to be the sea (its sacred center, whence emerged the snake that created the waters), the first tribe is represented by a single band that stands for the first straight stretch of the river; the second, by two bands separated by a horizontal line that indicates a change of direction in the river and, in abstract fashion, the boundary between adjacent tribal groups; the third, by three bands, and so forth for the remainder of the rivercourse.

Thus, the salient physical features of the territory can, maplike, all be condensed into a single schema, which also shows how the different tribes are disposed relative to each other along the waterway, each with its own relationship to a stretch of it (its own "pathway" or "route") as well as to the neighboring tribes upstream and downstream, and all of this is linked with the mythical identification of river and creator-snake.

This schema is significantly similar to the structuring of the territory based on the succession of separate tribes connected by a mythic zigzag route linking the sacred centers to the different tribal areas (*plate 67*).[30] In both cases, the boundaries are secondary in importance to the connecting link between different tribal areas, which gravitate, so to speak, around the principal ways of access to the mythic sources of life.

## JOURNEY AND DWELLING

### The Eskimos of North America and Greenland

The Eskimos' extremely detailed geographical knowledge extends far beyond their own hunting terrain.[31] As the coastline is the only truly significant landmark and remains constant with the changing seasons, a kind of two-dimensional schematization of it is often committed to memory and can be drawn with extraordinary precision, even for distances of hundreds of miles. At sea and inland, to get their bearings the Eskimos depend on an accurate analysis of every feature of the terrain, but above all on observation of the winds and by calculating their position with respect to the sun and stars. Contacts between groups occur during the good season but are for the most part individual in character: A hunter well acquainted with the territory can reach places where game is abundant; he can then have a wife in two or more bands, within whose territory, in consequence, he has the right to hunt.

Knowledge of the inland territory is essential for hunting caribou in summer. The hunters must travel to places where the herds pass year after year on their annual northward journey from winter to summer grazing lands. There, the herds are usually driven into a lake or river and attacked from kayaks that can be rowed much faster than the animals can swim. Salmon are caught during their mass migrations upriver, and again the fishermen travel to the most favorable places to secure them. For shelter in the summer camps there are tents of caribou or seal skins, which take different forms in different groups but are often sharply inclined so as to present less surface to the wind. At the end of the warm season, loaded with great reserve stocks of food, the group makes its way toward the center of the territory. There, traditionally, they inhabited permanent dwellings that had to be repaired and reinforced once a year, or even entirely rebuilt in the same place.

In more recent times, however, the permanent dwellings have been replaced by settlements composed of igloos built with blocks of snow (*plate 68*), which do not necessarily occupy the same site as the earlier houses and may be inhabited for several months in a row. The sites chosen for these winter dwellings fill the traditional requirements: layout that permits the group to live close together, position on the coast at a point easily accessible and convenient for both winter and summer hunting and in a spot sheltered from the cold. The substitution of the igloo for the semiunderground permanent house offers one real advantage: The Eskimos are now able to make use of the ice floes as dwelling places, which facilitates hunting the marine mammals (seals in particular) that are the staple of the winter diet.

To build an igloo, the hard-packed snow is cut into blocks with a knife of bone or ivory, and these are laid against one another in a spiral; the result is a cupola, whose keystone is inserted from the outside (*plates 68–70*). The gaps are filled in with loose snow, and the interior may be covered with skin stretched on sinews so as to leave

a circular chamber of cold air between the skins and the wall, a zone of insulation that makes it possible to heat the interior to a temperature of fifteen degrees centigrade (fifty-nine degrees Fahrenheit) without damaging the structure.

## The Nambikwara and Yanoama of Brazil

The relationship between territory and dwelling is particularly significant for populations that adopt complementary seasonal ways of life. One of the most widespread of such patterns of alternation is between sedentary agriculture and nomadic hunting and gathering.

During the winter, the Nambikwara in western Brazil gather in settlements on high ground near a river. Taking advantage of the rainy season, they settle down in roughly circular family huts, which they build in a semicircle or ring around an open space, and practice agriculture—specifically horticulture—near the riverbank. The men do the farming and build the huts. In the seven summer months of drought, however, there is a complete reversal in the life of the community. It breaks up into small nomadic bands that settle for only a few days at a time in provisional encampments, where the women (never the men) make shelters of branches or palm fronds arranged in a half-circle and joined at the top. When families are dispersed in this manner through extremely extensive territories, even the basic social structure often becomes unrecognizable. Thus, while the arrangement of the summer camp is analogous to that of the semipermanent winter settlement, there is a change in the position of the hearths and, indeed, of the family groups themselves because their membership is in constant flux. As with the Pygmies, the small shelter a Nambikwara woman puts up in the summer does not reflect any fixed spatial or social position. It merely expresses a relationship between the family and the group as a whole, which may be no more than momentary.[32] In the large encampments, this accidental quality results also from the fact that the families arrive separately—alone or in small groups.

During the nomadic period, the relationship with the territory becomes much more significant. It is heightened by a factor of fundamental importance for survival in an arid environment: water. Knowledge of the landscape can extend, for every group, as far as hundreds of miles and is based primarily on "reading" the territory as an ensemble of "water points," which are given, according to yield and position, specific geographical designations.

Water is present even in the names of the cardinal points of the compass. Since most of the rivers run from south to north, the south is called *ukenore*, "up," and the north *iokenore*, "down." The river journey is viewed as a string of localities, each identified by some aspect of water, each subject to precise location in a linear schema

71. *Paracana (Tupí): temporary shelter covered with palm fronds, Pará (northern Brazil).*

72, 73. *Xeta: roofed shelters, Serra dos Dourados, Paraná (Brazil).*

joining two places. These "maps"—or, more accurately, itineraries—are lists of names of places that, for convenience, can be traced out diagrammatically in the sand. Here, for example, are the fourteen stages of a journey from the Rio Papagaio to the Rio Juruena, marked as so many transverse notches on a straight line joining the two terminal localities, only three of which are without specific names: *krikrinékusu* (the starting point), *kadáreosu* (Rio Buriti), a nameless spring, *niákesu* (Rio Agua Quente), a nameless little brook, *kukútlie kukutreusu* (Rio Sapezal), *nouosenekesu* (small spring), *laiósu* (spring), a nameless brook, *sakéasu* (bank of the Rio Juruena), *iosidasu* (little water), *tukuredíkesu* (spring), *uriz inosu* (little water), *aitéasu* (little water), *unitíkesu* (spring).

Greater importance is accorded to the nomadic period, which is viewed as liberation from the monotonous life of the village. It is the period when the provision basket replaces the hut, when it is possible to meet other groups at journey's end. "We journey, we journey—we arrive at the water, we cross the water, we cross in journeying!—in journeying!—We go by the grassland, we cross the grassland—in forest we journey, once more descend the hill journeying—journeying, journeying we climb the hill, we cross the hill—on the crest we journey, we go down another hill, still walking on!"[33]

Another seminomadic population, the Yanoama, who occupy a forest zone at the upper Orinoco at the border between Brazil and Venezuela, set up a semipermanent encampment, the *chapuno*, made up of a near-circular open space surrounded by a more or less continuous wall of enormous lean-tos with a single rectangular roof sloping down toward the exterior (*plates 79–96*). Every shelter houses several families, and the central open space, considered sacred and the property of the entire group, is used for all social functions and can be enlarged or reduced for defence or because of changes in the number of members of the campsite.

As E. Biocca explains, "A *chapuno* is the product of an intelligent collective labor. Of particular importance is the choice of site, made with regard to the prevailing winds and rains, the danger of flooding, the presence of drinkable water, and the possibility of easy defence from attacks by other Indians or whites. The central plaza must be slightly elevated so that, when the great rains come, the water will not turn the terrain into a swamp, but run off. Moreover, in front of the hearths ingenious drainage networks are dug and these channel the water to the exterior of the *chapuno*. . . . The *chapuno* is also a temple. In the large plaza the shamans invoke the eternal spirits. . . in ecstatic poses reminiscent of flight or with frenetic expressions of collective exaltation. In the plaza, the dead are burned in the pres-

74. *Guató: framework of a shelter with two inclined walls covered with palm fronds, Mato Grosso (Brazil).*

75. *Guaraní: shelter of ogival section, Upper Paraná (Brazil).*

76. *Large elevated shelter (French Guiana).*

77. *Pilagá: plan of a settlement with huts curved around a central plaza, Chaco (Argentina).*

78. *Bororo: schematic plan of a circular settlement with the men's house in the center, Mato Grosso (Brazil). The lightly dotted lines indicate the divisions into "moieties," the heavy dotted lines mark the boundaries between the clans living upriver and downriver.*

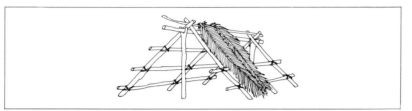

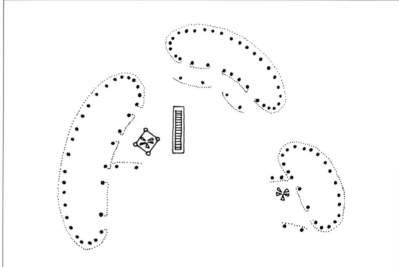

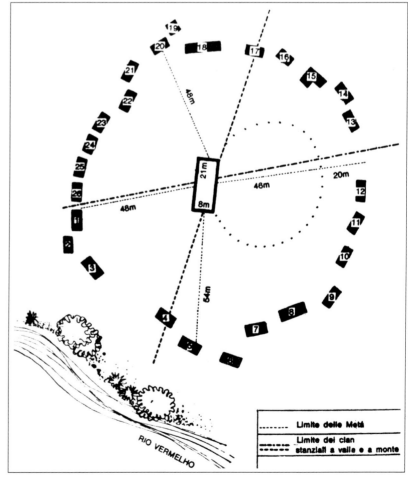

*Yanoama (Western Brazil): Axonometric Drawings of the Types of Multi-family Chapunos (plates 79–82)*

79. *Small, independent lean-tos* (tapiri).
80. Tapiri *with central shelter and a larger lean-to for the chief.*

81. *Large, independent lean-tos.*
82. *Lean-tos with joined roofs; at one end, the chief's hut (of* maloca *type) and a poultry coop, elements deriving from recent acculturation, Amazonas (western Brazil).*

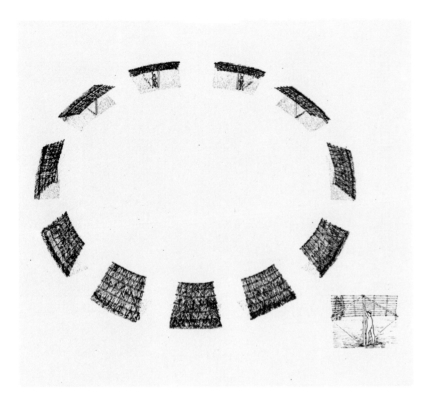

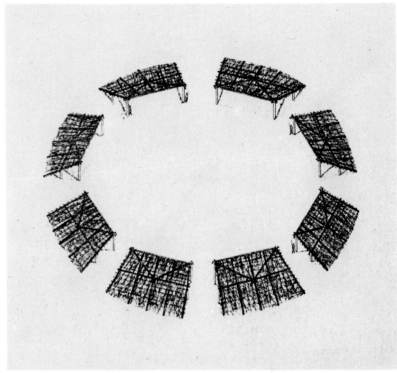

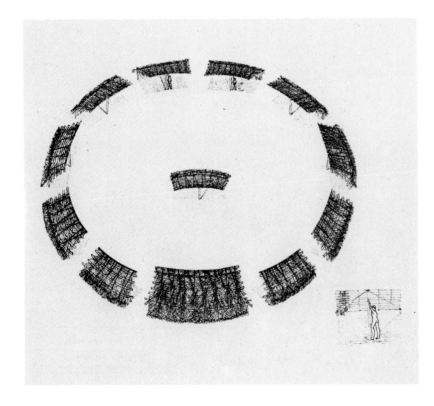

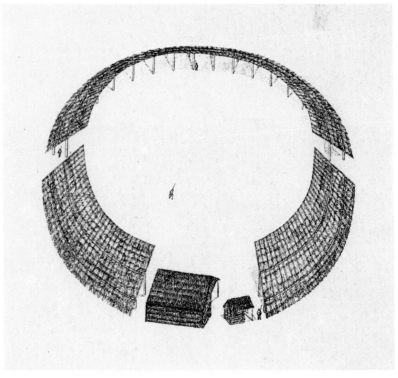

83. *Yanoama: small lean-to supported by a single pole (tapirí), Amazonas (western Brazil).*

84, 85. *Yanoama: family life and activities under a lean-to shelter, Amazonas (western Brazil).*

86. *Yanoama: plan and section of a large* chapuno *of the Kohoroshiwetari along the Rio Maturacá, Amazonas (western Brazil). Each number corresponds to a family unit; included are some family groups and individuals belonging to the Hereuteri, Wawanaweteri, and Amarokomabueteri tribes. Sector 14, in axial position, houses the chief and his wives, surrounded by brothers and relatives. The axes of symmetry of the complex are noted in dotted lines.*

87. *Yanoama:* chapuno *made up of independent lean-tos, Amazonas (western Brazil).*

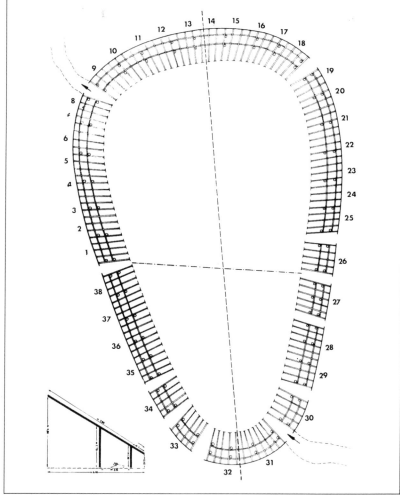

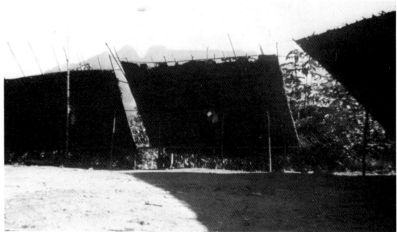

91. *Yanoama:* chapuno *made up of independent lean-tos, Amazonas (western Brazil).*

92, 93. *Yanoama:* chapuno *with continuous joined roofs, Amazonas (western Brazil).*

94, 95. *Yanoama:* construction used for funeral rites in the center of a *chapuno, Amazonas (western Brazil).*

96. *Yanoama:* dance in a chapuno, *Amazonas (western Brazil).*

ence of all; the plaza is the scene of the ultimate theatrical manifestation, the 'sung lament' "[34] (plates 94–96).

These large structures expand into major dimensions the type of temporary encampment made up of shelters with a single-pitched roof. Their circular plan is sacred in character, reflecting the conception that the hunting territory has the chapuno as its center. In settlements such as these, the group acts as a whole, an indivisible unit in counterpoise with the natural environment, experiencing a kind of exaltation in an effort of coordination that often, as with the Semang, culminates in a single collective work of architecture, a gigantic truncated cone open in the center, like a single unfinished hut.[35]

THE HUNTERS AND HORSEBREEDERS OF THE NORTH AMERICAN PLAINS
The life of the Great Plains Indians, whose economic base was buffalo hunting, demanded special kinds of territorial, political, and social organization. With the introduction of the horse, and especially among the numerous sedentary agricultural tribes displaced toward the west by white settlers, extensive changes took place in the social structure and in the economy, changes that led to greater mobility, to more efficacious methods and means of hunting, including firearms, and to a more efficient organization of the settlement and the tent, the tepee (plates 97, 98).[36] The tepee was in use in the western part of the Great Plains, which stretch between the Mississippi River and the Rocky Mountains, before the advent of the horse. The tribes of the northeastern part of that area—including the Mandan, Pawnee, Dakota, and Hidatsa—practiced agriculture before the conflict with the white settlers began, but those in the western area were already exclusively hunters, chiefly of buffalo. From the 18th and early 19th centuries, the agricultural populations were in far from intermittent contact with the white colonists. In the horse, they found a new and effective instrument for war, hunting, and transport, and it effected a fundamental change in the basis of their economy. By the time they began to resist the settlers, these tribes had become essentially horsebreeders and hunters. Tents reached notable dimensions, and the use of the travois—a very simple vehicle consisting of two poles supporting a platform or net and dragged along by horses—made it possible to transport very large loads during periodic migrations. Horses and firearms made hunting much more efficient but at the same time reduced the game, and this in turn encouraged and necessitated greater mobility. After the white men occupied all the tribal territories and decimated the tribes that resisted, the survivors were moved to or enclosed in reservations, and the ties the groups had to their hunting territories were more or less effectively destroyed. What did not disappear, however, was their traditional architecture, the tepee, which through the centruies had developed into a dwelling of extreme efficiency.

In its classic form, the tepee is a large conical tent consisting of a framework of four wooden poles tied together at the top by buffalo thongs, to which are joined other poles to complete the cone that supports the covering of buffalo hides (plates 97, 102). Laid out flat, the covering of a Blackfoot tepee is semicircular, with two flaps at the center of the straight border, which serve to protect the opening at the top of the tent from the wind. Every tent requires more than a dozen hides, and they are worked and sewn by the women who own them, who are also responsible for transporting and setting them up. To make the tent, the women enlist the help of others, whom they pay in food, the principal and most widespread means of payment for collaborators in many types of construction work in a large number of primitive societies.

The interior of the Blackfoot tepee is lined to a height of about five feet with skins, which shield the lower part of the tent from air currents. The hearth is laid on the axis of the entrance, almost in the center and just below the opening at the top that serves as chimney. Another hearth, this one ceremonial and used for making burnt offerings, is built on the same axis but near the rear of the tent, and it is there that the most sacred objects and the trophies are kept. The owner of the tent and his wife have their pallets on the left side of the tent, and their children occupy the other half. Often geometrical motifs are painted on the inner lining and the exterior of the tent.

### The Blackfoot
In the case of the Blackfoot of the northwestern plains,[37] the changes brought about by the new means of locomotion were gradually absorbed into their previous system of hunting and their form of territorial organization, which, in broad outline, remained unaltered. This was also the case with the Comanche and Cheyenne; in fact, these three tribes, which together extended from north to south over more than a thousand miles, developed a way of life that basically was much the same.

Detailed analysis of the Blackfoot, who hunted buffalo before the introduction of the horse, clarifies the connections between the earlier means of hunting and the great efforts, involving the entire productive community, that were called for in constructing .the huge buffalo traps in which entire herds could be slaughtered. This hunting group eventually undertook large-scale permanent works to transform zones of their territory into artificial enclosures for capturing game. Similar efforts are not unknown among fishing populations, who sometimes create artificial basins in rivers, but the constructions of the Blackfoot

97. *Sioux: camp of tepees (central USA). (Watercolor by Charles Willson Peale, 1819.)*

98. *Arapaho: drawing symbolizing four conical tents separated by a path with buffalo tracks (in the center); above and below, other tents and mountains; in the frame, chains of mountains and lakes (central USA).*

99. *Shoshone: drawing symbolizing the earth (the central rectangle) with a lake (the parallelogram) surrounded by four conical mountains (western USA).*

are noteworthy precisely because they made it possible to exploit to some extent the kind of animal husbandry in which livestock is permitted to run wild and then periodically assembled in corrals. The practice was feasible because of the great number of participants in every hunting group and because the hunting territories of the various groups were precisely delimited.

The Blackfoot were divided into three tribes that were independent but linked by common traditions and quite similar economic and social systems. As with other hunters of migratory game, the rhythm of the Blackfoot's seasonal movements was regulated by the movements of the herds of buffalo, which roamed eastward in spring to pasture lands that were particularly luxuriant between June and August. In that season, each tribe assembled in an enormous summer encampment for the great collective buffalo hunt and the annual feasts that renewed the bonds between the various groups. Thus, the social and cultural unity of the summer season had, as always, a specific economic basis. It was possible for all the groups in a tribe to gather for a prolonged sojourn in one place only because they all participated in the great hunt that assured them of adequate supplies of food. The differences between the groups were minimized by a strict social discipline. Each group was assigned a specific task in the hunt and each was assured of a role in the tribe as a whole and a well-defined location in the great camping ground.

Before considering the summer camp as it developed after the adoption of the horse, we must look at the way of life associated with winter hunting. When winter came and the great hunts were over, each group withdrew to its own zone where it set up camp in valleys and other sheltered places. During this more sedentary part of the year, hunting involved a small number of men only and consisted in inducing the wandering herds of buffalo to enter the group's territory and then diverting them into large traps. This system, which may have been current throughout the year before the introduction of the horse, required large permanent constructions, traps sited in carefully selected places that permitted even a modest party of unmounted hunters to slaughter a great number of animals.

The enclosing walls of these traps, built at the bottom of valleys or at the base of a hill, were made of tree trunks, earth, or stone. On the high ground two barriers of tree trunks or heaps of stones, some hundreds of yards long, were erected side by side. These barriers converged more and more sharply toward the enclosure and were made increasingly secure. Once the herd entered the passage between the barriers, the hunters frightened the animals; they rushed forward and tumbled into the trap from the top of a short but steep rise in the terrain. In the flatlands, where this procedure could not be followed,

wholly artificial traps were devised (of a kind used also by the Assiniboine and the Cree in southern Canada). A large circle of trunks and branches was laid down, with an opening a few yards wide on which converged the lateral barriers that would channel the moving herd. These were built higher as they neared the enclosure, whose walls were six feet or more in height. The enclosure was entered across a kind of bridge of tree trunks (rather like a gangplank) that slanted up about three feet at the end of the passage—enough to force the buffalo to fall into the interior and injure themselves as well as to prevent their getting out. As soon as the herd was trapped inside, the entrance was blocked with stakes.

The winter territory, thus, was the area within which a small band or group of hunters was recognized to have the right to hunt buffalo. The boundaries were precise, generally marked by watercourses, hills, rocks, and other natural features, and the group set up its tepees in a camp well inside them. But as time went on, the hunting territory became profoundly modified as more and more of these traps were erected in the vicinity of the paths most frequently traveled by the migrating herds and as more of them were built to last, requiring no more than annual restoration and reinforcement. In this manner, the hunt itself became transformed from a nomadic to a semisedentary activity through the architectural efforts of the group, localized in particular places that could be counted on to supply food for the band. Each band had a name of its own and lived in a single winter camp. Chieftainship was rarely hereditary, being awarded to the individual most skilled in hunting and therefore with the greatest prestige. However, because the members of these winter bands changed, much more political and cultural importance was attached to the great tribal assemblies that took place during the summer.

The summer encampment was made up of a vast circle of tents disposed in a number of concentric rings and reaching a diameter of several hundred yards, usually with an opening toward the east. Each group occupied a specific sector of the circle. Within the groups there were subgroupings by age, valid for the tribe as a whole, and these constituted societies to which all the men belonged with specific ritual and social functions, such as the preparation of feasts. In a Blackfoot tribe, for example, the groups, ranging from the youngest to the oldest, had such names as Pigeons, Mosquitoes, Braves, Brave Dogs, and so on, ending with the tenth degree, the Buffaloes. From the heads of these societies or age-groups were chosen each year those who would be responsible for the successful functioning of the hunt and the summer ceremonies, along with the council of group chiefs and the chief of the entire tribe. The heads of the societies set up their tents

at the center of the circle and kept an eye on the interaction between the groups and their respective positions. The ceremonies began after the first great hunt. The most important of these marked the passage of the men from one society to another, a younger man acquiring the marks of distinction of the member he would replace in the next higher society, who would himself move upward into another vacated position. For this ceremony, three large tepees were put up. At the end of the summer, immediately before the tribal groups went their separate ways again, the Sun Dance ceremony took place, a rite that lasted several days and marked the moment of most effective tribal cohesion.

*The Tepee and Encampments of the Cheyenne, Omaha, and Osage*
The highly structural summer camp at which all the bands of a tribe assembled, the Sun Dance, and the tepee were all characteristic of other Indian populations as well, those that adopted the horse and the big summer buffalo hunt early in the 19th century, much later than the Blackfoot. These were the originally sedentary or semisedentary groups from the eastern regions who gradually assumed the culture of the Great Plains Indians under the pressure of the colonial conquest, among them the Cheyenne.[38] Logically enough, given their late conversion to a seminomadic way of life, in what is known of the great Cheyenne summer encampment one can detect elements of order, geometrical and symbolic correspondences, that quite evidently had been part of their earlier sedentary and agricultural tradition.

The Cheyenne had a council of forty-four chiefs, each of whom was the oldest member of an extended family within one of the ten principal groups or bands of the tribe. These leaders were known as "peace chiefs," in contradistinction to the heads of each of the four men's societies to which the warriors belonged, who were called "war chiefs." The theme of the Sun Dance of the Cheyenne was the re-creation of the world in successive phases during which the void and infertile earth became filled in turn by water and plants and trees, and then populated by the buffalo, and, finally, the Cheyenne. Other ceremonies, such as that of the Medicine Arrows, alternated with the great hunts and had as their object the renewal of the community.

The organization of the great camp of the Cheyenne (*plate 103*) was determined by a precise, though not unchanging, ritual. The camp might include as many as a thousand tepees set up in several concentric rows within a circle often two-thirds of a mile or more in diameter. Particularly interesting is the relationship between camp and tents during the ceremony of the Medicine Arrows. The opening of the circular encampment faced northeast, the divine direction from which the tribe had arrived at the preordained site amid songs and

100. *Ojibwa: wigwam covered with bark and rush matting, Wisconsin (USA).*

101. *Navaho: group of hogans made of branches and logs and covered with turf (southwestern USA).*

dances, and each individual tent had the same orientation. Thus, the camp resembled a great tent, symbolizing the tribal unity that was reaffirmed annually in the solar renewal ritual and brought together thousands of separate family units. The camp was also identified with the vault of the sky, and its many tents with the stars. The individual groups, of course, occupied specific sectors, while inside the rows of tepees were situated the tent-lodges of the two large societies called the Medicine Arrows and the Buffalo Bonnets. In the center there was sometimes a single very large tent for the council or the tepee for the Sun Dance.

Symmetrical and dualistic organization, with the circle divided into complementary halves, was frequent among other Plains tribes. When the camp moved out, the chiefs of the two "moieties" of the Omaha positioned their own tents to either side of the entrance of the camp; on the return march, at the opposite side of the grounds, but the sacred tents were always disposed in the same fashion, toward the south.

In its elaboration, this ritual orientation far exceeded the requirements of efficiency in organizing the collective work and the simple expression of relationships between groups. Probably it was the expression of complex reciprocal relations within agricultural groups transplanted to the nomadic encampment. Certainly, the concept of territorial center as associated with a sacred edifice had been an integral part of the cultural and mythic patrimony of the Osage when they were farmers. In many tribes the tepee was not oriented by the door alone but by its whole structure. The tepee had four principal poles oriented to the four cardinal directions. Sometimes the four cardinal directions were acknowledged by a symbol, a star for instance, affixed to the outside of the tent. Thus, nomadic architecture—the tepee and its disposition—was here forced to assume significances that, in all probability, derived from the symbolic tradition of sedentary populations.[39]

A dualistic or triadic conception of the world seems to have been the basis of the distribution of the population in the villages of the Osage, a people of the Sioux. This tribe always resided in three villages, each of which was divided into halves by a street with an east-west orientation, mirroring the course of the sun. To the north were the dwellings of the representatives of the sky, to the south, those of the earth people. In the great hunting encampments, the tents were arranged in a single circle divided into three sectors: to the north, the seven groups under the aegis of the sky; to the south, the seven representing dry land; to the southeast, the seven corresponding to the waters of the earth. There was an analogous arrangement for the sanctuary, the House of the Mysteries (*Tsi wakondagi*), a hut erected in the south part of the

*102. Blackfoot (?): tepee (western Canada). Photograph of 1905.*
*103. Cheyenne: plan of a camp circle (western USA).*

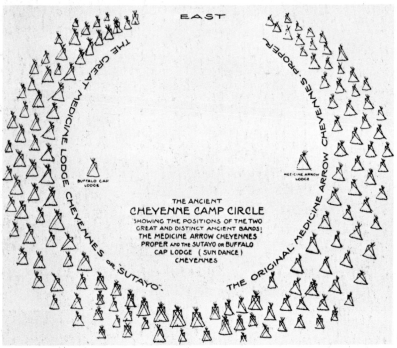

EAST

THE GREAT MEDICINE LODGE CHEYENNES or SUTAYO

THE ORIGINAL MEDICINE ARROW CHEYENNE'S PROPER

BUFFALO CAP LODGE

MEDICINE ARROW LODGE

THE ANCIENT
CHEYENNE CAMP CIRCLE
SHOWING THE POSITIONS OF THE TWO
GREAT AND DISTINCT ANCIENT BANDS;
THE MEDICINE ARROW CHEYENNES
PROPER AND THE SUTAYO OR BUFFALO
CAP LODGE (SUN DANCE)
CHEYENNES

camp. During the ceremonies, the representatives of the sky had their place north of the east-west axis, those of the earth and the waters to the south. To these three spheres belonged the symbols of maize (sky), red cedar (earth), and water. The House of Mysteries, ritually marking the center of the world, was identified with the spider, which in stylized representation resembled the intersection of the four directions of the world in the central point.

In similar fashion, the *huthuga,* the camp of the Omaha, another Sioux people, was divided between five sky lineages to the north and five earth lineages to the south, the first group symbolizing the cycle of human life, the second the cycle of productive activity, or, more specifically, the hunt and agriculture. Among the Cheyenne, lineages were distributed in the circle of tents, which was divided north-south, with an opening at the east. In the circle was a ceremonial hut, "the hut of new life," an edifice with a circular ground plan, cylindrical with a conical roof and a central supporting pole. The erection of this temple began with a ceremonial hunt, after which a tree was chopped down to make the central pole. The ceremonies that took place there comprised a dramatic representation of the re-creation of the world by the supreme being and were intended to assure the increase of the plants and animals. In erecting the central pole, the altar supporting a buffalo head, and the four principal poles that symbolized the four parts of the world, the Omaha ritually reenacted the formation of the earth by the creator-god when he threw mud collected from the bottom of the sea toward the four cardinal points of the compass, and the completed building represented the entire universe.[40]

PORTABLE PROPERTY
*Dwelling and Society in Central Asia: The Kazakhs*
In the constructions of the many seminomadic populations in the arctic and subarctic zones of Europe and Asia, one can find evidence of the transition from a hunting-and-gathering life to a stock-breeding economy. Usually, as the reindeer became increasingly domesticated, these groups tended to become sedentary and, as a result, their dwellings became more permanent in nature: a winter house built of tree trunks, a basic type in the seminomadic and sedentary (fishing) cultures, and a summer tent. Thus, like many other such groups, the Lapps of Scandinavia and the Kola Peninsula erect different types of constructions to meet the needs of their seasonal activities: tent, house of tree trunks, and elevated storage house for food (*plates 104–112*).

In the Central Asian areas the *yurta*—a type of tent with a more elaborate framework than the tepee (*plates 115–122*)—is the typical

105. *Lapps: log hut, winter season (Scandinavia).*
106. *Lapps: log hut in the form of a truncated pyramid (Scandinavia).*

107. *Lapps: diagrammatic sections of tent-huts built of branches and turf (Scandinavia).*
108. *Lapps: hut covered with turf and logs (Scandinavia).* ▷

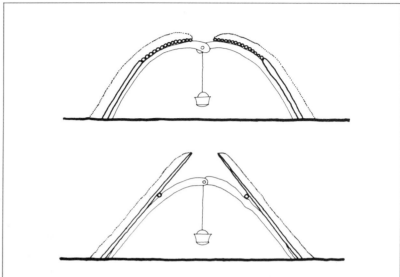

109. *Lapps: framework of a tent-hut (Scandinavia).*

110, 111. *Lapps: conical summer tent with barrier of dead branches to keep out wild animals (Scandinavia).*

112. *Lapps: framework of a tent-hut (Scandinavia).* ▷

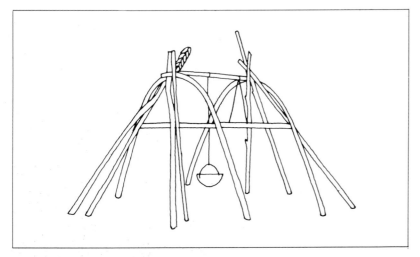

113. *Koryaks: framework of a tent, Kamchatka Peninsula (Soviet Union).*
114. *Chukchees: framework of a tent (kot), Siberia (Soviet Union).*
115. *Mongols: schematic plan of a yurta showing the disposition of furnishings and utilization of space (central Asia).*
*a. south zone: herders; b. west zone: household members; c. north zone: guest; d. east zone: head of family.*
*1. door, facing southwest; 2. path taken by guest on entering; 3. newborn animals; 4. herders; 5. food bin; 6. chest (abdar) containing the family wealth; 7. servants and the aged; 8. bed (or) for the daughters; 9. fireplace (tulha) or stove (suha); 10. firewood; 11. bed (or) for the sons; 12. chest (abdar) for the servants' clothing; 13. table; 14. chest*

*(abdar) for valuable clothing and objects; 15. table (shirée) for the guests of honor; 16. bench (zochini-suudal) for the guest; 17. cabinet for the holy images (burkhan-shirée); 18. casket for the images; 19. guest's bed (or-zochini-erentsab); 20. guest's bench (zochini-suudal); 21. chest for the clothing of the head of the family and his wife; 22. wardrobe trunk for coverings and rugs; 23. bed of the head of the family and his wife; 24. bench of the head of the family; 25. table 26. bench of the mistress of the house (gher-jin-suudal); 27. cabinet for the valuables of the head of the house; 28. bin for utensils and tableware; 29. tube leading to the smoke vent (turno) in the top of the yurta; 30. bench for herders and workhands (arduud-suudal); 31. goatskin for kumiss (mare's milk liquor).*
116. *Mongols: a yurta covered with felt (Mongolia). (Photograph of 1882.)* ▷

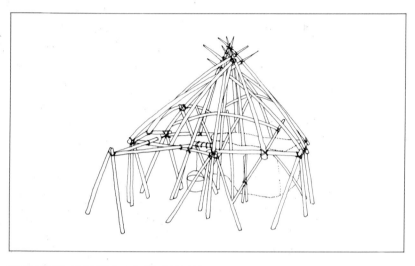

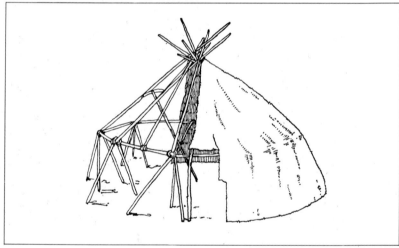

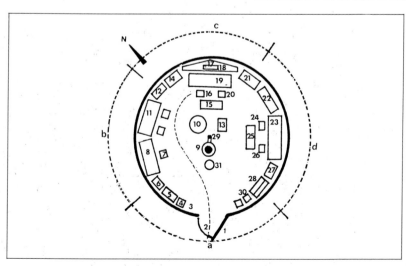

form of dwelling, and stockbreeding predominates. Here, as with every ethnic group, there is a traditional connection between the type of economy and the type of habitation, modified by the stratification of society and by the survival of economies that differ from the prevailing mode of production and of groups that do not belong to the dominant clans.

The Kazakhs are the largest ethnic group in Central Asia speaking the Turkish language, with an economy based almost exclusively on raising livestock.[41] Such sedentary activities as fishing along the rivers and agriculture (practiced chiefly in the southern regions of their territory) are considered secondary, the sort of thing done by the poorer groups to supplement stockbreeding. Until the Soviets took over, the political and economic organization was strictly dependent on ownership of livestock and, indeed, the basis for ownership of land.

The fundamental social unit is the clan (*taypas*), comprising several patrilinear extended families who recognize their common origin. The principal family, from among whose members the chief was selected (in the period before Soviet control), controlled the economic life and also held the richest pastures and most numerous herds. Each of the clans was distinguished by an emblem used as identifying sign on the *yurta* as well as on livestock and foodstores. Like a particular war cry (*uran*), this mark was used by all the members of a clan. Various clans together formed an unstable body, the brotherhood (*sök*), which in its turn could unite with others to form larger unions or tribes (*uruk*) and, by extension, "hordes," immense territorial bodies that, in the course of history, encompassed the Kazakhs in three semi-autonomous divisions: the Small Horde in the northwest, the Middle Horde in the center, the Great Horde in the east. All groupings larger than the clan had only a contingent economic and political character, and were generally formed in response to invasion from outside. The horde reflected what can be called feudal bonds between the families and the principal chieftains, but the foundation of social life continued to be the clan.

Breeding horses, camels, and sheep was the basis not only of the economy but also of social stratification and architecture. To provide grazing land for the livestock, seasonal migrations were imperative since it was virtually impossible to feed the animals from reserves of fodder. Thus, from November to mid-April, the Kazakhs took up winter quarters in encampments sheltered from the cold. In spring they migrated northward in quest of summer pasture lands, where they remained relatively stationary until mid-July because grass flourished in the then abundantly watered northern regions. In the hottest months, July and August, a scarcity of grass set the clans on the

117, 118. *Preparation of the framework of a yurta: oven and log used in bending the poles over heat, Akcha (northern Afghanistan).*

119. *Prefabricated parts of a yurta ready for assemblage: crowning wheel (in this case, two bundles of rods fastened at right angles), radial roof beams, and folding trellises that expand to make the walls, Akcha (northern Afghanistan).*

move again, but from September to October, when the rains began, the groups could be more sedentary again. Finally, at the end of October they quickly returned to the southern pasture lands and shelter from the winter cold.

The division of the territory among the clans reflected the clear separation between sedentary and nomadic periods. It was, in fact, during the winter season that boundaries between the individual territories became a matter of some importance, and they were marked by man-made signs or by obvious physical features of the landscape. Each clan had a specific portion of the territory that it was expected to defend against attacks from outside. A winter settlement comprised only a few *yurtas*, but the other settlements of the same clan were located nearby, only a few miles apart from each other, each within its territory. In colder zones some groups abandoned the *yurta* during the winter for a rectangular, semiunderground construction of stone, clay, or clods of earth that afforded protection for the animals at the front of the house as well as for the people who shared it with them and occupied the rear. The construction was surrounded by a stockade or a low wall of clods.

The route taken in the summer to better grazing land was agreed on each year by both families and clans. The localities selected varied from year to year, and whoever arrived first at a desirable place had the right to put his stock out to pasture there. The journeys might cover as much as four to five hundred miles and followed established itineraries along which the livestock could drink at the wells or waterholes owned by the nobles. The latter, called the White Bones (the lower class were the Black Bones), were members of the wealthier families with the longer genealogies; they had control of the principal economic resources and even made use of slave labor. The two classes were rigorously endogamous.

Because all Kazakhs led a nomadic life, class distinctions had little influence on the dwelling. Naturally, the wealthier families had more spacious habitations, more furnishings and utensils, and larger stores of food because they had plenty of animals to transport their *yurta* and household goods. The chieftains and nobles had wagons as well but the most common means of transport was the *travois*, two wooden trailing poles tied to the saddle and bearing some sort of platform on which goods could be loaded.

Because the Kazakhs did without burdensome and heavy objects they spent little time in fashioning utensils (for the most part acquired through exchange with urban centers and the villages of sedentary farmers in the southern regions) but a great deal in working wool for the felt used to cover the *yurta*. The felt is sometimes plain, sometimes assembled from separate, differently colored pieces sewn or otherwise

122. Turkmen: a yurta; *at the left, the cord for opening and closing the vent at the top (northern Afghanistan).*

123. *Lurs: tent in the vicinity of Khorram–abad (Iran).*
124. *Bakhtyars: putting up a tent, Caharmahal (Iran).*

attached, as in patchwork. Making the felt for the *yurta* is the women's task, while the men prepare the wooden parts of the tent-hut (*plates 117–120*). Construction has been standardized for centuries, for it would be difficult to improve or, indeed, vary this extremely lightweight structure, which is easy to set up, take down, and transport and is perfectly adaptable to both winter and summer conditions (*plate 122*).

The walls of the *yurta* are composed of collapsible trellises about four feet high (*plate 120*). For a hut twenty feet in diameter, six trellises are required. When the units are opened, the wooden staves form square diamonds about twelve inches on a side, and they are secured where they cross each other by leather thongs. The trellises are tied together, but a gap is left as a doorframe, which is covered by a felt curtain. The shallow dome over the structure is supported by stakes tied to each diamond at the top of the wall, and they meet at the top in a wooden wheel some two or three feet in diameter. The entire framework is further reinforced by crisscross ties on the outside, which are often fastened to carpets or cloths.

The *yurta* is set up and dismantled by the women or servants, and the large ones require two or three camels or horses to transport them. Like the North American tepee, the *yurta* is located in the center of a sacred space that is oriented with respect to the cardinal directions, as are the various sectors of the interior, which are occupied by different members of the family according to inflexible rule (*plate 115*).

*Tent and Desert: The Ruwala Bedouins of the Arabian Peninsula*
In the desert and semidesert regions of northern Africa and southwestern Asia, the nomadic breeders of camels, dromedaries, and goats use various types of tents. Of considerable diversity, they are always strictly functional, with every detail of material and form meticulously worked out; they are lightweight, an excellent protection from the rigors of the climate, and practical as regards the availability and use of material. Often acquired by barter with the sedentary populations with whom the Bedouins enter into contact seasonally, the materials are subject to considerable variation; the structure and dimensions of the tents, however, tend to remain unchanged, fixed once and for all in an age-old form determined by efficiency of fabrication and ease of transport.

The Ruwala[42] are considered to be the wealthiest of the Bedouins of the Arabian Peninsula, inhabiting its northwestern area in close contact with the hinterlands of Aleppo and Damascus. Theirs is an almost continuous nomadism. Traveling in groups guided by a dominant lineage (*ahl*) they follow a clockwise, circular itinerary that takes them through the prairies (*hamad*), the sandy desert (*nefud*),

126. *Kabábísh: axonometric drawing of a tent (northern Sudan).*

127–130. *Tekna: tent, showing details and furnishing (southeastern Morocco).*
  (127) plan; (128) position of the tent cloth at night and during the day; (129) topmost wooden element, supported by the two main poles crossing just below it; (130) trestle with sack hanging from it.

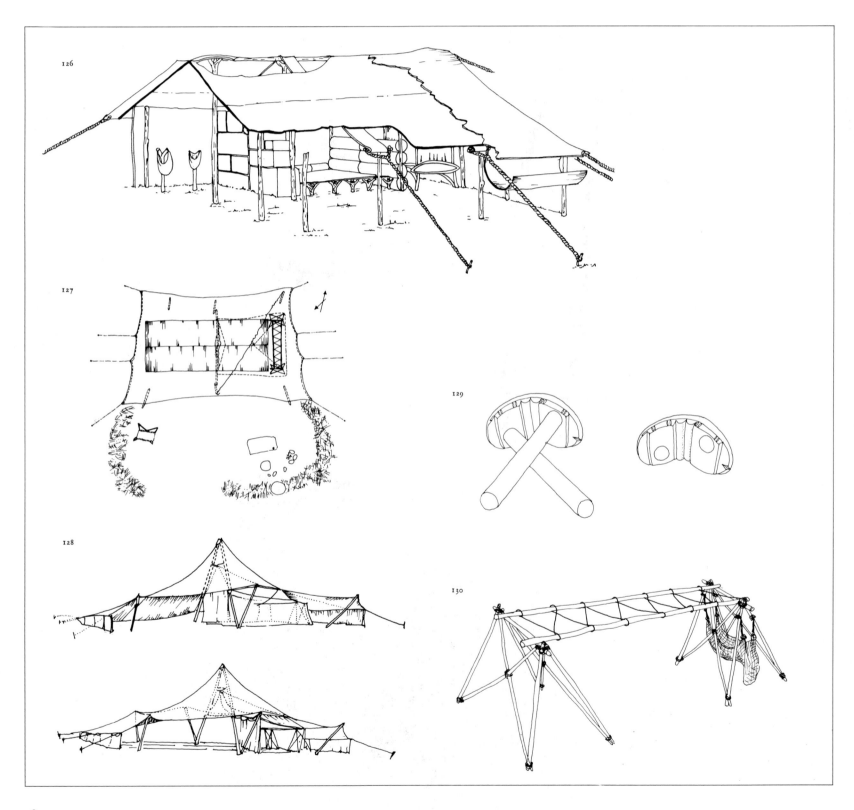

*131. Nomads' tent erected in an agricultural settlement, Gabès (Tunisia).*
*132. Tent with enclosure for cattle (zeriba), Fezzan (Libya).*

*134, 135. Ad Shek: keel-shaped tent; general view, and detail of the hanging mats closing the entrance, Eritrea (Ethiopia).*

*136. Transporting the disassembled tent, Eritrea (Ethiopia).*

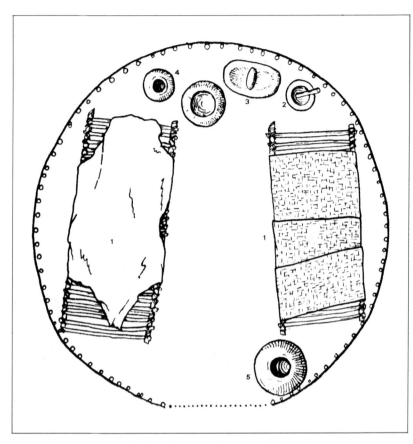

and a rocky zone (*hana*). In September, mounted on camels, the groups leave the villages of the coastal area where they have spent the hottest months, and move eastward to the pasture lands of the *hamad*, where they will pass the winter. In spring they move farther south, toward the desert and its oases, and with the onset of summer they turn north to spend August and September among the sedentary agricultural populations with whom they exchange some of their camels for grain, clothing, firearms, and tent cloth.

Along with camel raising, which gives them milk as well as a convenient means of transport for men, provisions, and tents, they do some hunting and gather wild grasses, berries, and locusts. The chief has the right to certain prized wild game such as antelopes, gazelles, and ibexes, which are caught by specially trained hunters using falcons. Camels—the index of the wealth of a head of a family—are important above all for the transport of foodstuffs: One camel loaded with cereals is needed for each member of the family, plus a few for eventual guests. For the more numerous and powerful families, the caravan may include more than fifty camels burdened with grain, barley, dates, and salt, products that must take care of all needs for almost a year.

Encampments are never made far from a water supply, often an artificial well a few dozen yards deep. The most favorable sites are occupied year after year, for periods of as much as several weeks at a time depending on the pasturage available. The large tents are disposed in parallel rows.[43] The covering is made of strips of goat's-wool cloth about two feet wide, which are sewed together. Six or eight poles with hitches of rope support the framework. The opening can be altered according to the climate. The tent of the chief, the most influential individual in the extended family, is larger than the others. The interior is divided in two by a cloth hanging; the smaller area is reserved for the owner and his guests, the larger for the women, children, and slaves and the larger also serves as kitchen and storeroom for the provisions. For furnishings, there are only carpets, quilts, and cushions but much importance is attached to utensils, in particular the receptacles for milk and food.

### THE SHEPHERDS OF CENTRAL AND SOUTH AFRICA

The pastoral cultures of central and southern Africa have developed a unique type of settlement, the circular kraal, which has an enclosure for animals in the center and human accommodations around the pen. The type is quite uniform across a large area, and it is found, varying only as specific solutions for installation and construction differ, among the Tsonga of Mozambique, the Masai of Kenya and Tanzania, and the Zulu of South Africa (*plates 150–151, 153–160*).

84

139. *Dankali nomads: tent in the plain of Dakka (Somalia).*

140. *Bezanozano: hut of bent branches with the open side covered by mats (northeastern Madagascar).*

141. *Tent-hut covered with matting, Wadas (Chad).*

142. *Teda: circular tent with enclosure of canes for cattle, Tibesti region (Chad).*

143. *Teda: habitation of canes with granary in stone and earth, Tibesti region (Chad).*

144. *Berbers: village of Gabr-on, Fezzan (Libya).*

### The Masai and Tsonga

In the *muti* of the primarily agricultural Tsonga[44] (*plate 150*), motifs belonging to different productive and cultural stratifications almost classically coexist. Circular in form, it is large enough to house an entire extended family (whose oldest and most respected member is recognized as chief). The surrounding stockade has one main opening as well as other secondary gates, and in the center is the circular enclosure for livestock, often subdivided to segregate various kinds. The dwellings of the individual families are disposed in rings around this enclosure. They are cylindrical huts with conical roofs and a door opening toward the center of the complex; in front is a small open space for domestic activities. On an axis with the principal entrance of the stockade are the huts of the wives of the chief, and often he has another hut especially set aside to receive guests and to rest. As is universally the case, the village considers itself the focal point of the link with the territory, which is represented by the sacred tree. Here, as at an altar, sacrifices are offered periodically, notably during the feast of the dead (*chirilu*) when the horns of sacrificed oxen are hung on it. In this prevailingly woodland area, where trees must be cleared before new settlements and plantings can begin, this sedentary village type reflects the link between the group (patrilinear, in this case) and the sacred tree but has as well the concentric arrangement of dwellings around a space for animals that is characteristic of populations raising livestock.

The kraal of the Masai,[45] a semiprovisional structure put up and then abandoned during the periodic seasonal migrations in search of grass for the herds, has the same basic arrangement (*plate 151*). Around the enclosure, divided into pens for different kinds of animals, is a concentric shelter of branches and thorny bushes with two, sometimes four, diametrically opposite entrances. The small huts grouped symmetrically to either side of the enclosure are built of bent branches and covered with dung, clay, and vegetable matter, and have a characteristic opening that doubles back in a spiral. Building the kraal is entirely the women's affair, and they also own the family huts. A special institution of the Masai is the subdivision into age-groups of men from sixteen to thirty years of age; they are segregated from the group as a whole in a complex similar to the domestic kraal but without defensive walls. This institution is of military character, for the young men are intended to defend the territory, to augment the herds by raids on other villages, and so on; nonetheless, here again the women, the mothers of the warriors, have to build the huts of their camp.

### The Zulu

The encampment of the Zulu[46] reflects an even more nomadic way

145. *Nyangatom: aerial view of a village (Ethiopia).*
146–148. *Nyangatom: final stages in building a hut with a framework of branches and covering of bound bundles of grass (Ethiopia).*

149. *Nyangatom: cookhouse in disuse (many of its materials have been reutilized elsewhere); in the foreground, the hearth composed of pieces of clay from an anthill (Ethiopia).*

of life (*plates 156–158*). Their domed huts—called *indlu*—are portable. The kraal is not substantially different from those just described: a circular defensive wall (here, with a single entrance), a ring of huts, and a circular enclosure for the livestock in the center. However, we know that gigantic encampments were set up in the past, by Zulu kings in the center of a territory subjugated by them, functioning as permanent military camps from which raids could be launched in all directions. The battle order of the Zulu, the *impi*, was a half circle with the concavity toward the enemy, who could thus be caught in a pincers when the outer wings of warriors closed in—a technique originating in the hunt, no doubt. The same arrangement was maintained in the great royal encampments, one of which was described in a 19th-century account:

The king's kraals are of enormous dimensions, and are several in number. Panda, for example, has one kraal, the central enclosure of which is nearly a mile in diameter. This enclosure is supposed to be filled with the monarch's cows, and is consequently called by the name of *isiBaya*. Practically, however, the cattle are kept in smaller enclosures arranged along the sides of the *isiBaya*, where they can be watched by those who have the charge of them, and whose huts are placed conveniently for that purpose. The vast central enclosure is used almost exclusively as a parade ground, where the king can review his troops, and where they are taught to go through the simple maneuvers of Kaffir warfare. Here, also, he may be seen in council, the *isiBaya* being able to accommodate an unlimited number of suitors.

Around the *isiBaya* are arranged the huts of the warriors and their families, and are placed in four or even five-fold ranks; so that the kraal almost rises to the dignity of a town, having several thousand inhabitants, and presenting a singularly imposing appearance when viewed at a distance.

At the upper portion of the kraal, and at the further end from the principal entrance, are the huts specially erected for the king, surrounded by the other huts containing his harem. The whole of this part of the kraal is separated from the remainder by lofty and strong fences, and its doors are kept by sentinels . . . at that time Panda had thirteen of these great military kraals, and he had just completed a fourteenth. He takes up his residence in these kraals successively, and finds in each everything he can possibly want—each being, indeed, almost identical in every respect with all the others. As a general rule, each of these military kraals forms the residence of a single regiment; while the king has many others which are devoted to more peaceful objects.[47]

150. *Tsonga: circular settlement, or kraal (Mozambique).*

151. *Masai: schematic plan of a circular kraal with the huts disposed symmetrically to either side of the axis indicated by the dotted line (Kenya, Tanzania).*
    *Livestock enclosure: 1. sheep; 2. calves; 3. adult cattle.*

152. *Nyamwezi: quadrangular habitation (wagogo) of branches and earth built around a courtyard, near Dodoma (Tanzania).*

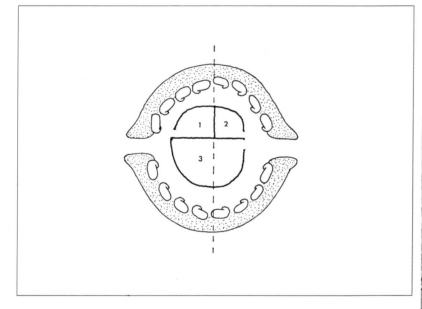

153. *Walled farm with habitations and pen for the livestock (Rwanda).*

154. *Reconstruction of a fortified farmhouse with sunken inner courtyard for the livestock (Rhodesia).*

155. *Ambo: schematic plans of two labyrinthine kraals (Namibia).*
   *a) 1. sacred fire and central plaza; 2. residence of the chief; 3. wives' huts; 4. guest huts; 5. granaries.*
   *b) 1. central plaza; 2. residence of the chief; 3. wives' huts; 4. guards; 5. main entrance.*

156. *Zulu: drawing representing a labyrinthine kraal with the royal hut in the center (Republic of South Africa).*

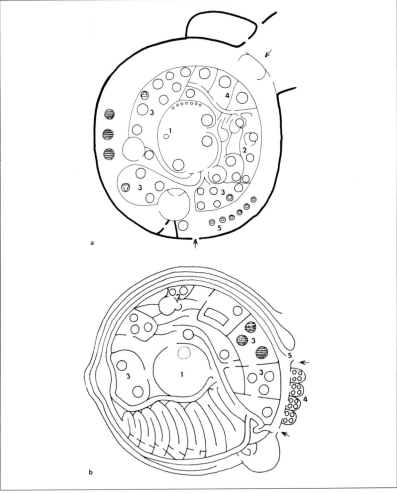

157. *Zulu: aerial view of a kraal (Republic of South Africa).*

158. *Zulu: diagram of a hut* (indlu) *with the names of its principal structural elements (Republic of South Africa).*
  *1.* umtwazi; *2.* uqunga; *3.* ibaxa; *4.* isicaba; *5.* isicholo; *6.* umjanjato; *7.* umshayo; *8.* insika; *9.* izi thungo; *10.* umsele; *11.* iziko; *12.* isilili sokudla samadoda.

Life in the common encampment also followed hierarchical patterns, with a clear "dualistic" matrix.

In the good old days, when wives were cheap and many, a high-class Kaffir kraal was organized in two distinct sides or branches. There was the *ekuNene* (or right-hand side) whose huts ran up on the right side from near the kraal entrance till they reached and included the *iNdlunkulu* (or Great Hut), occupying exactly the central position at the top of the kraal (under the dominion of the Great Wife and her son); and there was the *iKohlo* (or left-hand) branch, whose huts formed the opposite side of the circle.[48]

ARCHITECTURE AND THE DIVISION OF THE HUNTING CATCH

Ways and means of building and of organizing space, developed from an immense variety of spatial and territorial experiences by hunting and gathering populations, live on as a continually reinterpreted and modified historical substratum by stockbreeders and agricultural peoples. Naturally, not only are types of construction involved but systems of relationship, which mediate between the productive systems and the social structure and physical environment. Despite profound mutations in the systems of production, we can still recognize the vestiges of a people's very earliest conceptions of space and of their territory. Thus, among seminomadic farmers, hunting often is considered the heritage of an older (and therefore superior) system of living. In the majority of cases, there exists a stratification of different systems of production that are more or less archaic and of greater or lesser importance, each having a precise spatial, mythological, and architectural conception.

Generally speaking, the provisional architectural structures of hunters and gatherers, whether private (family) or public (clan, tribe), precede the edifices of agricultural peoples in time and social significance, and even as building types. Among the latter, the constructions for initiatory rites must be considered an integral part of architectural activity, although they are built only for particular ceremonies.[49] Indeed, they are complete works of transformation of the myth and the social structure in terms of collective architecture. They mediate between territory and residence, human activity and nature. Even if they only involve displacing earth or shifting sacred images or edifices of some sort from one place to another, they establish ritual relationships between territorial space and society that are not obliterated but transformed in the later experience of the agricultural populations, given the natural tendency to celebrate, to glorify whatever happened and was done in the past. The economy and culture that go with hunting are therefore never completely left behind, not even by those

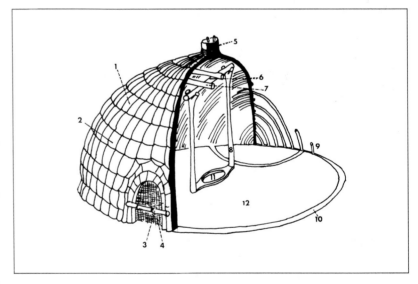

*159, 160. Hottentots: the tent-hut and the kraal (South Africa). (Engravings by Naanheurige, 1727.)*

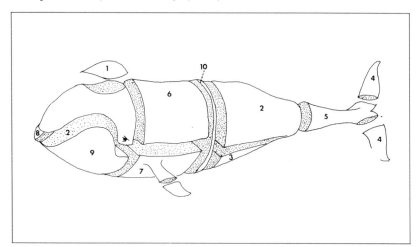

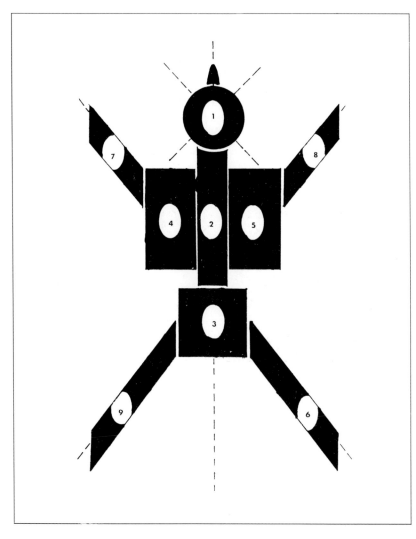

societies that abandoned the activity long before; together with the totemic animals that were its object, many of its consequences remain to symbolize the power of man (as chief) over the animal species and over other men as well.

One important aspect of this continuity derives from the manner in which the quarry is divided up among the participants in a hunting party. Undergoing a profound change in significance, this act becomes transformed from simple food distribution into a ritual parceling of power, which remains perfectly evident in the way highly organized agricultural populations continue to plan and subdivide their dwellings, cultivated fields, and territory. Few actions succeed better than the division of the great catch in expressing the relationships of hierarchy and symmetry within the hunting group or team in terms of what we may call organic relationships. The latter are symbolized architectonically, so to speak, in the dismemberment of the animal into specific cuts according to precise rules. Having taken the initiative in the enterprise, the chief by right obtains the most important part (the head or the most appreciated piece). The others, according to their degree of relationship and participation, receive the other parts. Such procedure is carried out on the kangaroo by the Australian aborigines, on the elephant by the Pygmies, on the whale by the Eskimos of Tigara in Alaska (*plate 161*).[50] When dividing up a sacrificial animal substitutes for the division of the hunt quarry, the parallels between social system and animal body, between members and member, and between the chief and the head of the animal survive to leave their mark on many of the foundation rituals among primitive peoples (*plate 162*) as well as on the power relations within agricultural and herding societies. As with the problem of the representation of the power of god, clan, or state in human form, here too we are confronted with an ensemble of relationships which, because they appear in a great variety of cultures, constitute a valid means for identifying, in a historical rather than geographical sense, the significances of the various architectural traditions.[51]

THE COLLECTIVE HOUSE AND LONGHOUSE

The collective house[1] represents an important stage in the emergence of the clan and family from the community, a process that has taken many different forms in the course of history. For Western ethnologists concerned with architectural typology, the collective house in its purest form has long represented the dwelling most characteristic of communistic societies in which inequalities and privileged positions do not exist among the family nuclei and, instead, agricultural work is shared equally, as are all other activities. This state of affairs is reflected in the basic features of the collective house: specifically, large dimensions and limited decoration. The dimensions of such a building can be taken as an index of cooperation in the work of construction in which all the members of the collectivity took part. The limited use of decoration may be attributed to the fact that in such societies there is little incentive to competitiveness and, in consequence, little exploitation of myths for family or individual purposes or profit. Housing all the members of a tribal clan or kinship group, the collective dwelling reflects the closed structure of that clan or group, whose membership is both limited and predetermined. The fundamental economic parity between the families is expressed in the fact that no single family group produces for itself alone and that private property is limited. All of the inhabitants participate in the collective administration and maintenance of their joint "territory." This is why the collective house can be considered a factor counteracting the tendency of agricultural societies to become stratified and, consequently, to foster more or less pronounced internal inequalities. Instead, it affirms the separation of the clan or family group from others, which assumes the perpetuation of its direct relationship with the territory.

The ideal is by no means easy to achieve, and thus in only a few forest areas does a single isolated house shelter an entire clan nucleus. More commonly, a limited number of constructions assembled around a clearing or along a streetlike plaza compose that more complex unit, the village, that the collective type of house would seem to obviate. But even in such cases, what remains the potent factor as regards centralization of power, defense, and organization of work, is the unity of the clan, evidenced and kept vigorously alive precisely by the house that shelters all of its members. The fact is, such communities lack what one expects to find in a village: some sort of public edifice for assemblies and ceremonies and the type of building known as a "men's house." All needs have to be met by the single structure of the collective dwelling, whatever its size.

The interior is divided into compartments for the individual families, each with its own hearth, and an area is set aside for the chief. Perfectly self-sufficient, the collective house may be regarded as the dwelling that most fully draws the human groups living in a specific territory into a centralized structure; nevertheless, it does not at the same time involve a hierarchical partition of the economic and social life.

*The Tupinamba of the Brazilian Coast*

There are two geographical areas where the collective house was not completely supplanted by the village with its family dwellings, public edifices, chief's house, and the like: southeast Asia and the American continents, and it is in the latter that we find the most developed and unequivocal examples of the institution. Isolated in the South American forest, the *churuata* of the Piaroa and the *maloca* of the Desana represent the kind of complex and fully developed social and architectonic solutions that are possible only in a theoretically unlimited natural environment such as the middle Orinoco and upper Amazon basins. There, each house is the center of a territory that expands in concentric rings: habitation, garden plots, cleared area, hunting grounds. But in addition to these and other close to archetypal examples, the collective house comprehends innumerable varieties of the so-called longhouse, its most widely diffused type. As early as 1519, Antonio Pigafetta was struck by their uniqueness and described them in his account of the life of the coastal populations of Brazil. "They live in certain long houses that they call *boii* and sleep in slings of cotton called *amache* [hammocks] slung inside the house from sturdy wooden supports at one end and the other; they make fires on the ground between these. In each of these *boii* live a hundred men with their wives and children, all making a great racket."[2]

About the middle of the 16th century another traveler, Hans von Staden,[3] grasped in its essentials the anthropological significance of the longhouse of the Tupinamba on the Brazilian coast (*plates 163–165*). He described the "village" as composed of a few collective houses, in each of which the authority of the head was as uncontested as that of a king, though it was restricted to exceptional occasions of special importance for the group as a whole. The site was changed every four or five years when the resources of the territory became exhausted and the *pindo* palm fronds covering the houses had deteriorated.

Once it is decided to build the shelters the head of the group assembles some forty men and women or as many as he can find, commonly from among his relatives and friends. These erect the cabins which measure about fourteen feet in width and a hundred and fifty in length, according to the number of persons to be lodged there. The cabins are around two toises in height [twelve feet] and are curved above like the vault of a cellar, being covered with a thick layer of palm leaves so as to keep out the rain. Inside there are

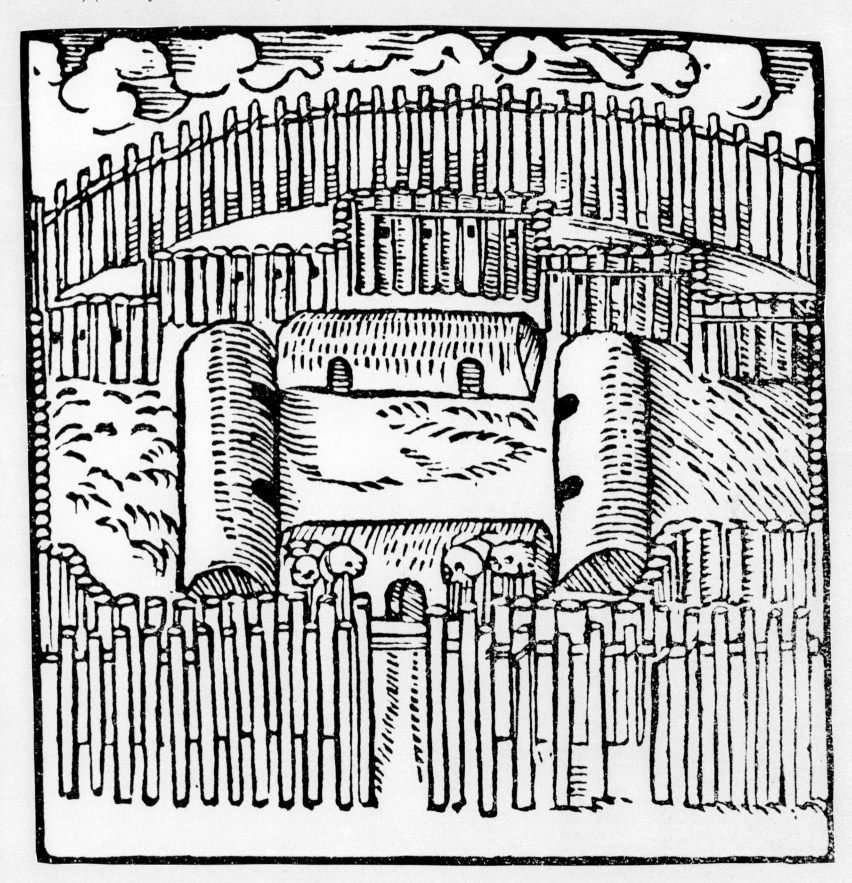

163. *Tupinamba: fortified village with barrel-roofed longhouses (eastern Brazil). (Woodcut from Von Staden, 1557.)*

no dividing walls so no one has a separate room, but each couple, man and woman, have their own space twelve feet in length on one side of the room, and the same amount of space is occupied on the opposite side of the room by another couple. Thus these shelters are crowded with people, and each couple has its own hearth. The head of the group has his place in the center. Every shelter has, as a rule, three small doorways, one at each end and one in the middle, so low that one must bend down to enter or leave.[4]

The architecture of the Tupinamba at that time included, along with the collective house, such elements as organization around a central open space, a multiplicity of dwellings, and a palisaded enclosure, all of which would seem to be inconsistent with the apparent political and social autonomy of the group. Absent was the "oneness" that characterized the relationship between group and territory. In the course of time, the longhouse underwent an important change. Still capable of lodging several dozen individuals linked by blood, it developed from a structure divided into a series of single-family cells into a type of building marked off into a very few sectors belonging to a limited number of families.[5]

### The Desana of the Upper Amazon Basin

The dwelling of numerous groups of hunter-farmers in the Amazonas region, on the other hand, is perfectly expressive of the relationship between clan and territory (*plates 166–169, 171, 174–178*). The *maloca* is a house lodging all the members of a patrilinear clan; among the Desana,[6] its framework and plan are identified with the spatial and temporal structures of the universe, within which the clan has its place and through which it is assured that life will continue and nature remain fruitful.

The Desana think of their territory as an ensemble of "houses" belonging to the various animal species, each of which receives from the sun the fecundizing force: the male principle, the energy required for reproduction. The hills are conceived as great *malocas* where the animals of the forest reproduce themselves; the rapids in the rivers are the subaqueous *malocas* of the fish; the *maloca* of the clan is the residence of man, the uterus within which the human species is born and perpetuates itself. A subterranean house corresponds to these terrestrial "houses," a uterine paradise called *Axpikon-diá*. Symbolically and materially, the house of man is linked to these sacred places that make the territory of the clan a complete and self-sufficient universe.

Around the *maloca* a series of protective barriers, visible and invisible, are interposed between inner and outer spaces. Around the house is an invisible stratum that covers it like a placenta. The circular clearing is surrounded by a wall of stakes, likened by the Desana to the aureole around the sun, that delimit a sacred area—thus, a true cosmic boundary. Outside this magic circle, paths branch off to connect the *maloca* with the sacred places of the territory: most importantly, with the "port," the crucial link between terrestrial world and subterranean world. Here, too, is that umbilical connection between the local group and the sacred places in the hunting territory, a link that again is identified with the path uniting the settlement with the water hole, with the vortex that represents the passage into the subterranean world and where the events of the myths are concentrated. Situated near a rapids where the water forms whirlpools, the "port" is the seat of Waí-maxsë, the lord of the fish, who resides there in his underwater *maloca* and is protected by Diroá-maxsë, the divinity who maintains the sanctity of life. The port is also the point where the umbilical cord of the individual is connected with the subterranean *maloca* of *Axpikon-diá.* The central zone of this port (*dexhó-maha perá*) is the place of unity, sacred to the rites of the shaman; upriver is the "port of the men" (*ëmë-ya perá*) and downriver the "port of the women" (*nomé-ya perá*).

An additional network of paths radiates outward to connect the collective house with the fields, the *chagras,* owned by the individual family nuclei, some as much as a few miles distant, where manioc, bananas, yams, potatoes, and other produce are grown. The paths, like the space around the *maloca,* are considered a protected zone, the terrain of man, in which all his productive and ritual activities take place.

Both as a whole and in its structural and decorative details, the Desana *maloca (wi'i)* is thought of as an integral model, summing up the social structure and the patrimony of myth.[7] It has a rectangular ground plan, sometimes rounded off at one or both ends in an apse, and a peaked roof. It always faces south, toward the river and the port to which it is linked (all the rivers in the area of the Rio Vaupés are thought of as running eastward). The main door opens in that direction, the secondary door, on the opposite side, toward what is thought of as north. Four to eight family nuclei have their quarters in the rear, the front normally being reserved for guests (*plate 166*). The building consists of a wooden framework covered by palm fronds. The three transverse wooden "portals," each made up of two tall poles yoked at the top by a crossbeam (*plate 166, and see plates 167, 168*) are called "red jaguars" in tribute to the great mythical jaguar, the being that transmits to earth the fertilizing virtues of the sun; for this reason, they are often painted in red with black spots. A longitudinal beam connecting these portals represents the ladder, the cosmic pillar that joins the different levels of the world. The rafters (*waxsúni*) are identified with the men of the clan because wood is considered a con-

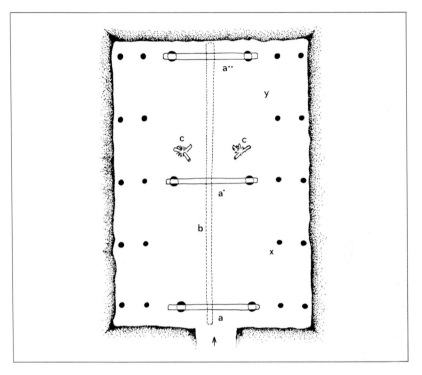

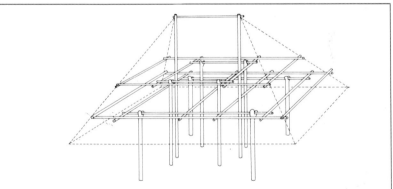

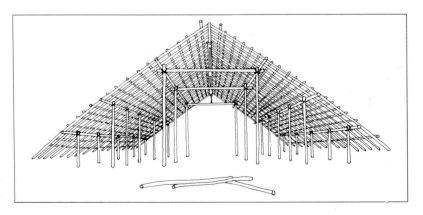

169. *Jivaro:* jivaría, *a rectangular maloca* with rounded ends, upper *Amazon (Peru).*
170. *Araucano: rectangular* ruka *with rounded ends under construction (Chile).*

171. *Tucuna:* maloca *with rounded corners, Rio Ygarape (northern Brazil).*

172. *Hixkaryana: rectangular huts with rounded corners and pyramidal roofs, Rio Nhamunda, Amazonas (northern Brazil).*

173. *Piaroa: framework of a churuata (Venezuela).*
174. *Muinanï:* maloca, *upper Rio Cahuinari (Colombia).*
175. *Rectangular* maloca *with rounded corners under construction (Colombia).*

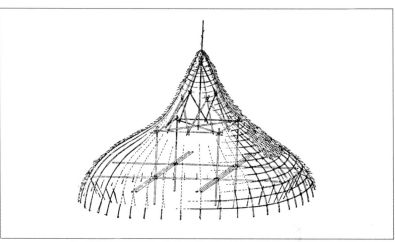

centration of male energy (the forest represents a masculine principle). Over the rafters is laid the covering of palm fronds, personified as Maxsí-maxsë, lord of the roof and the fronds.

The front of the house is decorated with symbolic motifs representing the subterranean world, *Axpikon-diá,* painted in yellow clay and charcoal, among them the mythical serpent-pirogue that conveyed the first men to earth. This vehicle of primordial humanity is believed to have passed along the median transverse line of the *maloca,* which is, in fact, the second jaguar portal. The latter symbolizes the primordial crossing, from east to west, and marks the most sacred point in the center of the building, which, in the course of the ritual ceremonies, functions as cosmic support. The front part of the house is considered masculine and is associated with the color yellow; the rear is feminine and red. The hearth, constructed from tubular supports that hold the pots and the dish for preparing manioc and cassava, is the symbol of birth, of the union between the male and the female sexual organs.[8]

The significances inherent in Desana architecture express many fundamental connections between territory and residence, clan and mythic beliefs, which, in turn, reveal the coexistence of different economic and cultural stratifications. The background, the general environmental picture, is still that of a hunting society, and, indeed, the Desana consider themselves as such: The places where animal species reproduce, the passages between the visible and the invisible world are still the fundamental underpinnings of the organization of their world. But only a quarter of their food is hunted. The rest comes from fishing and gardening in roughly equal measure. Thus, the Desana residence is stable, linked directly to the most significant point in their territory, and a radial network of paths expresses the basic relationship between residence and fields that is characteristic of agricultural activity. The complex of significances that they attach to their dwelling reflects, therefore, two parallel interests: the territorial elements that must concern them as hunters and the primordial concept of fertility, reproduction, and the male and female principles that are associated with agricultural production.

Some peoples such as the Witoto and the Bora in the Colombian area of the Amazon[9] conceive of the *maloca* as a crouching human being, male or female. The equilibrium between the architectural elements, the walls and their covering (*plates 177, 178*)—the supporting and the supported elements—is part of a concept involving the entire natural and human equilibrium, with constant reference to the clan, which makes a concentrated joint effort in building the collective house-temple. In this manner, though the building put up by men constitutes an intrusion into the natural environment, it is none-

*177, 178. Witoto: views of the interior of a maloca, Amazonas (Colombia).*

theless conceived of as something belonging in essence to that environment. Just as for hunters the camp is the mobile center of their territory, so the *maloca* of humankind is thought of as having the same value and significance as the *malocas* of the various animal species, which, like the human dwelling, have a sacred and indissoluble link with the place in which they are situated.

*The Iroquois and Lenni-Lenape of Eastern North America*
The longhouse of the Iroquois and other eastern North American Indians is not, properly speaking, a collective dwelling in the classic sense of the term but rather a multifamily house, which reflects a certain hierarchy. Its community ties are external, delegated to the village and the territorial sanctuary. Its internal structure centers on hearths, each usually serving four families, two to either side (*plate 187*). An aggregate of relatively self-sufficient units, the multifamily house has neither the function and character of territorial sanctuary nor that of cosmological model characteristic of isolated collective edifices. It is the residential function that is important, detached from the significance inherent in the group, clan, or "nation." By definition no longer center of the territory, the longhouse has remained intrusive in an economic context associated with such levels of organization as the village, the chief's house, the intertribal sanctuary.

Given the marked similarity among North American Indian ritual edifices and the areas allotted within them to the different kinship groups (each with its own distinguishing totemic emblem), one must assume the existence of a widespread mythic-ritual tradition, connected until the arrival of the white man with an agricultural society; later, the various populations separated into farmers and hunters. The obvious contrasts between economic systems, modes of production and utilization of the territory, and architectural traditions of these Indians by no means conceal the fact that there is a consistency in their ritual harmonization of space and time that derives from the pre-Columbian period. The basis of this equilibrium is the village whose agricultural economy was more or less thoroughly integrated, seasonally, with the hunt. The sanctuary, whether tribal or intertribal, has as its chief function the expression and affirmation of the interconnection between the various clans, traditions, and cultures—a role in which political and territorial factors assume no marked importance. On the whole, the sanctuary can be said to play the role of a spatial-temporal focal point for groups dispersed across broad regions and so reinforces their spirit of cohesion through the acceptance of a common myth explaining their origin. Among the northern tribes, however, as was not true in the area of the Moundbuilders culture in the south, the weblike structure of villages was never spanned (even in the case of the Iroquois League of Five Nations) by economic and political structures with a specific architecture to express the interconnection.

Intertribal unity and common divine origin are underscored by a common symbolic and ritual language and given overt expression in the annual celebrations that take place in the tribal Big Houses of the Lenni-Lenape (Delaware) Indians. Because of the relative cultural similarity of the dozens and dozens of tribes that recognize the supremacy of the institution, the Big House has the function of a religious center of the type found in South America among, for example, such tribes as the Desana. Its significance is substantially similar, too, for the various populations that maintain relationships only through the cosmogonical rite of the Big House. The architecture of the "temple" represents every aspect of the succession of the mythic events but receives its deepest significance from the presence of the men who take part in the ceremony according to established procedure.

The division of the cosmos into celestial world, human world, and infernal world is reflected in the symbolism of the structure of the large rectangular cabin—the roof, the walls, which represent the four parts of the world, and the floor—and this tripartition is echoed in the brotherhoods of the Turkey, Turtle, and Wolf, which symbolically represent all of mankind.[10] Together, the building and the ceremony represent the re-creation of the world by the creator-god after its destruction in a cataclysm. "The twelve planes or terraces that rise above the roof lead up to the twelfth heaven, the dwelling of the Great Spirit. Ten faces carved by the sky powers ornament the ten upright supports and another two the central support that rises through the entire structure, symbol of the pillar of the world and, at the same time —as center of the quadripartite cosmos—seat and representative of the creator-god. Two masks are hung on it, the one on the right painted red, the other black. . . . The doorway at the east symbolizes the primordial beginning of all things; that at the west, direction of the setting sun, symbolizes their end and, unlike the east door, remains closed at all times. . . . Around the two fires and the central support an oval, well-trampled space for dancing is traced on the floor, beginning at the east and circling back through the north, west, and south to end at the central upright, which is the seat of the Great Spirit. This the white path of life on which the participants walk in the twelve nights following an ecstatic dance ritual, broken by brief declamations."[11]

*Structure and Family: The Ngadju of Borneo*
The longhouse can be expressive of the main lines of kinship and production. It is necessarily the product of collaboration on the part

*179. Dayak: longhouse (Borneo).*

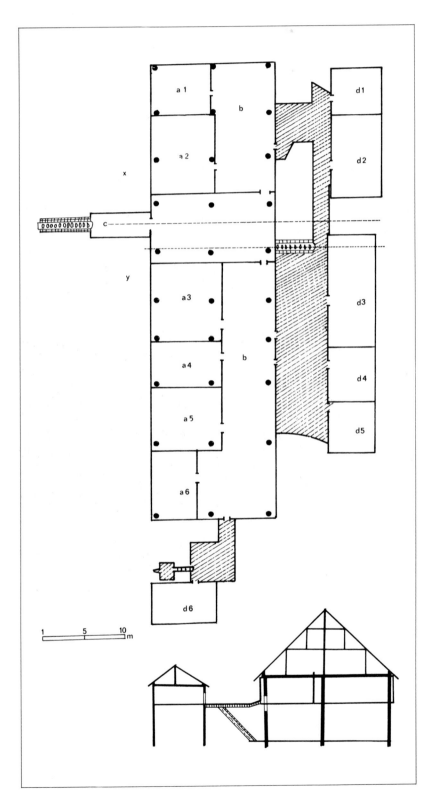

180. *Ngadju: ground plan and section of the longhouse of the Antang and Ideng families, Tumbang Gagu (Borneo).*
x. *section of the house belonging to the descendants of Ideng: (a1, a2) their family room..; (d1, d2) their kitchens.*
y. *section of the house belonging to the descendants of Antang: (a3–a6) their family rooms; (d3–d6) their kitchens.*
b. *galleries, c. entrance: common areas.*

of an entire clan or kinship group, since only the efforts of a large number of individuals make it possible to build and maintain such an edifice: Social unity is the premise and, at the same time, the guarantee of an investment of labor that is always heavy because of the large size of the building.

That technical means and economic factors (principal food source and its acquisition) differ so widely in different places and times is demonstrated by the fact that there are innumerable solutions to the problem of the coexistence of different families under a single roof. Even within a restricted geographical area there are traces of different ways of organizing society and labor, with a greater or lesser accentuation of the role of the community as opposed to that of the lineage group, and of the clan as opposed to that of the individual. Each of these factors has its specific influence on the way the interior of the house is organized. On the one hand, the longhouse may be equivalent to an entire village; in this case, the interior is divided into compartments for the family units, as in the house-villages of the Dayak in Borneo (*plates 179, 181*). On the other, the longhouse may merely shelter an extended family; in this case, the longhouse is simply an elongated dwelling with no transverse partitions between the nuclear families that share it (as in Polynesia). Despite very precise analogies between building techniques and forms, the relationships of production and architecture as reflected in the longhouse never find identical expression. Within a single population many changes take place in the course of time and according to location. Finally, it must be kept in mind that building a longhouse requires a very considerable number of hands and, because of this, a distinction must be made between the situation in which all of the members of a group lend a hand in the task of building and the very different situation in which specialized artisans are recruited to do the job and are paid in gifts and food.

The longhouse in Tumbang Gagu, Borneo, built less than a century ago by certain Ngadju families (*plate 180*) is a large construction supported by thirty posts of very strong ironwood (*Eusideroxylon zwageri*).[12] It houses six family units, each with its own room and a place for cooking on the opposite side of the broad gallery that runs the length of the house. Each family is responsible for maintaining its own private sector of the house, while all the occupants are expected to take care of the areas held in common, specifically, the entrance, galleries, and part of the uncovered platform. This particular longhouse is exceptional among the Ngadju. Normally, individual family units have their own separate dwellings, built with a system of recruiting called *hindjam* (used also for ceremonies and special agricultural tasks) in which the workers are paid with cooked fowl, pork,

181. *Bidayuh: portion of a longhouse with the common room* (balai) *projecting, Sarawak (Borneo).*

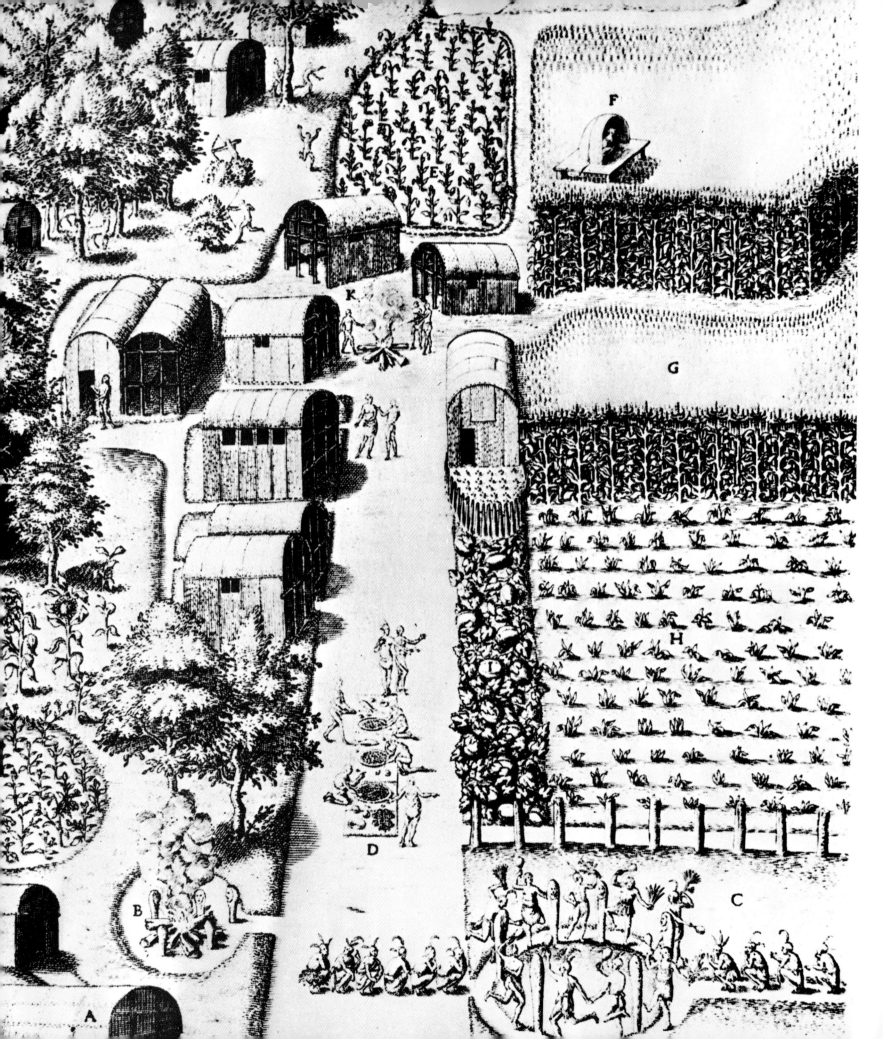

◁ *182. Algonquin: village of Lecotan, with its barrel-roofed longhouses, Virginia (USA). (Engraving by Théodore de Bry, c. 1585.)*

*183. Algonquin: funeral rite inside a longhouse (eastern USA). (Engraving by Théodore de Bry, c. 1585.)*

and beef. Obviously numerous cattle were required to pay for the labor involved in building the Antang and Ideng longhouse with its thirty extremely heavy pillars.[13]

According to the reconstructed oral tradition, the longhouse of Tumbang Gagu came about through the initiative of two individuals, Antang and Ideng, heads of two extended families differing in both wealth and number. Thus, the former is said to have paid for the erection of eighteen of the pillars, the latter for twelve. The descendants of Antang became proprietors of the larger portion of the house, occupying four sectors; the heirs of Ideng, two. The imbalance between the two groups of family nuclei is fully reflected in the architectural plan, in which a transverse gallery divides the house into two unequal sectors.[14] When the initial link between the two groups grew slack over the years, the areas held in common deteriorated from lack of proper upkeep.[15]

Although the Tumbang Gagu collective house is in fact exceptional, the universal significance of the longhouse can be detected in it: It represents a historical experiment, widely diffused, which ran counter to the prevailing tendency toward social stratification, toward "celebratory" architecture, and toward the increasing separation between architecture and the prevailing means of production. In this experiment there seem to survive within an agricultural environment the social bonds and symbolic interpretation of the territory that in hunting and gathering societies make the territory equally available to all the members of the community.

### THE PUEBLO VILLAGES OF THE SOUTHWESTERN UNITED STATES

Twenty-five villages distributed in two main groups in the semi-desert regions of Arizona and New Mexico constitute the remnants of a type of agricultural community that underwent its greatest development about the 13th century A.D. and was given the name *pueblo* by the 16th-century Spanish invaders (*plates 5, 188–200*).[16] The seven Hopi villages, constructed on the summits of three mesas, the flat-topped rocky hills where the plains population took refuge from the colonialist invasion, belong to the western group. On the first mesa is the village of Oraibi; on the second, the three settlements of Shipaulovi, Mishongnovi, and Sihmopovi; on the third, the villages of Walpi, Sichomovi, and Hano (*plate 188*). Farther east, on the border between Arizona and New Mexico, the Zuni occupy a village that is the only one of seven existing at the time of the conquistadors to survive. In the central zone between the two groups are the villages of Acoma and Laguna. In the basin of the Rio Grande are the villages of the eastern group: of the Keres tribe (Santa Ana, San Felipe, Santo Domingo, Sia, and Cochiti), of the Towa (Jemez), of the Tiwa (San-

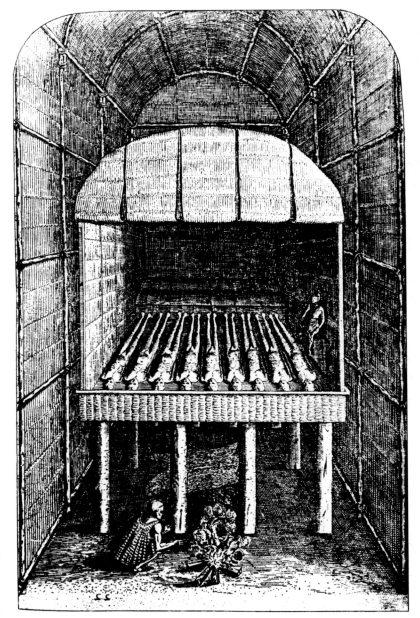

184. *The fortified village of Pomeiock, North Carolina (USA). (Engraving by Théodore de Bry, c. 1585.)*

185. *Mandan village (central USA). (Oil painting by George Catlin, 1832.)*

186. *Ceremonial dance in an Indian cabin, Kansas (USA). (Watercolor by Seymour, 1819.)*

187. *Iroquois: drawing and plan of a longhouse (northeastern USA).*

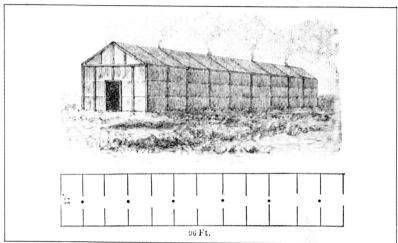

188. *Hopi: schematic plan of the settlement and cultivated fields of the Walpi, Sichomovi, and Hano pueblos, Arizona (USA). The pueblos are on the mesa in the center; the fields are in the plain below and belong to these village clans:*
*1. Kachina; 2. Sun; 3. Tobacco; 4. Stick; 5. Parrot; 6. Sand; 7. Pine; 8. Water; 9. Mustard; 10. Deer; 11. Badger; 12. Rabbit; 13. Bear; 14. Snake; 15. Coyote; 16. Reed; 17. Cloud; 18. Maize; 19. Pumpkin.*

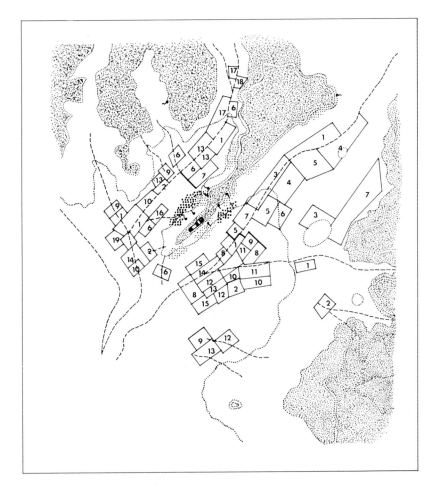

dia, Isleta, Taos, Picuris), and of the Tewa (Tesuque, Nambé, San Ildefonso, San Juan, Santa Clara).

The common basis of subsistence (chiefly cultivated maize, beans, and squash) and the nearly uniform environmental conditions—the climate is so dry that irrigation to supplement the infrequent rains, especially in the eastern zone, is required—have resulted in a notable homogeneity in the use of the territory as well as in the architectural tradition of these different populations, which belong to very different language groups.

Characteristically, each village controls a particular unit of territory, and this custom must have been even more widespread when the earlier plains settlements, of which a good deal of archaeological evidence survives, were flourishing. At the conquest at the end of the 16th century, there were at least seventy settlements, some of notable dimensions. Property, both cultivated land and dwellings, is divided among the various clans that compose each village. There is no social stratification, but special prestige is attached to the groups of priests whose primary function is to keep alive the traditions and rites of the tribe.

The impoverishment in material culture that has taken place among the Pueblo societies in recent centuries makes it impossible to compare in depth the world of mythic beliefs and its spatial correspondences (today still extremely subtle and complex) with the present-day architecture, which is very much simpler than what existed in the past. A profound qualitative dichotomy exists between, on the one hand, the ceremonies, the cosmogonical and cosmological myths, and the spatial, territorial, and geometrical interpretations of time and space, and, on the other, the groups of compact villages in which the last authentic traces of the traditional mode of dwelling are well on the way to disappearing. For this reason, the complex of spatial myths must be compared with the architecture of some centuries ago in which the geometrical organization of the general plan and the steplike downward displacement of the dwellings toward a sacred place in the interior of the village, and even the orientation of the settlement all reveal extremely precise relationships between spatial concepts and their architectonic realization.

The ancient villages, with their simple ground plans and habitations gathered around central plazas containing kivas—the semiunderground sanctuaries where the *kachina* spirits dwell—are a perfect realization of the desire to bring the world of man into harmony with the physical world and the cosmos. The plans may be rectangular, as in the Aztec pueblo (*plate 191*), circular as in the Tyuonyi pueblo, or semicircular, as in the Bonito pueblo (*plate 189*), but in all of them the rectangular dwelling units are fit into a rigorously detailed design.

*189. Plan of the ancient settlement of Bonito pueblo showing habitations and circular kivas, New Mexico (USA).*

*190. Hopi: model of the Tegua pueblo, Arizona (USA).*

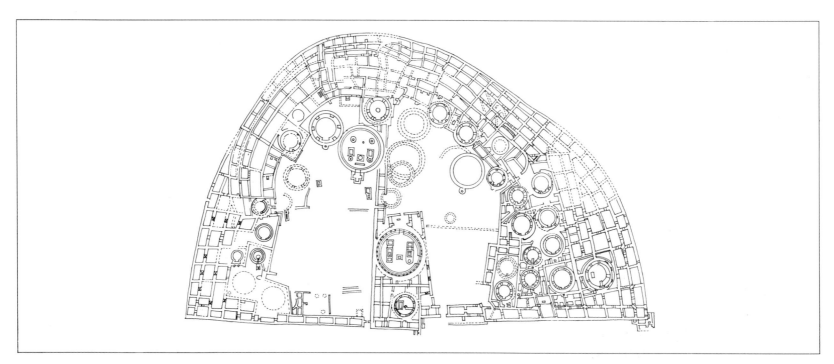

191. *Model of the Aztec pueblo, abandoned at the end of the 13th century,*
*New Mexico (USA).*

192. *Reconstruction drawing of a pueblo habitation protected by a round tower at Mesa Verde, showing entrances to two underground kivas, Colorado (USA).*

193. *Partial view of Cliff Palace pueblo, built under overhanging rock, Mesa Verde, Colorado (USA).*

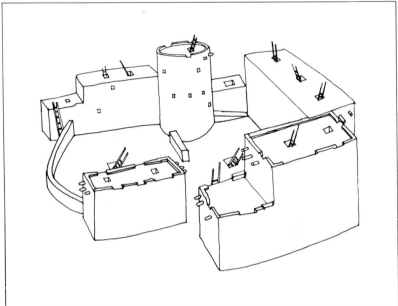

196. *Tiwa: Taos pueblo, New Mexico (USA). (Drawing of 1886.)*
197. *Tiwa: Taos pueblo, with hemispherical kilns in the foreground, New Mexico (USA).*

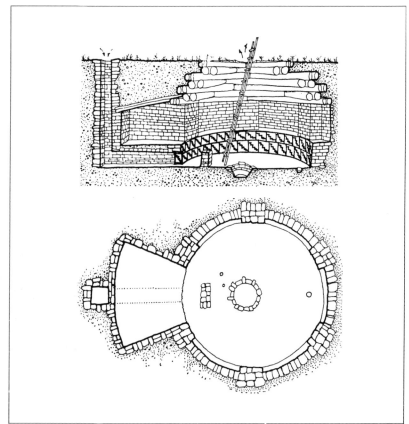

198. *Section and ground plan of a kiva with a ladder from the entrance above and an air conduit for the central fireplace, Mesa Verde, Colorado (USA).*

199. *Tewa: Nambé pueblo, New Mexico (USA).*

200. *Hopi: ceremonial altar inside a kiva, Arizona (USA).*

201. *Navaho: ceremonial drawing in colored sand and colored flour (USA). The four female personages depicted inhabit the House of the Dewdrop and are associated with the four cardinal points, as is indicated by their respective colors, and there is a rainbow around them.*

202. *Navaho: ceremonial drawing in colored flour representing the Cavern of the Bears (USA). The four male figures are in the colors of the cardinal directions (east: white; south: grayish blue; west: yellow: north: black) and are encircled by a rainbow.*

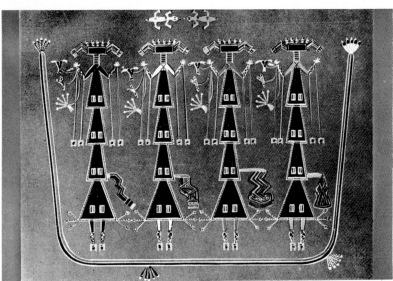

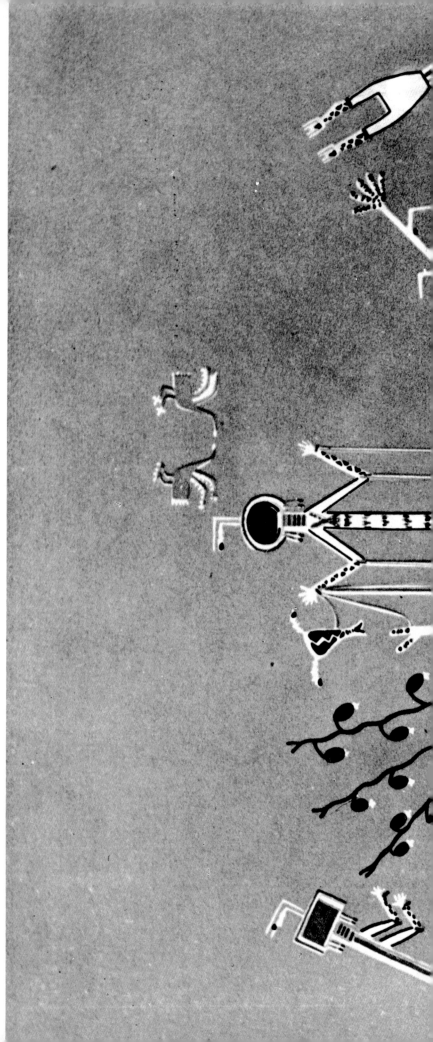

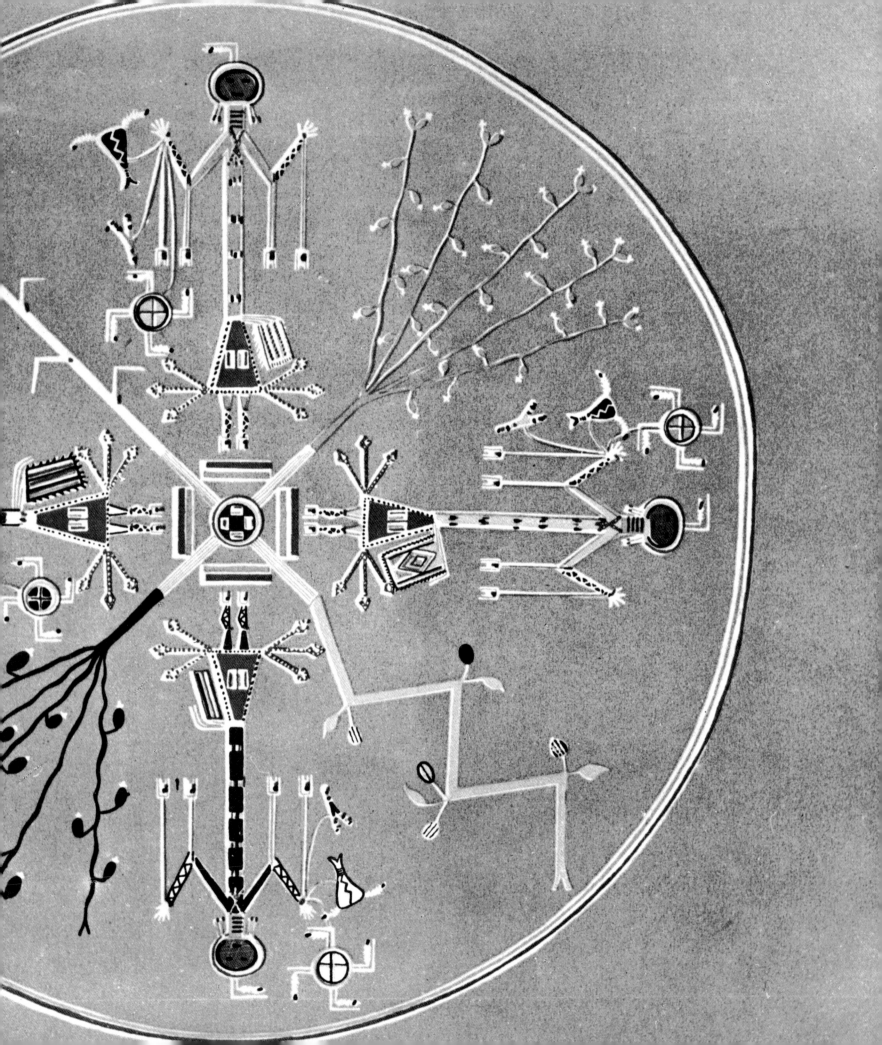

203. *Geometrical designs drawn in sand, New Hebrides (Melanesia).*
204. *Sand-drawing entitled* netömwar *(adultery), New Hebrides (Melanesia).*

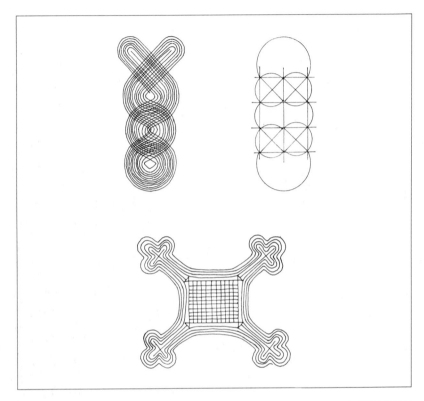

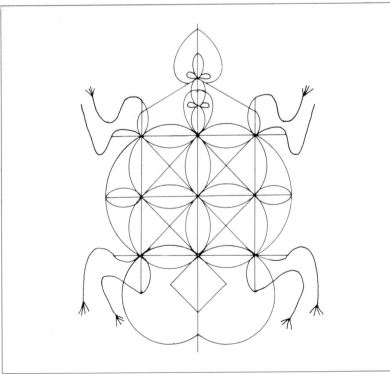

In the three pueblos just mentioned, the traditional spatial factors are especially apparent: Every mythical event, each alternation of the seasons, is related to the six fundamental astronomical directions—the four cardinal points, zenith, and nadir. In the mythological tradition of the village of Acoma, there is a series of correspondences between the cardinal directions, colors, and seasons: north-winter-yellow, west-spring-blue, south-summer-red, east-autumn-white.[17] Beasts of prey, and divinities protecting the hunters also find a place in this scheme. This type of quadripartite organization of time and space is common to the Pueblo Indians as well as to the nearby Navaho, whom they have profoundly influenced during the past two centuries. The complicated designs executed by the Navaho with sands and flours of different colors (*plates 201, 202*) bring the mythological tales, cosmogony, and the relationships between the human, animal, vegetable, and celestial worlds into such a fundamental schema.

The extreme importance of the spatial and temporal coordinates is also shown in the attention paid to the position of the sun on the horizon line as it rises and sets on different days of the year. The calendar of the Sihmopovi pueblo, which takes into account the irregularity of the skyline,[18] serves essentially to regulate the times of sowing and harvesting and the dates of the principal sacred ceremonies marking the phases of the annual cycle, the chief of which coincide with the summer and winter solstices. But it is in the traditional ceremonies that take place in the kiva (*plates 192, 198, 200*) that the link between myth and architecture can be most directly perceived. According to a mythological tradition, the creator-god Iatiku, after having taught men to construct the first village by showing them a model, had them put up an altar around which the *kachina* spirits would dispose themselves ritually at the four cardinal points. As a final revelation, he taught them to enclose the altar in a semiunderground circular kiva, the sacred place where the *kachinas* can rest during their sacred visits to mankind. The architectonic elements of the kiva thus signify the celestial world of the spirits as they come into contact with the terrestrial world of man: The covering is the Milky Way, the entrance ladder represents the rainbow, and the ledge running along the wall is the bank of cloud where the *kachinas* have their home.[19]

CLAN AND VILLAGE IN MELANESIA
*Men's Houses and Prestige Symbols in the New Hebrides*
Although Melanesian society is quite rigidly structured according to clan and has no class stratification, the position of the individual within the society may nonetheless be very thoroughly differentiated by degree of personal prestige and power, regardless of age. In the northern part of Ambrim Island in the New Hebrides, thirteen social grades

205. *Drums and personal altars surmounted by wooden birds, Vao Island, off South Malekula Island, New Hebrides (Melanesia).*

◁ 206. *A rectangular, pitched-roofed men's house* (nagamal) *under construction, Pentecost Island, New Hebrides (Melanesia).*

207. *Framework of a clan house under construction, North Malekula Island, New Hebrides (Melanesia).*

form a hierarchy (*mage*), and their tokens are displayed by the individuals who have the right to them.[20] These tokens should not be regarded simply in terms of secular art as opposed to ritual or religious art, but as symbols codified by the entire tribal group, which are acquired by an individual according to his personal wealth. Although most of these emblems of prestige can be bought and resold at will, it is significant that their conventional use remains restricted by a code that, broadly speaking, may be defined as artistic and superstructural in character. The code permits neither an unlimited accumulation of the symbols nor their variation in any manner.

Here, certainly, is a form of private property; however, because the unity of the clan remains the higher value, ownership of the symbols does not affect the fundamental structure of ownership of the land. The first grade (*fangtasum*) enables the member to set up a kitchen apart from the family dwelling. The second grade (*mwel*) is indicated by a *cycas* palm planted at the edge of the space for dancing; the third grade (*wer*) by a stone painted black; the fourth grade (*sagran*) by a sculpture of tree fern surmounted by a small platform for dancing; the fifth grade (*liun*) by a stone painted with red spots and black circles; the sixth grade (*gulgul*) by a sculpture representing a human face or by a stone on a small mound; the seventh grade (*wurwur*) by a large human-faced sculpture surmounting an animal and topped by a dance platform; the eighth grade (*simok*) by a white and black stone; the ninth grade (*hiwir*) by a large male sculpture surmounted by a dance platform; the tenth grade (*wet ne mweleun*) by a white and black stone on a mound; the eleventh grade (*mage linbul*) by a hole with two statuettes, male and female, covered by a small single-pitched roof; the twelfth grade (*loghbaro*) by a rectangle of stones with a larger stone at one end. The ultimate grade (*mal*) is represented by all the stones of the preceding grade plus two carved poles supporting an arched crossbeam carved with the figure of a falcon, the largest stone representing the door; this is a small-scale reproduction of the men's house.[21]

There are two other significant cases in the New Hebrides in which personal prestige, acquired within a precise system of rules, is linked with artistic and architectonic activity. The drawings on sand found in the northern New Hebrides and called *tu* on Ambrim Island (*plates 203, 204*) certainly have a ritual origin, though their collective significance has been partially lost since making them has become competitive. These drawings represent totemic, ritual, and mythological subjects, but their high degree of abstraction makes them analogous to such highly conceptualized spatial-temporal representations as the Australian schematic territorial renderings, though they lack the complex connotations of those "maps." Within the center of a grid,

*208, 209. Men's houses with sacred stones and trees in the foreground, Little Namba, South Malekula Island, and the village of Mand, Southwest Malekula Island, New Hebrides (Melanesia).*

the members of an animal, human, or mythological figure are intertwined, in extremely stylized representation, making a virtually abstract design. The most elementary characterization defines them as parts of a body, but because the abstraction grows in logical manner out of their relationships to one another, the result is recognizable as a geometrical transposition of the intrinsic properties of the subject.[22]

Competition for position and prestige between the men of Pentecost Island, north of Ambrim, has given rise to a very special architectonic feature, a high tower made of a trellis of poles that serves as a springboard for flights through the air, head downward, with nothing but the flimsy protection of a liana cord tied around an ankle to break the fall.

The organization of the local groups with respect to reciprocal relations and authority is given full expression in the spatial and architectonic concepts in this Pacific archipelago. Thus, the men's house, the *nagamal* (*plates 206–209*), is the communal, ceremonial, and ritual center of the restricted community, and its significance extends also to the adjoining open clearing. It is in fact identified with a patrilocal and patrilinear group. When a number of local political and ritual groups come together, they have as their symbol another clearing called the *nasara*, a flattened area serving mainly for the dances and the inaugural ceremonies of a chief recognized by several *nagamal* groups.[23] Large carved drums are set up either horizontally or vertically, and the ceremonies associated with the larger-than-local group take place there. The order is more evident when the *nasara* is the property of a single individual who exploits the religious assemblies to his own profit, or when *nasara* and *nagamal* are located side by side with a precise boundary between them that the women (who are always excluded from the *nagamal*) cannot cross. As a building the *nagamal* is therefore the visible symbol of the unity of the clan, whereas the *nasara* represents a space that is an independent instrument of individual or tribal power and is used only on such occasions as the consecration of a chief on the sacred stone or the great ceremonies that are celebrated at intervals of many years.

In point of fact, the men's house regulates the life of the community. It is also the index of the status of the individuals belonging to it, whose rank is confirmed by particular sculptural and architectonic symbols. By a complex mechanism of balance, the men's house can exercise efficacious control over any too clear-cut disequilibrium between individuals of different status, assuring the separation between the political (and kinship) unit and the ownership or exploitation of specific territory. The preservation of the socioeconomic nexus, which extends also to landed property, guarantees each lineage a role

210. *Dani: cleared and cultivated mountainside (New Guinea).*

211. Dani: settlement surrounded by palms in a valley bottom (New Guinea).

that, despite differences in prestige, is officially recognized and relatively secure.

On other islands, there are also various distinctions in grade or rank, for the most part connected with the erection of specific monuments, as on Ambrim. On the small island of Vao northeast of Malekula there are only two such grades. The first is merely designated by a platform of stones; the second by a stone slab resting at the back on a block of coral, at the front on a post carved in anthropomorphic form. The horizontal beam is carved to symbolize the fishing eagle (nabal), and the supports and stone slab are protected by a roof.[24]

In the New Hebrides, then, the highest grade is most often distinguished by a miniature men's house, symbol of the achievement of maximum participation in the rituals and corporate life of the group. Often the upward progression from the lowest to the highest grades is marked by increasingly complete images of the men's house (amèl): first, four corner poles secured together by a rope; second, stone enclosure; third, a small building complete with door and roof. The representation of an eagle or falcon on the crossbeam—symbol of the highest grade on both Ambrim and Vao—exactly reproduces the main crossbeam in the men's house (plate 205). These grade distinctions constitute a system alternative to, but not incompatible with, that of hereditary power. Essentially, their purpose is to bind the individual closely to the mythic tradition, giving him at the same time an increasing dignity within the society. That dignity corresponds, of course, to his economic position, most notably to the number of pigs he owns. Indicative of this religious and social duality is the fact that the stone slab signifying the second grade on Vao represents the god Lehevhev, guardian of the way that leads to the realm of the dead; moreover, the carved post on which it rests is symbolic of the ancestor who was first to carry out the ritual sacrifice.[25]

*The Mountain Villages of New Guinea*
The villages in the interior of New Guinea lack such communal buildings as decorated men's houses and clan edifices that are found in the wealthier coastal regions.[26] Even the collective house is quite rare and, where present, is not large enough to shelter more than a few family units. Whether rectangular or round (plates 211, 215–218), it has only a single room in which the men are often segregated from the women, as among the Sayolof and the Yarumui, for example. A village usually consists of no more than a few dozen huts scattered around an open area (plate 211) or along a length of road: that is, either a circular disposition of round houses and clearing or a serial alignment with rectangular houses all facing in the same direction. In either case, the village is often fortified (plate 214). The building materials

212, 213. *Dani: bridge of lianas with catwalk of planks and split logs (New Guinea).*

216–218. Dani: round habitations with and without an outside portico (New Guinea).

are chiefly tree trunks, lianas, and bamboo, and these are also used for the suspended bridges indispensable for communication between groups separated by deep valleys. The bridges may be made entirely of ropes or lianas or else have a catwalk of tree trunks suspended longitudinally, as in the territory of the Dani (*plates 212, 213*). In a heavily forested environment where the limited food supply from pig-breeding and kitchen gardening does not permit any great density of population or especially close relationships between the different groups and villages, these bridges certainly constitute the most important permanent architectural structures in the territory.

In the dwellings, there are innumerable variants in the use of materials as well as in general plan; the range includes the round houses with walls of wooden planks cut by stone axes that are found among the Dani (*plates 215–218*) and the houses of the Telefolmin set up on squat piles. In the latter, each family unit has a hearth on a mound of earth rising well above the floor level so as to limit the dangers of fire while making it possible to cook directly on the ground.

### The Abelam Tribes of New Guinea

In the Maprik area of northeastern New Guinea, between the Sepik River, the north coast (Wewak), the Torricelli Mountains, and the Prince Alexander Mountains, the tribes of the Abelam[27] maintain an extremely interesting architectural tradition whose principal expression is the huge ceremonial house. The villages each contain a few hundred inhabitants, and each village has one of these immense houses with a characteristic triangular facade covered with paintings. The economic base is kitchen gardening, and in the social system the clan is the predominant structure around which the economic and political activity of the village revolves. The clan system is supplemented by a system of dualistic correspondences dividing the society into two groups (*ara*) that are in competition with each other as regards food production and ceremonies. There is a chain of even more important relationships between the various villages of the region (the entire Abelam population is about 30,000). Villages are "twinned," and this connection involves an exchange of foodstuffs and attendance at each other's ceremonies. Each person has two companions (*chambara*), one in his own village, the other in the twin village. Each person seeks prestige deriving from usefulness to society. Every structure above this individual level—clan, *ara,* twinship—encourages the development of a spirit of competition between groups and a constant circulation of mythic and cultural motifs. These emphases are clearly reflected in the importance of the role of art in society.[28]

An Abelam village[29] is characterized by a disparity in scale be-

220. *Schematic plan of the coastal village of Boru, Baxter Bay (New Guinea), showing the grouping of the habitations belonging to the various clans (dubu).*

1. Orimu, 2. Lapi, 3. Gundubu, 4. Womong, 5. Warata.
*Elements of acculturation: a. church and missionaries' house; b. trader's house.*

221. *Schematic plan of a village on the island of Mailu, Papua (New Guinea), showing the division into four clan groupings, each comprising various subgroups.*

*x.* Morau *clan: 1.* Maraoraed Dubu; *2.* Mageva Dubu; *3.* Buma Dubu; *a. men's house* (Koporaoro).
*y.* Maradubu *clan: 4.* Arisadubu; *5.* Motodubu; *6.* Maradubu; *7.* Baraudubu; *8.* Dibodubu; *b. men's house* (Danilea).
*w.* Urumoga *clan: 9.* Banagadubu; *10.* Gonudubu; *11.* Bariidubu; *12.* Boiladubu; *13.* Diadubu; *14.* Garagoiledubu; *c, d, e. three men's houses* (Abauoro, Onibuoro, Dariavara).
*z.* Bodeabo *clan: 15.* Udadubu; *16.* Abidubu; *17.* Arisadubu; *18.* Banidubu; *19.* Gabinadubu; *20.* Warasadubu; *f. men's house* (Goiseoro).

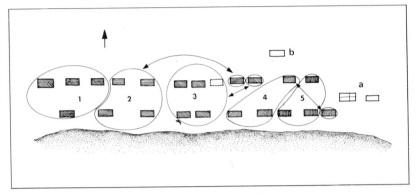

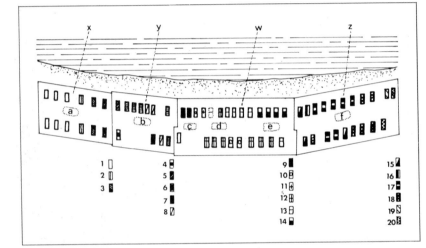

tween the common dwellings and the enormous sacred edifice. The center of Kalabu, a settlement stretching out in a line across the summits of several hills for nearly two miles, is divided into two parts. In the center rises the cult edifice. The ordinary houses, along the central street, are covered by double-pitched roofs that extend to the ground, slope up toward the front of the building, and are covered with the leaves of the breadfruit tree. Each family owns a number of houses, one strictly for the men, one for the women and small children, one used as kitchen, and one a storage place for food.

Among the Abelam and in other villages of the Sepik River and Ramu Valley, the huge public building that serves both as cult house and men's house (*plates 223–236*) is a construction with a framework of poles and rafters covered by an extremely steeply pitched saddleback roof whose sides come down so far as to constitute, to some extent, walls as well. At the rear, the roof may end at more or less the height of the ridgepole, some 6½ feet above the ground, or rise steeply as does the front end, which sweeps upward to form a triangular facade as much as 59 to 72 feet high and 33 to 39 feet wide. The facade is overhung by the roof, which protects the painted decoration. The marked sweep of the roof is further emphasized by the ridgepole, which shoots up at an angle of about 45 degrees to terminate in a small caplike projection high in the air. Beneath this bell-shaped turret hangs a long chain of osiers; above it rises a wooden pinnacle. The supporting framework holds up this combined roof-and-wall of woven bamboo. Access to the interior is via a small tunnellike aperture that can be entered only on all fours. Wooden images of ancestors and gods are preserved in the gloom of the interior. The men's assemblies actually take place outdoors in the open clearing, sometimes under a lean-to shelter or in the field in front of the house. The emphasis is entirely on the exterior of the cult house as if to underscore the social function of the ritual art.

From the ground to a height of 16 to 20 feet, the facade of the Abelam men's house has no painted decoration but is covered with paneling of interwoven strips of bamboo in elegant geometrical patterns, generally bands of zigzag motifs. Between this lower zone and the crowning peak the front is painted, and the two zones are separated by a horizontal molding semicircular in section and consisting of a wooden beam with a succession of carved and painted human masks, birds' claws, and human feet. At either end, there is a face that represents an ancestral tutelary spirit (*plate 233*), as do the sculptures in the interior of the house (*plate 232*).

The entire upper zone is covered with pictorial decoration painted on panels made of the bracts of sago palm fronds opened out, smoothed, and sewed together. In the lower part of this enormous

222. *Garden and community house, Nomad River (New Guinea).*

223. *Vestiges of an ancient men's house (New Guinea).*　　224. *Tambanum: framework of a men's house under construction, Middle Sepik River region (New Guinea).* ▷

225. *Men's house with saddleback roof with double cusps, Middle Sepik River region (New Guinea).*

surface are painted six identical human faces representing the spirits of the six clans (*Ngwalndu*), and each face has a name of its own. Above this, various series of decorations composed of parallel bands with representations of human bodies and geometrical motifs are crowned, beneath the bell-shaped peak of the roof, by yet another face like the ones below (*plate 234*). Such faces are also often found on the generally triangular panels hung up in the cult houses during ceremonies (*plate 236*). The interest of these faces goes beyond their relationship with the facade and the character they lend to the building as a whole. They are, in fact, extremely significant from the standpoint of the relationship between figuration and abstraction in primitive art and architecture.

The various Abelam groups have different "styles" that they follow consistently in decorating the fronts of their cult houses.[30] Certain villages in the north of their territory chiefly use the mask motif, whereas in others in an eastern zone the decoration is considered "abstract." The same graphic elements deformed in different manners, and above all with different significances according to different groups of the Abelam, can be variously interpreted as human faces, men's hair, human figures, and so on (*plate 234*). Modifications in form and color imperceptible to the outsider's eye can completely alter a painting's significance for the inhabitants of the Abelam area as well as for the groups in immediate contact with them. As A. Forge has shown, the continuity of meaning occurs as signs are inserted into different contexts. Nevertheless, despite all the stylistic and semantic variants, the paintings on the front of cult houses always represent the element "man" as related to the clan and its mythology, to the function of the sacred dwelling (forbidden to women and therefore also a "men's house"), and to the connections between individual and artist and clan. The social structure that calls for the twinning of villages and individuals and the exchange of visits on ceremonial occasions has favored a considerable give-and-take of experiences, including artistic ones, between different areas. However, when an artistic motif of one group is copied by another it does not, nor cannot ever, result in a simple repetition of form and content but rather in a recomposition of the imitated motif.

Despite the large scale of these paintings—the masks can be ten to thirteen feet high—they are no different stylistically from the pictorial decoration of small objects (*plates 234–236*). This indicates that the decoration applied to architecture is a faithful enlargement of motifs and figures well established in the artistic repertory associated with both ceremonies and the objects of daily use. One can in fact find a double correspondence: on the one hand, the perfect stylistic consistency between large-scale and small-scale decorations; on the

226. *Men's house with saddleback roof with double cusps, Middle Sepik River region (New Guinea).*

227. *Front of men's house with anthropomorphic elements (human face), Middle Sepik River region (New Guinea).*

228. *Kanigara: men's house, with carved pillar in the foreground, Middle Sepik River region (New Guinea).* ▷

other, the identical nature of the motifs painted on the ceremonial houses and those set up for specific ceremonies, which are also painted on surfaces made of the bracts of the sago palm. This implies that before the specific type of cult house with decorated front was firmly established, decorated panels were hung up provisionally on the fronts of such buildings. By rendering such decoration definitive and permanent, the group availed itself in everyday life of that efficacious instrument of cohesion and persuasion that is ceremonial art. The role of sacred architecture as container of masks and ritual objects is in part modified, transformed into a permanent public proclamation (always of high artistic quality in its execution) of the group's own particular mythic, ritual, and social principles.

### The Big Hut in New Caledonia

In New Caledonia, the "big hut" is the permanent symbol of the unity of the clan, the power of the chief, and the bond between the community and its mythic traditions. It is a "men's house" as well, but is conceived as a public edifice in contradistinction to the family dwellings. In front of it there is a sacred hearth. Its purely architectural and carved elements make the entire structure visible evidence of the constructional capacity (in the ritual and political sense as well) of the clans who worked together in building it.[31]

The ground plan is circular. Over a low wall punctuated by supporting posts rises a very high conical roof terminating in an ornamental pinnacle (*plates 251, 252*). A central pillar, symbol of the unity of the village, is the main support of the structure.

To mark the link between the hut, the mythic ancestors, and society, every important architectural element is decorated with sculpture. Most important of all is the doorway (*plate 253*), which faces the central plaza of the village and is the element of contact between the sacred interior, forbidden to the women, and the outside plaza, accessible to the community as a whole. The lateral doorposts (*jovo*), made up of two semicylindrical sculptures terminating in a human face, are ancestor-images (*katarah*), also often found on minor lateral pillars or in the center of the threshold. The architrave (*pweretu*) is likewise often decorated with a carved frieze, and another ancestor-image or mask is hung on the central pillar facing the entrance. But the most diversified and interesting feature is the upper end of this main supporting pillar, which pierces the roof, becoming a kind of decorative pinnacle or spire. It is sometimes carved with a mask of a human face but more often in various manners with geometrical motifs that together with propitiatory symbols reproduce the emblem of the group. The collaboration between the clans in building the hut is commemorated by the anthropomorphic elements in the guise

229. *Interior of a men's house, Middle Sepik River region (New Guinea).*

230. *Anterior platform of a spirits' house with carved and painted corner pillar, Middle Sepik River region (New Guinea).*

231. *Reconstruction of a spirits' house, Sepik River region (New Guinea). Museo Etnologico, Musei Vaticani, Vatican City.* ▷

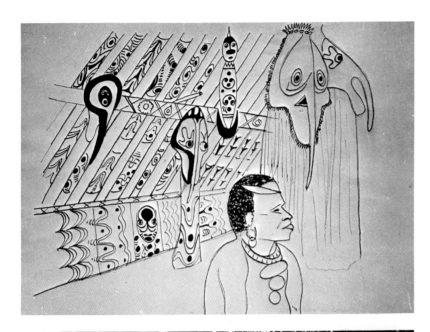

of bearded human faces quite different one from the other, which often decorate the inner side of the posts supporting the outer walls, each of them corresponding to a particular clan. Then too, the space set aside in the interior for divinatory trance is delimited by a wooden wall, whose principal feature is a richly carved horizontal beam (*boedu*).

The New Caledonian village is dominated by the "big hut," where the chief and his men live. In front of it is a narrow rectangular plaza, about 16 to 40 feet wide and from 33 to as much as 200 feet long. This serves for ceremonies as well as for dances and feasts. The plaza is slightly elevated and is flanked by coconut palms and araucarias, which—like the plaza and the "big hut"—have male significance. Along the sides are the family huts, linked by small pathways shaded by poplars, which are female in significance. The huts are surrounded by an enclosure of branches, sometimes adorned with trophies of enemy skulls. Each hut maintains contact with the vital forces of the group, represented above all by the ancestors, by means of certain objects placed in front of the door: sacred stones, which are seats of the ancestral spirits, and a very high post set up alongside to ensure contact with the invisible world. Near the house, a yam or taro is planted to guarantee the fertility of the soil through the intervention of the ancestors.

The collective life of the village is centered in the plaza, and this focus is particularly evident on the occasion of the great festival of *pilu-pilu*, during which part of the excess food accumulated during the year is consumed. The equilibrium between the wealth of the individual family nuclei, that of the clans, and that of the chief—three factors mutually controlling and interacting with each other—makes the New Caledonian village a singularly significant organization, a precise reflection of the rules governing the society and at the same time a factor that determines them. It is not by chance that the life of the village with its big huts, plazas, and cultivated fields was a favorite subject for the bamboo carvings done chiefly in the 19th century, which constitute priceless examples of spatial representation only in part influenced and contaminated by the first contacts with the European colonizers (*plates 249, 250*).[32]

MYTH, COLLECTIVISM, AND HIERARCHY IN SOUTHEAST ASIA AND MADAGASCAR

Among the sedentary agricultural populations of Southeast Asia, there is always a close connection between myth, agriculture, and dwelling. Ritual and sacred considerations influence the rhythm of farming and also the construction and utilization of the house. Between field and house—both owned property—there exists a close connection, the

232. *Interior of a spirits' house, Sepik River region (New Guinea). Museo Etnologico, Musei Vaticani, Vatican City.*

233. *Wooden mask from the front of a men's house (height c. 48"), Sepik River region (New Guinea). Musée de l'Homme, Paris. ▷*

234. *Abelam: detail of the painted front of the men's house, with repeated motifs interpreted as "men's hair" and "cassowary," village of Wingei (New Guinea).*

235. *Painted wooden emblem from a dwelling, Middle Sepik River region (New Guinea). Museum für Völkerkunde, Basel.*

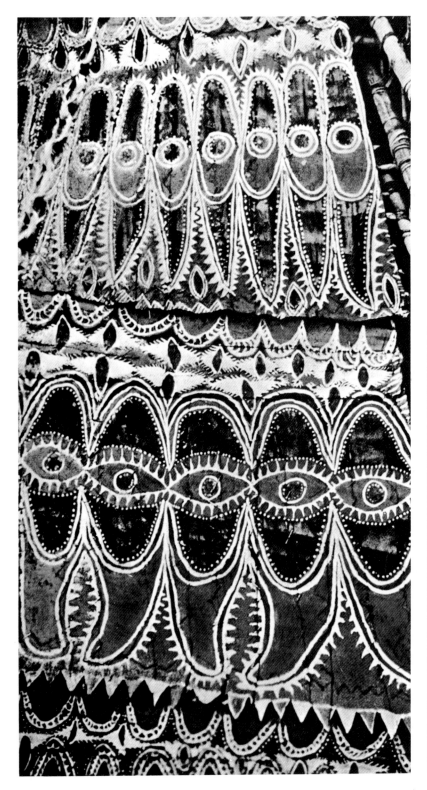

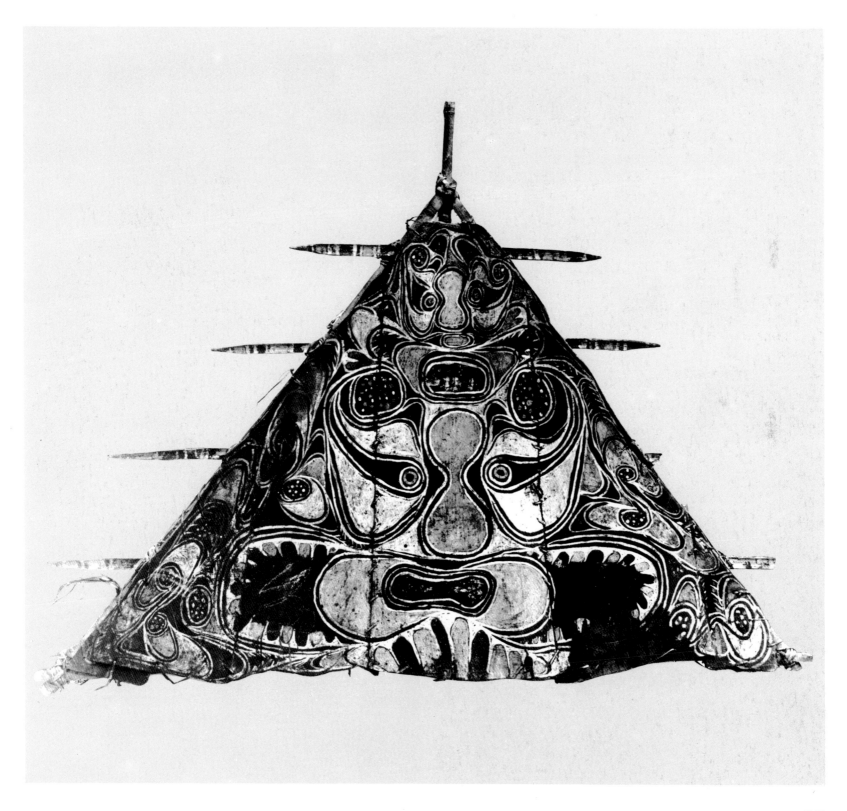

237. *Mono: schematic plan of the village of Omarakana, Trobriand Islands (Melanesia) (dwellings drawn in outline, storage places for yams in solid black).*
   1. *chief's hut;* 2. *chief's storehouse;* a. *burial ground;* b. *plaza for dances.*

238. *Village raised on piles with huts of ogival section facing a veranda that also serves as wharf, Admiralty Islands (Melanesia).*

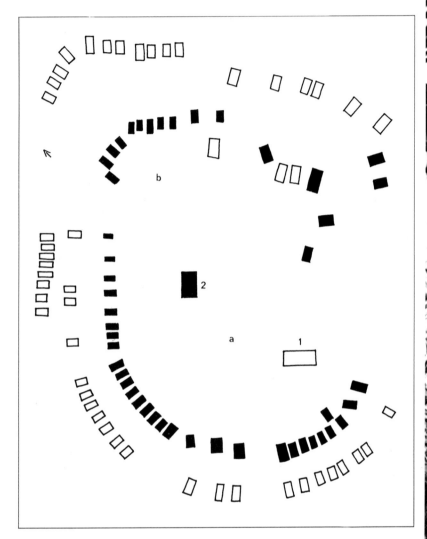

field being the place of production, the house the place where the agricultural products are worked, consumed, and conserved.

Certain non-Asian areas have been influenced by the agricultural cultures of Southeast Asia and among these is Madagascar, where there is a high level of integration between village, habitation, and territory. This relationship is expressed in the plan of the dwellings, which are ritually oriented toward the cardinal points. The walls and corners correspond not only to directions but also to temporal subdivisions (the twelve months of the year). In the interior each area is either assigned to different members of the family or has a specific ritual function (*plate 259*). Although dwellings are relatively uniform in type—rectangular huts with double-pitched roofs—there is considerable refinement in the execution of houses, tombs, and food storehouses that recalls the Indochinese and Indonesian world, as does the widespread use of vegetable-fiber matting and roofing and the practice of supporting buildings with piles (*plates 254–263*).

Village communities in India, Burma, Cambodia, and Vietnam have well-defined traditions of building that differ according to linguistic and tribal grouping. Stratification and successive waves of influence have resulted, even in small areas, in an extremely diversified panorama of settlement and construction types. Thus, in South Vietnam every group has its own traditional way of resolving the problem of the relationship between the human community and the habitat: that is, its own architectonic tradition that testifies to age-old cultural influences that left their mark unequally across the area. The analogies between the different traditions are general rather than particular and do not involve details of construction; instead, they reflect a conception of the house and village as an expression of the social compactness of the group, of its individuality, and of the wealth of its members.

*The Family House as Model: The Sre of South Vietnam*
The architecture of one of the South Vietnam tribes, the Sre, gives an excellent idea of the nature and range of building activity in the area as a whole. For this information we are indebted to a study by J. Dournes,[33] who examines in parallel fashion the architectonic traditions of the Sre and the Jörai, comparing them with those of nearby populations such as the Södang, Ma', Ködu, Jölöng, and others (*plates 266–271*).

A Sre village is made up of a number of large rectangular family houses (*hiu rôt*) with double-pitched roofs, disposed irregularly in parallel rows, set on piles and entered by a staircase (*ntung*) near one end of the long front (*plate 266*). Above all, the house has the function of storing and conserving the personal property of the family—from clothing to precious objects. The villages are built in clearings in the

241. *Framework of a hut under construction, Stewart Island, Solomon Islands (Melanesia).*

242. Dwellings raised on piles, Stewart Island, Solomon Islands (Melanesia).

*243. Dwelling covered with pandanus leaves and matting, Stewart Island, Solomon Islands (Melanesia).*

244. *Detail of the internal structure of a dwelling, Buka Island, Solomon Islands (Melanesia).*

245. *Nasioi: crown of a funerary post in the form of a hut in which offerings are left, Popoko Island (Melanesia). Museo Etnologico, Musei Vaticani, Vatican City.*

246. *Men's house with decorated facade and portico, Admiralty Islands (Melanesia).*

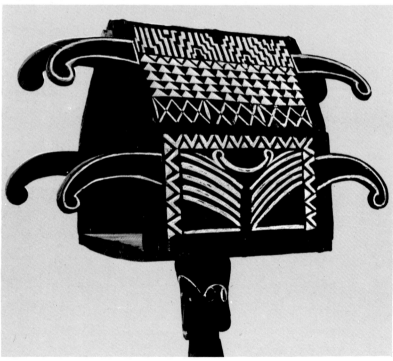

247. *Lateral posts of a door, with female and male figures (heights 69 1/4″ and 80 3/4″), Pitiliu Island, Admiralty Islands (Melanesia). Museum für Völkerkunde, Basel.*

248. *Reconstruction of a funerary cult house with* malanggan *statues, northwestern New Ireland (Melanesia). Museum für Völkerkunde, Basel.*

249. *Kanaka: incised drawing on bamboo representing "big huts" facing a rectangular plaza, New Caledonia (Melanesia).*

250. *Kanaka: incised drawing on bamboo representing a double row of huts, New Caledonia (Melanesia).*

251, 252. *Kanaka: circular huts with conical roofs of different heights and with carved pinnacle ornaments, New Caledonia (Melanesia).*

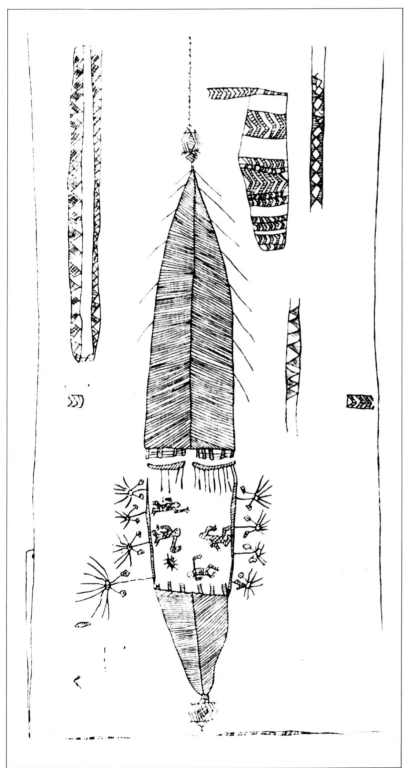

253. *Kanaka: carved pieces from the entrance of a "big hut" (jambs, cross-beam, sill, lateral anthropomorphic figures, and, in the center, the mask from the central pole of the interior facing the entrance), New Caledonia (Melanesia). Musée de l'Homme, Paris.*

254. *Betsimisaraca: view of a mountainous region with slopes cleared for cultivation and a village in the valley, with axial street lined by huts on low pile foundations (east coast, Madagascar).*

255. *Betsimisaraca: hilltop village reached by a road raised on piles (east coast, Madagascar).*

256. *Bezanozano: central plaza of a village (northeastern Madagascar).*

257. *Sacred enclosure with live trees and a palisade (Madagascar).*
258. *Sihanaka: dwelling (Madagascar).*

259. *Bezanozano: schematic plan of a traditional dwelling (northeastern Madagascar).*
*1. central post; 2. silo; 3. children's sleeping area; 4. parents' sleeping area; 5. window for the circumcision rite; 6. mortars; 7. jar; 8. poultry; 9. hearth; 10. entrance.*
*The sections of wall marked off by the radial dotted lines are associated with the twelve months of the year.*

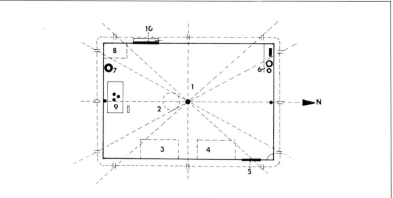

260. *Sakalava: dwelling (west coast, Madagascar).*
261. *Antaisaka: dwelling and storehouse for rice (Madagascar).*

262. *Mahafaly: pit graves covered with stones and topped by zebu horns and carved pillars (aloalo) showing episodes from the life of the deceased (Madagascar).*

263. *Betsileo: model of a funerary pillar with ox skulls (Madagascar). Museo Etnologico, Musei Vaticani, Vatican City.*

264. Brou: framework of a dwelling under construction; nearby, prefabricated components including walls of interwoven strips of bamboo and a gable covered with bamboo leaves (Khmer Republic).

265. Brou: community house (Thui-mbol), Ratanakiri province (Khmer Republic).

forest. A group of storehouses for rice (*ddam*)—buildings on piles, reproducing on a small scale the family dwelling—is situated at a distance from the houses, for protection from fire among other reasons. The open space underneath a storehouse is a sacred place (*rum*) used chiefly during the agrarian rites that follow the rice harvest and conclude with filling the *ddam*. The storehouse is thought of as part of a single, indivisible unit with the dwelling and the cultivated fields that belong to a particular family group.

The plan of the family house is also reflected in the seasonal shelters in the rice fields, the *ku* in the irrigated paddies near the village and the more elaborate *mir* built farther away in the fields on the hillsides and mountain slopes.

Specific founding ceremonies are called for when any of these are built, but especially in the case of a large house. The choice of site is tested by placing a grain of rice on a leaf: Only if it is still there the morning after can work begin, though that must wait for a "good," odd-numbered day (*leh*). The work is done collectively by the men in the village, all of whom are capable of building a house, as there is no sort of craft or trade specialization. When it is finished, an inaugural ceremony marks official entry into the completed dwelling. The words spoken in the analogous ritual of the Jörai people reveal a profound relationship between architecture and the natural world, between village and forest. The latter is the realm of mysterious forces, the *yang,* which must be invoked and induced to be favorable to the new house. These forces reside in trees and—after a tree has been chopped down and cut and fashioned into the various components of a house—in the building material itself. Wood thus passes from a natural state to a human condition, from a link with the *yang* to one with man. More than a consecration of nature, this is an insertion—requiring caution and propitiatory rites—of a human activity (building) into the equilibrium of natural forces, an equilibrium vital to maintain.

The cemetery is located in the realm of the *yang* forces, in the forest. The tombs are covered by a small provisional shelter, which once again echoes the form of the house, being composed of four sticks covered by a small peaked roof. The ritual functions that, among the Jörai, for example, take place in a large open lean-to in the cemetery are carried out among the Sre in the cabin for assemblies (*hiu wer*), essentially the periodic feasts and ceremonies. These large sheds are composed of two parallel rows of stakes covered by a double-pitched roof. The agrarian rites that take place there are conceived as a complement to the family rites performed in the dwelling: The former are linked to the earth, to the level of the ground, whereas the latter have their place on an upper level, in the dwelling raised up on

266. *Sre: diagram of framework, drawing of exterior, and ground plan of a house, with the names of the main elements (South Vietnam).*

Framework: *1.* jörong; *2.* röpas; *3, 5.* bla; *4.* töwör; *6.* dra; *7.* rökang; *8.* öp.

Exterior: *a.* ntung; *b.* mprap; *c.* rum; *d.* kölik; *e.* rököm.

Ground plan: *a.* passageway; *b.* main living quarters; *1.* guests' hearth; *2.* family hearth.

267. *Jölöng: exterior of the community house* (rong), *village of Kön Jökoi (South Vietnam).*

268. *Jölöng: trusswork supporting the roof of the community house* (rong), *village of Kön Jökoi (South Vietnam).*

269. *Jölöng: detail of the exterior of the community house* (rong), *village of Kön-Möhar (South Vietnam).*

270. *Jölöng: community house, village of Yanlo (South Vietnam).* ▷

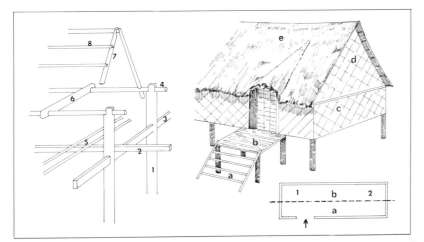

piles. Such dualism is common to much of the architecture of Southeast Asia and leads to solutions that, for all their variety, always reflect the complementary relationships of high and low, of upper plane and lower, of man and his foodstuffs, of sky and earth.

The Sre house is the symbol of the family's wealth and well-being; a precise index of this is the number of upright supports (*jörong*) that are used (in effect, its length). The interior is ritually divided into longitudinal halves: the main ("noble") area and the passage area near the entrance (*plate 266*).[34] In the former are kept foodstuffs and clothing, and visitors are received there. When asleep, the occupants of the house lie with their heads toward this principal area and their feet toward the passage and, in fact, the area is called the "head" of the dwelling. The passage serves as storage place for utensils and firewood. Usually there are two hearths (*bönha*) near the center of the principal area, one near the door, for receiving guests, the other to the back, for normal domestic use. Above the latter, there is a crisscross framework for preserving dry foods (*pönhör*).

## The Villages of Nias Island

The territorial organization, the settlement plan, and the architecture found in the southern part of the Indonesian island of Nias[35] all bespeak a village society based on social stratification. At the summit of the hierarchy is the divine chief, who governs through sub-chiefs representing the various lineages in the village. An especially great abundance of food, the ownership of slaves by the chiefs, and the development of a complex craftsmanship in wood and stone all play a part within the ritual framework.

In the Nias Islanders' cosmology, two opposed but complementary twin deities represent not only the complex of natural and social antitheses but also the inseparable unity underlying every dualistic principle. Lowalani stands for the positive forces: sun, light, life, the cock, the color yellow; Latura Dano for the negative forces: moon, darkness, death, the serpent, the color black. The world is divided into nine superimposed planes, on the highest of which resides Lowalani and his consort, a mediating divinity. The layout of the village and the positions of the chief's house and of the individual family lineages express on different levels, and with a series of symbolic articulations that draw on such diverse concepts as rivers, cardinal and astronomical directions, a tree, and the cosmos, both hierarchy and the transmission of political power from above. A correspondence between artificial space and mythic prototypes manifests itself through the axial plan of the village, consisting of a slightly elevated rectangular plaza flanked by dwellings that terminates in the chief's house in axial position (*plates 274–276*). Through the cen-

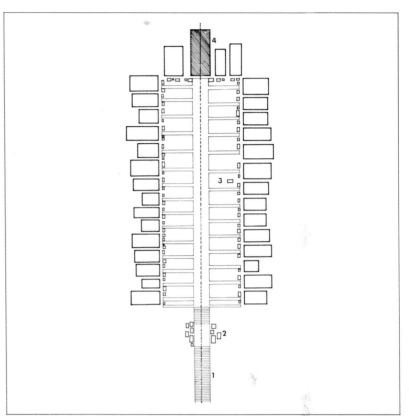

273. *Garoet: huts in a village, Java (Indonesia).*

274. *Schematic plan of the village of Bawamataluö, Nias Island (Indonesia).*
   1. *entranceway;* 2. *megaliths;* 3. *stone for the ritual leap;* 4. *house of the chief.*

275. *View of the inner plaza dominated by the chief's house, village of Hili Mondregeraja, Nias Island (Indonesia).*

276. *House of the chief, village of Bawamataluö, Nias Island (Indonesia).*
277. *Batak: central plaza of a village, Sumatra (Indonesia).*

278. *Receptacle with compartments for betel, woven in colored vegetable fibers in the form of a typical house, from Timor (Indonesia). Musée de l'Homme, Paris.*

279. *Batak: large house and storehouses for rice, Sumatra (Indonesia).*

280. *Batak: village, Sumatra (Indonesia).*
281. *Batak: carving on the corner of a house, Sumatra (Indonesia).*

ter of the plaza runs a street, the ceremonial axis from the entrance on the "lower" level to the seat of power at the "highest" level. The orientation of this axis is generally determined by the cardinal directions. The ritual foundation of the village consists in the choice of a suitable site, the careful clearing of the terrain, and the placement of the "umbilicus" of the new settlement, its central point (*fuso newali*). Wooden stakes, thought of as fragments of the cosmic tree (*eho*), mark off the plaza, which is its most important component. This tree is the support of the social structure: As the beneficent god resides at the highest level of the world, so too the chief is equated with the top of the tree. Its branches are identified with the family lineages linked to and favored by him. Correspondingly, the hierarchical structure is reiterated in the language of the "lower world" in the identified images of cosmic serpent, river, crocodile, Milky Way, and rainbow.

Both the tree and the serpent, which should probably be read in superposition, furnish a model by which to interpret the overall plan of the village. The trunk of the tree and the serpent are both represented in the central thoroughfare; the branches correspond to the terraces and houses along its sides; the treetop (or the head of the serpent) coincides with the chief's house; and the root (or the tail) may be equated with the terrain at the "lower" level—the entranceway and stairway that give access to the "upper" part. While the "celestial" figure of the cosmic tree seems to predominate here (the word designating the village, *bahmua*, signifies sky, or cosmos), the general ground plan of the village appears clearly also to have been influenced by the zoomorphic figure of the crocodile (equated with the serpent), which is often carved on the stones placed at the sides of the entranceway.

The whole complex of terms having to do with an analogy between the watercourse, the social structure, and the village is another aspect of this spatial symbolism, here, as always, linked to the complementary concepts of "higher" and "lower." Thus, the high part of the village is called *sibaloi* (upper stretch of the river; the chief is called *si ulu*, he who stands at the top of the river), and the entranceway is *jou*, the lower stretch of the river. The principal street is therefore also the celestial river (identifiable with the Milky Way), which, in the center of the village, as *fuso newali*, connects the upper world with the lower; its course begins at the source—the chief's house—and ends, as does the settlement itself, with the village gate and the thoroughfare leading to it.

The connection between settlement and spatial directions derives more from myth and social structure than from any real fixed orientation; the nobles are associated with the south (*raja*), so the zone to their right is considered to coincide with the east and that to their

191

284. *Minangkabau: wooden models of a house and a granary, from Sumatra (Indonesia). Musée de l'Homme, Paris.*

285. *Minangkabau: model of a house in brass, from Sumatra (Indonesia). Museum für Völkerkunde, Basel.*

286. *Minangkabau: a large house covered with carving and other decoration, Sumatra (Indonesia).*

287. *Minangkabau: detail of a corner at the back of a house, Sumatra*
   *(Indonesia).*

left is consequently thought of as west. But the residences of the nobles are most commonly placed to the north, and therefore they do in fact have the east to their right.

This complex of interconnections, prototypical forms, and balanced counterpositions testifies to the importance of myth as the instrument justifying social imbalances. The two halves into which, in practice, the village is divided in this region are not so much two rows of houses facing each other in mirror-fashion along the sides of the central street as an "upper" part inhabited by the nobles and a "lower" part left to the commoners. This means that the prototype from which the village takes its form originated from the fact that the codified disequilibrium of the society was equated with the disequilibrium of the cosmos constructed in its image. Like an animal or vegetable organism, the mirror-halves represent the doubling, so to speak, of a linear structure, which, however, in reality is divided into a governing part (the head, the treetop and the upper part of the trunk and branches) and a subordinate part (the lower limbs, the lower part of the trunk and branches, and the roots). But, as with many other societies that have developed correspondences between mirror-image parts (for example, between right hand and left hand), the hierarchy is contradicted by the symmetry of the village plan as we see it, and this is probably the residue of a type of dualist organization without a "head," such as one finds in collective longhouses.

The areas to either side of the central thoroughfare and along the front of the more important dwellings are paved with stones and contain stone monuments, megaliths erected in honor of the ancestors of the respective lineages. These take the form of seats (osa osa) and what resemble our capitals (njogadij) and columns (behoe), and were the sites of periodic sacrifices by means of which the chiefs used to make public display not only of their own genealogy but also of their personal wealth.

In Sumatra, Timor, Borneo, and the Celebes, too, there developed specific architectonic styles (using that word broadly) out of an age-old stratification that had resulted from successive waves of migration, coming for the most part from the continental coasts, and from local cultures that had already developed bold and complex architectonic solutions (plates 277–289). In this region, the art of building the large structures of the village chefferie (a form of hereditary chiefdom) has survived nearly unaltered to the present day. They include not only dwellings but also streets, plazas, fortified enclosures, altars, and tombs. Ironically, this tradition, because of its extensive use of stone, is commonly defined as megalithic.

## THE POLYNESIAN-MICRONESIAN UNIVERSE
### The Myths of Origin and the Science of Navigation

In Polynesian culture (and its variant in Micronesia), sea and sky are the matrices within which the small patches of dry land emerged. Thus, fish and islands are thought of as similar—a notion reflected in the myth that tells how the islands were fished up by a hero. There are other versions of the origin myth. In the Hawaiian poem Kumulipo, the origin of the islands is traced back historically to Tahiti, the source of the population of all of Oceania. According to the poem, the islands were created one after the other, in order of importance, by the divine couple Wakea and Papa: "From them was born first Tahiti-ku of the rising sun, then second was Tahiti-moe of the sinking sun; born third were the stones of foundation and born too was the stone [vault] of the sky. Fifth to see the light was Hawaii."[1] However, in the collectivity of Polynesian myths, the marine element assumes a key role because of the importance of fish as the principal foodstuff for most of the archipelagoes.

The myth Tkana Maui tells how the northern island and principal center of the New Zealand archipelago was caught on a hook and fished up by the youngest of the five Maui brothers. We are told,[2] the canoe used in that miraculous catch was stranded on the chief mountain of the island, Mount Hikurangi; the hook of Maui is represented by the bay of Hawke, between the peninsula of Mahia and Kidnappers Cape; the fish he pulled up—the island—is called Fish-of-Maui (te Ika-a-Maui) and likened in form to a stingray (Dasyatis pastinaca), with the southern extremity of the island representing the head, the eastern extremity of East Cape and the western headland of Taranaki the two large lateral fins, and the narrow peninsula of North Auckland the tail. Thus, every natural feature, every particularity of the landscape became part of a model that made it easier to understand the shape of the territory and the hierarchical relationships between its parts as well as to distinguish between populations of different districts. That the myth was made use of in the political and territorial division of the land is demonstrated by the example of the island of Aitutaki, whose territory, though not resembling a fish in its contours, is nonetheless subdivided into the same organs: head, body, tail, and fins.[3] This zoomorphic subdivision also fulfills mnemonic needs, making sense out of natural structures and groups that otherwise would appear to be merely casual. Thus, according to a local myth, the Society Islands "emerged floating one near the others and from the depths of the ocean like an enormous fish with many protuberances on its back."[4]

The need to fix the islands in space—tiny scraps of land lost between sea and sky—often led the Polynesian settlers to conceive the

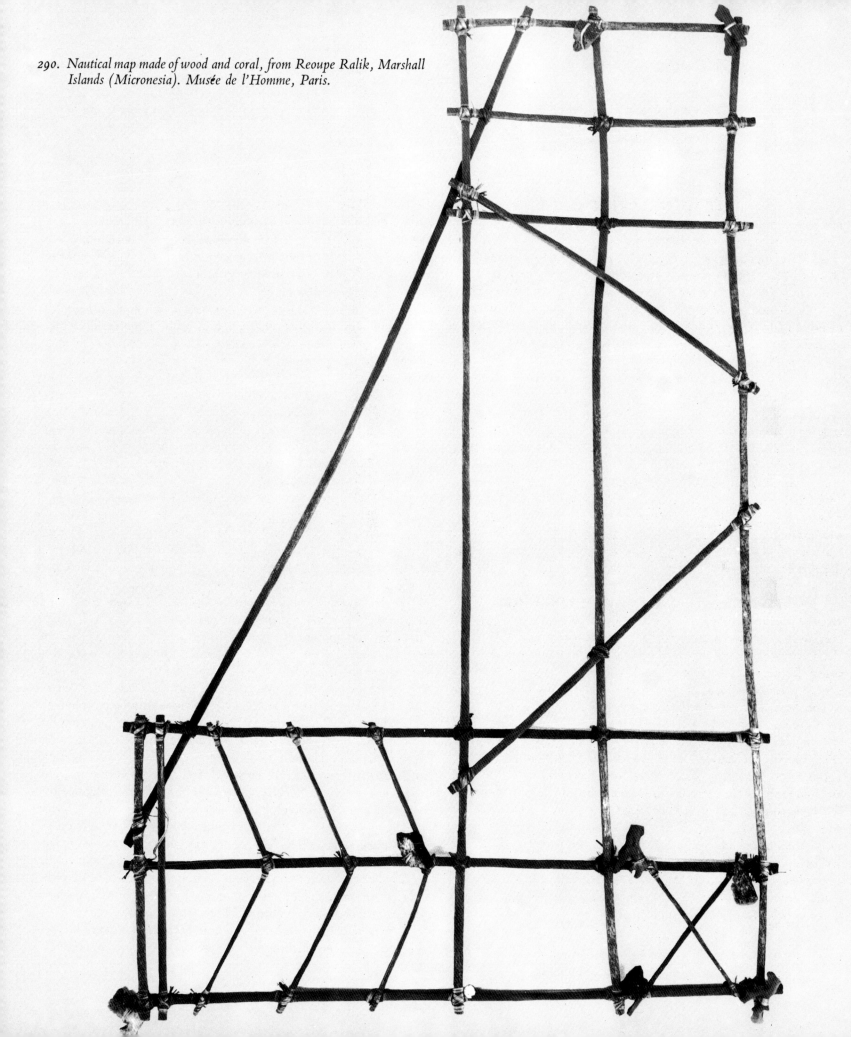

290. *Nautical map made of wood and coral, from Reoupe Ralik, Marshall Islands (Micronesia). Musée de l'Homme, Paris.*

291. Schematic drawing of navigation stones on Arorae Island, Gilbert Islands (Micronesia).
1. successive lines of beach; a. stone aligned in the direction of Onotoa Island; b, c. stones aligned in the direction of Tanana Island; d. stones aligned in the direction of Nukunau Island.

292. Decorated facade of a men's house, Melekeiok, Palau Islands (Micronesia). (Watercolor by Kramer, 1908–10.)

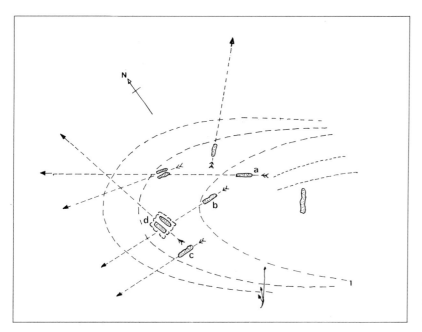

relation with the two dominant elements of the environment as an umbilical thread. As in the case of Aitutaki, often a liana was thought to anchor an island (almost always considered to be floating) to the ocean floor, while a star suspended in zenith position above the island connected it with the sky—as in the case of the star Hokulei shining above Hawaii.[5] This conception can be interpreted as an identification of each island, particularly its center or highest mountain, with the original cosmic axis of space that links the sky with the earth and the waters and is the pole of a system of coordinates radiating out in all directions through space, a belief held, for example, in Tikopia,[6] a Polynesian colony in Melanesia, and on Easter Island. Yet, again, because the sea is of life-giving importance, the part of the island that faces the sea is most highly charged with sacred significance.

For the early Polynesian and Micronesian navigators, acquaintance with the territory of Oceania was by no means a marginal aspect of their culture but, in fact, the very basis of their survival.[7] Voyages over routes covering hundreds of miles were made regularly to exchange goods, establish new colonies, and broaden spheres of influence that extended over incredibly vast stretches of ocean speckled here and there with minuscule islands. In the same way as we map continental territory—although usually with more specifically practical motivations—the people of Oceania made cartographic representations of marine territory that take into account everything that might be useful to the navigator: ocean currents, birds that might signal the proximity of land, winds, and stars. The most noted of these "modules" of navigation are the nautical maps of the Marshall Islands, the medo, which take the form of lattices of wood, small ropes, and shells with representations of the currents, routes, and islands (plate 290). These show, for the different seasons and under different meteorological conditions, the path that a boat should follow both by day (with reference to the position of the sun) and by night (with the help of the stars). Between two stars grazing the horizon, an alignment was determined and plotted out to show relative shifts in position during the successive hours of the night. Even if his boat strayed from the planned route, the navigator could steer by the zenith stars above the various islands and navigate by meridians and parallels.

This navigational expertise, practiced by the governing and priestly class, forged a link between each island and the archipelago to which it belonged, encouraging the islanders to maintain close contact with the nearest or most important islands. Testimony to this tendency are the so-called navigation stones—slabs set up on the shore, at the point where voyages began—indicating the exact direction of the nearest islands, often dozens of miles away and invisible to the naked eye. Some of these stones have been found on the northwest coast of Arorae, in the southern Gilbert Islands, and these point toward Onotoa, Tamana, and Nikunau, fifty-two to eighty-six miles away (*plate 291*).[8]

*Social Stratification: Lineage and "Chefferie"*

In the Polynesian and Micronesian world, whose history is threaded with voyages of exploration that resulted in colonization and exploitation of native populations of the islands or of prisoners of war, division into classes has been the most widespread form of social organization. M. D. Sahlins[9] has stressed that it was only in the relatively few volcanic islands where there were more extensive agricultural resources that such stratification came about between the nobles (direct descendants of the tribal ancestor) and the lower stratum of the population, composed of either the more recent nobility, the small landowners, the subjugated tribes, or the slaves, depending upon the particular circumstances. In the atolls, where irrigation is not possible (rainwater is collected in holes in the ground) and there are no reserve stores of wood, society continued to have a merely segmentary character. Thus, the larger islands came to be ruled by a hereditary chief belonging to a lineage claiming divine descent; in some cases, the society resembled a kingdom, based not only on a complex internal stratification but also on regular commercial exchanges with other archipelagoes; a relatively democratic tribal system continued in force in the lesser islands. In reality, however, the latter became subordinate to the larger islands, with tribute paid in the form of foodstuffs.

A brief description of the conditions that gave rise to a social hierarchy in the chief islands and centers of culture in Micronesia and Polynesia is indispensable to the understanding of the architecture there. It was under the auspices of the nobles—those who could legally or by indirect means hold land—that an architecture developed in the form either of assembly houses with community functions (though always with the ulterior purpose of celebrating the power of the chief) or of royal residences and sanctuaries. Both types were built in stone and administered in autocratic manner by an elite or by a king.

In all the large archipelagoes of Polynesia, society was stratified historically into two or more classes.[10] In the Society Islands there were nobles (*hui-ari, ariki*), nonhereditary landowners (*raatira*), farmers and fishermen in the service of the upper classes (*manahune*), and slaves. Mangarevan society was divided into nobles (*togoiti*) and commoners (*urumanu*), with an intermediate class of warrior-landowners (*pakaroa*), and finally workers (*kiore*). Supreme power was shared between the king (*akariki*) and the high priest (*tahura-tupa*). In New Zealand there were hereditary nobles (*rangatira*), the people (*tutua, whare*),

295, 296. *Exterior and interior of a traditional house with trusswork covered with colored vegetable fibers, Fiji Islands (Melanesia)*

297. *Chief's house with shell decoration, Fiji Islands (Melanesia).* ▷

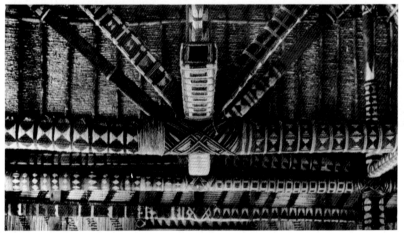

and slaves, who were prisoners of war (*taurekareka*). In Easter Island, the *ariki,* the dominant class from which the king was chosen, constituted the principal clan (the *Meru* clan). In Samoa, operating above the structures of the semiindependent villages, was the governing class of *matai;* however, they had to heed the counsel of the assembly of nobles (*fono*). In Hawaii, power was in the hands of the nobles, who were district chiefs (*alii*) and were the hereditary owners of the land; below them were the *menehune* (the subjugated aboriginal population, similar to the *manehune* of the Society Islands), and the slaves (*kauwa*).

In Micronesia there was a much more marked social difference between atolls and volcanic islands; the latter, at various times in their history, exercised more or less extensive hegemonies. The population of Ponape was divided into four classes: nobles (*mundjab*), nobles of inferior rank (*jau-liki*), workers (*aramac-mal*), and prisoner-slaves (*litu*). There were three classes in the Mariana Islands: the nobles (*matua*), the intermediate class (*achaot*), and the lower class. In the Gilberts, there were noble landowners (*te-tokker*), a farming middle class (*ao-matta*), the common people (*te-torro*), and the serfs of the nobility (*te-bei*). In the Marshalls, not only were there the greater nobles (*irodji*), the lesser nobles (*burak*), an intermediary class (*leadakdak*), and the populace (*kadjur*) but also clans, of which only the first two were considered noble. In Yap, the two classes were subdivided into nine subclasses, four among the upper class, five among the lower. Despite the division between village chiefs (*rupak*) and populace (*arabuiyk*) in the Palau Islands, the importance of the clans and the men's societies made the stratification less clear, and it is there, in fact, that the men's house reached a high stage of development (*plate 292*).

*Political Organization and Monumental Architecture*
In Polynesia the hierarchical organization of power and the absence of "marginal" territorial zones (due, among other reasons, to the limited availability of land) account for the fact that the different social classes, populations, and clans lived in separate areas of the territory. Such a dislocation is always hierarchical in character, even when it involves merely the simplest division of the territory into halves since these, by definition, are unequal, one being superior to the other. The Fiji Islands are subdivided into a western area, which cuts through the island of Viti Levu from north to south and is considered Melanesian, and an eastern, Polynesian, area. The former is more agricultural in character, the latter depends more on fishing. The inhabitants of the former are known as *Ra* (those who live below), while the easterners are *Natuidhara* (those who live above). This is by no means a merely conventional division, for it is in the eastern zone, where chiefdom is

298. *Model of a house in interwoven cord, from Fiji Islands (Melanesia).*
*Musée de l'Homme, Paris.*

299. *Above: reconstruction of two maraes, Tahiti, Society Islands (Poly-*
*nesia). Below: plan of the plaza for assemblies, Nanauhi, Marquesas*
*Islands (Polynesia).*
*1. large house; 2. house of women and small children; 3. visitors' house; 4.*
*warriors' house; 5. priests' house; 6. entrance; 7. large drums; 8. house of the aged.*

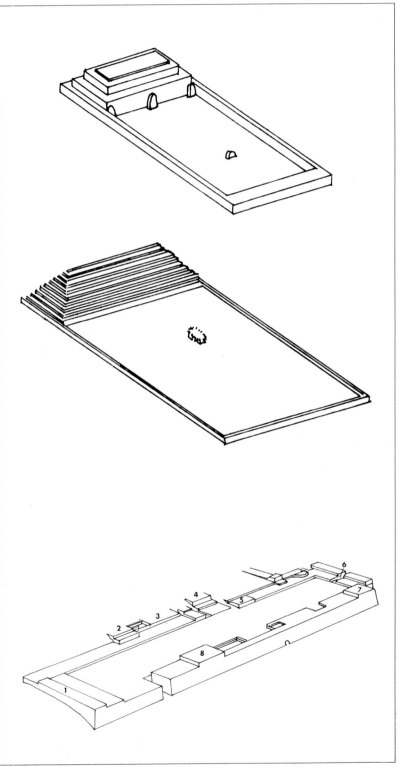

*300, 301. Rectangular dwellings with rounded ends, bamboo walls, and roofing of pandanus leaves, Tahiti, Society Islands (Polynesia).*

302. *Festivity in honor of General D'Entrecasteaux given on March 30, 1793, by King Toubau, Tonga Islands (Polynesia). (Contemporary watercolor by Piron.)*

303. *Habitation partially walled in by logs, Futuna Islands (Polynesia).*

304. *View of a village from above, Samoa Islands (Polynesia).*

hereditary and the social structure more rigidly hierarchical, that the myths locate the sanctuary from which mankind arose. Similarly, the chiefs in the southeast part of the Solomon Islands clearly maintain a higher grade of control over the village populations than do those in other sections. In the Marquesas, the islands of Hivaoa and Nukuhiva are each divided into a western part (*nuku*) and an eastern part (*pepane*), a division that, the myths say, can be traced back to two brothers, and the same is true in Hawaii and Rarotonga. Probably these divisions were the product of successive migrations that resulted in the partitioning of the islands between indigenous populations and immigrants. According to tradition, the division of the land in Easter Island in the 17th century caused a ruthless struggle between the "fat men" (*hanau-eepe*) and the "thin men" (*hanau-momoko*), who arrived later and occupied the eastern part.

In general, in both Polynesia and Micronesia, the division of the islands into from two to ten or more districts was based on a criterion of inequality between clans or classes of the different areas. Considering that the district chiefs invariably belonged to the hereditary nobility, the clan (or stirps) living in a particular sector was that which reserved to itself the privilege of commanding and was therefore the royal clan. This was the case, for example, in Truk. Similarly, the dominion of one island over others was exercised by forcing the defeated people to accept an inferior role and requiring the payment of tribute. The power of Yap extended to many islands of Micronesia, and a Yap legend with some historical basis explains the fact by a migration organized by eight couples, each belonging to one of the eight clans (*kailang*) into which the island was divided. Since the various Yap clans resided in separate villages organized in a rigid hierarchy, it is clear the legend offers an attempt to reproduce the same criterion of political and territorial control in the subject islands.[11]

Given such social organization, it is understandable that monumental architecture, especially in stone, which was built for the king or the dominant aristocracy, should have been concentrated in only a few districts in the major volcanic islands. The erection of large stone structures, whether for religious purposes (sanctuaries and *maraes*) (*plate 299*)[12] or more specifically for royal use (palaces and tombs), always depended on the availability of slaves or cheap labor, which was in turn contingent upon the formation of "kingdoms" that comprised one or more islands and were based on a system of regular tribute in men or foodstuffs from the various *chefferies*. The basis of the power of the supreme chief or king was his ability to provide free food to his guests and to the workmen involved in building the edifices proclaiming his power. In Mangareva the king kept in his own storehouses the tribute of breadfruit imposed on nobles and

305. *Guest houses, Samoa Islands (Polynesia).*
306, 307. *Details of the interior structure of a guest house roof, Samoa
Islands (Polynesia).*

308. *Detail of the interior structure of a guest house roof, Samoa Islands (Polynesia).*

309. *House of a chief and a screen to protect the fire at the left, Easter Island (Polynesia). (Drawing by Pierre Loti, 1872.)*

310. *Vestiges of a stone house with small conical tower, northwest coast of Easter Island (Polynesia).*

311. *Vestiges of the foundations of long, boat-shaped huts, south of Ahu Te Peu, Easter Island (Polynesia).*

*pakoara* alike, and these food reserves were drawn on for the great banquets during the principal festivals that were the occasion for the periodic renewal of hierarchical ties. At those festivities, the principal personages were the nobles (*rongorongo*), who sang the deeds of the mythic heroes, and the carpenters (*taura rakau*) entrusted with putting up the buildings and the decorations required in the ceremony.[13]

### Village, Royal Residence, and Sanctuary

In some islands where agricultural production was particularly important, the inequalities between different clans and different territorial groupings resulted in a struggle for land that came to be reflected in the structure of the territory and the settlement. In New Zealand there were frequent wars between the districts, and many of the villages (*pa*) were fortified (*plates 318, 319*). High palisades surrounded these settlements, which were situated on heights and on cliffs rising steeply from the sea and therefore difficult of access. The technique of terracing used in cultivating taro was used to prepare the slopes and hilltops as sites for dwellings, the chief's house, and the plaza for assemblies. The different family groupings of the dominant class of Rapa contended for ownership of the territory, which was subdivided into separate areas, dominated by the residence of the chief on the highest hilltop, for example, the fortified settlements of Karege and Te Vaitau. Mountainous Rapa with its fortified villages provides significant evidence as to the way strategic natural resources were once exploited in an environment much like that of New Zealand. From an authentic source we learn that a mountain range with a high peak was selected and its summit leveled off to become the highest terrace. The flanks were cut down with digging tools and crude adzes of basalt until a second terrace wide enough to accommodate huts took shape. Excavation continued with successive terraces that needed high walls to back them up. Deep moats were dug to either side of the citadel, cutting through the main ridge; on the secondary ridges leading to the principal fort, other terraces were carved out for dwellings and defensive outposts. On the highest terrace of the citadel was the residence of the great chief who, in case of war, acted as supreme commander.[14] The royal palace was built in stone and, from what can be deduced from archaeological remains, derived at least partially in style from large wooden constructions.

Only in Tonga (the Friendly Islands) does there seem to have been complete unification of society under a royal dynasty of divine origin. To honor his two sons, the thirteenth king, Tuitatui, is traditionally supposed to have erected a trilithon, a gigantic portal in coral stone, called *Haamonga-a Maui* (Yoke of Maui) on Tongatabu. His aim probably was to reproduce the form of a crossbar with two weights hang-

312. *Vestiges of a ground-level kiln, south of Ahu Te Peu, Easter Island (Polynesia).*

313. *Vestiges of a stone building covered by a false vault, sanctuary of Orongo, Easter Island (Polynesia).*

314, 315. *Petroglyphs representing a bird-man, south of the sanctuary of Orongo, Easter Island (Polynesia).*

ing from it. The twenty-ninth king of Tonga, Telea, is said to have been responsible for the most imposing of the royal tombs on the island, which are large, pyramidal, terraced stone constructions (*langi*). In Matolenim, the easternmost district of the island of Ponape and the seat of the king, imposing remains in stone testify to the sumptuousness of his palace. In the Marianas, too, there are vestiges of colonnades with pyramidal shafts and round capitals, which are thought to be from the palace of the king (*maga-lahi*).

More widespread and, on the whole, better documented is stone architecture of religious character. Administered by the nobles, these edifices were more directly linked with the social life of the community. The Polynesian sanctuary, the *marae*, consists of an open rectangular plaza surrounded by a wall and terraces and containing at one end the *ahu*, a stepped pyramid that is its principal and most sacred element (*plate 299*). Probable prototype of the *marae* is the complex dedicated to the god Oro in Opoa on the island of Raiatea, the political and religious center of the Society Islands before the rise of Tahiti. This *marae*, called *taputapu-atea,* had an *ahu* whose base measured 144 by 24 feet and was about 10 feet high. Near it rose a stone pillar used during the solemn investiture of the king of Opoa (*te papa-tea-ia ruea*). Here were associated the architectural and symbolic complexes connected with the two highest authorities, the king and the class of nobles and priests. The same arrangement is found in Rarotonga, where, in addition to the *marae*, there were enclosures with unmistakable civil-political functions, notably the *arai-te-tonga*, a court where the royal enthronement took place close to the stone of investiture (*taumakeva*).

Within the precinct of the Tahitian *marae* were planted certain sacred trees, including the casuarina. Access to the enclosure was strictly forbidden to the women. Here, as in all large-scale architectural undertakings involving working stone with stone axes, it was of utmost importance to command a slave labor force and to keep them at their task at a rigorously organized worksite. Besides governing through the chiefs, the noble Tahitian families exploited the work of the *manahune* (the productive classes) to maintain the slaves during the building of these large religious complexes and private *marae*.

In New Zealand and certain other archipelagoes, notably Samoa and Tonga, there was no collective sanctuary. Among the Maori, its place was taken by village plazas called *marae* but having more limited functions since the offerings to the gods were made in a sacred place outside the settlement (*tuahu*). In the Fiji Islands, the *nanga*, stone altars in an open enclosure, served for initiations.[15]

This exclusion of the sanctuary from the normal functions of social and political life—evidence of a separation between cult places

316. *Eighteenth-century drawing by La Pérouse showing anthropomorphic statues still erect on a platform* (ahu), *with cylindrical elements superimposed on their heads, Easter Island* (Polynesia).

317. *Statues abandoned on the west flank of the Volcano Rano Raraku, Easter Island* (Polynesia).

(linked to the myth of origin and to the tribal identity) and governmental places—is found in numerous instances, from Micronesia to Easter Island. The sanctuary remained the "place of origins," which, in this marine environment, meant the point of contact between each separate island and space as a whole, both sea and sky. In the Gilberts, every island had a temple on the shore dedicated to the god Tabuarik, a "house of the spirits" (*bata n'anti*), with stone walls and a door opening toward the west.[16] The sanctuary of Orongo on the southwest point of Easter Island was dedicated to the cult of Tiki-makemake, the god presiding over the increase in foodstuffs, who assumed the form of the sea bird *manu-tara* (*plates 313–315*). Here, too, the use of stone—for these constructions with false cupolas and petroglyphs—is linked to the fact that it was a cult center. Larger in scale are the monumental terraces connected with the activity of the clans of the dominant class, which were erected near the seashore. These, dominated by rows of gigantic anthropomorphic statues, were intended for ceremonial and burial use (*plates 316, 317*). They were symbols of the power of the nobles who exalted their own genealogy by exploiting the poorer classes; the statues (*moai*) in all probability represent the ancestors of their family.

In the Marquesas Islands, the use of stone became widespread not only for community edifices but also for dwellings. The basement of these buildings included seats and also anthropomorphic representations. However, as a rule throughout the Polynesian area, the family house is raised above the ground on a stone platform: a sign of the constant relationship between public architecture and private architecture, both exploited as evidence of its power by the dominant class. Often the important families owned more than one hut, each with specific function as private parlor, kitchen, or public gathering place. In Samoa, as we shall see, building a house for guests was an economic effort that no family eager to increase its prestige could afford to evade.

*The Carpenter-Architects*

The construction of wooden buildings and boats is the prerogative of individuals who are at one and the same time architects, carpenters, and sculptors and who occupy a position at a remove from the other classes. The fact that they are in the service of the king, the chiefs, and the influential families confers privileged status on the Polynesian artisans, who not only perpetuate technical knowledge and skills but also keep alive the more significant aspects of the mythology in a society in which every undertaking, whether long ocean journey, construction, or war, depends in highly selective manner on the rational application of complex technological principles. This is why

the associations of artisans not only have their own tutelary gods but sometimes act as bodies distinct from the social classes with priestly functions of greater importance than the practical ones. Thus, in Tahiti the god of the carpenters, Tane, is the son of the supreme being, Tangaroa, and of Atea, who represents Space. The Polynesian word *tahunga* and its related local forms mean "expert," or "specialist," and apply equally to priests and to architects.

The link between house, power, myth, and craft specialization is clearly demonstrated by the Samoan chief's guest house, a large privately owned building for social use in which the chief receives guests, offering them a libation of *kava* and a meal.[17] Here, too, prestige is maintained on the part of the dominant lineage by offering food, an unmistakable sign of wealth. The association of artisans entrusted with building the guest house is in this case the pivotal and mediatory point of the social system. In form, the guest house derives from the first mythical model erected by the god Tagaloa in the sky and thereafter faithfully reproduced on earth. Direct descent from the god who is protector and founder of the line of artisans is emphasized in the names assumed on the various islands by the different branches of the association of house builders: *Sa-Tagaloa, Aiga-sa-Sao* (family of Tagaloa, family of Sao). Rigid norms control the relationships between the artisans and the individuals for whom they work: A product defined in every element and made in conformity with strict professional rules must be paid for according to the demands of prestige and tradition by regular and adequate outlays of food, rounded out by gifts and banquets offered by the owner at critical phases of the construction.

The Samoan guest house (*plates 305–308*), built by preference from the wood of the breadfruit tree, is a rectangular construction with rounded ends and a roof shaped in a continuous domelike curve on a framework of crossbeams and elements bent to shape. The number of crossbeams, in direct proportion to the length of the house, testifies to the importance of the owner. The supporting poles, between which mats may be tied to make a continuous wall, are also a sign of the chief's prestige since each of them makes a backrest for his guests.[18]

*House and Gods Among the Maori of New Zealand*

In Maori mythology, the supreme god, Io, lives on the highest of the twelve terraces of the sky in a sumptuous palace, Rangi-atea, behind a sacred precinct called Te Rauroha. His dwelling is the model for the earthly residence of the *ariki*, the supreme chiefs among men, who, with the entire aristocratic class of the *rangatira*, descend directly from the mythical progenitors.[19] The gods, who were descendants of

Rangi (Space or Sky) and Papa (Earth), in the course of time took on more human characteristics, and in line with this the architectonic features found elsewhere in Polynesia here lost some of their mythic and sacral associations and assumed a more social and political character.[20] An example of this is the *marae* (called *malae* by the Maori), which in New Zealand, as in the Samoan and Tongan islands, is not a temple where religious rites are celebrated in an enclosure forbidden to women, but a plaza within the village itself, in front of the chief's house, which is used for public assemblies.

A rigid subdivision into two classes makes the specialists (*tohunga*), among whom the house builders have a primary place, the principal intermediaries between governors and governed. They transmit the values of the traditional society through a highly codified language, which is well adapted to convey very technical information.

The fact that agriculture predominates over fishing has also meant that the social status which, in smaller islands, is more directly associated with the various types of boats, is reflected here in the architecture of the house and the village.

A function of the taboos and magical prescriptions in the art of architectural woodcarving is to impart technical knowledge. A class art, carved decoration is used lavishly on assembly buildings (*plate 321*),[21] storehouses for food, and village gates, but above all it serves the purposes of the noble families and the chiefs. The carved panels and figures transform a uniform and simple architectural type (a rectangular cabin with double-pitched roof and front veranda) into an extremely rich construction with variations in style that correspond to the different districts and the different social ranks of their owners (*plates 320–328*).

Each district has its own myths to explain the origin of the art of architectural sculpture. It was always gods or demigods who built, in one of the celestial realms, the first model that thereafter was imitated on earth.[22] According to the populations on the east coast, the art was introduced by the artisan-priest Rua-i-te-Pu kenga, who had learned it in the next-to-last of the twelve heavens, the realm of Rangi-Tamaku. Another tale explains how the god Rua was first to try his hand at architectural carving (*whakairo rakau*) and so became the predestined protector of the association of artisans. Rua built the first house ever decorated with carved beams in competition with Tangaroa, the great and powerful god of the sea and fish, who had put up a house decorated only with paintings. Tangaroa was so deceived by the carvings that, mistaking the figures for real persons, he came right up to them and rubbed noses with one of the sculptured faces. The particular expression of the faces of the ancestor figures that decorate the walls of Maori houses is explained by a particular mythic

321. *Maori: large assembly house built at the end of the 19th century (New Zealand).*

322. *Maori: diagram of an assembly house* (whare) *with the names of the various parts (New Zealand).*
1. ama amo; 2. maihi, mahihi; 3. koruru; 4. teko-teko; 5. parata, maui; 6. pare; 7. whaka-wae, waewae; 8. korupe; 9. matapihi, pihanga; 10. tatau; 11. pou-koukou aro, pou-tou-aroaro; 12. teko-teko aro; 13. rapa-rapa; 14. pae-pae kai awa; 15. paepae; 16. heke; 17. poupou.

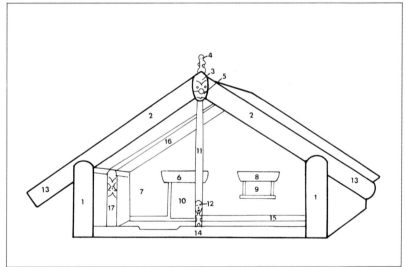

episode. The figures have round, wide-open eyes made of shell, which give them a fixed stare like that of an owl (*plate 324*). Rongo, the craftsman to whom the origin of this trait is attributed, after having learned the art of architectural sculpture by reproducing the divine model of a house called *whare-kura,* sacrificed an owl to the gods and buried it under the rear wall of the house; this is said to explain the wide staring eyes, which ever since have characterized the carved faces of Maori ancestors.[23]

Similarly, the anthropomorphic pinnacle crowning the frontal pillar of houses (*plates 322 [4], 323*) was the consequence of a legendary feat attributed to a chief named Ruapupuke. Tangaroa had kidnapped the chief's son with the intention of putting him up on the roof of his house, but Ruapupuke contrived to liberate him and at the same time make off with the most important decorative elements of the divine house of the god. Thus, the pinnacle (*teko-teko*) represents the protagonist of this feat, and the story, as do other tales, emphasizes the divine origin of architectural sculpture.[24]

*Maori Architectural Sculpture*

The anthropomorphic wooden relief panels make up the principal decoration of the house, both outside and inside (*plates 321–328*). In addition to the penetrating fixed gaze, the power of the word (expressed by showing the tongue stuck out) and the power of tattooing are emphasized; tattooing is an important feature of the carved faces, calling attention to the rank of the personage represented. These figures alternate along the walls in the interior of the house with extremely elegant panels of reedwork called *tukutuku,* which are woven in horizontal and vertical directions and painted (*plate 327*). Although quite without figural form, the geometrical motifs resulting from the intersection of ties and reed strips have names that relate to details of the animal world: The zigzag is called by the name for ribs, *kao-kao,* and the triangles by that of the teeth of mythic monsters in the shape of gigantic lizards, *niho-niho taniwha.*[25] The other customary decorative motifs are also related to the world of myth: spirals, which have a diversity of significances, the lizard (personification of Whiro, god of evil), the whale, the Manaia (a hybrid of man and bird), the Marakihau (a fish-man with tubular tongue to suck up men and ships), and so on.[26] Every panel and every carved part of the house, especially in the large assembly buildings, has its own name (*plate 322*).[27] In large measure determining the general appearance of the house are the carved panels and beams that frame the portico.(*plates 321–323*): the *amo* (upright panels to either side), the *pae-pae kai awa* (the sill of the veranda), the principal rafters (the length of which is called *mahihi* and the ends projecting beyond the walls, *rapa-rapa*). The

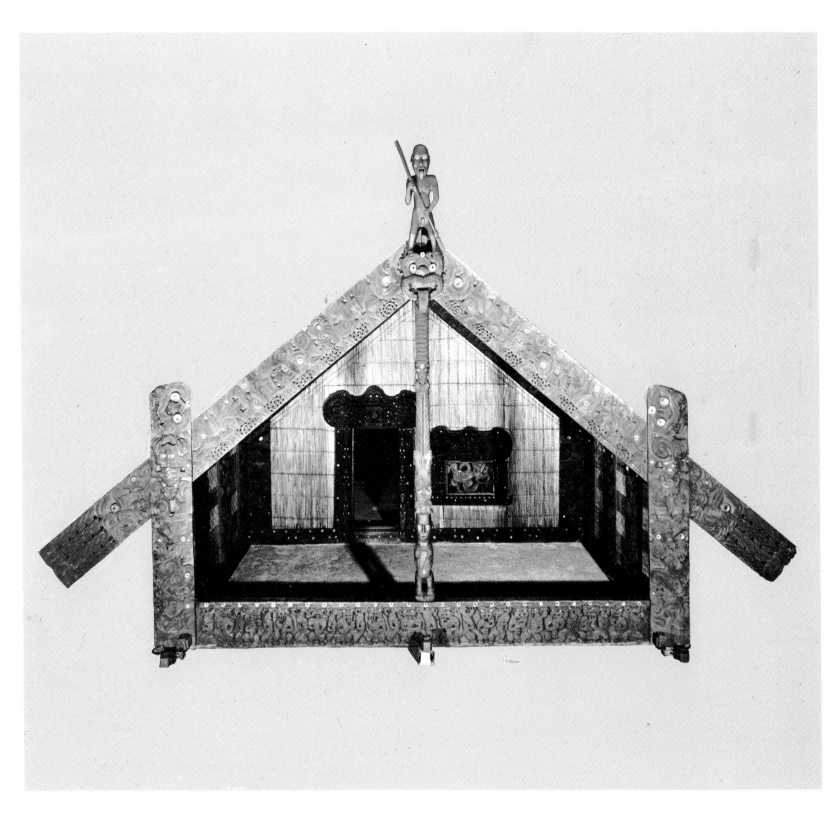

324. *Maori: detail of the wood and mother-of-pearl frieze on the beam of the porch of the assembly house in plate 323, showing figures entirely covered with tattooing (New Zealand). Museum für Völkerkunde, Hamburg.*

325. *Maori: tattooing on the face of a chief, 19th century (New Zealand).*

326. *Maori: interior of an assembly house (whare) (New Zealand).*

327. *Maori: reconstruction of the interior of a house with carved wooden panels, painted beams, and panels of colored straw woven in geometrical patterns (New Zealand). Museum für Völkerkunde, Hamburg.*

pivotal element of the facade is a central pillar (*pou-koukou aro*) whose top and base are ornamented with anthropomorphic figures, the *teko-teko* and the *teko-teko aro*; a human mask conceals the point of junction (*koruru*) between the two principal sloping rafters. Every sculptured detail of the facade has its own technical and symbolic place; however, the artisan can introduce numerous variants at the request of his patron.

More invariable, because of the religious significance associated with it, is the decoration of the *pataka*, the village food storehouse, which is a small-scale version of the dwelling but is set high above the ground on a post or posts. The carved portions are still intimately linked to the most important concerns of the tribal community: production and conservation of food, fertility of the soil, the benevolence of the gods. For this reason, when there is threat of enemy aggression these panels are dismounted and carefully hidden away in inaccessible places so that, even in case of defeat, the relationship between the group and the natural forces will be preserved. As one would expect, the decoration of the *pataka* tends to be inspired to a greater extent by fertility symbolism, which is found on the vertical frontal panels, *te puawai-o-te arawa* (flower of the arawa) as well as on the horizontal ones, *te oha* and the rafters on the facade.[28] Among the themes depicted are the coupling of the mythic first man and woman from whom the tribe descends, as well as other sexual symbols and images such as the whale. Similar motifs are used on the carved gates of the village.

A series of taboos regulates the activity of the sculptor working in wood (chiefly, totara wood).[29] The initial aim, as we have seen, is to preserve the technical knowledge of a complex art, which is exploited by the nobility as ornament and justification of its own power. Until the 19th century, the tools used were exclusively of stone,[30] and there were three basic colors: red obtained from burnt ocher, white from clay, black from soot, all of which were mixed with shark-liver oil.[31] The technical mastery exhibited in this architecture, in which the decorative element is superimposed on the structure and masks and enriches it, is evidence that the dominant class had firmly in its grasp the means of communication, which they exploited to glorify their own power and to legitimize, after the fact, their monopoly of the means of production. This control, however, did not result in making the village community obsolescent but rather in strengthening it through the solidarity imposed by the hierarchy.

As for the motifs: Again, symbolic elements already present and established in the decoration of domestic wares (particularly, in the boxes for feathers, the *wakahuia*, which are entirely covered by them) were enlarged to the scale of architecture, a process found, albeit in dif-

ferent forms, in almost all the decorative languages applied to primitive architecture, here as elsewhere. Another source of inspiration was tattooing. Not only are the distinctive anatomical features of the sculpted figures less important than the tattooing, which is the real key to their symbolic and social meaning (*plates 324, 325*), but, indeed, a display of carved decoration spreads over the structure of the building like a tattoo, covering every inch of the facade and those architectural parts of more social importance. The artistic language of this decoration has peculiar characteristics and is extremely significant within a larger context. Although the motifs were drawn from myth, the decoration was not utilized to reinforce the unity and power of the clan or the equilibrium between different clans. Instead, it was placed at the service of the family (*hapu*) as a result of unilateral control over the labor force and as a means of visual proclamation of the glories of the ancestors and of the direct descent from the progenitor of the tribe to which the owner of the house laid claim. This occurred in conjunction with the development of family (and individual) private property which, in Maori society, came more and more to replace land held in common by the entire community.

It was thus indispensable to extend the visual account of the lineage back in time as far as possible, to the divine progenitors themselves—and this was carried out through architecture, which is the perfect art by which to tie materials to each other (it is not by chance that in many environments of the Pacific the ligatures are the most significant decorative feature of the house, and indeed make incarnate the very rite of construction [*plates 294, 296, 306, 307*]), myth to reality, and the living to the dead.

> The lineage goes back,
> Back to the period of the parent sky.
> The descent traces back,
> Back indeed to the line of Atea.
> Bind the knowledge securely,
> Let the tying be firm,
> Let the knotting be fast,
> That it hold.[32]

The measure of this art is always the human body because its principal dimensions constitute ideal units of measurement easy to apply to the artificial (constructed, man-made) universe.[33] It is the human body that establishes the rules for the sacred measurements of buildings, those hidden relationships that sum up in themselves the indissoluble interconnection between rite and architecture.[34]

When a visual language takes shape it also to some extent vitiates

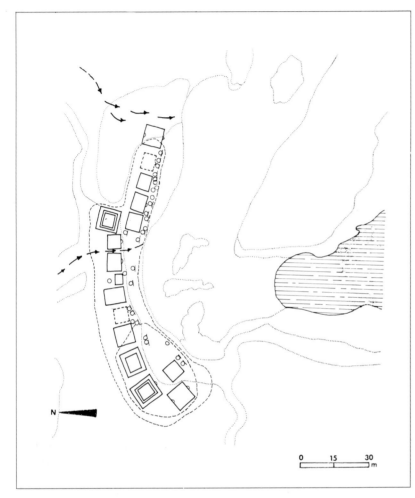

the verbal meanings attached to the repertory of signs and figures connected with myth—an advantage, inasmuch as the same ingredients are then recast and fused again into a unified overall context, though always in a somewhat novel manner and more consistently. Because of an increasing emphasis on the artistic and workmanlike values of the house, in the visual language as in myth, there takes place a continual distortion of the original versions, which are generally considered to be the matrices from which the more complex models grew.

Architecture was the last to develop, after the decorative arts of tattooing and of ornamentation, and this was the consequence of a particular economic link between construction and ownership of land. The aim was to make conspicuous, through the artistic refinement of an object intended for use (the house), not only a social status but an economic status. From that standpoint, architectural decoration is the perfect field on which to squander one's reserves of food, especially when they are abundant, can be conserved, and are concentrated in the hands of a few. The function of decoration thus came to be transformed from ritual reconfirmation of the essential oneness of the group to an after-the-fact demonstration of the family's well-being. In this sense, it is an art whose progress can be traced historically, introduced as it was directly into a socioeconomic world in rapid transformation, whose members were no longer aiming to repeat the mythic model but to transcend, quantitatively and qualitatively, the standards already attained by other family groups and their own as well.

## ARCHITECTURE AND POWER: THE INDIANS OF THE NORTHWEST COAST OF AMERICA

In a very different geographical area, the northwest coast of North America, there is a native architectural tradition based on an even more extensive development of the artistic and social potentialities of a house (plates 329–358). While the tradition has socioeconomic determinants analogous to those in Polynesia, here their effects are highly pronounced. (The historical contacts between groups on the transoceanic routes are still very far from clear, though they are nonetheless incontestable; certainly, though, the Northwest Coast Indian culture came to manifest analogous developments in the interrelationship of art, architecture, and society, and did this with a wealth of variations.)

An environment with exceptionally rich natural resources, a social organization based on a clear-cut hierarchy, a spirit of competition between the various lineages within a clan: These formed the basis on which the architecture of these Indians developed.[35] From

331. *Haida: village of Yan, Queen Charlotte Islands, British Columbia (Canada).*

332. *Haida: village of Massett, Queen Charlotte Islands, British Columbia (Canada).*

333. *Haida: village of Kasaan, Alaska (USA).*

334. *Village on the Salmon River, British Columbia (Canada).*

335. *Village with painted house fronts, British Columbia (Canada).*

northern California to Alaska an aggregate of tribal groupings, *chefferies*, and village units occupying a narrow coastal strip and nearby islands shows a common tendency to express differences in rank, prestige, and wealth through an architecture that became the integral expression of all their artistic gifts. On the other hand, the great social importance attached to architecture and sculpture is directly linked to the extensive development of crafts, which can only be explained by the very special economic organization that prevails in this region.

Until the end of the 19th century, hunting and, particularly, fishing brought in such abundant supplies of food as to permit not only a notable accumulation that could be preserved by drying and smoking but also a vigorous expansion of nonessential activities. The latter were both instrument and cause of a clear-cut social differentiation based, more evidently than among the peoples we have observed so far, on specialization of labor and on private property. Each of the sedentary populations in this region developed a style of its own, but with variations and aims that were by and large comparable and which transcended otherwise profound ethnic and linguistic differences. Thus, architecture plays the same fundamental social role among the Skokomish, Quileute, Makah, coastal Salish, Nootka, Kwakiutl, Bella Coola, Haisla, Tsimshian, Haida, and Tlingit populations settled from south to north along the coasts of the state of Washington, British Columbia, and southeastern Alaska.

*A Competitive Society: Potlatch and Craftsmanship*
The accumulation of surpluses by families of higher rank (from among whose members comes the chief of a village or group of villages) is limited by rules that control the most excessive imbalances. The *potlatch*, a feast offered by the wealthier families to their adversaries and intended to humiliate the poorer among them, is one such instrument, but there are also large architectural undertakings such as the decoration of house fronts, ornamental sculptures, and huge totem poles, which also have as their ultimate aim the dissipation of vast holdings and the encouragement of nonessential labor in order to keep within well-defined limits an equilibrium between families and between chiefs. Evidence for the underlying function of these activities is the spirit of competition behind both the potlatch (particularly strong among the Kwakiutl) and the obsessive quest for the most efficacious way to show superiority over one's opponents by means of a distinctly individual style and the large scale of architectural undertakings.

It was not profit but prestige that motivated the Northwest Coast Indians to adopt from the early 19th-century colonizers a number of means of reinforcing even further the tendencies already present within their society. For example, the coins (of hammered copper, introduced by the white man were used by the Indians to exaggerate the systems of credit—involving interest of 20 to 200 percent—habitually resorted to by those intending to offer a potlatch. The introduction of metal tools in the early 19th century prompted the full-scale development of all sorts of carving, totem poles in particular. It is impossible to distinguish between an autonomous development and one induced by external factors (encouragement by the white man, touristic exploitation) when considering the later examples of these monumental artistic expressions, divorced as they often were from their traditional community functions. But from the technological, social, and cultural point of view, the architecture of the Northwest Coast Indians can certainly be said to show how the various craft activities, though not controlled by a definite class, did lend themselves as in Polynesia to becoming an instrument of social differentiation.

As in Polynesia, in the architecture of these Indians there is a connection between the evolution of the specific characteristics of the dwelling (the products of artistic craftsmanship) and the ownership of the land. Because these fishing, hunting, and gathering populations have been able to pursue a completely sedentary life (apart from the annual migration between summer and winter dwellings which, in any case, are similar in layout), the tribal territory is divided up among private owners. This is perfectly comprehensible if one remembers that ownership of the land is the real economic basis of every tendency to consider architecture as the central activity with respect to all the other artistic activities. Moreover, the territory is depended on for the supply of cedarwood used in constructing artistic and ritual objects, habitations, tombs, totem poles, traps for salmon, boats for whalehunting; it is understandably the jealously guarded source of the raw materials that contribute to the wealth of the owner, when transformed into useful implements or, even more clearly, into instruments of prestige.

The usual Northwest Coast dwelling is a multifamily construction of logs and planks, rectangular in shape, with peaked roof and front entrance. The development of quite different architectural traditions, which was favored by the fact that families of artisans undertake different specializations and transmit their craft from father to son, has resulted in an extreme diversity of techniques, decorative styles, and standard schemes. Woodworking reaches extraordinary heights of refinement, as for example, when the trunks of cedar trees, utilized for the principal beams of the house, are thinned down with an ax alone to an impeccable cylinder from one end to the other. Such craftsmanship shows that the house is regarded as an artistic object

337. *Carved and painted totem pole topped by a falcon, Alaska (USA).*

338. *Haida: structural diagram of a house with door through a totem pole in front, and with the parts below ground level shown by dotted lines, Queen Charlotte Islands, British Columbia (Canada).*

339. *Haida: house with frontal totem pole seen against a slope with visible evidence of trees split and chopped to obtain building lumber, Queen Charlotte Islands, British Columbia (Canada).*

340. *Haida: small model of a house with frontal totem pole, from Queen Charlotte Islands, British Columbia (Canada). Musée de l'Homme, Paris.* ▷

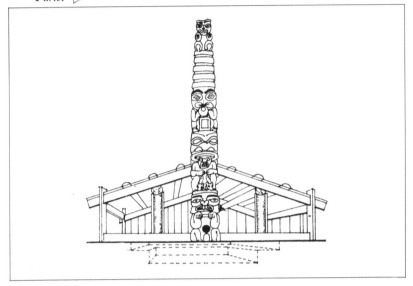

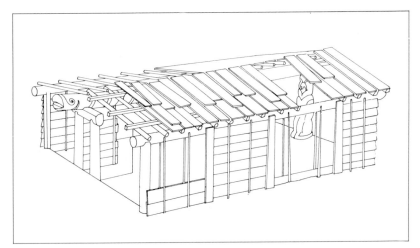

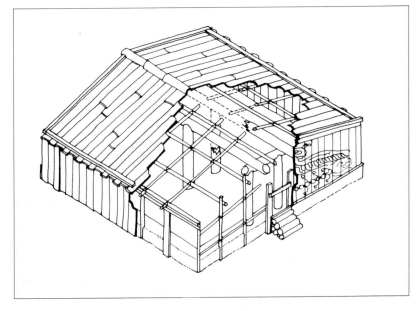

and therefore deserves the same meticulous care as small carved and painted objects. In fact, both the carved and the painted decoration applied to architecture are derived, with only a difference in scale, from such objects as masks, boxes, pipes, and the like, and this is true as regards their meaning, too (*plates 352–355*).[36]

*Building the House*
The carpenters' high degree of specialization was particularly evident in the period preceding the introduction of metal tools, when they were still restricted to using wedges, chisels, and hatchets of bone, stone or jade. In their splendidly solid houses of red cedar (*Thuja*

*plicata*), the Nootka have achieved a well-balanced relationship between permanent elements—the posts and beams of the supporting structure —and removable ones—the planks covering the walls and roof (*plate 341*).[37] Because the seasonal migration necessitates transferring the dwelling from the winter sites along the inland creeks and inlets to summer places on the shores of the open sea, the planks are dismounted, loaded in canoes, and reassembled on frames of exactly the same dimensions as those left behind. By reducing to a minimum the elements to be transported, it is possible to have in every season a large house with richly decorated structural members (the supporting posts and roof beams) while at the same time preserving the seasonal mobility required by the very different activities of hunting and fishing.

The Nootka use a remarkable technique for making cedar planks with the simplest of tools and without having to chop down a tree. Choosing a cedar with a smooth straight trunk, the woodsman makes two longitudinal notches with his chisel, the first about three feet above the roots, the second as much higher as the length of the board desired. After widening the upper cleft with wedges, he then forces a pole into the gap and, little by little, as the tree sways, the split extends down to the bottom notch. As much as half the trunk can be removed in this way without chopping down the tree. The wood is then worked on with wedges and hatchets.

Whole tree trunks are floated downstream, and the heavy structure is erected by a large group working under the direction of the head of the family, who has to provide them all with food during the entire period of work. In Nootka houses (*plate 341*), figural sculpture is restricted to the two principal structural elements: the rear post, which is carved into anthropomorphic form, and the front end of the ridgepole. But care is lavished on other components as well. The corner posts and the two central uprights of the facade and the short beam connecting them are thick and sturdy and worked with great care so as to last many decades, whereas the boards used for the walls and roofs (those removed annually) are less durable. The planks are not merely superposed but, to make them tight against rain and snow, are laid like roof tiles, with the joinings of every two adjacent planks covered by a third, and fastened in place with ties made from cedar bark. They are connected and finished with stone drills, dogfish skin (to smooth them down), and sandstone adzes; sometimes they are bent by steam or treated by charring. For measuring, there are ten different modules derived from the human body, in particular the finger, hand, and arm; the smallest corresponds to a finger's breadth; the largest to a span.[38]

The division of the building process into two parts—fixed structure and portable covering—reveals a fundamental aspect of the way

*343. Kwakiutl: main structural supports of a house; the logs have been painstakingly grooved with an ax, Memkumlis, British Columbia (Canada).*

344. *Kwakiutl: structural supports of a house, Memkumlis, British Colum-*
*bia (Canada).*

in which the Northwest Coast Indians conceive of architecture. The fixed elements are given more painstaking treatment and adorned with sculpture, whereas the planks of walls and roofs are thought of as merely utilitarian (*plates 338, 343, 344*). Consequently, the supporting structure—along with the tombs of chiefs and the great totem poles—is of more significance than the complete house as the sign that a tribal group or family is asserting its possession of a particular site.

*Art, Myth, and Family Power*
"The flooring of the house was made of stone. Then the chief broke it, seized the boy, and threw him down on our earth. The water was still high, and above the surface of the water emerged only the tip of his totem pole. The boy fell on the tip of the pole crying, 'Kaw,' and took the form of a raven. The pole split into two when he fell on it. Then the waters began to recede, and he set forth on his wanderings."[39] In this passage from a Haida tale, the house of the creator-god, the demiurgic hero (the raven), and the architecture of the house—whose outstanding feature is the great totem pole at the front, broad enough for the oval aperture of the door to be cut through it (*plates 338, 340*)— are brought together in a style intermediate between an origin myth and a simple story of everyday life. Particularly among the Indians farthest to the northwest—the Tlingit, Haida, and Kwakiutl—art and architecture reflect rather complex developments in the representation of the mythological personages and tales that are at the basis of both social structure and art. The figures most frequently encountered are the totemic animals of the exogamous clans, and they correspond to the two moieties (Raven and Eagle, Raven and Wolf) of the Haida and Tlingit or to the four exogamous groups of the Tsimshian (Raven, Eagle, Wolf, Bear). But from here the mythological material proliferates to accommodate the genealogies of more restricted family groups, assuming a function that can be called heraldic since every line of descent has its own animal insignia and its own inherited repertory of tales, which accounts for the great number and variety of figural subjects.

The finest carving is done by the Haida, the finest architectural painting by the Kwakiutl, and both achieve the utmost in the heraldic rendering of the predominantly totemic figures of the myths as a means of increasing the prestige and social rank of the wealthy house owners for whom these totem poles and paintings are done. The figures differ only in the treatment of a few details—eyes, claws, tail, wings, fins—but include all the major species of animals: birds (crow, falcon, eagle, vulture, cormorant), land mammals (wolf, bear, goat, beaver), marine mammals (seal, whale, sea lion), mollusks (snail),

346. *Kwakiutl: totem pole showing a bear seizing a man in its paws and a figure, below, that holds two large pieces of copper money, from Hope Island, British Columbia (Canada). National Museum of Man, Ottawa.*

347. *Tombs with carved images of the dead, Salmon River, British Columbia (Canada).*

348. *Tsimshian: freestanding totem poles, British Columbia (Canada).*

349. *Freestanding totem poles in front of dwellings, Queen Charlotte Islands, British Columbia (Canada).*

350. *Carved and painted totem poles, Vancouver Island, British Columbia (Canada).*

351. *Large sculptures and a totem pole, Alert Bay, British Columbia (Canada).*

352. *Haida: tattoo representing the sea monster Ts'um'àks, British Colum-*
*bia (Canada).*

353. *Haida: painting on a box representing a frog, British Columbia*
*(Canada).*

354. *Kwakiutl: painting on a house front representing a thunderbird, British*
*Columbia (Canada).*

355. *Kwakiutl: painting on a house front representing a crow, British*
*Columbia (Canada).*

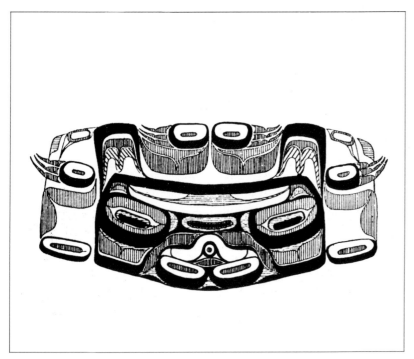

356. *A chief with the insignia of power, British Columbia (Canada).*

amphibians (frog), fish (shark, salmon), and even fabulous beasts (dragon, sea monster, merman, thunderbird). On the totem poles of the Haida (*plates 338–340, 345*), the vertical succession of the subjects, often treated in an extremely condensed style, sometimes culminates at the top in the heraldic animal of the family or clan, thereby proclaiming their divine descent. The human figures are depicted realistically and intermingle with the animals in a narrative that is anything but unequivocal in interpretation: It may concern the myth of the origin of the particular clan or tribe or else the glories of a particular family—most conspicuously the humiliation inflicted on rival families on the occasion of a potlatch.[40] When the house, like the canoe, furnishings, and personal objects, became a symbol of private wealth, the images decorating boxes, prows of canoes, and wooden masks were taken over into architecture, with the artistic idiom unchanged and only the scale enlarged.

The Kwakiutl also make extremely beautiful totem poles (*plates 344, 346*), always isolated from the house, and heraldic insignia carved on the peak of the roof and the sides of the gable. But their distinctive specialty is found on their house fronts, where they paint enormous, highly stylized decorations of great elaboration and quality, found elsewhere only on small objects of daily and ritual use, on textiles and canoes (*plates 342, 354, 355*). This indicates a profound transformation in the conception of the house itself. Pure architectural decoration always draws upon artistic motifs used on a much smaller scale, and when applied to the dwelling it implies that the house has a distinctly private significance. The process of disintegration in the unity of the tribe becomes plain to see when art is used competitively to enhance the accumulation of wealth. But this same tribal unity, which tends to restrain imbalances by imposing rules of competition, is responsible for the fact that the architecture of the Northwest Coast Indians still remains very much a part of the activities of the village as a whole, despite the absence of an embryonic state system to promote public works through obligatory levies of labor. The differences in social level between the heads of families, the younger family members, and the slaves do not manifest themselves through stratification in the way they live but simply, within the individual family group, in personal power relations. Thus, every family—and the slaves are included in the family unit—participates in the system in equal measure when it comes to the contest for a supremacy that is reflected, among other things, in architecture.[41]

VILLAGE, SANCTUARY, AND "CHEFFERIE" IN WEST AFRICA

Cultural unity—the bond between different peoples who, though not perhaps linked politically, recognize a common origin in a place they designate as center of the world—is given a very particular expression in the sanctuary, the place where the group believes its history began in a creation they celebrate in periodic commemorative rites (*plates 359, 360*). The similarities between the cosmological and cosmogonical myths of numerous tribal populations of West Africa (among them the Mandingo, Bozo, Bambara, Dogon, and Fali) go well beyond mere analogy and, indeed, involve the innermost secret core of spatial symbolism. However diverse their architectural traditions, social structures, and productive resources (this is true of the Dogon and the Fali in particular), the mechanism by which these people interpret reality—the way they represent the world in all its spatial and temporal aspects—is by and large comparable.

The Keita, in the region occupied by the Mandingo, celebrate the creation of the world every seven years by redoing the paintings that cover the walls of the intertribal sanctuary known as the "vestibule of the Mande." The profound symbolism of these images is revealed in the order in which they are painted. The sanctuary at Kangaba has a circular ground plan, and its straw roof with six crests represents the spiral development of the seed of the universe, which unfolded to give origin to the world. The symbolic figures on the exterior present the explanation of the relationships and correspondences between everything in creation, from men to animals to fields, cultivated plants, stars, ancestors. "But when we looked on during the painting of the figures, their hidden meaning became clear: With her face turned to the east, the woman responsible for the work painted a black circle to begin with; then, turning toward the north, a circle above a vertical line followed by an analogous figure, but with a transverse bar in the shape of an arm; in a fourth, another bar symbolized the legs. These four works, in short, were intended as elementary personages. Consequently, what was being depicted across the wall was the beginning of creation. The initial seed (the point) bursts open under the action of a first vibration (the line) followed by a second (the arm), which generates the four cardinal directions, or, in other words, the physical setting of the universe; a third furnishes the lower members of all earthly creatures and generates their sex. Briefly, the figures continued to have this incomplete aspect, which vanished once the edifice was complete, the initial sketches having become personages."[1]

For the entire area occupied by the populations roughly designated as Sudanese the problem is to distinguish between the real stratification and differentiation of the sociopolitical, territorial, and architec-

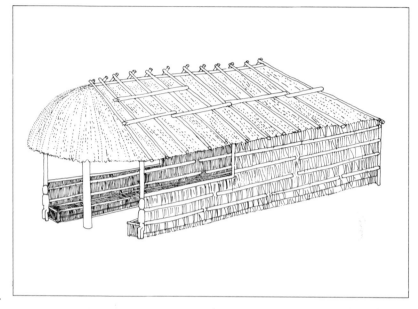

359. Sanctuary hut (Gabon).

360. Ibo: sanctuary hut (eastern Nigeria).

361. Bamum: door frame, Fumban (Cameroon).

362, 363. Bamum: posts carved with ancestor figures, Fumban (Cameroon).

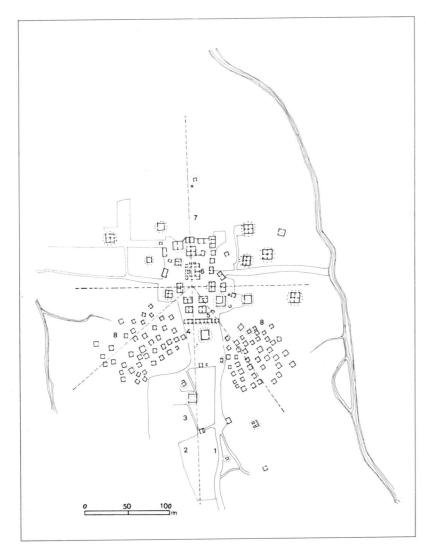

364. Bamileke: plan of the village of Batufam (Cameroon).
1. main access; 2. market; 3. skulls and statues of ancestors; 4. entrance gate; 5. guest house; 6. chief's house; 7. site of the puberty rites; 8. wives' huts.

365. Bamileke: a chief seated at the door of his house, Jang (Cameroon). ▷

tural structures and their symbolic interpretation as furnished by the various peoples themselves. In no other cultural area, perhaps, are the meanings attached to the various architectural types so utterly at odds with the semantic reality and social use and so difficult for us to grasp because of a very different conception of language. These peoples find substantial differences in details that, to us, appear to be of no importance whatsoever and, at the same time, insist on analogies between forms that are, in our eyes, completely different. The systems of construction, the techniques of settlement, and the basic building types are a "given," which, however, has been completely reexperienced, reinterpreted, and joined indissolubly with the general complex of myths and the economy. Dwelling, field, and village are all viewed as entities in formation, pulsating with vitality, participating in the life of the cosmos. Yet every detail of social life, of sacred edifices, of granaries, and of dwellings, has a precise role, even if its interpretation can never be pinned down to a single meaning. The way inhabited space is construed seems to be a decisive instrument for maintaining a universal dynamic equilibrium, quite apart from the tensions that arise through the events of history. The concept of architectural type would appear to be the key factor here, not because of the form it takes in any particular sociocultural context but because it is a fundamental instrument for transmitting traditional values. The type, if we can use that term here, is not valid so much in itself, in its physical configuration, as in relation to all the other aspects of cultural reality, in the significances with which it is charged.

A quasi-historical explanation of the mythic partitioning of a territory into seven parts, corresponding to seven villages, is found in the tradition of the Samake, a tribe of the Bambara group: The seven villages were founded by seven sons of the initial founder of the line. Three are situated in the northern part of the territory (Jitumu), four in the southern part (Kurulamini). Each of the northern villages was subsequently divided into twelve villages, as were the four in the south. Each of these groupings has its own capital: Sanakoro in the "north" (though in reality in the east) and Zabagu in the south. This partitioning obviously goes back to a myth of first sacrifice, and every territorial element contains some sort of reference to it. The division of the territory into two parts recalls the primordial female twins, disposed cross-fashion. A modest rise in terrain near the plain of Kurula is thought of as the cosmic mountain, the first stone, or the Star of Fire, which gave origin to the cosmos, and the entire territory of the Samake is believed to revolve around it. In addition to annual sacrifices performed both in the plain and at the base of this hill, a rite is carried out every seven years to renew the world.[2]

366. *Bamileke: chief's house with ancestor statues and carved pilasters, lintel, sill, and jambs, Bafussam (Cameroon).*

367. *Bamileke: door frame of a chief's house, from Banganete (Cameroon). Musée de l'Homme, Paris.*

368. *Bamileke: ancestor statues at the sides of the door of the chief's house, Jang-Baham (Cameroon).*

369. *Bamileke: detail of the portico of a square house with conical roof, Bafussam (Cameroon).*

370. *Bamileke: detail of a chief's house showing external supports, walls of bamboo bound with vegetable fibers, and carved corner post, Bafussam (Cameroon).*

371. *Matakam: building a clay house and granary (Cameroon).*

372. *Carrying a prefabricated conical roof to the site of a cylindrical hut (Chad).*

251

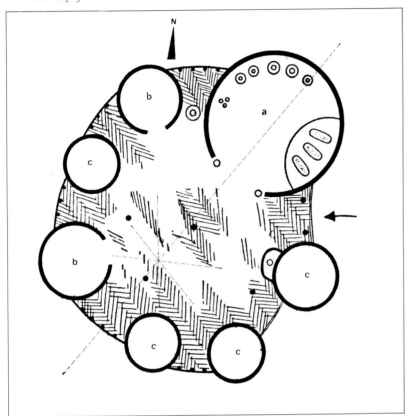

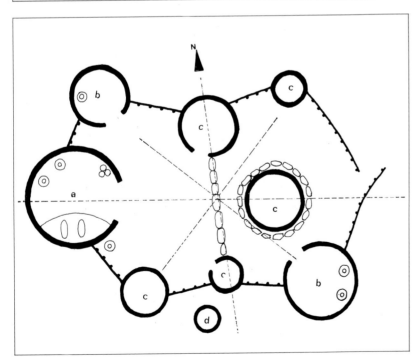

Inside almost every village is a cosmic image shown in its essentials: a stone placed in the center of a small pool. The stone-as-mountain and the pool are the complementary symbols of the unity of the cosmos, territory, and village. The settlement was established in its entirety by the founding ancestor, but, like the world and the territory, it broadened out by subdividing centrifugally. Thus, in the village of N'Tintu, there are eight distinct outlying quarters founded by the eight wives of the progenitor, who founded the central nucleus. In other villages, the rationalization of the process of growth is similar to that of the division of the territory as a whole: the ritual subdivision of the body of the ancestor into seven parts, each giving rise to a sector of the settlement.

The architecture of the *chefferies* of the forest area in central West Africa, particularly in the settlements of the Bamum and the Bamileke (*plates 361–370*), indicates a stratification of power. The plan of the village is axial, with the large houses of the chief and dignitaries dominating the ceremonial plaza (*plate 364*). The entire plan is ruled by symmetry, by hierarchical order, by the geometry of the buildings. The architectural sculpture—door frames, pillars, freestanding statues—distinguishes the dominant dynasty, which maintains its authority by emphasizing, in its genealogy, the distinction between those of divine descent and the ordinary run of mankind, the two inseparable poles of power.

*The Fali of the Northern Cameroons*

History and myth, architectural typology and architectural significance, these are the two opposed and complementary interpretive registers in the organization of the "constructed universe" of the Fali, a small population living in the mountains of the northern Cameroons (*plates 373–383*). An exemplary informative study by J.-P. Lebeuf,[3] distinguished by a careful and thorough critical rethinking, has made it possible for us to grasp the fundamental rapport between society and architecture, in an economic context that is not particularly unique and is therefore all the more open to general and cross-cultural comparison. The basis of subsistence—chiefly, the cultivation of various kinds of grasses—and the social organization, based on the extended family are both, in fact, common to many other peoples in the sub-Saharan area. Also common is the Fali type of settlement: an isolated enclosure composed of a number of cylindrical huts with conical roofs and of granaries disposed around one or more covered courtyards. Within the various groups there are no real economic and political stratifications, nor is there competition between the several lineages, each of which participates in the assemblies through its oldest member. The aged hold the power and have the burden of transmit-

375. *Fali: schematic plan of the dwelling of a patriarch (Cameroon).*
    *a. kitchens; b. sleeping quarters; c. granaries; d. storage places.*

376. *Fali: anthropomorphic conception of a residential enclosure (Cameroon).*
    *a. sleeping quarters; b. granaries; c. central granary; d. vestibule.*

377. *Fali: elevation and section of the sleeping quarters of an adult (Cameroon).*

378. *Fali: ground plan and section of an aggregate of units (tim ǫyu) with a granary in center, two bintin silos, and two areas used as kitchens and separated by a low wall (Cameroon).*

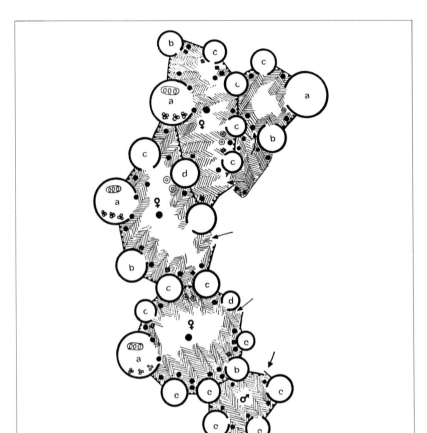

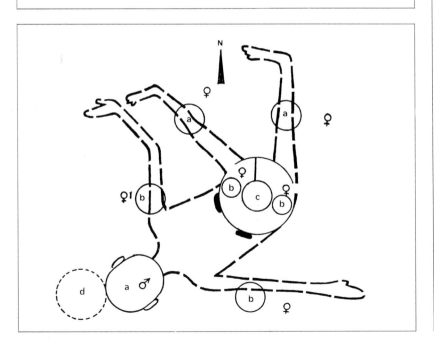

379. *Fali: elevation and ground plan of a granary of* ma beli *type with a hearth, two grinding stones, and a small* bintin *silo as annexes (Cameroon).*

380. *Fali: section of a granary of* bal do *type (Cameroon).*

381. *Fali: two granaries of* ma *type (Cameroon).*

382. *Fali: granary painted with the mythic toad motif (Cameroon).*

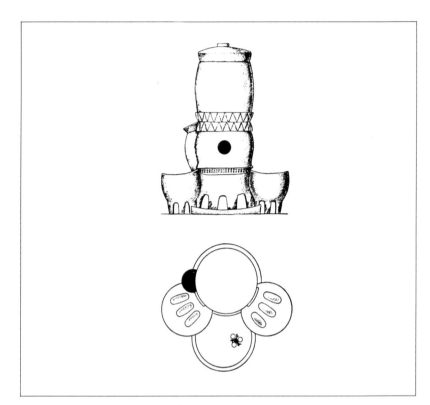

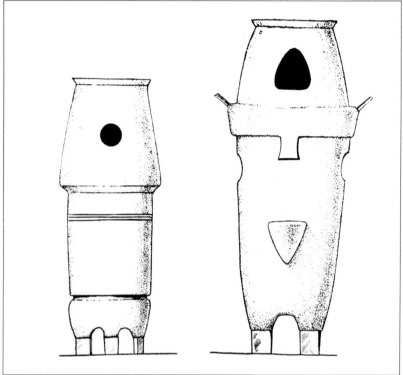

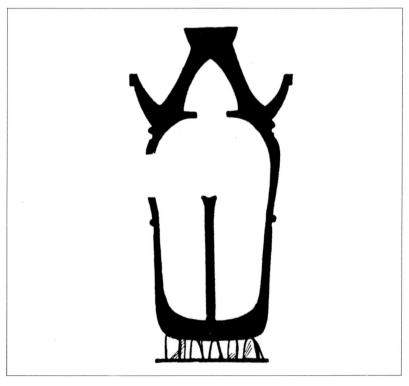

ting and organizing the religious and mythological heritage, but always within a segmentary system of relationships between the villages, the village subdivisions, and the families.

The present geographical distribution of the Fali seems to be the result of successive migrations that took place between the 16th and the 19th centuries, which brought about continual changes in the inner and outer organization of the various groups. Despite the accidents of history, there exists a myth that explains the common origin of the four groups (from north to south, the Bossum, Bori-Peské, Kangu, and Tingelin) and proposes a complete interpretation of all the aspects of spatial reality, from the territory down to architectural details. Through the agency of relatively vague correspondences, this complex of beliefs provides the cohesion between disparate elements, the "historical" unity fixed once and for all among forms of organization in continual change. The chief organizational principles are a division of space into four parts and a hierarchical cohesion between the diverse elements based on the form of the human body.

Every interpretation can be brought back to the myth of the creation of the universe through the balanced correspondence between the two cosmic eggs: of the tortoise and of the toad. This subdivision into two unequal parts corresponding to tortoise and toad is also reflected in the organization of human society, which is subdivided into two corresponding groups, the organization of the territory (with its inhabited part and its wilderness), and the organization of the dwelling. Every successive differentiation came about through a series of "vibrations" of alternate and contrary movements, which guaranteed the universal self-perpetuation of the equilibrium between the opposites. Every region, every group, every architectonic element either partakes of one of these virtually complementary movements or is thought of as a fixed point that acts as pivot for the motion of the parts around it. This reciprocal dynamism of all the elements, subdivided into male and female, represents a virtual rotary motion, clockwise or counterclockwise, that affects, first of all, the two essential parts of the habitation: the feminine, cylindrical part in masonry and the masculine conical covering made up of rafters and straw, which circle in inverse direction to each other. It was, in fact, the tortoise that gave man the model for his house: Under its tutelage the first couple built the primordial house, whose constructional and decorative detail was established for all time and which must be faithfully imitated in all the dwellings of the Fali.

The human figure is the preferred reference in interpreting the territory, the house, and the granary (*plates 40–42, 373–376*), but not as a static scheme. The scheme is, rather, what we may call functional: the different parts of the human body can be considered in their re-

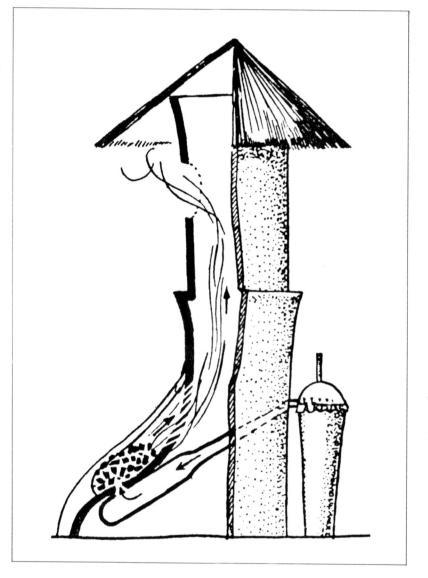

384. *Musgum: schematic plan and section of a family enclosure (Cameroon). a. hut of the head of the family; b. entrance; c. kitchen; d. hut of the favorite wife; e. shed for animals; f. hut of a wife and joint kitchen; g. hut of a wife; h. kitchen; i. hut of a wife; l. hut of two wives and a tool room. Between the huts are the granaries.*

385. *Musgum: huts and granaries of a family farm with inverted Vs modeled on the exterior walls (Chad).*

386. *Musgum: renovating the upper part of a clay-covered hut with isolated, modeled vertical projections (Chad).*

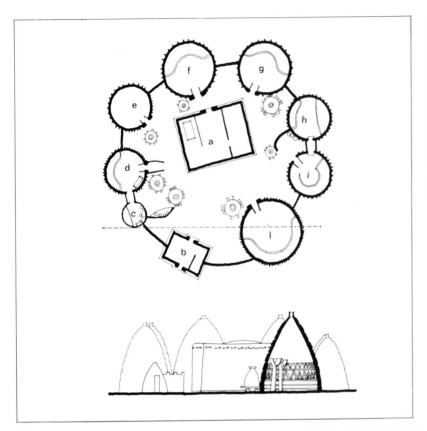

387. *Musgum: interior of a farm enclosure, with a deteriorated hut at the left and a recently renovated one in the center (Chad).*

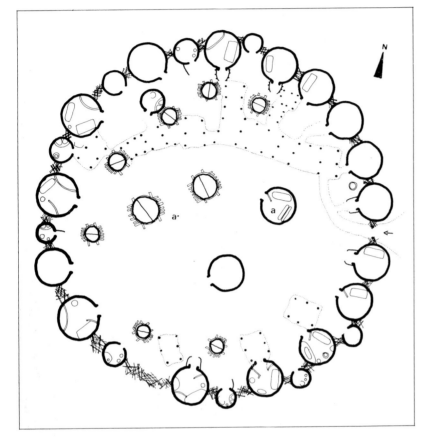

388. *Massa: schematic plan of a large farm enclosure (Cameroon).*
a, a'. hut and granaries of the head of the family.

ciprocal relationship but also separately, and the members can be dislocated in plane and in space in an order of importance that does not always take into account their real connection to each other. In addition to the frontal view of the human form, with the members converging symmetrically on the trunk, there are also anthropomorphic representations in which the figure appears compressed, the members interwined, and with such principal articulations as the clavicle detached.

The four Fali groups think of themselves as situated at the four cardinal points of their territory. Within each group the different "subdivisions" are disposed anthropomorphically according to four complementary, symmetrical modes. The macrocosmic order (the earth is subdivided into four parts: head, trunk, upper limbs, lower limbs, with its center represented by the sexual organs) corresponds to the different positions assumed by man-the-microcosm representing the four different groups during the act of procreation (*plate 40*). All of reality is involved in a series of correspondences that have the human body as reference. Every element of the dwelling is susceptible to such an interpretation, from the entire enclosure (*plate 376*), to its components, with a constant oscillation between masculine and feminine, tortoise (*plates 373, 374*) and toad (*plate 382*). Decoration too, as a whole and in its details, is interpreted anthropomorphically, as also are the interior furnishings and the details of the altars, blast furnaces (*plate 383*), and utensils. The pivotal point of the entire interpretation is constituted by the granaries.[4] Here, the organic connection between the various structural and decorative elements is explained by the human figure, which is directly associated with the exterior aspect of these buildings and the complex subdivisions inside them (*plates 41, 378–382*).

Viewed within this comprehensive mythic interpretation, the architecture of the Fali reveals itself to be not only the product of adaptations to the environment, to the social structure, and to the materials available, but also a complex and independent expression of an ideology. The projection of a design upon space is not merely a secondary act but is central with respect to the vital needs of society. The coherence between the various formal solutions does not derive from aesthetic assumptions but from necessary and logical proofs of the unity of everything real, manifesting itself above all in the inner congruence of all the material objects made by man. This, then, is a specific cultural "mode of production" intended for the maintenance of the material "mode of production"; but because it enters into (informs) real, concrete structures (the material interconnections of production and relation) it cannot be confined to a purely "superstructural" role.

*390. Interior of a farmhouse enclosure (tata) (Chad).*
*391, 392. Detail of roofs and exterior view of the tata of Lamido, Lere
     zone (Chad).*

393. *Ground plan and section of the doorway of a clay hut with seats to either side and a low wall to keep out animals (Ghana).*

394, 395. *Cylindrical family huts with both conical thatched and terraced roofs; detail of the doorway of the wife's hut shown in plate 394, Wagadugu (Upper Volta).* ▷

Building a Fali house does not require specialized artisans. The work is the collective undertaking of the family group concerned; however, the labor is divided, with the men taking on the heavier tasks, the women chiefly gathering and transporting the materials: clay and straw to make the mud-plaster medium *torchis* used in the cylindrical walls, stones for the flooring, thatch for the roof. The units of measurement used in building are constant within each group and are all based on the human body: the distance between the elbow and the middle of the open hand, between the elbow and the farthest point of the closed fist, between tip and tip of the fully outstretched arms, between the navel and the soles of the feet, between the shoulders and the feet, between the chin and the feet, between the top of the head and the feet, and between the thumb and the middle of the open hand. These measurements are directly reflected in the dimensions of the architectural elements, whether interior areas or wall openings, and thereby help to affirm material reality by supporting the myth.

As among the other populations of the northern Cameroons, the Mandara for example, Fali sleeping rooms and kitchens (*plates 377, 378*) are furnished with built-in elements—shelves, hearth walls, beds, the low tables used for pounding and grinding foodstuffs, small tables —which are all made of *torchis* built up and shaped plastically into curving forms and connected in such a way as to give the impression of being all part of a single block.

Inexhaustible invention is lavished on the plans and shapes of the granaries, so much so that any attempt to reduce them to conventional types produces at best, a vast number of possibilities (*plates 41, 378–382*). These are the most important Fali edifices, from the symbolic standpoint as well. As places where edible seeds are stored they represent the ark that descended from the sky in the mythic age and contained, among other things, all the vegetable species. Like the granaries of many other African populations (*plates 23, 26–28*), those of the Fali are conceived as enormous fixed jars raised above the ground and are constructed with the same technique as the houses and the rough-ware vessels. Internal subdivisions make it possible to store many different grains in a single receptacle. The different varieties go into separate compartments according to what is thought of as a ritual order of correspondence among the foodstuffs themselves. Thus, in the same granary—the *ma beli* type of the Bossum, for example (*plate 379*)—yellow millet, white millet, red millet, white sesame, wild melon, and rice can all be stored. Construction involves first placing the supporting stones and then making a solid round platform as base for the silo (*plate 371*). The large receptacle is then built up in successive rings of mud plaster (*torchis*), leaving a circular opening on one side that can be plugged up with a clay pot. The height of

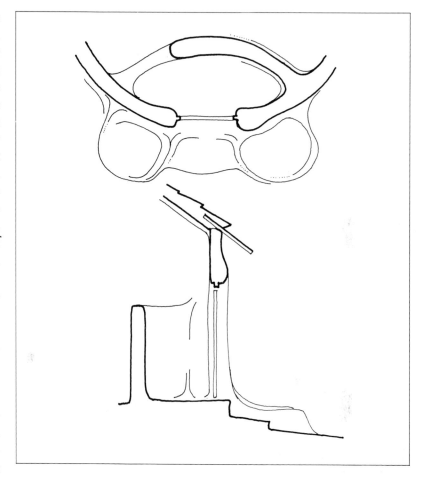

396. *Gurunsi: fortified enclosure with exterior decoration (Upper Volta).*

397. *Gurunsi: fortified enclosure with granary-shed (left rear) and dividing wall punctuated by conical pilasters (Upper Volta).*

398. *Farmhouse of castle type built of horizontal bands of clay, with conical altars and sacred plants in front of the entrance at the left (Dahomey).*

399. *Farmhouse of castle type, with cultivated field in the foreground (Dahomey).*

400–402. *Somba: farmhouses of castle type, Taiakon region (Dahomey)*.

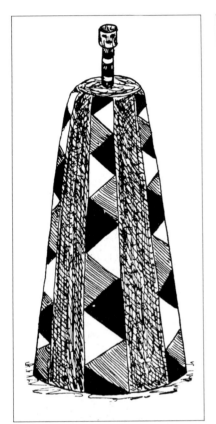

the granary is roughly that of a man, and it has a certain likeness to the human figure, which is borne out by all the structural and decorative details as well as the complex interior structure, from the head at the top through the neck and body down to the lower members, the supporting stones on which the building rests (*plate 41*). The application of pottery-making techniques to architecture gives a rather special character to the interior of the huts and kitchens, and the results are even more interesting in the complicated and articulated structure of the granary. A schematic classification of the various forms these Fali storehouses take gives some idea of the diversity of types: among the Kangu, for instance, there are seven, known respectively as *dǫ* or *doy, doy tasa ta, porom, ma, bal do, bemdi* (small interior silos), and *do*. All told, the Fali build eleven principal types, to which the different groups give different names. In practice, considering all the local variants, annexes, and differences in dimensions and arrangement, the granaries represent a construction whose infinite variability serves as an index to the various groups, village subdivisions, and even individual family complexes. Small silos, slabs for grinding stones, hearths, and low walls are often connected with the granary (*plates 378, 379*). The relationship of all these plastic forms is perfectly evident, running an uninterrupted gamut of size from utensil to architecture, from interior to exterior, from movable to fixed furnishings. The walls vary in thickness according to functional requirements, and a conical roof of rafters and thatch similar to that used for the huts provides protection from the weather.

In the architecture of the Fali and other populations in the Sudanese cultural area, an important role is played by woven mats, which are used not only to cover the courtyard on which the various parts of the house open but also quite regularly as lightweight partitions in the interior and as doorway coverings. Circular or conical mats are used as additional roofing for the granaries, to shade verandas, and to protect the dried mud walls of the individual buildings from rain damage. As the family nucleus grows, the huts and enclosure are added to, expanding from the small living quarters of bachelors and young couples, with no more than three or four huts and a single granary, to the elaborate residences with several courtyards of the patriarchs and men with many wives (*plates 373–375*).

In the numerous areas of West Africa where an agricultural economy and segmentary political structure prevail, the most widely diffused type of residence is the fortified farmhouse occupied by all the members of a family (*plates 384–402*). The most frequent architectural characteristic of these is a plastic fusion (emphasized to varying degrees) between the single constructional element (the dwelling cell typical of each group, the ritually repeated "primordial house")

406. *Dogon: foundation altar (momo), lower village, Ogol (Mali).*

407. *Dogon: village of Banani seen from above, with typical family houses*
    (ginna) *(Mali).*
408. *Dogon: village of Diamini Na (Mali).*

and the outer wall that unites the individual dwellings and their granaries into a single articulated organism (*plate 388*). For the most extreme example of such solutions one must look to the so-called castles of Dahomey and Togo (*plates 398–402*). In these, the huts lose their individuality with respect to the whole, which is conceived as an integral, indivisible unity. The entire structure can be thought of as the architectural expression of the conception of the family as superior to the individual: The true individual is the family, an organism that is perfectly definable and coherent. It is in this idea, therefore, that one must seek for the origins of the architecture that constitutes the highest form of creative activity attained by these people.

### The Dogon of the Upper Niger

According to a cosmogonic myth of the Dogon, an agricultural population in the mountainous region of the upper Niger basin, the earth—circular, surrounded by the waters of the ocean and by a gigantic serpent (*yuguru-na*) biting its own tail—is one of the fourteen levels or terraces of the universe. It is the highest of the seven lower disks and is surmounted by the seven upper ones, each with its own sun and moon. Each disk revolves around its own center through which passes the cosmic pillar, *amma dyi* (*dyi* is the name of the forked post supporting the roof of the house; Amma is the creator-god). The lower worlds are inhabited by men with tails, the upper by men with horns, and each heaven is governed by an Amma.[5] All things come from the creative act of Amma: earth, sky, water, the genie Nommo, the chameleon and the tortoise, the Yeban genies who dwell in the rocks, the Gyinu genies whose home is in the great trees, the animals, plants, and men.

The Dogon myths describe a migration from the Mande country to the place where they now live, the mountainous region of the Bandiagara and the plain below it. This migration was connected with the temporary death of an ancestor, Lébé, who was subsequently resuscitated in the form of a serpent. The Dogon brought with them sacred earth from the tomb of the revivified ancestor with which they made a conical altar, thereby initiating the cult of Lébé. Each of the groups that settled an area of the new territory took with it a part of that first altar. Four principal tribes descend from the two sons of Lébé: the Dyon, Domno, Ono, and Aru. The Dyon set up an altar to Lébé in each village, whereas the Aru had a single altar at Aru near Ibi, which thus became the religious center for the entire tribe. The altars are all now entrusted for cult purposes and maintenance to the *hogon*, the oldest man in the village, whose function is to direct the community of villages. However, according to the practice of their particular tribe, the groups obey the local *hogon* who heads the

410. *Dogon: village of Pegue seen from below, with granaries and the "caves of the ancestors" in the rock face above it (Mali).*
411. *Dogon: storage place with supply of wood under a rock cliff (Mali).*

council of elders or, in the case of the Aru, the *hogon* of Aru near Ibi.[6]

The Dogon have a segmentary political structure; the various groups consider themselves related through the myths of origin they hold in common and through their religious beliefs. But the link of every group to its own area is extremely significant: Economic activity, ritual activity centering on the sacred places, which are the points of connection between the group and the mythic ancestors, and architectural activity—all of these are intimately interconnected and linked with features of the landscape, especially in the rocky zone of the Bandiagara.

To understand Dogon architecture it is particularly useful to distinguish between the "theoretical" sphere of the ideal solutions that form part of the mythic ritual and the "practical" sphere, the actual building. But, as is not true of other populations that attribute symbolic significances to architectural and landscape forms that are diffused over a broader area than their own and are therefore open to diverse interpretations, among the Dogon creative activity is closely bound up with a specific culture. It is therefore of particular importance because of its fully realized and highly original artistic language, in which the myth is never intrusive into the spatial and architectonic reality but constitutes, purely and simply, its rational explanation. Three factors—a stimulating environment, cultural roots that are complex but nonetheless connected to those of the other populations in the Sudanese area, and a flexible and refined technique of building in wood and clay—have made Dogon architecture not only one of the best known and successful artistically but also fundamental to the understanding of the more "cultivated" developments in the Islamic cities and monuments in the Nigerian area. For these reasons, it must be analyzed for the logic behind its construction—which is intimately bound up with the philosophy of the origin myth—and also because of the adaptation it reflects to the environment, to continually varied social demands, and to the materials at hand.

The most important public edifice is an open-sided shed in which the men's assemblies and council meetings are held. Every village has at least one, and at the time of settlement the largest and most important, the *toguna*, is built on the main plaza; others are also put up in particular places, such as a rocky elevation or open space in the inhabited sector.[7]

The ideal ground plan of the *toguna* is rectangular, oriented according to the cardinal directions. However, there are numerous variants in both form and use of the materials, and one type built in stone is round or rounded. In general, *togunas* are low constructions

413. *Dogon: detail of the paintings at the temple of Binu under a rock cliff, village of Diamini Na (Mali).*

414. *Dogon: front of a temple built against a rock wall, with checkerboard decorations and remnants of sacrifices (Mali).* ▷

on three rows of supports (wooden uprights or stones) covered by trussing that supports a roof of heaped-up layers of vegetable matter, usually millet stalks, and their practical function is really only to provide shelter from the sun without blocking ventilation, since the assemblies take place in the hottest hours of the day (*plates 33, 416, 426–430; compare plates 32, 34*).

The *toguna* is intended to reproduce the shelter where the eight primordial ancestors met together, and in fact each of them is identified with one of the supporting pillars. Three rows of uprights—the side rows with three pillars, the middle one with two—frequently bear out this mythic association and, indeed, are often carved into anthropomorphic shapes representing the eight ancestors. The uprights are lined up from northwest to south, ideally following a spiral line associated with the mythic serpent. The principal *toguna* is often situated in the most dominant position in the settlement and in relation to its most sacred place. At Yugu Dogoru it crowns a gigantic rock about sixty-six feet high in the center of the village, at whose foot is the principal sanctuary, built partly in the rock.

The sacred places of the Dogon are, broadly speaking, points of condensation of the vital force (*nyama*) inherent in all living beings. The origin of these vital centers is believed to be connected with specific mythic events. Their power is continually renewed and maintained by sacrifices of animals, whose blood above all keeps the store of energy located in the altar in sufficient quantity.

The altars may belong to a clan that inherited them from mythic times or acquired them at some later date. The sacred centers that serve an entire territory generally contain inherited altars of ancient origin. Different categories of sacred places and altars call for different kinds of architecture or for a deliberate effort to integrate them into what are thought of as special places in the territory. Thus, there are sanctuaries in caves (where the masks are stored) and others beneath steep rock faces, which are often covered with paintings of masks and totemic subjects (*plates 410, 412–414*); there are foundation altars in the villages (*plate 406*), private altars, and altars for the mask cult; and finally there are the more complex so-called totemic sanctuaries.[8] Among these special types is the *buguturu* altar, which commemorates the killing of a lion after a young Andumbulu girl had been maimed by it (*plate 403*). Over a lion's paw, an altar is erected in the shape of a truncated cone topped by a small cylindrical pole, the *dannu*, and the entire structure is decorated with geometrical motifs in red, white, and black. The impression of a claw emerging from the top of a mass of clay piled up around it is conveyed, and the colors are those that conventionally designate the lion. The animal's energy (*nyama*) accumulated in the altar can be drawn on by laying a great mask upon it.

415. *Dogon: conical clay granaries under a rock overhang, village of Yugo Dogoru (Mali).*
416. *Dogon: village of Yugo Dogoru viewed from below, with a toguna on the top of the rock at the right (Mali).*

◁ *417. Dogon: granary of torchis (mud plaster) with relief decorations, including the* kanega *motif (Mali).*

*418. Dogon: straw-roofed granary with pinnacle and relief decorations, village of Banani (Mali).*

*419. Dogon: wooden granary door (24 3/8 × 18 7/8″) with anthropomorphic figures and, on the latch, the primordial couple. Musée de l'Homme, Paris.*

More complex in significance and structure is the altar of the *donikere* type, which is set up inside inhabited centers. The *mama* altar of the village of Barna (*plate 405*) is composed of an enclosure of unmortared stones; in the eastern corner is a small rectangular construction, inside which is an altar made of *pisé* (mud brick), its back to a corner and with a hearth in front.[9] The principal feature is a hemispherical construction of *pisé* isolated in the center of the enclosure, and this is the altar proper. It is about five feet in diameter and rests on a circular platform. Once a year, before the rainy season, its surface is renewed and repainted with images of *kanaga* and *satimbe* masks, which are geometrical schematizations of the human figure. Two objects are inserted into the hemisphere: a forked pole (*dannu*) painted with red, white, and black circles, and a jar. The pole symbolizes the horns of the *waru* antelope and is the altar of the initiated (*olubaru*); the jar holds medicinal roots.

The extreme variety of the sanctuaries in the Dogon region is matched not only by the complexities of the myths but by the complexities of the landscape. The most interesting sanctuaries are isolated edifices covered with symbolic paintings, true temples of the myth. These are usually rectangular buildings, with the facade framed by round corner towers and with a door surmounted by two niches, so that the central part looks like a house, or like a house reduced to its essentials (*plates 424, 425*).

The sanctuary of Binu Sangabilu in the Do quarter of lower Ogol[10] represents the tomb of Lébé and the forge of the mythical blacksmith (the primordial anvil appears on the upper part of the facade); the terrace symbolizes the first field ever cultivated; the paintings on the facade, renewed ritually in the course of the ceremonies, present a synthesis of mythic thought in the form of figures and ritual objects. Thus, a checkerboard painted above the door is the image of the rational organization of the world, symbolizing the lines of descent from the eight ancestors, the cultivated fields, the facade of the family house with its niches, and finally the plan of the village or, more extensively, of the whole of the territory inhabited and organized by human beings. Such ensembles of paintings (*plates 412–414*) constitute a veritable terrestrial system and are intended to encourage the germination of the plants the community cultivates and, in general, to ensure the balanced continuation of life.

The temple, even more than the house, is a sculptural construction, modeled—like the altars, forge furnaces, and house fronts—directly in the material to form a single block (*plates 424, 425*). Every form is connected and fused with the adjacent ones in a continuum that the annual waterproofing of the surface merely enhances. Here, architecture seems to become half-construction and half-natural

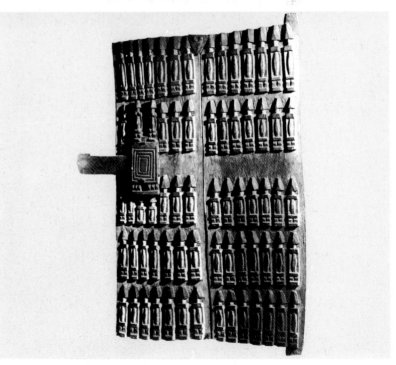

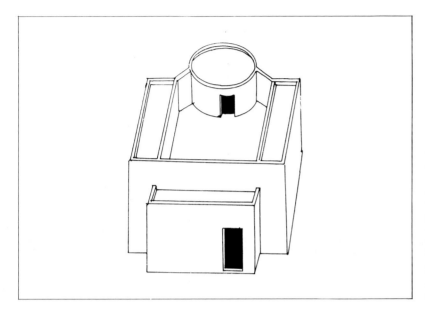

form, no longer obviously and assertively man-made, and this organic look results from the adoption, on an urban scale, of the processes of shaping and molding used by the potter, clay sculptor, and decorator of utensils and masks. The conspicuous emphasis is on the mass of clayey *pisé* rather than on the complementary relationship between the supportive function of the wooden beam and the plastic wall, as in certain house fronts. This characteristic is particularly evident in the sanctuaries beneath rocks, where the clay wall seems virtually a continuation of the natural rock (*plate 414*).

Painting and low-relief decoration play a considerable role in Dogon architecture and are widely used to designate altars and natural sites as sacred places. In its ritual and more significant aspect (*bammi*), painting most often reproduces masks, and low reliefs, in the same clay as the walls of the granaries on which they are customarily found, have analogous subjects (*plates 417, 418*).[11] Like the repertory of the masks themselves, such huge painted rock surfaces as the celebrated shelter of Songo (*plate 412*) give an idea of the highly diversified, though well-ordered, body of motifs and figurations current among the Dogon. Two masks directly involve architectural models: the *sirige* mask, resembling a multistoried house and therefore a symbol of authority, since ownership of such houses is restricted to the *hogon*, and the *ammala* mask, which represents the Door of Amma, a granary door on the head of a horned animal. Often, too, the granary doors are richly carved with motifs derived from myth (*plate 419*).

The common family residence is the *ginu sala* (ordinary house), which comprises an enclosure with stalls for animals, granaries, and the dwelling itself.[12] A door opening on the street leads into a vestibule (*dolu*) and a courtyard (*gono*); the latter is divided into an area for the animals and another for the granaries (*guyo togu*) and the dwelling. Access to the house is by an entrance (*day*) that leads into a central room (*deu bere*) flanked by two side rooms and a circular kitchen (*obolo*) through which one goes up to a terrace on which open one or two storerooms. The entire construction is of *banco* (beaten clay shaped into the desired form) with wooden supports and beams to hold up the roof, and it is interpreted symbolically as an anthropomorphic figure.

The soil of the ground-floor. . . is the symbol of the earth and of Lébé, restored to life in the earth. The flat roof, square like that of the flying granary, represents heaven, and the ceiling which separates the upper storey from the ground-floor represents the space lying between heaven and earth. The four small rectangular roofs around it indicate the four cardinal points, as does the hearth itself.

426. *Dogon: a* toguna *with continuous wall of mud plastered over stone and covered by a thick roof of vegetable matter, Tonyogu (Mali).*

427. *Dogon: detail of a* toguna *with anthropomorphic pillars, Dyankabu (Mali).* ▷

The hearth derives its living flame from the celestial fire that came from the fire purloined by the smith. When the house is correctly sited, that is to say, is open to the north, the pot on the fire indicates the same point, the stones indicating east and west, while the wall, the third support for the pot, marks the south.

— Inside the house, the several rooms represent caves of this world inhabited by men. The vestibule, which belongs to the master of the house, represents the male partner of the couple, the outside door being his sexual organ. The big central room is the domain and the symbol of the woman; the store-rooms [to] each side are her arms, and the communicating door her sexual parts. The central room and the store-rooms together represent the woman lying on her back with outstretched arms, the door open and the woman ready for intercourse. The room at the back which contains the hearth and looks out on to the flat roof, shows the breathing of the woman, who lies in the central room under the ceiling, which is the symbol of a man, its beams representing his skeleton; their breath finds its outlet through the opening above. The four upright poles (feminine number) are the couple's arms, those of the woman supporting the man who rests his own on the ground. . . . The earthen platform that serves as a bed lies north and south and the couple sleep on it with their heads to the north, like the house itself, the front wall of which is its face.[13]

In this famous passage by M. Griaule, the links between the structure of the house, the motifs of the myth, and the humanized interpretation of architecture appear as so many fixed points in the primitive interpretation of a type of cross-shaped building widely diffused in northern Africa south of the Sahara. In the Dogon house certain elements, the circular kitchen for one, are still directly inspired by the human form (the head in this instance), but the process of abstraction is already well advanced. The type of house in human form is thus perpetuated through the linkage and harmonious unity of various rooms, and their functions take on added vitality through the interpretation of the house itself in terms of the living being. This conception is of some importance, for we shall find it again, virtually unchanged, in the dwellings and religious edifices of the towns in the Nigerian area, only slightly disguised by an overlay of Islamic reinterpretation.

By recognizing in the house connotations of the human figure and, indeed, of the couple (of whose fertility the house is not only custodian but also inducer), the Dogon stress the value of the family within the social organization. Prestige and the power to hand down decisions are reserved to the elders and, in architecture, are translated

into the facade—the face—of the house itself. The oldest member of the extended family (*ginna bana*) resides in the building specifically designated as family house (*ginna*, from *ginu na*, large house) which differs from the ordinary houses in its breadth and height and, most of all, in its facade, the outer wall of the vestibule, which marks it as the residence of the head of the family.[14]

The facade (*plates 420, 421, 423*)[15] is divided symmetrically by the central axis marked by the main door and, on the upper story, the door of the principal granary, the special property of the master of the house (*jele*), a sacred depository where the altar of the ancestors (*vageu*) is stored. The door of this granary is, by tradition, carved all over in low relief with representations of the primordial couple, on the lock, and the successive generations who peopled the earth, on the panel (*plate 419*). Thus, the granary above the entrance constitutes a sanctuary sacred to the family, entirely similar in appearance to the totemic sanctuary described above (*plates 424, 425*) with its door, two upper niches, and a crown of small pinnacles continuing the vertical line of the "pilasters" spaced across the house front. A number of vertical struts and transverse bands divide the surface of the facade into several compartments or niches, oblong on the ground floor and smaller and squarer on the upper story. These are called "swallows' nests" and are believed to be the dwellings of the ancestors; offerings are left to them there. Their number, implying the increase of the generations, is conventionally a multiple of eight, the number of the ancestors of the Dogon. The same conventional number applies to the projecting pinnacles above the line of the terrace, which are conical or cylindrical and surmounted by a flat stone; like the analogous elements of the sanctuary, these are interpreted as the altars of the eight ancestors. The pilasters, however, are conventionally ten in number, "like the fingers of the two hands." The general concept expressed by the house front is the multiplication of men and their works, with reference also to the cultivated field and the tilled earth in the symbol (found also in the temples) of the "blanket of death" with black and white squares (*plates 413, 414*). The succession of generations is read from the top to the bottom row of niches and is explicitly depicted in the carved door of the granary.

Treated very differently in the various Dogon villages and even within the same settlement, these niches (*vele komo*) are the most original motif in the architecture of the *ginna* facade. They are used as personal altars, as for example the *ku togolo* (the skull) sacred to the *nyama*, the individual vital force, and the *jabie*, symbol of the body of the individual.

The doors with their wooden panels are provided with latches of two types. The first, called *duro kunu* and chiefly used for the main door of the house leading to the large central room, is concealed in the interior, and to open it one must put one's arm through a hole at the left of the door and insert the key from inside. The second type, *ta koguru*, is found for the most part in the granary doors on the upper story of the *ginna*. This latch is on the outside and is the major decorative element on the door, with representations of animals or the mythic twin-progenitors.[16]

Taken as a whole, the habitation of the Dogon is a balanced structure that makes constant reference to the mythic tradition, yet is nevertheless open to a great variety of solutions and interpretations. Though it is chiefly built in *banco*, some limited use is made of stone (for foundations, but also, in some areas, for the granaries, dwellings, and sacred enclosures) and of wood—the latter more sparingly because of its rarity. Wood, however, is used for the core of the horizontal beams, which are then plastered over with *banco*, a building material that can be likened to reinforced concrete. Wood is a material in which it is easy to express complex mythic and social significances (as in the granary doors and masks); put to this use, it acts in counterpoint to the rigorous architecture of the structures themselves, in which the builders give shape to a continuous flow of plans and forms, finding a constant variety in the possibilities offered by the natural surroundings and the social situation. If art is a kind of writing capable of transmitting a cultural complex, then the architecture of the Dogon is only partly art: It models itself over and over again, following the concrete interweavings between the uniform "history" of the myth and the "accidents" of sociocultural reality.

The clear layout of the Dogon house is also found in the ideal plan of the village, in which myth again is the linchpin of an association between the form of the human body and the arrangement of objects in space. At the basis of a Dogon village is the body of the first ancestor as represented by eight stones marking the principal anatomical articulations, plus a ninth for the head: The eight are the eight descendants, four men and four women, founders of the lineages of all living men (*plate 43*).

"The seventh ancestor," Ogotemmêli explained, "swallowed the old man head-first, and brought up the *dugué* stones, putting them in the shape of the stretched-out body. It was like a drawing of a man picked out with stones. . . . He organized the world . . . by vomiting the *dugué* stones in the outline of a man's soul." He placed the stones one by one, beginning with the one for the head, and with the eight principal stones, one for each ancestor, he marked the joints of the pelvis, the shoulders, the knees, and the

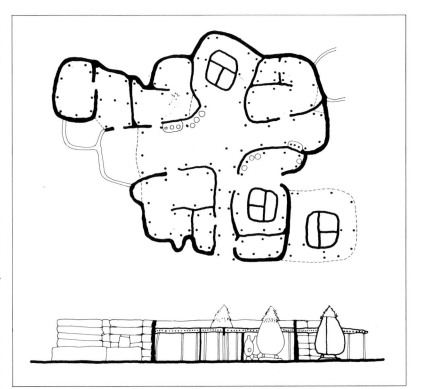

elbows. The right-hand side came first; the stones of the four male ancestors were placed at the joints of the pelvis and shoulders, that is, where the limbs had been attached, while the stones of the four female ancestors were placed at the other four joints.[17]

This structure reflects the Dogon anthropomorphic view of the world and the village and also regulates the kinship relationships; it is therefore an eminently social mnemonic figure.

In the schematic plan of the village, M. Griaule distinguishes the essential organs: the smithy, plaza, and council house to the north (head), the women's houses to the east and west (hands), the family houses in the center (chest), with the stone for oil (female genitals) and the altar of foundation (male genitals) and the altars (feet) concluding the figure to the south. More interesting than this abstract scheme is that of the social system, inasmuch as it touches on the central point of the relationship between architecture, structure of the society, and human form. In Dogon mythology, the eight families that descended from the eight ancestors placed themselves to the sides of a north-south axis terminating in the north with the forge and house of the smith, and the arrangement reproduces that of the first field ever cultivated. Among so many oscillations in significance, what is decisive is the hierarchical relationship between the eight family units (the social body) and the ninth element (the head), the symbol of the unity of the village and of political dominion, which is the prerogative of the council of the elders.

Although the mythic interpretation of the ideal conception of the village relates the Dogon to the other populations of Mali (which, as V. Pâques has shown, includes settlements right up to the level of the cities in partially Islamized societies), in reality their settlements have a great variety of overall plans and of positions within the territory. Often they comprise more than one of the four historical groupings of the Dogon people, each of which lives relatively autonomously in a quarter of its own.

The most characteristic and best-known settlements lie at the base of the overhanging cliffs of the Bandiagara range. There, where every inch of agricultural terrain is precious, the dwellings are built on the rocky slope between the great masses of fallen rock wall. Below, on the lower slope and the plain at its foot, are the fields—rectangular plots carefully divided up into sectors (in imitation, as we have seen, of the primordial rectangular field or the "blanket of death" with its white and black squares); higher up, in the steepest places and under overhanging rocks where advantage can often be taken of natural shelters are the granaries, sanctuaries, storage places for the masks, and burial grounds (*plates 409–411, 415, 416*). Visually, certain villages,

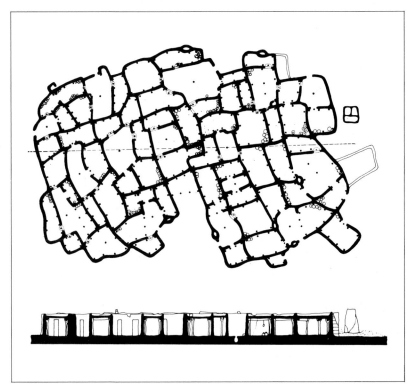

433. Aerial view of a village with curvilinear walled houses, Bobo-Julasso (Upper Volta).

Banani for one (*plate 407*), seem to heal over the fracture between the imposing natural formation looming above them and the farming plots below, almost as if employing architecture as a means of mediating between the divine presence (known *a priori* to reside there) and human productive activity.

THE PRIMITIVE TOWNS AND CITIES OF AFRICA

*History and Myth*

In Africa south of the Sahara there are no traditional terms to designate a town or city as distinct from a village or royal court. In most cases, no qualitative distinction is made between types of settlements; the only emphasis is quantitative. A town may be designated as a large village. Its name may also refer to the myth of its origins.[18] The name of the capital of the kingdom of Congo, Banza (Mbanza Congo), signified only "court," residence of the king, according to the account published by the explorer Filippo Pigafetta in 1591.[19]

Rarely does the absence of a word conceal as many problems as in this case. Were the cities of the African kingdoms true cities or only semiurban agglomerations exercising basic directive, political, and administrative functions over the surrounding territory, but without sufficient distinctive traits to permit us to consider their historical development by the same criteria we apply to the urban history of the Occident and Orient? The question has had the most diverse answers. But while it is true that each case must be examined individually, the logical comparability of the phenomena having to do with the concentration of the economy, population, and power appear to justify the use, as a working tool, of the words "town" or "city," at least for the large centers, the historical capitals of the Sudanese area.[20] That the question is not merely one of terminology but involves the nature of the territorial, urban, and architectonic values becomes clear, however, as soon as one analyzes one of these centers in detail and discovers that it cannot be reduced to any standard model of the Western capitalist city nor to any in the historical and geographical area of Asia.

The case is different in central southern Africa where, in the absence of Islamic influence, one can more appropriately speak of royal courts, which functioned for varying periods as territorial poles, drawing together the diverse political components of the "states." Those cities were primarily residences created to reflect the familial and bureaucratic power imposed on a number of subject lineages by the dominant lineage. Such a court, intimately connected with the person of the king, directly administered all nonagricultural activities and the judicial and military systems without ever bringing about the development of an intermediary class, a bourgeoisie that could confer

434. *Plan of a family residence in a large circular enclosure (Upper Volta).*
*1. entrance; 2, 3, 4. main living quarters.*
*The utility areas, storerooms, and fixed kitchen furnishings are hollowed out of the thickness of the walls.*

435. *Aerial view of part of the oasis of Siwa showing stone houses with curvilinear ground plans (western Egypt).*

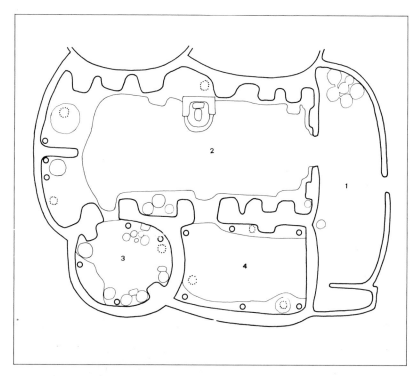

urban characteristics on a central settlement—and these therefore remained much like the *chefferie*.[21] Viewed thus, the court-city represents an extreme expansion of the concept of the dominant lineage, which uses totemic forms to lend credibility to its own power. An extremely clear example of this may be found in the plan of the ancient capital of the Lunda kingdom in central Africa, where the royal court buildings were organized according to the zoomorphic model of the tortoise (*plate 439*).[22] Bearing in mind the meanings attributed to that animal, we may visualize that capital less as a city than as an enormous house in which the familiars of the king and the most important functionaries assembled to exercise their power over the entire territory. Still present in its organization, and in extraordinarily overt form, was the concept of the dissection of the sacrificial animal as basis for the division of space, and for the division of the territory according to the cardinal directions. Here it was royal power that exploited the cultural substratum to demonstrate its own legitimacy to perpetuate the dynasty. Architecture was at the service of a single chief at the top of the social pyramid, although it continued to make use of such figures and meanings as we have found, for example, in the myths of the Fali.[23]

In the forest kingdom of the Ashanti in present-day Ghana, economic ties to the commercial world of Islam have not prevented the autonomous development of an architecture that, in all its aspects, from decoration to typology, represents an exemplary compromise between the demands of the Islamized class and the traditions of the animistic populations (*plates 440–444*). The traditional house is still related to the type common in West Africa. It is an open rectangular courtyard surrounded by four roofed rooms, with obvious analogies with the plan of the Dogon *ginna* (*plate 442*). During the last two centuries, this elementary form has undergone a progressive increase in size, and there has been a marked change in the traditional decoration and materials. The residence of the ruler of each *chefferie* of the Ashanti nation had all the features of a royal court but on a smaller scale, having a number of courtyards and being somewhat isolated from the dwellings around it (*plates 440, 441*).

The comprehensive study by M. Palau Marti on the kingdoms and capitals of Ife, Oyo, Ketu, Benin (Edo), Alada, Porto-Novo, and Dahomey shows what importance was attributed to the royal palace, which covered a great area, was built for permanency, and was quite isolated from the inhabited zones around it.[24] The town of Ketu, for example, is surrounded by a large oval-shaped stone wall and is divided into halves: the right one to the west, the left one to the east of an imaginary line running north to south. Though the fortified wall confers an obvious unity on the settlement, nevertheless a clear inter-

436. *Berbers: aerial view of part of the ksar of Bukhais with curvilinear stone houses (Algeria).*

437. *Throne of a dignitary representing the court of the king of Dahomey, from Kana. Musée de l'Homme, Paris.* ▷

438. *Carved pillars from the royal palace of Ketu, now destroyed (Dahomey).* ▷

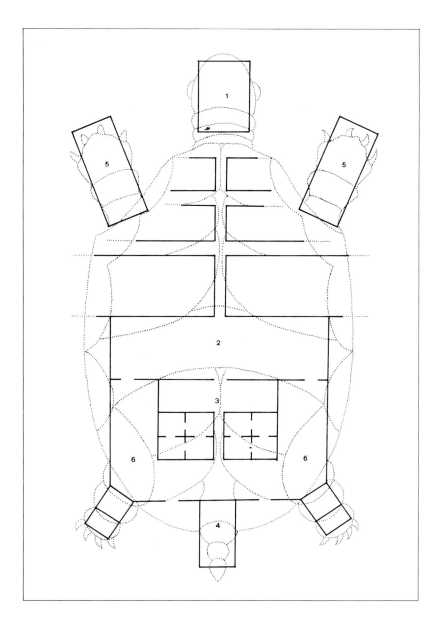

*439. Schematic plan of the court buildings of the capital of the Lunda kingdom, showing the disposition of the principal clans (Angola).*
*1. Mesu; 2. Ambula; 3. Shimene; 4. Mazembe; 5. Mucano; 6. Manga.*

nal differentiation sets the royal court apart from the rest of it, which in character is little more than a large village. According to legend, the fortifications were erected under Sa and Epo, the fourteenth and fifteenth kings of Ketu, with the help of two giants, the smith Ajibodun and the miner Oluwodu, who carried out the work at night. The earth used for cementing the stones was mixed with palm oil, which, along with their unpaid labor, Epo extorted in great quantities from his subjects, who, not unexpectedly, revolted and killed him.

Of all the gates, the one at the north (Idena) is the most important. It marks one end of the imaginary north-south axis, the southern end being the royal palace (*afin*) itself. Sacrifices were offered to the Idena gate as though to the tutelary divinity of the city, and it is significant that the name means not only "defence rampart" but also "sentinel." It was through Idena that the king entered for his enthronement, following a ritual route which throws some light on the internal equilibrium of the city's structure. He was required to stop in four sacred huts inside the town but close to the wall, remaining in each a full three moons and thereby taking an entire year to reach the royal palace. The route began in the northwest with the Ilé Era, the house of the sorcerers, where he learned magic, continued to the Ilé Jjumo Ketu, west of the main axis of the town, to the Ilé Alalumon, located symmetrically to the east of the axis, and ending with the Ilé Eru at the south, close to the royal palace.[25]

This royal progression was thought of as the king's taking possession of his capital—of its east and west halves but, above all, of its two cosmic axes, north-south and east-west, which also symbolize his appropriation of the territory as a whole. The route took the shape of a large **S**; the upper and lower parts were opposite and symmetrical with respect to the center. All this, however, has no real connection with the physical structure of the town except that it reveals, through the rite, significant meanings often in contradiction to apparent reality. In addition to other symbolic implications and complications we shall look into below, the hidden structure of the town is reducible to the cross of orthogonal directions pinpointing the four cardinal points and, as it were, linking the city to the territory.

Since these interpretations are so independent of the real physical plan of the settlement, it is not surprising that a city built under colonial, not native, direction could nevertheless be interpreted in this traditional manner despite the fact that its structure was entirely different. The capital of the Haussa state of Gobir—laid out in 1946 on a European plan with a radial structure and streets fanning outward—is thought of by the indigenous inhabitants not as it is but rather according to the traditional model with a gate at each of the four cardinal points.[26] Thus, distinct from the real city, and superimposed

440. *Ashanti: plan of the village of Kwamo with houses built around courtyards (Ghana).*
  1. main plaza; 2. residence of the chief; 3. burial ground; 4. sanctuary (abosomfie).

441. *Ashanti: plan of the palace of a chief (Ghana).*
  1. entrance courtyard; 2. guests; 3. courtyards for audiences; 4. kitchen–dining room.

442. *Ashanti: ground plan and section of a traditional house with courtyard (Ghana).*

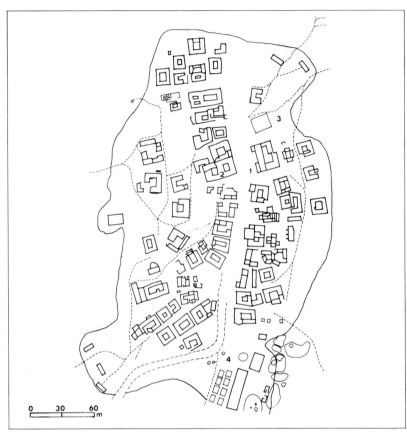

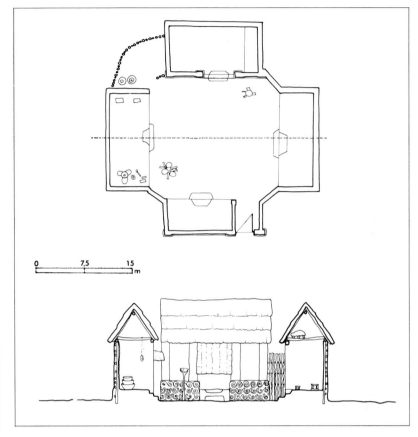

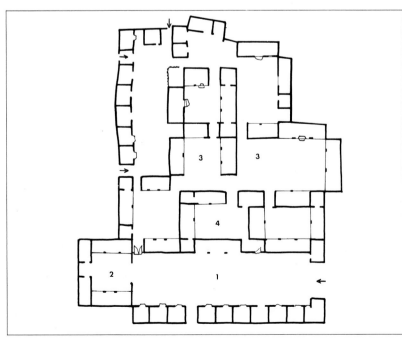

443. *Ashanti: ground plan and sections of the sanctuary (abosomfie) of Bawjwiasi (Ghana).*

444. *Figural and nonrepresentational decorative motifs (Ghana).*

445. *Schematic plan of the town of Matari (Chad).*
*1. central zone (Holmé); 2. Halaka moiety; 3. Alagué moiety.*
*Positions of the groups: a. Gocelo; b. Bodo; c. Daji; d. Maguio;*
*e. Hargué; f. Modo; g. Wagaji; h. Welia, i. Mada.*

446. *Aerial view of Lagone-Gana (Chad).*

447. *Plan of the royal palace of Kusseri (Chad).*
*1. entrance; 2. courtyards; 3. audience chamber and residence of the Me; 4. women's quarters; 5. servants' quarters and storerooms.*

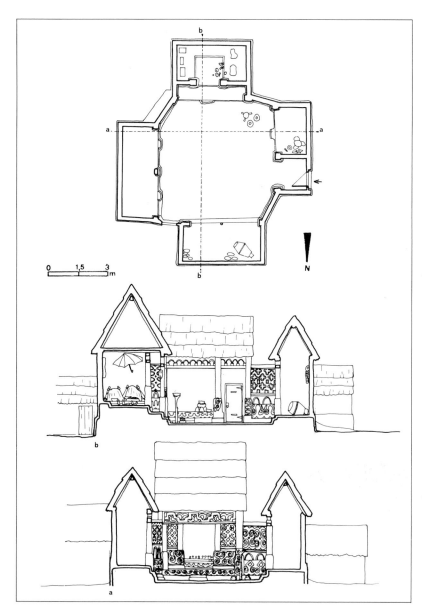

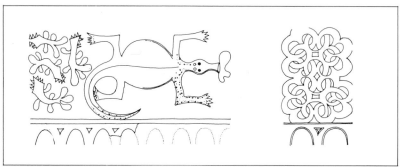

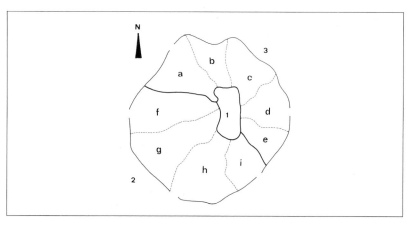

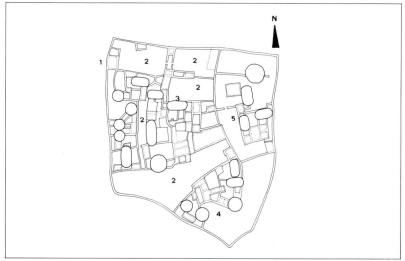

on it, there exists an invisible city whose structure is marked only by five points—the center and the four gates in the four chief directions—where, at the foot of sacred trees and stones, are repeated the traditional propitiatory sacrifices intended to protect the city from harm and to assure its safety within its invisible ring of wall.

The localization of the regional divine principle—the *genius loci*—in a sacred tree is one of the main connections between the conception of the village and that of the city in the Sudanese area. The tree always figures in the foundation of the settlement and remains thereafter the principal sign of the divine protection extended to the local authorities. In Ketu the tree is in the east part of the town, near the sacred hut known as Ilé Alalumon. Often when a group settles in a new place the most important initial point of reference is such a tree, considered almost as the host welcoming the group into the new territory.

Two examples throw light on the importance of this conception, which, in fact, is the prelude to the more complex notion of the cosmic tree. The first thing a Bambara (West African) group does when settling in a new place is to choose a tree that thenceforth will represent the tutelary spirit of the community. The warriors hang their weapons on its branches, the workers lean their tools against its trunk, the chief offers sacrifices to it. The sacred tree will protect the new village and its inhabitants from harm. In return, periodic offerings renew the relationship of dependence of the inhabitants and their chief on the tutelary spirit of the tree, called *nyana dugu dasiri,* the guardian spirit of the place.[27]

If the settlement develops, and differences between the various lineages in the community become more marked, this focal point where the group is, literally, rooted to the place in time assumes the character of a center of political power and is therefore appropriated by the chief and his family. The tree then becomes the seat of the divinity protecting the family of the chief, and they defend it against the rival families as their own source of strength and power, preventing outsiders and possible enemies from even approaching it. Thus, in more elaborate communities such as the *chefferie* and, still more so, the kingdom, the tree becomes an integral part of the compound or royal palace. Sometimes it is replaced by a log, which is likewise protected by a series of taboos that, in reality, are designed to keep it exclusively under the control of those holding the power.

The legend of the foundation of the kingdom of Baguirmi in the Sudanese area tells that the founder, the first king (*mbag*), having arrived in the area with twenty-two companions, carried out the sacrifice of foundation—the ritual killing of an ox—under a ficus tree (*mbaya*), though another tradition has it that the sacred tree itself

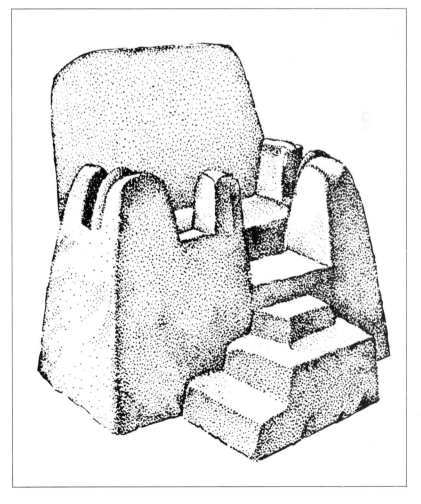

450. *Gate in the city wall of Zinder (Niger).*

452. *Drawing of a house front in Zinder (Niger).*

451. *Drawing of the upper part of a decorated house in Zinder (Niger).*

453. *Residence of the Sultan Barmou, Tessawa (Niger).*

454, 455. *Changes in a compound associated with the growth of the family, Zaria (Nigeria).*
  *Schematic plans (a–d) showing the gradual replacement of round huts by more commodious rectangular houses, and detailed ground plan.*
456. *Drawing of a decorated house front in Zaria (Nigeria).*

457, 458. *Renewing the plastered surface of a house, Kano (Nigeria).*

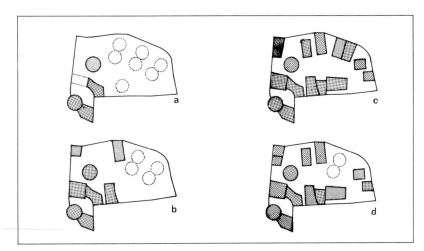

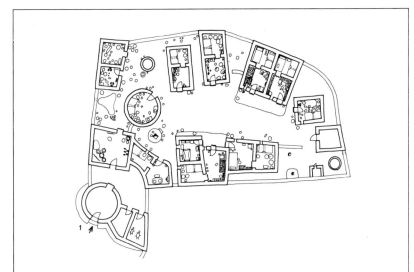

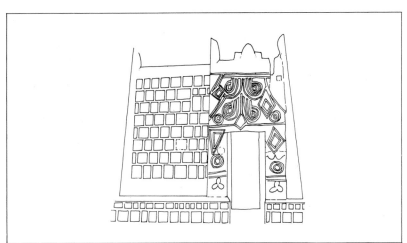

*459. House in Kano (Nigeria).*

465. *Schematic plan of Timbuktu showing its symbolic structure (Mali).*
   *1. market (belly); 2. tomb of Sidi Mahmud; 3. (head); 4. (feet); 5. (left arm); 6. (right arm).*
   *The crosses mark the tombs of Moslem saints and have correspondences with planets, stars, or constellations.*

466. *Elevation and ground plan of a house in Timbuktu (Mali).*
   *1. entrance and vestibule; 2. servants' quarters; 3. large courtyard; 4. woman's bedroom (belly); 5. man's bedroom (belly); 6. large bedroom of the woman (heads of woman and man); 7. small courtyard with utility rooms.*

467. *View of a street in Timbuktu with a typical house front and, at the rear, a minaret (Mali).*

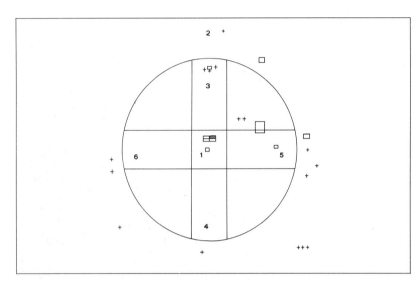

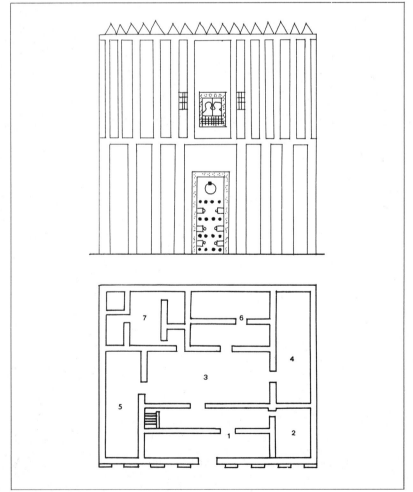

(*jan*) gave origin to the kingdom by dividing itself into six radial parts.[28]

The multiplicity of significances of the sacred tree includes its identification as the burial place of the ancestor-founder associated with it. By and large, the tree is the natural territorial axis to which the urban structures and also the political power remain connected. It is by no means rare in the ritual of the foundation of a city that one or more trees may be planted on the spot where the first propitiatory human sacrifice was offered. In the myth of the foundation of Logone-Birni, also in the Sudanese area, the two chiefs of the ethnic groups, Saldoma and Roudama, sacrificed two of their children, burying them at the sides of the west gate of the city. Near their tombs were planted an acacia (*lufu*) and a fig (*zara*) whose branches intertwine.[29]

If the tree is the symbol of the relationship of the group with the *genius loci,* that is, of its connection with the earth, the imaginary orientation according to the cardinal points represents the relationship with the celestial regions. Both of these locational devices are evidence of an attitude that considers every village and every town as the precise center of the territory, so that, by definition, every settlement is situated at the center and point of origin of space. The first device, the tree, so often the distinctive sign of place, is complemented by the second, the distinctive sign of space. At the extremities of the so-called cross of directions there are almost always points of external origin—older settlements, for example—which delimit the area in whose center the new town is situated and which have the function of focusing the axes themselves on places endowed with a precise function and precise significance. The two Kotoko cities of Logone-Birni and Makari are thus situated in the "center" of a territory having four external points of reference that correspond, by and large, with the cardinal points: They are, counterclockwise from north to east, for Logone-Birni and Makari, respectively, Gala, Malafana, Zemade, Unkwal; and Mosso, Ngame, Fima, and Selo.[30]

But it is above all in the residence of the king that the visible symbols that proclaim it the central point of the territory and the social system are concentrated (*plate 447*). One of the most imposing royal dwellings was the ancient palace of the king of Benin, described in the early 18th century by Willem Bosman on the basis of the report of a voyage to Benin by Van Nyendael.

The king's court, which makes a principal part of the city, must not be forgotten: It is upon a very great plain, about which are no houses, and hath, besides its wide extent, nothing rare. The first place we come into is a very long gallery . . . sustained by fifty-eight strong planks, about twelve foot high, instead of pillars. . . . As

**469.** *Schematic drawing of a typical house front in Jenné (Mali).*
1. loburu; 2. kadye; 3. saraf har; 4. gu; 5. hume; 6. titi; 7. potige; 8. potige-tita; 9. potige-diye.

**470.** *House front in Bandiagara (Mali).*

471. *Aerial view of part of Agades with the mosque in the middle distance (Niger).*

soon as we are past this gallery, we come to the mud or earthen wall, which hath three gates, at each corner one, and another in the middle, the last of which is adorned at the top with a wooden turret, like a chimney, about sixty or seventy foot high. At the top of all is fixed a large copper snake, whose head hangs downward: This serpent is very well cast or carved, and is the finest I have seen in Benin. Entering one of these gates, we come into a plain about a quarter of a mile almost square, and enclosed with a low wall. Being come to the end of this plain, we meet with such another gallery as the first, except that it hath neither wall nor turret. . . . This gallery hath a gate at each end; and passing through one of them, a third gallery offers itself to view, differing from the former only in that the planks upon which it rests are human figures . . . my guides were able to distinguish them into merchants, soldiers, wild-beast-hunters, etc. Behind a white carpet we are also shown eleven men's heads cast in copper, by much as good an artist as the former carver; and upon each of these is an elephant's tooth, these being some of the king's gods. Going through a gate of this gallery, we enter another great plain, and a fourth gallery, beyond which is the king's dwelling-house. Here is another snake, as upon the first wall. In the first apartment, at the entrance of the plain, is the king's audience chamber, where, in presence of his three great lords, I saw and spoke with him: He was sitting on an ivory couch under a canopy of Indian silk.[31]

## Jenné

Besides the residence of the king or chief and the principal religious edifice (mosques in the Islamized towns), the populous centers in the Sudanese area always have a market, the true driving force behind the urban activities, and it is this institution that, both symbolically and economically, distinguishes a town from a mere seat of a chief.

The inhabited area of the centers is divided into family units, each of which, in a reciprocal system of interrelationships but with considerable internal autonomy, repeats the structure of the compound inhabited by all the members of a clan or lineage group; this structure is subject to constant alteration according to the changing needs, numbers, and rank of the family components. It is significant that in the cities, as is not true in the isolated complexes, external conditions and limited space rule out the continuous growth of the family dwelling by the addition of new dwelling units. From the outset, the house is delimited by spaces that have to be left open for public passage, and therefore whatever transformations are made (primarily the gradual occupation of all the available space as the family increases) take place behind an enclosing wall in an area which is clearly and exclusively private (*plates 454, 455*).

These limitations imposed by urban conditions have led to the close massing of buildings, virtually pushing into their neighbors, and to the loss of the architectural diversity one might expect from the fact that the city is made up of so many different populations. The result is a highly uniform architectural language based on boxlike volumes and on a kind of dense compression of the units within the house, so that all the artistic, symbolic, and compositional qualities of the house must be concentrated in one place, the street front of the main body of the building with its door giving access to the interior (*plates 451–453, 456–461, 468–470*).

The cities of the central Nigerian region, in which the major activities have been commerce and crafts, have each developed a complex type of urban habitation that is based on the traditional dwelling of the farming population but in its decoration and functional aspects reflects the requirements of the Islamized dominant class. Some of the Islamic decorative elements and schemes are, in point of fact, popular —that is, local folkstyle—variations (*plates 456–463*). They are expressions of the wealthy native bourgeoisie, who have introduced into the local architecture elements derived directly from objects produced in the Islamic countries along the Mediterranean or brought back from pilgrimages to Mecca. Thus, the internal structure and the facade decoration of the urban houses represent the enrichment of a preexisting decorative and mythic heritage by geometrical motifs that originated elsewhere.[32]

Jenné (Djenné) and Timbuktu (Tombouctou), the twin cities of the Niger basin, have a diversified architectural tradition, stratified by class: The building types are not characteristic of a specific ethnic group but, rather, of a class pursuing a specific activity. For Jenné and its territory, the basic information has been gathered by C. Monteil, who has described the varieties and technical procedures used in construction there.[33] For Timbuktu, there is the more recent comprehensive study by V. Pâques.[34] Emphasizing the profound similarity in the conception of territory, city, and house in the various regions of northwest Africa, she attributes less importance to Islamic influence and, instead, reveals the persistence of mythic associations typical of village cultures, which makes it possible to define the architecture of this vast region of Africa as still fundamentally primitive.[35] As is plain to see in the 19th-century view of Timbuktu by Caillé (*plate 464*),[36] there were then, as now, three essential types of habitation in the city, its outskirts, and the territory: the hut made of vegetable matter, the one-story house of *pisé,* and the urban house.

The nomadic Peul (Fulbè) population has easily assembled huts of branches covered with straw (*sudu*), whereas the sedentary populations of the region occupy houses of *pisé* that are rectangular in shape with one entrance. These houses are built of crude bricks roughly $1^5/_8$ to 2 inches high, 16 to 20 inches long, and 8 to 9 inches wide, made of clay mixed with crushed straw. The roof rests on a wooden framework supported by beams resting on split poles and is covered first with leaves and branches and then with a layer of clay.

The urban house has a large inner court (*batuma*) approached through a vestibule (*sifa*) and a small corridor (*sorodyide*), and a stairway (*kalikali*) leads to the upper story. The rooms surround the court, and above the front part of the house, directly above the door, there is usually a second story. The flooring between the two stories is made of webs of branches laid down according to the width of the room: a simple crosswise web for the corridors, a diagonal web with a strip interwoven perpendicularly for wider rooms (*Al Maruba*); for even larger rooms the corners are covered and then the central part is overlaid with a crosswoven layer (*tafarafara*); some rooms, however, are covered only at the four corners (*barmame*). In these upstairs rooms the women can work without having to come down into the courtyard; they can even bathe there since the flooring is watertight so the bath water simply runs off. The walls are built of cylindrical bricks (*tufa*) $3^7/_8$ to $4^3/_4$ inches high and wide.

But the most interesting aspect of these houses is the facade (*plate 469*), a direct reflection of the social position of the occupants as well as the expression of a complex architectural language. The central part is strictly symmetrical, with the door (*hume*) and the decorated panel above it (*potige*) absolutely centered. To the sides of the door are, symmetrically, a feature that can be called a pilaster strip (without base and capital), and these taper upward. These are spaced across the entire front, marking off the central, most important, part of the facade and terminate at roof level in a small pyramid some fifteen or twenty inches high. Sometimes, too, they support a protective canopy over the door. These uprights (*kadye*) are a dominant motif in Jenné and elsewhere and are not confined to dwellings but are a fundamental element in religious architecture, most notably the mosque. The corner verticals terminate at the top in a conical motif and are called *loburu* (man-tip), probably with phallic significance.

A square window (*gu*) opens above the door, and higher still is the *potige,* an oblong panel bisected by a vertical strip, at either side of which is a relief (*potige-tita*). On the transverse strip at the lower edge of this *potige* the ends of the ceiling beams project through the wall to make handy grips and supports (*potige-diye*) for the masons when repairs are needed, something similar being found in most tall earth-built edifices in the Sudanese area, including mosques and minarets. Finally, at ground level, there is often a fixed clay bench (*titi*) to either side of the door.

### Timbuktu

With no rupture of any sort, the cosmogonic myths of those regions that have converted to Islam continue to use the essential motifs that characterize the architecture of the animistic primitive populations: the cosmic mountain linking sky and earth, the sacrifice at creation, which, following the division of a sacred body, gave rise to an orderly system of natural phenomena, social structures, and exercise of power.

From the study by V. Pâques on Timbuktu it would appear to be myth that accounts for the organization of the city and territory, its history as an urban center, and the structure of its dwellings.[37] In

Timbuktu, as in many other places in northern Africa, the borders between "primitive" and "popular" are extremely labile. Certainly the Islamization that this region underwent overlies a very much earlier body of myth and architectural tradition that distorts even its most characteristic features. Only certain motifs can be described as manifestations of "popular" religion and these always have to do with the cult places—the mosques—and the tombs of the holy men who protect the city.

In the local myth of creation, the dominant theme is the sacrifice of the divine serpent-mountain (*minia*), which resulted in the division of its body, the invention of arithmetical calculation (division by three and by four), and, in substance, all the phenomena and all the correspondences growing out of subsequent subdivisions.

The fundamental structure of the world is said to be based on the division of space into six parts, the first six words spoken by God. This corresponds to an anthropomorphic image with the head as zenith, the limbs as the four cardinal points, the sex organ as nadir. The words are: *Ina Ateinaka* (associated with east, white, division by six, the world), *Al Qasara* (west, yellow, division by four, the progenitors), *Fasalli* (south, white, division by four, water), *Li Rabika* (north, white, division by four, cereals and other foodstuffs), *Wen hari* (the zenith, green, division by four, salt water), and *Walabtar* (the nadir, yellow, division by six, devils, djinns, etc.).

The sacrifice of the *minia* is the guiding thread of the familial and social organization and the different stages in the life of individuals as well as of the historical and political interpretations of the city. But it is on the plane of the territory and the relations between different cities that we find an anthropomorphic model applied that is perfectly in line with the kind of interpretation of the territory we have encountered elsewhere. The human figure is characterized in different manners, but in all cases Timbuktu itself marks the principal point, the head. One interpretation considers the twin cities of Timbuktu and Jenné as, respectively, the head and the belly, connected by three towns—necks—functioning as intermediaries: Mopti in the center and San and Sofara to the right and left. In another version, the entire group of five towns is the head, with Tinduf as the belly of a rather more extended organism of which Tawdeni is the neck. Then again, viewed in relation to Kabara, its port on the Niger, Timbuktu is the head and the port the belly.

The legend of the founding of the city attributes to the sacrifice of a woman named Tim Buctu the draining and drying-out of the swamps and the emergence of an island of land with the sacred tree in its center, the future site of the settlement. Nine sacred water holes or pools remained in the drained territory, and these were identified with the body of the sacrificed woman. Her slayer was Sidi Mahmud, founder and protector of the urban community, who by his act dried out the zone and instituted agriculture there. The city itself represents his body, which is divided into five parts (the center, which is double, and the four cardinal points) in imitation of the division that took place in the moment of creation: The central zone is the belly, the head is at the north, the right and left arms to the west and east, the lower limbs at the south.

A particular constellation and activity is associated with each of these zones. Outside the city, to the north, is the tomb of the founder, Sidi Mahmud, and this is identified with the polestar. In that direction, and also in the other principal astronomical directions, there are a number of tombs of historical personages thought of as minor protectors, and these form constellations, so to speak, of sacred centers that guard the city from malevolent influences. Traditionally there are 333 saints who, like the sacred serpent, surround the city in a vital belt.

The five parts of Timbuktu originating in the members of the bodies of Buctu and Sidi Mahmud are the five districts of the city, although they are in fact very different from each other and grew up in quite different historical periods. These are Sakore at the north, Bella Faraji at the east, Sarakaena at the south, Jingareyber at the west, and Baga Jindo (Ba Jnde) in the center. The latter, thought of as the heart (or belly) of the city, contains the principal mosque, Sidi Yayah.

Every district has its own complex internal subdivision related to the residences of the principal families, the ethnic groups, and the corporations or guilds of the arts and trades. However, it is only in the central district, the vital nucleus of the city where three leading families live, that the organization can be traced back to a structure clearly connected with the myth of origin and, in particular, with the cosmic tree. The three families consider themselves to represent the center, the right arm, and the left arm. To the north of the mosque in this central district is the market, the true center of a city whose population is made up, in overwhelming majority, of merchants and artisans.

The ground plans of two of the three chief mosques are also conceived according to an anthropomorphic image. That of the mosque of the Jingareyber quarter represents a man in prayer with head turned to the north, that of the Sakore district a praying woman with her head at the south—the two in perfect symmetry.

For the mosque of Sakore there are two different anthropomorphic conceptions by which the real structure of the edifice is interpreted. The marabouts, guardians of the mosque, see the plan as a praying woman, with the minaret (to the south) as head, the central court as belly, the west gallery (the one reserved for women) as the lower limbs, the chamber at the north as the left arm. Every gallery (as is true of the mosque of Jingareyber, too) symbolizes a position of prayer. The outer wall protects this extended figure as does the presence of the tombs of three saints: Sidi Belgasem at the east, Nana Mama at the west, Amma guna Arasul at the south.

The masons' tradition is quite different. They visualize the edifice as divided into twelve rectangular parts, the twelve parts of Ali, master-builder of the mausoleum and the house of Sidi Mahmud. The *mihrab* (the niche in the east wall toward which prayers are addressed) is the head, the east galleries are the chest, the court is the belly, the west galleries the feet, the chamber at the north the left arm, the chamber at the south (the living quarters of the officiating priest, or *imam*) the right arm. The minaret represents the penis of the master-mason or, alternatively, the man himself in erect position. The first interpretation is more closely bound up with the religious function of the edifice; the second (and more important) has traces of the myth of the division into parts of the primordial organism (or of the sacrificial animal or of the blacksmith) that gave rise to cultivated fields and to buildings.

The position of the various social classes at prayer inside the mosque clearly reflects the hierarchical organization of the city's population. Thus, in the mosque of Jingareyber the *imam* has his place in front of the *mihrab*; in the first gallery are the marabouts and the descendants of the founder, Sidi Mahmud; in the second gallery are the civic notables, the head of the city, the heads of the districts, and the heads of the various age groups; in the third are the *gabibi* (the class of slaves subject to the principal families); in the fourth are the slaves, foreigners, and women.

Despite the strongly hierarchical organization of the classes, the unification of the different populations by the Islamic religion, and widespread commercial activity, the social structure of the city still reveals some of the significant traits of village organization. Every district is relatively self-sufficient and, as in a *chefferie* (every district here is dominated by a family and a head), holds its own principal ceremonies that involve daily life and the development of the individual. The decisive factor is the separation into groups according to age, based on the rites of circumcision (those of excision have been abandoned for centuries now), which, with their ceremonies, constitute the focal point of urban life. All circumcised males belong to the *kodey* society commanded by a *gabibi*, the eldest within that class being head of all the societies in the city. Economic in character, this grouping answers the need for mutual assistance that underlies every classification of individuals by age group. Each of the various family lineages occupies a compound of its own within the various districts.

These lineage groups are also ordered into a hierarchy headed by the most powerful family group, whose members, by convention, are held to be descendants of the founder of their particular district.

Finally, each of the various groups of artisans not only has a precise location in the city plan but also a specific role in the government of the city and the district. They are also an integral part of the mythic structure, having their place on the cosmic tree. In fact, fixed, clear-cut relations exist between the various types of economic activity, the families that practice them (among whom the slaves are especially important), and the urban sociocultural context. Even the market is divided up in orderly manner, according to the different trades, with four parts marked off by two streets intersecting at right angles: butchers at the northwest, shoemakers and tailors at the northeast, cloth merchants at the southwest, ironmongers at the southeast, with the food market (run by the women) stretching along the two principal arteries.

The typical house in Timbuktu is a rectangle oriented according to the cardinal points and entered usually from the south or the north (*plate 466*). It represents, symbolically, the body of the smith whose sacrifice gave origin to the world and the tomb of Sidi Mahmud (also anthropomorphically conceived), which was the first edifice of *banco* constructed in the city. The anthropomorphic image has its arms open and head turned toward the south, which connects it to the cultivated fields and the ritual subdivision effected in the primordial sacrifice. Sacred stones and offerings are buried in the four corners of the house and beneath the central pillar and the jambs of the main door, and propitiatory objects are placed under the stones.

Traditionally, the house should have twelve (or nine) doors and be built entirely of clay except for the pilasters of the doors. The rectangular space of the interior should be partitioned into nine rectangular areas corresponding to the pieces of the sacrificed man with the vestibule as his head. As in the Dogon house, the anthropomorphic image is androgynous, representing not only the smith but also his wife. The central court is the belly, the lateral rooms the arms and legs, though these parts are identified differently in different types of houses. The division into masculine and feminine elements may be said to coincide with the Islamic division of the house into two parts by gender. There are still other interpretations of family houses, some based on the form of the mythic serpent.

As usual, the front of the house (*plates 466, 467*) is considered the face, and the upper coping is therefore the turban. In the example cited by V. Pâques, the facade represents the cosmic tree, the sacrificial being subdivided into parts, which is stressed by the subdivision of the front by pilaster strips, while the door is a representation of the

479. *Aerial view of a modern quarter of Kutyala showing the streets laid out in modern colonial fashion and the mosque and compounds built in the traditional manner (Mali).*

480. *Aerial view of part of the town of Mopti (Mali).*
481. *Detail of the mosque at Mopti (Mali).*

482. *Mosque at San (Mali).*

483. *Great Mosque of Timbuktu (Sidi Yayah) in the 19th century. (Engraving by Caillé, 1830.)*

484. *Detail of the roof of a mosque, Jenné (Mali).* ▷

face. In the totality of its parts, the facade is also thought of as representing the constellations and the movements of the stars.

### THE PRIMITIVE MOSQUES OF WEST AFRICA

When the Arab traveler Ibn Battutah (1304–77) visited sub-Saharan West Africa in 1352–53, Jenné was already a fortified city. By then almost fully Islamic in faith and culture, its governing class, and in particular the king, Koy Komboro, had not long before promoted the construction of the Great Mosque and had, in every possible way, encouraged the populations of the adjacent regions to move into the city. As elsewhere in the complex and variously evolving city-states, urban development and, above all, the quality of urban life were bound up with Islam. In Timbuktu also the mosques were erected

at the time the city took its definitive shape, in the 14th and 15th centuries. However, like the Great Mosque of Jenné[38] and those of so many other cities, they have not come down to us in their original form, whereas the tombs of the kings have undergone less remodeling and often show their earliest structure virtually unchanged simply because they have no function other than to be the visible sign of the sacred continuity of power.

Even when redone in modern times the mosques as well as the tombs of the saints and kings have continued to be built of clay and wood by a technique that is adaptable to edifices of large dimensions (*plates 471–486*). The basic module for tombs and mosques alike is an elongated pyramid: Prime examples are the 16th-century tomb of Askia Mohamed in Gao,[39] the 15th-century minaret of Agades in the Niger region (*plates 471, 472*), and the mosques of Sakore and Jingareyber in Timbuktu, reconstructed in the 16th and 17th centuries (*plate 483*).[40] The tapering square towers in mud and wood common to all Islamic architecture in the Sahara region are probably of Arabic derivation, as is plain to see in Yemen (*plate 16*), but they are not the only type of public edifice. Often such buildings were incorporated into the older tradition of the local populations that remained animistic in belief and had never been assimilated into Islam and an urban way of life. While it is true that verifiable history in the Sahel and the Sudan begins only with Islamic history, of which they became more and more a part after the 11th century (though the introduction of writing has much to do with the fact that what happened there is known chiefly from that time on), it is also true that the primitive world remained the general background against which the cities emerged as points of concentration of mercantile wealth and territorial power within the new urban perspective.

Thus, it is safe to claim that certain characteristics of the architecture of these mosques (as regards not only symbolic significances but also formal plastic language) are the outgrowth of the primitive architecture of this region. This is consistent with our general premise that it is preferable to give more weight to the facts of architecture as seen within its own territory than to any theoretical criteria. This holds, too, for the royal residences that likewise undergo continual renovation. For all that they contain motifs that are not part of the local building tradition, as a whole they reflect the political and administrative autonomy of the *chefferie* and the city-state and can therefore be considered a direct continuation of primitive village architecture.

Like the religion, political organization, and economic structure of these urban societies, the architecture of the mosques in this region cannot be thought of as the exclusive product of a mercantile

class in power. It is the result also of pagan traditions that were already well established and widespread within the individual populations that later became part of the urban community. We have already seen how the symbolism and technologies reflected in residential architecture were taken over into the urban house within the family compound. We can find somewhat the same process in effect in the mosques, with their characteristic conoid pilasters, recognizing in this specifically Islamic type of building the extension of a repertory already brought to maturity in the Sudanese "castles" and villages. Especially in the less imposing examples, the mosque in the form of a sacred enclosure extends the conception of both the family house and the territorial sanctuary. Thus, what we can call the elementary mosque often follows the model of the rectangular room with "head" (apse) facing in the sacred direction, which gives it an anthropomorphic plan very like that of the Dogon *ginna* (*plate 44*).[41] The numerous conoid pilasters within the enclosure and along the outer walls and ends of the mosque are simply an elementary constructional and symbolic form: the altar of pyramidal or conoidal profile made out of a mass of beaten clay (*banco*) with or without a wooden framework, whose exterior is renovated annually (*plate 473*). We have seen the Dogon variant of this, the *buguturu* altar (*plates 403, 404*), but the village foundation altars are also conceived as a rounded mass of clay and have overt phallic-cosmological significance (*plate 406*). The use of this form as a repeated, rhythmic architectonic element—a form whose original purpose was to act as visible evidence of the sacred attachment of a population to a particular place—is essentially the same in the terraces and surrounding walls of these Islamic mosques as in the animistic sanctuary and the facade of the *ginna* of the Dogon people (*plates 420, 421, 423–425*). What is repeated in the mosques is, in reality, a mud pilaster, with or without a wooden core and more or less markedly tapering upward, though chiefly, in its most archaic form, of oval or circular cross section. Together they give a rhythmic vertical scansion to the buildings, and they are linked horizontally by beams covered with mud. That these pilasters are so similar in form to the primitive altars and related domestic motifs is not merely a reflection of local material resources and of building practices; it is their traditional symbolic and mythic significance (which, as we have seen in the plans of both the city and the house in Timbuktu and Jenné, extends to every aspect of reality) that explains their use in the Islamic mosque—particularly in this region, which for so long has been influenced by the social stratification, the craft specialization, and the purist separation of architectonic volumes so characteristic of Islamic culture. In this commingling of tendencies—countering the movement by the ruling powers to impose a uniform model of house and of mosque, an effort that is also reflected in the syncretism of the religious and sociocultural models—the other face of the historical interrelationship of animism and Islam finds concrete expression, in the architectural structures and decoration.

The arabesque motifs that are prevalent in cities from Walata to Kano (*plates 451, 452, 456, 457, 460–463*), are sometimes reduced to figural compromises in the kingdoms in less direct contact with the trans-Saharan caravans that were the means by which the Islamic culture of the Mediterranean coast and of Morocco made its way into the West African region. In this way, the traditional architecture of the Ashanti, a pagan kingdom linked through commerce to the northernmost chain of cities of the Sahel, absorbed Islamic decorative elements, which exist there side by side with totemic motifs (*plates 443, 444*).

The roots of this architecture of conoid pilasters (*plates 474, 475*), of which perhaps the major expression is the mosque at Bobo-Julasso in Upper Volta, are to be found among the agricultural populations grouped in villages and farms that shelter an entire clan or family. Various types of construction, among them the granary (*plate 415*) and the altar (*plate 473*), are likely to have contributed to the formation of this language; it was adopted to support the enclosure walls in the quite elementary compounds of the Nabdam people in Ghana.[42] There is certainly some semantic connection here with the fact that the vertical constructional element, the pilaster, is known over a very vast region as typifying an anthill.

We may conclude that in the historically well-defined phase of reciprocal acculturation between village societies and the state and religious systems that tend to superpose themselves on such societies, architecture may develop a broadened repertory of building types, while maintaining such deep roots in its territory as to prevent it from losing ground to the dominant new culture. This is a phase that, in the course of modern colonization, has usually been of only fleeting duration because of the brutal suppression of the "alien" cultures by the colonizers. In this part of Africa, however, where the local kingdoms were able to resist because they had already achieved cultural and economic integration of village and city, that phase persisted until only a few decades ago.[43] Primitive architecture, in consequence, continued to develop in the service of the dominant local lineages, and though integrated for many centuries into the Islamic tradition, showed itself capable of pursuing without interruption an approach whose origins were rooted in the "internal" history of an indissoluble relationship between mythology and power.

# NOTES

*Titles of publications included in the bibliography are given here in condensed form with author's name and date of publication only, followed between parentheses by a capital letter referring to a specific section of the bibliography and, in some cases, also by a small letter indicating a subsection.*

## INTRODUCTION

1  For some of these influences, see OLIVER 1969 (A), pt. 1: "Attitudes in the Modern movement," pp. 16–21; and RYKWERT 1973 (A).

2  RUDOFSKY 1969 (A).

3  FORDE 1934 (A), a work notable for its historical orientation, observes, "How far that history is known will make all the difference to the degree of our understanding; but unless there is realization of the existence of that specific history, both of internal change and external contact in one or several specific environments, understanding cannot begin" (p. 466). Forde also rejects the concept of economic "stages" in the analysis of specific cultural ambits. "Peoples do not live at economic stages. They possess economies; and again we do not find single and exclusive economies but combinations of them" (p. 461).

4  As FORDE 1934 (A), p. 468, affirms, the simple techniques and those less bound up with the social complex are the ones that change most rapidly.

5  See, for example, DAVEY 1961 (A) and M. Collura, *Architettura del legno* (Palermo, 1968).

6  This problem, which is of the most vital importance today, is approached from different points of view, but with common agreement that it creates a need for a complete revision of the role of anthropology, in R. Jaulin, *La Paix blanche: Introduction à l'ethnocide* (Paris, 1970); N. Zitara, *Il proletariato esterno* (Milan, 1972); G. Leclerc, *Anthropologie et colonialisme* (Paris, 1972); and V. Lanternari, *Antropologia e imperialismo e altri saggi* (Turin, 1974), pp. 349–410.

7  H. Kühn, *Die Kunst der Primitiven* (Munich, 1923); BOAS 1927 (A); L. Adam, *Primitive Art* (Harmondsworth, 1940; 3d rev. ed., London, 1963); BIEBUYCK 1969 (A); FORGE 1973 (A).

8  FRASER 1968 (A), OLIVER 1969 (A), RAPOPORT 1969 (A).

9  FRASER 1968 (A), introduction, conclusion, indexes.

10  RAPOPORT 1969 (J-a).

11  In RAPOPORT n.d. (G), the author himself proposes numerous classifications relative to the use of territory and space. On the predominance of sociocultural factors and the concept of the relativity of the diverse elements, FORDE 1934 (A), pp. 6–7, is already quite explicit.

12  For the relationship between the "nonconstructed" and architecture, see C. Norberg-Schulz, *Intentions in Architecture* (Oslo and London, 1963).

13  GUIDONI 1968 (A).

14  LANTERNARI 1965 (A).

15  GUIDONI 1968 (A): "Il segno spaziale non è mai disgiunto da una forte carica semantica, che riguarda l'aggancio mitico, e quindi essenzialmente storico, alla realtà naturale . . . di cui l'interpretazione spaziale è un valido strumento ordinatore, sia al livello dell'inserimento nell'ambiente che al livello del riferimento cosmologico." Translator's note: The thought and its expression here are so extraordinarily dense, and of such exceptional complexity, that it seemed advisable to reproduce the original.

16  Here we have in mind especially LÉVI-STRAUSS 1958 (A), chap. 8; and LÉVI-STRAUSS, "Le Symbolisme cosmique dans la structure sociale et l'organisation cérémonielle de plusieurs populations nord et sud-américaines," in *Le Symbolisme cosmique des monuments religieux* 1957 (A).

17  This state of affairs is felicitously described in PÂQUES 1964 (M) as "a system belonging to the old African foundations . . . covered over by a thin Islamic crust."

18  LEBEUF 1961 (O-f).

19  We refer chiefly to the studies published during the past twenty years or so in the *Journal de la Société des Africanistes* by C. Dieterlen, G. Nicolas, A. Masson-Detourbet Lebeuf, C. Meillassoux, M. Izard, and V. Pâques. Fundamental for their methodology are PÂQUES 1964 (M) and LEBEUF 1969 (O-b), in which architecture is often viewed as a key factor in social relations, historical development, and ritual significances.

20  L. Morgan, *Ancient Society* (London, 1877); F. Engels, *Der Ursprung der Familie, des Privateigentums und des Staats* (1891; *The Origin of the Family, Private Property and the State,* in numerous English translations); MEILLASSOUX 1964 (N-c); TERRAY 1972 (A); M. Godelier, *Horizon, trajets marxistes en anthropologie* (Paris, 1973).

21  On the possibility of using the material of myth and spatial models in a historical sense, regarding physical structure as a necessary point of comparison in understanding the economic structure, see E. Guidoni, "Storia dell'urbanistica e società 'precapitalistiche'," in papers of the congress "La Storia dell'Architettura: Problemi di metodo e di didattica," Florence, May 16–18, 1974 (forthcoming). For the importance of territorial disposition, stressed by Morgan as far back as 1877, see EVANS-PRITCHARD 1940 (N) and the remarks in BALANDIER 1967 (A). Concerning the concept of space in relation to architecture, B. Zevi, "Architecture," in *Encyclopedia of World Art,* vol. 1, col. 649 remarks: "The modern definition of architecture as the art of space does not deny the findings of traditional interpretations, though it evaluates them simply as particular aspects of a single problem. Rather, it brings together all the phenomena of architecture and forms them into a unified, harmonious system. Political and social conditions, the wishes of the client, civil customs, religious aspirations, technical knowledge—all the influences respectively emphasized in cultural, psychological, symbolist, functionalist, and technicist interpretations—are presuppositions of the spatial program. Although such data are extrinsic material from the artistic point of view, they are of substantial importance in the genetic reconstruction of architectural practice."

22  Here we must stress how very important it is to work out research methods based on the broadest possible range of specialized studies, any of which might conceivably furnish proof of one or more potentially significant correlations adopted as working hypotheses, which in turn may be applicable to other research problems. For example, for the interlinkage of "capital" and territory in Inca civilization, see E. Guidoni and R. Magni, *Civiltà Andine* (Milan, 1972), pp. 126–38.

23  LÉVI-STRAUSS 1958 (A), chap. 8, reports the case of a dual interpretation, diametrical and concentric, of a Winnebago village, gleaned from informants belonging to its two "moieties."

24  FORDE 1934 (A), p. 6: "The spread of crafts and customs are but contributing factors, the movements of the raw materials, as it were, out of which human life is built up."

25  In the light of analyses carried out in other areas of African culture, the following "riddles" of the Kikuyu appear, for example, not as gratuitous associations of concepts but as fragments of the historical relationship between myth and architecture, now dissolved from their original contexts: "The white sheep of my father on which you

cannot count the ribs" is the granary hut; "a hut with seven windows" is the head; "I tried to cut down a tree but it was not possible" stands for a stream; "I found a hut without supporting pole" refers to the sky; "an enclosure for the livestock made only of posts of *muiri*" is the eyelashes; "an eagle sitting on three trees" is a pot. See V. Merlo Pick, *Ndai na gicandi, Kikuyu Enigmas—Enigmi Kikuyu* (Bologna, 1973).

26  GUIDONI 1974 (A).

27  B. Malinowski, *A Scientific Theory of Culture and Other Essays* (Chapel Hill, N. C., 1944), p. 136, insists that any discussion of symbolism divorced from its sociological context is futile, as is every affirmation that culture can arise without the simultaneous appearance of manmade articles and of techniques, organization, and symbolism. This is the most that can be conceded to functionalism. The symbolistic, gestaltist, prossemical, semiological, and typological formulations produced in such numbers in recent years are all open to dispute if not utilized in an instrumental context that is rigorously historical. On the deep-lying motives of the "personification" of the "higher community" (tribe and state) to which surpluses must be consigned, see K. Marx, *Pre-Capitalist Economic Formations,* trans. Jack Cohen, ed. E. J. Hobsbawm (New York, 1965) and Godelier, *Horizon, trajets marxistes (op. cit.),* introduction and "Parties mortes, idées vivantes dans la pensée de Marx sur les sociétés primitives: Marxisme et évolutionnisme," pp. 133–73. Regarding the relations between tribal figure and supreme being, one must keep in mind the role of the latter as producer of food; thus, R. Pettazzoni, *L'Essere supremo nelle religioni primitive* (Turin, 1957), pp. 121–22: "Just as in the primitive agricultural civilizations the supreme being is the earth mother because man's sustenance comes from the earth, just as in the pastoral civilizations the supreme being is the celestial father because it is from the sky that the rain comes that gives life and growth to the grass necessary for the grazing lands of the herds and for the existence of human beings, so too in the hunting civilization the supreme being is lord of the beasts because on him depends the capture of wild game and the outcome of the hunt, which has vital importance for man."

28  OLIVER 1969 (A), Pt. 1. For folk art in general, see G. Cocchiara, in *Encyclopedia of World Art,* vol. 5, cols. 458–66, where the parallelism with primitive art is denied, to support the argument that only "folk," or popular, art is the product of adult individualities and that to it alone can be applied the historical method. On the concept of primitive, see F. L. Hsu, "Rethinking the Concept 'Primitive'," *Current Anthropology* 5 (June, 1964): 169–78. FRASER 1966 (A), p. 113, n. 1, uses the term "primitive world" as a "conventional designation for the traditional societies of Africa, Southwest Asia, Oceania, and the New World that, until recently, had not been strongly influenced by the high cultures of Europe, Asia, or pre-Columbian America."

29  Regarding popular culture, the definition of Gramsci, founder of the Italian Communist Party, in *Letteratura e vita nazionale* (Turin, 1950), p. 215, is still pertinent: "[a] conception of the world and of life, in large measure implicit, of specific strata of society (*specific in time and in space* [italics mine]), in contraposition (this too for the most part implicit, mechanical, objective) to the conceptions of the 'official' world (or, in a broader sense, to the cultivated parts of the historically determined societies) that have followed one another in the course of the historical development." The contraposition is insisted on by A. M. Cirese, "L'antropologia culturale e lo studio delle tradizoni popolari intese come dislivelli interni di cultura delle civiltà superiori," in *De Homine,* nos. 17–18 (1967), pp. 239–47, and in his *Folklore e antropologia tra storicismo e marxismo* (Palermo, 1972). E. De Martino, *Naturalismo e storicismo in etnologia* (Bari, 1941), supports the historical approach.

30  This is how Cirese, *Folklore e antropologia (op. cit.),* p. 32, defines the term "people" (*popolo*): "If one rejects all metahistorical conceptions, the notion of 'people' can preserve a significance only if it is thought of as a summary designation of the complex of

classes, groups, subgroups, individuals, who in the course of history have been or are vehicles of the forms and cultural contents that constitute the imbalances." In the context of our subject, to Cirese's "imbalance" (*dislivello*) (corresponding to "popular") must be added "otherness" (*alterità*) (corresponding to "primitive"). Colonialism tends to transform the otherness into imbalance and to tolerate otherness only with the connotation of imbalance, of something on a lower level.

31  LEBEUF 1969 (O-b), p. 8: "We resolutely reject the method which consists of detaching from a culture one or more elements so as to establish points of similarity and of going on to conclude that there are influences when no analysis has been made of the institutions in which they are comprised. The analogy of certain cultural traits does not entitle us to presume anything about the particular civilization in which they are observed, and the accumulation of arbitrarily isolated facts gives rise to more problems than it throws light on when it comes to understanding a system."

32  GUIDONI 1968 (A).

## CHAPTER ONE

1  For the Mbuti Pygmies, see C. Turnbull, *The Forest People* (London, 1961); "The Mbuti Pygmies: an Ethnographic Survey," *Anthropological Papers of the American Museum of Natural History* 50, pt. 3 (1965): 137–282; FRASER 1968 (A), pp. 11–13; and COON 1971 (A). Not considered here are the ties that those hunting groups using the bow and arrow especially have long established with agricultural communities.

2  Turnbull, *Forest People (op. cit.),* p. 194, ground plans. In net hunting, an activity that involves all able-bodied members of the group, the hunters move together in a ringlike formation analogous to that of their encampments. According to COON 1971 (A), pp. 99–100: "The nets are about four feet wide and vary from one hundred to three hundred feet in length. Between seven and thirty such nets are set up in a semicircle, tied to bushes and creepers, and each man conceals himself behind his net. As a rule the older men are stationed in the center and the younger men on the flanks, and brothers like to be next to each other."

3  For the Semang of the Malay Peninsula, see FORDE 1934 (A), pp. 11–17.

4  An analogous example of the private ownership of single trees is found in Queensland, Australia. The *bunya-bunya (Araucaria bidwilli)* bear fruit every three years, and their proximity and abundance make it possible for several hundred persons to settle down in one place for a number of months (COON 1971 [A], p. 168).

5  For the Bushmen of South Africa, see FRASER 1968 (A), pp. 15–17, and MARSHALL 1960 (Q).

6  In the middle of the 19th century, Sir Francis Galton described one of these enclosures in his *Narrative of an Explorer in Tropical South Africa* (London, 1853), p. 160 (cited in COON 1971 [A]). "We passed a magnificent set of pitfalls which the Bushmen who live about these hills had made. The whole breadth of the valley was staked and bushed across. At intervals the fence was broken, and there deep pitfalls were made. . . . When a herd of animals was seen among the hills, the Bushmen drove them through this valley up to the fence; this was too high for them to jump, so that they were obliged to make for the gaps, and there they tumbled into the pitfalls." Further details on this system of hunting are given by Coon in his discussion of the Blackfoot Indians.

7  RAPOPORT n.d. (G), p. 9: "Aborigines structure their *existing* physical landscape

mentally, mythically and symbolically without building it." Even if one refuses to consider as architecture such temporary works as ceremonial camps, carving in trees, rock paintings, and so forth, which in their way do modify the environment, an architectonic quality in the narrow sense of the word must be conceded at least to aboriginal alignments of stones. See, for example, I. McBryde, "An Unusual Series of Stone Arrangements near the Serpentine Bay, Ebor District, New South Wales," *Oceania* 34, no. 2 (1963): 137–46 (bibliography to date on pp. 145–46).

8  Archaeological investigations indicate the Australian aborigines have experienced unusually constant living conditions through the millennia. See R. A. Gould, "Living Archaeology: The Ngaljara of Western Australia," *Southwestern Journal of Archaeology* 24, no. 2 (1969): 101–12. See also GOULD 1971 (G): The author points out that at Puntutjarpa, in the territory of the Ngatatjara, excavations have demonstrated the continuous presence of man for ten thousand years.

9  ELIADE 1972 (G), pp. 172 ff. (French edition), argues for the diachronical nature of the religious manifestations, which often, and especially in recent times, have had extremely rapid diffusion; indeed, he insists that there is no civilization without a history, without transformations, and an evolution brought about by influences from outside (p. 76, French edition). See also STANNER 1964 (G), a work extremely rich in references to the cosmological, symbolic, and spatial aspects of religion among the primitive Australians.

10  ELIADE 1972 (G), pp. 37–52 (French edition).

11  ELKIN 1964 (G), p. 166, speaks of a "personalization" of nature.

12  W. Arndt, "The Australian Evolution of the Wandjinas from Rainclouds," *Oceania* 34, no. 3 (1964): 161–69. Arndt hypothesizes a stylistic, geometrical, symbolic derivation from the naturalistic image on the basis of comparisons with other cultural environments; see especially fig. 2, p. 168.

13  W. Arndt, "The Dreaming of Kunukban," *Oceania* 35, no. 4 (1965): 241–59.

14  *Ibid.,* figs. 2 and 3 of plate 2, p. 248. For the "scientific" aspect of classificatory totemism, see ELKIN 1964 (G), p. 186.

15  ELKIN 1953 (G), p. 68; with this also *gina* (foot) and *mil* (eye). The statistics for place names reveal not only a predominance of names of plants and animals but also a frequency of names having to do with parts of the human body (head, nose, neck, and so on). The names of campsites are often derived from social life; for example, Yee Warra means "the place of assembly for sport" and Urandagie means "to meet and sit down." See B. J. S. Ryan, "Some Aboriginal Place Names in the Mid-North Coast of New South Wales," *Oceania* 34, no. 4 (1964): 278–307, especially 284.

16  In some cases, the links with the outside are broken off. Thus, among the Aljawara all the mythical itineraries it has been possible to identify—paths of the kangaroo, of the fire, of the honey-bearing ants, of the cockatoos, of the dingo, of the lizards, and places sacred to honey and to the emu—are entirely inside the territory. See C. L. Yallop, "The Aljawara and Their Territory," *Oceania* 39, no. 3 (1969): 187–97.

17  ELKIN 1953 (G), pp. 176–79 and *passim.*

18  *Ibid.,* p. 179.

19  For the Walbiri, see M. Meggitt, *Desert People: A Study of the Walbiri Aborigines of Central Australia* (Sydney, 1962). See also MUNN 1973 (G), and "Gadjari Among the Walbiri Aborigines of Central Australia," *Oceania* 36, no. 3 (1966): 173–213; 36, no. 4 (1966): 283–315; 37, no. 1 (1966): 22–48; 37, no. 2 (1966): 124–47.

20  Concerning the intertribal "network of roads" in Tasmania linking particularly the places from which stone and ocher were obtained, see COON 1971 (A), pp. 172, 198.

21  RAPOPORT n.d. (G), p. 3.

22  SPENCER and GILLEN 1904 (G), p. 388; E. De Martino, "Angoscia territoriale e riscatto culturale nel mito Achilpa delle origini," *Studi e Materiali di Storia delle Religioni* 23 (1952): 52–66; ELIADE 1972 (G), pp. 60–62 (French edition).

23  ELKIN 1953 (G), p. 265.

24  ELIADE 1972 (G), pp. 42–43 (French edition).

25  *Ibid.,* pp. 77 ff.

26  R. H. Matthews, "The Bora or Initiation Ceremonies of the Kamilaroi Tribe," *Journal of the Royal Anthropological Institute of Great Britain and Ireland* 24 (1895): 411–27, summarized in ELIADE 1972 (G), pp. 92–93 (French edition). See also the circumcision ceremony of the Djunggan among the Waiwilak of Arnhem Land as summarized in COON 1971 (A), pp. 351–59, fig. 31, on the basis of WARNER 1937 (G). The ceremonial terrain reproduces the snake in an elongated triangle that terminates in a circular "sacred house."

27  MUNN 1973 (G), figs. 6a and b, plate 5, pp. 208–10, and see also fig. 4.

28  *Ibid.,* pp. 211–15.

29  C. G. von Brandenstein, "The Symbolism of the North-Western Australian Zig-zag Design," *Oceania* 42, no. 3 (1971): 223–38.

30  R. Piddington, "A Note on Karadjeri Local Organization," *Oceania* 41, no. 4 (1971): 239–43, and drawing on p. 241.

31  For the Eskimos, see FORDE 1934 (A), pp. 107–28, based on the classic works of Boas, Mathiassen, and Wissler. For their maps and other representations of the landscape, see HOFFMAN 1897 (B-a).

32  LÉVI-STRAUSS 1948 (K), pp. 46–50, figs. 12–14. The plan reproduced in that book is curved, with an isolated "internal" focal point. Lévi-Strauss is rightly reluctant to admit the absence of rules of residence (p. 49) and is inclined to think such an assumption may be attributed to inadequate investigation.

33  *Ibid.,* pp. 127–28.

34  BIOCCA 1969 (K), pp. 36–39. For the subdivision of the villages, see pp. 78–79.

35  *Ibid.,* p. 39: "The particular form of the large constructions that form the perimeter, with roofs sloping to one side and no roof covering the center, makes it very easy to enlarge and reduce the *chapuno* in response to immediate needs and without compromising the whole construction; even very large groups can assemble there, which is doubtless of enormous importance for defense. At the same time, the central plaza surrounded by hearths guarantees that nothing can happen without everyone's knowing it and responding accordingly at once." For the solution to constructing a unified truncated cone, see especially figs. 45, 46.

36   C. Wissler, "The Influence of the Horse in the Development of Plains Culture," *American Anthropologist* 16 (1914): 1–24, and LAUBIN 1957 (J-c).

37   For the Blackfoot, see FORDE 1934 (J-c), a synthesis based on studies of C. Wissler.

38   For the Cheyenne, see FRASER 1968 (J-c), pp. 19–22, which includes relevant bibliography.

39   For the information that follows and for the agricultural basis of the organization of the settlements, see C. Korvin Krasinski, *Mikrokosmos und Makrokosmos in religionsgeschichtlicher Sicht* (Düsseldorf, 1960), and MÜLLER 1956 (J-c) and 1970 (J-c).

40   Korvin Krasinski, *Mikrokosmos und Makrokosmos (op. cit.),* pp. 210–11.

41   For the Kazakhs, see FORDE 1934 (C), "The Kazak . . . ," pp. 328–44, and TOKAREV 1958 (B).

42   For the Ruwala, see FORDE 1934 (C), "The Ruwala Badawin . . . ," pp. 308–27, based chiefly on the studies of A. Musil published between 1927 and 1938, including MUSIL 1928 (C).

43   FORDE 1934 (C), "The Ruwala Badawin . . . ," p. 317: "The Ruwala scorn to camp in a circle like the weaker Badawin, who thus endeavour to protect their stock by herding them at night inside this compound of tents."

44   For the Tsonga village, see A. Jorge Dias, in *Ethnologie régionale,* vol. 1, 1972 (A), pp. 950–53, and fig. 6, p. 951.

45   For the Masai, see FORDE 1934 (P), pp. 287–304.

46   See BIERMANN 1971 (Q), pp. 96–105.

47   *Ibid.,* pp. 98–99.

48   *Ibid.,* p. 100.

49   True buildings are erected for the initiation ceremonies of the Yaghan fishermen of Tierra del Fuego: a long oval hut with two entrances placed longitudinally, formerly large enough to accommodate eighty or more persons during the "rite of the great hut," and a conical log structure used for the "rite of the men's house." Both of these were oriented carefully to the encampment of dome-shaped huts; see COON 1971 (A), pp. 361–68.

50   *Ibid.,* pp. 176–80, fig. 29 (division of the kangaroo), and pp. 125–26, fig. 21 (division of the whale).

51   GUIDONI 1974 (A). Further discussion in Chapter 4, below.

## CHAPTER TWO

1   We are referring here to a particular organization of production, society, and architecture that, within certain limits, can be considered representative of the constructional activity of each group under consideration. A detailed analysis of the differences between longhouse, multifamily house, and collective house would have to take specific social stratification and local developments into account and would therefore go beyond the scope of this survey. However, it is our intention to discuss not merely a type of building but a social and architectural system that emerges out of the totality of economic and architectural activities.

2   A. Pigafetta, *Il primo viaggio intorno al mondo* (1519; Milan, 1929, pp. 83–84).

3   H. von Staden, *Wahrhaftige Historia* (Marburg, 1557; Italian translation, Milan, 1970).

4   *Ibid.,* pp. 173–74 (Italian translation).

5   Classically, this dislocation will result in one family settled in each corner of the house. With the minimum number fixed, other nuclei can be added by lengthening the side walls. This arrangement has been observed not only among numerous Siberian populations but also among the American Northwest Coast Indians (see Chapter 3).

6   For the Desana, see REICHEL-DOLMATOFF 1968 (K).

7   For the symbolism of the *maloca,* see *ibid.* (French edition, pp. 133–39), and for the references to anthropomorphism, see GUIDONI 1974 (A).

8   REICHEL-DOLMATOFF 1968 (K) (French edition, pp. 136–37).

9   "Recherches ethnographiques dans les bassins des Rios Caqueta et Putumayo (Amazonie Colombienne)," *Journal de la Société des Américanistes* 58 (1969).

10   C. Korvin Krasinski, *Mikrokosmos und Makrokosmos in religionsgeschichtlicher Sicht* (Düsseldorf, 1960), pp. 202–3.

11   *Ibid.,* pp. 214–16.

12   MILES 1964 (E-b). This article gives tabular information on the habitations of the Iban, Dayak, Kenyak, Kayan, Tagal-Murut, and Kelabit on p. 49.

13   According to the sources, an animal would have been required for every pillar. MILES 1964 (E-b), pp. 55–56, stresses how rarely cattle were sacrificed (as a rule, only on the occasion of the funerary *pesta tiwah* rite).

14   MILES 1964 (E-b), pp. 56–57: "One was originally part of the joint estate of Antang's extended family; the other was part of the joint estate of Ideng's extended family. The foyer was part of the joint estate of the extended family of Antang, who financed its construction. Thus the households of this Ngadju longhouse represent two corporate groups, each with a joint estate."

15   The difficulty of organizing the construction work and of assembling a large group of men and necessary food explains the retarded spread of the longhouse as a type; it persists through inertia in areas where it represents the normal expression of the relationships of production.

16   For the Pueblo cultures, see FORDE 1931, 1931, 1934; RAPOPORT 1969, with bibliography on pp. 78, 79; SEBAG 1971; WHORF 1953; MINDELEFF 1891 (all J-a). For the relationships between settlements and the cultivated fields belonging to the clans, see FORDE 1934 (J-a), figs. 74, 78.

17   SEBAG 1971 (J-a), table on p. 90, fig. on p. 131.

18   FORDE 1934 (J-a), schema of the landscape on p. 227.

19  SEBAG 1971 (J-a), schema, p. 84.

20  GUIART 1951 (H-c), 1952 (H-c), 1963 (F), and 1972 (H-c).

21  GUIART 1963 (F), p. 108.

22  See DEACON 1934 (H-c), which has about a hundred schematic drawings. These are figures, more or less secret, whose subject derives from a code of symbols that includes all the potentially spatial aspects of the human and natural world. From the architectural point of view, it is important that they almost always reproduce the "ground plan" of the subject, whether it be a copulating human couple, an animal (often the tortoise), or a drop of water falling on a stone. A different but comparable code is reflected in the string figures of New Guinea, for which see H. Maude and C. H. Wedgwood, "String Figures from Northern New Guinea," *Oceania* 37, no. 3 (1967): 202–29; note especially the rectangular plan of the "big house," fig. 8 on p. 210.

23  GUIART 1972 (H-c), especially pp. 1156–58, planimetric schema on p. 1157.

24  J. Layard, *Stone Men of Malekula: The Small Island of Vao* (London, 1942); GUIART 1963 (F), p. 52, and 1972 (H-c), pp. 1156 ff.

25  GUIART 1972 (H-c), p. 1167.

26  See especially HATANAKA and BRAGGE 1973 (H-a); it has schematic plans of the houses of the Sayolof and the Yarumui. For the valley of the Whagi, see VILLEMINOT 1966 (H-a), pp. 99–100, 108. For the Telefolmin, *ibid.*, pp. 200–205, and CRANSTONE 1971 (H-a).

27  For the Abelam, see P. Kaberry, "The Abelam Tribe, Sepik District, New Guinea: A Preliminary Report," *Oceania* 11, nos. 3, 4 (1941): 233–58, 345–67; WHITEMAN 1965 (H-a), pp. 102–20; VILLEMINOT 1966 (H-a), pp. 293–310; and FORGE 1973 (H-a), pp. 169–92.

28  VILLEMINOT 1966 (H-a), p. 296.

29  For this description, *ibid.*, pp. 296–300.

30  FORGE 1973 (H-a), fig. 1, p. 176, and *passim*.

31  For New Caledonia, see LEENHARDT 1930 and 1937 (both H-b), and for its architecture, GUIART 1963 (F), pp. 252–54.

32  Fragments of bamboo incised with scenes of village life appear in *Ethnologie régionale*, vol. 1 1972 (A), fig. 3 on p. 1108, fig. 8 on p. 1121; and in GUIART 1963 (F), fig. 88.

33  DOURNES 1971 (D).

34  *Ibid.*, fig. 21, p. 304.

35  For information concerning the structure of the villages of Nias and for comparisons with other Indonesian regions, we are indebted to FRASER 1968 (A), pp. 35–40, figs. 36–45.


CHAPTER THREE

1  LANTERNARI 1959 (F), p. 454.

2  BUCK 1938 (I), p. 267. See also the version of the legend of Maui in LANTERNARI 1959 (F), pp. 472–86.

3  BUCK 1938 (I), p. 56.

4  LANTERNARI 1959 (F), p. 378.

5  G. Puglisi, *Navigatori senza bussola* (Rome, 1971), pp. 45–55.

6  This small island has been the focus of the most penetrating efforts at interpretation of the Polynesian conception of space, beginning with the fundamental contributions of FIRTH 1957 (I-e) and the same author's *History and Tradition of Tikopia* (Wellington, 1961). Since then there have been, notably, EYDE 1969 and PARK 1973 (both I-e).

7  In addition to the many specific and general contributions to the understanding of Polynesian and Micronesian nautical science, among which see especially DRÖBER 1903 (A), there have been some very interesting experiments in traveling on indications by experts in the traditional techniques of navigation: see P. S. SMITH, "Notes on the Geographical Knowledge of the Polynesians," in *Australian Association for the Advancement of Science* 1, (1891), pp. 280–310, and A. Sharp, *Ancient Voyages in Polynesia* (Los Angeles, 1964; 1st ed., 1956). The thesis that the islands were casually discovered is more and more definitively being disproved by work such as GOLSON 1963 (I). More recent studies have demonstrated the extreme complexity and precision of Polynesian navigational systems: see D. Lewis, "Stars of the Sea Road," *Journal of the Polynesian Society* 75, no. 1 (1966): 84–94, and S. H. Riesenberg, "The Organization of Navigational Knowledge on Puluwat," *Journal of the Polynesian Society* 81, no. 1 (1972): 19–56. The diagrams of routes used by the inhabitants of Puluwat, an island of the central Carolines, are identified with large fish made up of a series of squares superimposed according to the diagonals. On the divine origin of the nautical science on the Micronesian island of Ifaluk, see LANTERNARI 1959 (F), p. 543.

8  Puglisi, *Navigatori* (*op. cit.*), pp. 48–50, fig. on p. 49; and GOLSON 1963, (I), pp. 84–88.

9  SAHLINS 1958 (I). See also R. Williamson, *Religion and Social Organization in Polynesia* (London, 1937), and B. Finney, *Polynesian Peasants and Proletarians* (Wellington, 1965), about the Society Islands. A recent synthesis is B. Danielsson, "La Polynésie," in *Ethnologie régionale* vol. 1 1972 (A), pp. 1126–1329. Note that the atolls and the volcanic islands often had different divinities; see BUCK 1938 (I), p. 128.

10  For information on the social stratification, we are particularly indebted to LANTERNARI 1959 (F).

11  *Ibid.*, pp. 362 and 496.

12  From the very considerable bibliography on the *marae* we single out EMORY 1970 (I).

13  BUCK 1938 (I), p. 211.

14  The preceding description is taken from BUCK 1938 (I), pp. 176–77.

15  LANTERNARI 1959 (F), p. 363: "The *nanga* (literally 'beds') are quadrangular stone enclosures found on the island of Viti Levu, especially in the central region (with offshoots toward the west and the south) inhabited by the Nujamalo, Nujakoro, Nujaloa tribes and others. The *nanga* is oriented from east to west and divided laterally into two or three sections; at the corners inside are usually found four heaps of stones ('altars') in pyramidal form."

16 *Ibid.*, p. 511.

17 Buck 1938 (I), pp. 295–97.

18 *Ibid.*, p. 296.

19 *Ibid.*, p. 266.

20 For the architecture and architectural sculpture of the Maori, see especially Hamilton 1896–1901, chap. 2 (1897), pp. 69–171; Firth 1925; and Buck 1921 (all I-a). On New Zealand society in general, see Buck 1949 (I-a).

21 For the history and detailed significance of one of these "public" edifices, see Phillips 1970 (I-a). The house under discussion, inaugurated in 1906 with the traditional rite, was renovated in the 1930s.

22 *Ibid.*, p. 83: The name of the house was that attributed to the dwelling of Maui (*whare whakairo*) situated in the twelfth heaven and could therefore be used only by a chief considered to be among the direct descendants of Maui.

23 T. Barrow, in Bühler, Barrow, and Mountford 1962 (F), p. 199.

24 Lanternari 1959 (F), p. 480: The *teko-teko* is the highest element, the one closest to the sky (as well as to the earth) in the cosmogonic myths recounting how the house was fished up out of the sea: When the hook of Maui was descending along the carved beams to bury itself finally in the threshold, the first thing it touched was the *teko-teko*.

25 T. Barrow, in Bühler, Barrow, and Mountford 1962 (F), p. 196.

26 *Ibid.*, p. 204.

27 The nomenclature is that reported in Mead 1967 (I-a), chap. 8, diagram on p. 22.

28 T. Barrow, in Bühler, Barrow, and Mountford 1962 (F), p. 202 and plate on p. 205.

29 Hamilton 1896–1901 (I-a), p. 80, describes the preparation of the material for building a house. "A *whare* consisted of a framework of timber, carefully notched, and lashed together with flax, the wall spaces being filled in with screens made chiefly of *kakaho*, the reeds of the *toetoe* plant (*Arundo conspicua*), the whole being covered with bundles of *raupo* (*Typha angustifolia*), bound on with strips of flax (*Phormium tenax*). For months, and perhaps years, the materials would be sought for, collected, and prepared. Suitable timbers would be slowly and laboriously dressed down to the required size by the application of fire and stone tools. The timber most desired for building purposes was that which had been brought down by floods and then buried for years in the bed of the river, and in course of time had lost its sap wood and become well seasoned. . . . The *kakaho*, or reeds, the flower stalks of the Arundo (*toetoe*), had to be cut at the proper season, if possible from a forest locality, and carefully dried. Huge stores of the leaves of the Typha or bulrush (*Raupo*) would be required for the sides and the roof of the house, together with quantities of the invaluable Phormium or *Muka*, the so-called New Zealand flax. In the northern districts, the wiry creeping fern (*Lygodium scandens*) *Mange-mange* was utilized to fasten down the outside layers of thatch on the roof; in other districts, plaited ropes of flax, or a light lattice of thin *manuka* rods. If suitable timber could not otherwise be obtained, it was necessary to fell some huge totara or other pine, and to do this, fire and the stone axes (*toki*) had to be used. The branches were removed, and the trunk then split with wedges made of hard wood."

30 From the difficulties encountered in chopping down the trunks needed for Polynesian buildings and canoes was born a series of rules, myths, and taboos. Buck 1938 (I), p. 113, adduces an example of these from the tale told on Rarotonga of the building of the canoe of Te Ara-tanga-nuku: The tree chopped down without following the rules was brought back to life again by the god Tangaroa, and only after the reconsecration of the adze could it be chopped down once and for all and transported to the place where a "spirit carpenter" with eight assistants carved it into a canoe in a single night.

31 T. Barrow, in Bühler, Barrow, and Mountford 1962 (F), p. 194.

32 Buck 1938 (I), p. 128.

33 Hamilton 1896–1901 (I-a), p. 81: The units of measurement were, on the east coast, the *maro*, a length of about 5 feet 9 1/2 inches, and on the west coast, the *takoto*, "the length from the foot to the hand extended beyond the head as the measurer lay at full length on the ground."

34 On the tracing of the plan of a house, *ibid.*: "The lines for the two ends, known as *roro*, the front, and *tuarongo*, the back, were first laid down, and the building squared by measuring the diagonals *hauroki*. Finally, for some occult reason, the corner on the right-hand side of the *roro*, looking into the house, was displaced a very slight distance towards the *tuarongo*, or back."

35 Forde 1934 (J-b), pp. 69–95; Boas 1955 (A), pp. 183–298; Drucker 1951 and 1955 (both J-b); Fraser 1968 (J-b), pp. 23–62, based in part on J. Vastokas, "Architecture of the Northwest Coast Indians of America" (Ph. D. dissertation, Columbia University, 1966); and Coon 1971 (A), pp. 31–37.

36 Boas 1955 (A), *passim*.

37 Coon 1971 (A), pp. 35–37 and fig. 9.

38 *Ibid.*, p. 35.

39 Pettazzoni 1948–63 (A), vol. 3 (*America Settentrionale*, 1953), p. 52.

40 See the example in Boas 1955 (A), pp. 209–212, fig. 199.

41 Against the naively "capitalistic" interpretation of the potlatch, which along with architecture should be considered as an instrument for reestablishing social equilibrium, see C. Meillassoux, "Ostentation, destruction, reproduction," in *Economies et Sociétés* 2, no. 4 (1968).

CHAPTER FOUR

1 M. Griaule, "Africa," in *L'Arte e l'Uomo*, vol. 1 (Turin, 1959), pp. 87–88.

2 Pâques 1964 (M), pp. 175–79.

3 For information concerning the architecture of the Fali and its interpretation, we are indebted to Lebeuf 1961 (O-f). For certain aspects of its symbolic significance, see Guidoni 1974 (A), where the Fali are discussed in parallel comparison with other agricultural populations.

4   Concerning the granaries, see LEBEUF 1961 (O-f), *passim.*

5   GRIAULE 1938 (O-a), chap. 1, and fig. 15 on p. 44. See also PALAU MARTI 1957 (O-a).

6   GRIAULE 1938 (O-a), pp. 25–39 and 45.

7   Concerning the *toguna,* see examples in GRIAULE 1938 (O-a), pp. 18–20, fig. 9 on p. 19; for the symbolism, see GRIAULE 1965, (O-a), pp. 97–98.

8   GRIAULE 1938 (O-a), pp. 743–62.

9   *Ibid.,* pp. 756–58, figs. 255, 256.

10   Concerning the sanctuary, see GRIAULE 1965 (O-a), pp. 101–14.

11   Concerning masks, see GRIAULE 1938 (O-a), pp. 419–604, and concerning paintings, pp. 618–98.

12   Besides the cited studies by M. Griaule, and especially 1938 (O-a), pp. 14–18, figs. 5–8, see CALAME-GRIAULE 1955 and N'DIAYE 1972 (both O-a).

13   GRIAULE 1965 (O-a), pp. 94–95.

14   N'DIAYE 1972 (O-a), *passim.*

15   GRIAULE 1965 (O-a) and N'DIAYE 1972 (O-a).

16   Concerning the doors and latches, see CALAME-GRIAULE 1955 (O-a).

17   GRIAULE 1965 (O-a), p. 50.

18   On the precolonial urban terminology of the "Sudanese" area, see B. Kamian, "L'Afrique Occidentale pré-coloniale et le fait urbain," *Présence Africaine* 22 (1958): 76–80.

19   F. Pigafetta, *Relatione del Reame di Congo et delle circonvicine contrade* (Rome, 1591), bk. 2, chap. 1.

20   For the Nigerian area, see E. W. Bouill, *The Golden Trade of the Moors* (Oxford, 1958; 2d ed., 1968) and MABOGUNJE 1968 (O-e), in both of which the emphasis is on commerce. Both also recognize the urban quality of the centers. See also MORTON-WILLIAMS 1972 (O).

21   We are in agreement with the opinion of RANDLES 1972 (L), p. 895: "We would hesitantly suggest that all three [the centers of São Salvador, Musumba, and Zimbabwe] may be called 'towns,' but more because they were centres of political control that attracted settlement through the advantages offered of personal security and hopes for political advancement, rather than as economic centres of specialization and of division of labour."

22   MARGARIDO 1970 (P).

23   Concerning these problems, see GUIDONI 1974 (A).

24   PALAU MARTI 1964 (O-e), to which we are indebted for the material that follows.

25   *Ibid.,* p. 54 and fig. on p. 45.

26   G. Nicolas, "Fondements magico-religieux du pouvoir politique au sein de la principauté hausa du Gobir," *Journal de la Société des Africanistes* 39, no 11 (1969): 199–231, plan on p. 227.

27   MONTEIL 1932 (O-a), p. 137: "For the choice of the new dwelling, again they have recourse to the soothsayer. By means of signs traced on the sand, the soothsayer divines and designates the propitious site; at that site he indicates the one or several dwellings of the one or more local spirits. Often the *genius loci* inhabits a tree that will thenceforth be held sacred by the newcomers; they consider it, according to the native expression, the host who offers them hospitality."

28   PÂQUES 1967 (O-b), *passim.*

29   LEBEUF 1969 (O-b), p. 57.

30   *Ibid.,* pp. 56–64, figs. 4 and 5.

31   W. Bosman, *A New and Accurate Description of the Coast of Guina,* 2d ed. (London, 1721).

32   An important contribution to our knowledge of the process of formation of this architectural decoration, taking the traditional body of decorative motifs as point of departure, is now available in WENZEL 1972 (M), a highly detailed, critical presentation of the "popular" art that flowered in the 20th century in the Nubian villages that were finally submerged by the waters of the Aswan Dam in 1964.

33   MONTEIL 1932 (O-a), pp. 184–97.

34   PÂQUES 1964 (M), pp. 181–289.

35   In her study of 1964, Pâques quite rightly adopts the term "primitive," since symbolic thought is discovered there under the unifying Islamic interpretation, though this, as we have seen, she considers no more than a "thin crust."

36   R. Caillé, *Journal d'un voyage à Tomboctou et à Jenné dans l'Afrique Centrale* (Brussels and London), 1830.

37   The descriptions that follow and the symbolic interpretation are drawn from PÂQUES 1964 (M). See this work especially for fig. 47 on pp. 241–42 and fig. 48 on p. 259.

38   The mosque of Jenné was destroyed in 1830 by Sheik Amadou but rebuilt in 1906–7; see S. M. Cissoko, *Histoire de l'Afrique Occidentale, Moyen-âge et temps modernes, VIIe siècle–1850* (Paris, 1966), pp. 71 (with reconstruction of the 14th-century edifice), 110.

39   *Ibid.,* fig. 9 and pp. 113 and 275.

40   *Ibid.,* fig. on p. 168.

41   DEFFONTAINES 1948 (A) illustrates certain Islamic houses of prayer in the zone west of Lake Chad (figs. on pp. 84, 85). These are small mosques (as for example that of N'Guigmi) or *m'salah,* places of prayer that are enclosed but not roofed over (as the

(*m'salah* of Borrua) and often have rectagular ground plans with apses that can be interpreted anthropomorphically.

42  ARCHER 1971 (O-d), figs. on p. 49.

43  The recent decadence of the architectural tradition in West Africa may be compared with what took place in the architecture of the Northwest Coast American Indians and the Maori, which flowered only after the initiation of foreign commerce and the introduction of new tools, and which became a product of imbalance—influenced in a variety of ways by the white man—only in the second half of the 19th century, after the colonial occupation of those territories had become irreversible.

APPENDIX: PRIMITIVE PEOPLES AND THEIR ARCHITECTURE / SELECTED BIBLIOGRAPHY / INDEX / LIST OF PLATES / PHOTOGRAPH CREDITS

## ARCTIC AND SUBARCTIC REGIONS

### LAPPS

Seminomadic reindeer herders, formerly an exclusively hunting and fishing people, in the European arctic regions of Sweden, Norway, Finland, and the Kola Peninsula of the Soviet Union, their principal habitation is a tent-hut, which they use in the summer season and during their nomadic peregrinations. It exists in two main types: the *kohti*, in the form of a full or truncated cone on a round plan, and the *goatte*, a cone with an arched internal framework on an elliptical plan. The first type has a diameter of about thirteen feet and a frame consisting of a forked upright on which rest peri-metric crosspieces, with a smoke vent at the top for the hearth, which is set up in the center of the tent-hut behind the larder, opposite the entrance. The internal structure of the *goatte* is based on two parallel wooden arches formed from four poles that are bent and brought together and then connected by three stakes, with other poles set against them. The tent is covered with wool or other cloth or reindeer skins, and birch branches are strewn over the ground to make a flooring. Another type of *goatte*, used for winter quarters or as a storehouse, has a framework of two intersecting pairs of arches whose upper parts are held at a fixed distance by two crosspieces and smaller poles that lean against the whole obliquely. Here there is a double covering, with a layer of bark plastered over on the outside by a layer of turf, which acts as insulation. The entrance is closed by a wooden door. Seen from outside, this construction on a squarish ground plan takes the shape of a truncated pyramid. In the forest regions, winter huts are built of logs, with low walls and a truncated-pyramidal, pitched roof, again with an opening at the top as vent. For stor-ing provisions, a small wooden hut is set up on a post (*njalla*) and is reached by steps cut in a log used as ladder.
*Plates 104–112*

### KHANTS (OSTYAKS), MANSES (VOGULS)

Fishing and hunting peoples in the northern valleys of the Urals and the basin of the Ob River in Siberia (Soviet Union), the Khants used to inhabit a type of hut sunk into the ground to a depth of about $1^1/_2$ feet, with pyramidal roof, door on one side, and interior fireplace. More original, however, is the *kot*, a conical tent-hut with supporting skeleton made up of a series of tripods holding a ring of horizontal beams on which rests a depressed conical roof often reinforced by sup-plementary stakes. The tent is covered in hides, which are tightly cinched by strong horizontal ligatures. During the winter, the *kot* is to all intents and purposes a semiunderground hut since snow is piled up around the cylindrical base to help keep in the heat, and the wooden door is shifted to the roof. In older types, blankets were hung around an area in the interior to make a well-insulated room heated by oil lamps.

### KET

The Ket are hunters and fishermen in the lower and middle basin of the Yenisei River in western Siberia (Soviet Union). The winter house is half-buried to a depth of about five feet. The summer tent, conical in shape, is covered by strips of birch bark softened in boiling water and stitched together.

### NENCHES

Nomadic reindeer breeders of Samoyed stock, the Nen-ches live in the area between the Mezen River in northern Russia and the Yenisei in western Siberia (Soviet Union). The traditional dwelling is a conical tent of large dimensions (up to thirty feet in diameter) similar to that used by the Tungusic-speaking groups. The framework of slender poles is covered with skins in winter, with birch bark in summer. There is a place for the fire in the center of the interior.

### YAKUTS

Herders of eastern Siberia in the basin of the Lena River (Soviet Union), the Yakuts have a traditional dwelling, the *balagan*, that is a complex quadrangular construc-tion with walls leaning into the interior and a flat or slightly convex roof, so that the exterior appearance is of a truncated four-sided pyramid. Structurally, there are four (or eight) corner posts connected at the top by crossbeams. The walls are made of logs and are plas-tered over first with brushwood, clay, and dung, and then with an outer insulating layer of earth, in summer, and of hard-packed snow in winter. The entrance is usually on the east side of the cabin, and in the south and west walls there are windows that, in summer, are cov-ered with animal bladders or horsehair, in winter, with sheets of ice. Often at the north side of the cabin there is an outside annex for the animals. Along the walls in the interior runs a raised wooden shelf divided into compartments for the members of the family and guests. To the right of the entrance is the stove in a rectangular clay box complete with chimney. In the northern areas, a cone-shaped habitation used to be made of slender poles covered with turf; in the south, a lighter type with birch-bark covering sometimes served as second home during the summer.

### CHUKCHEES

These people are reindeer herders located at the extreme northeastern tip of Siberia (Soviet Union). The seden-tary fishing population along the northern coasts used to build a type of half-underground hut out of the ribs and jawbones of whales, as do some Eskimo groups. The habitation of the nomads is quite different: a com-plex two-coned tent consisting of two concentric struc-tures. The inner cone is higher and supports the highest part of the roof, while the outer structure is a truncated cone solidly connected to the inner framework. The frame of slender poles is covered by two tent-cloths of reindeer skins stitched together. In the interior, in front of the entrance is a stove made of a wooden casing closed by reindeer skins, and this is heated by an oil lamp.
*Plate 114*

### EVENKS

These hunters, fishermen, and stockbreeders of Tungu-sic linguistic stock are found in a vast area of the Soviet Union between the Ob River, the Pacific Ocean, the ice-locked Arctic Ocean, and Manchuria. Their char-acteristic conical tent, the *chum*, is similar to that of other Siberian and North American nomads. A frame-work of branches fixed in the ground and tied at the top is covered in summer with birch bark and in winter with pieces of felt or, more often, reindeer skins sewed together. A flap of the covering is left hanging loose to close the entrance, and there is a smoke vent at the top. The hearth is in the center, and along the walls are benches covered with skins serving as seats and beds.

### KORYAKS

The Koryaks are fishermen and reindeer herders in the northernmost part of the Kamchatka Peninsula in Soviet Siberia. The sedentary groups live along the coast in small settlements of semiunderground houses, and the nomads have easily dismantled tent-huts. The house is a large octagonal, semi-interred construction about fifty feet long, forty feet wide, and up to twenty-three feet high, with wooden framework and an entrance at the side in summer, through the roof in winter—the latter serving also as smoke vent, a function often helped along by a funnel-shaped rise in the roof. The tent-hut of the nomads is very similar to that of the Chuk-chees, a complex structure of slender poles covered with skins.
*Plate 113*

### ITELMAS (KAMCHADALS)

This sedentary fishing and hunting population inhabits small villages along the shores of the sea and the rivers of the Kamchatka Peninsula in Soviet Siberia. The multifamily winter house is rectangular with ceiling and walls of planks and earth-covered roof. It is semi-interred so the main entrance is at the top, through a rectangular opening against which a stout pole carved into steps is propped; a side opening is reserved for the women. The summer dwelling, a low, broad conical hut set on a platform, is much like those in the large village of about a hundred families described in the 18th century by G. W. Steller: The round houses rested on square platforms that were held up by nine or twelve piles. They were roofed in straw and had two doors, one at the north, the other at the south, and the dwell-ings were packed closely next to each other.

### NANAS, OLCHAS, OROCHES

These largely sedentary fishing populations of Tungusic

linguistic stock are settled in the Amur River region of Soviet Siberia in villages of semi-interred houses stretching along the river banks. Thanks to Russian and Chinese influence, this traditional winter dwelling has undergone some change. In the basin of the Imin River there are peaked-roofed houses of logs cemented with clay. The summer dwelling is a rectangular hut covered with larch bark. The Oroches on the Pacific Coast also use a type of tent covered in fish skins smeared with grease. No longer in use among the Nanas and the Olchas is a traditional dwelling similar to the North American wigwam with a hemispherical structure of curved poles fixed into the ground and tied at the top and covered with bark.

## GILYAKS

This sedentary fishing people in the northern zone of Sakhalin Island and at the mouths of the Amur River in Soviet Siberia have seasonal settlements of limited extension sited along the rivers or seashore. The traditional winter dwelling is a house set into the ground to a depth of about five feet, rectangular in shape but with rounded corners. It has a central fireplace and an entrance corridor. Along the walls, large elevated benches provide sleeping accommodation for from one to three families. Chinese influence in recent times has introduced a system of heating by terra-cotta pipes that carry the smoke under the wall benches and then out a chimney set against the house. As so often in the Siberian area, there is a window closed by fish bladders. The summer dwelling is a large rectangular plank-hut set up on piles and covered with bark. The front area is set aside as storage place. In summer the conical tent is also used.

## AINUS

The Ainus live by hunting and fishing in the southern half of Sakhalin Island, the Kurile archipelago (Soviet Union), and almost all of Hokkaido Island (Japan). The old Siberian architectural practice of building semi-underground winter houses with a round ground plan and entrance through the wall rather than the roof and conical summer tents on a framework of three poles has been altered under Japanese influence: Permanent settlements of rectangular cabins are now built at ground level. The wall and corner posts support a framework on which is placed a roof pitched in four directions, constructed separately and set into position as a finished product. The walls are sealed with layers of interwoven reeds reinforced with matting both inside and outside. The roof is held up by two three-pronged struts fixed at the ends of the rectangular frame and connected by a ridgepole. It is covered with laths sheathed in straw and laid like tiles in parallel bands. The ridgepole juts out in front and back to form a small shelter above the two lesser slopes of the roof. The main axis of the house is oriented from east to west, and the main entrance, sheltered by the overhang, is usually at the south. There are windows in the north and west walls. Inside, the hearth is set up in the center, within a rectangular en-closure, and kept perpetually burning from the day the house was first inhabited. Hanging mats partition the interior into sectors, the north for the parents and the domestic objects, the southeast for the children. The east wall, and in particular the northeast corner, is considered sacred and reserved for guests. The house itself is believed to be the property of the Kamui genii, with the wood used in building belonging to the Kamui Shiramba and the hearth to the Kamui Fuchi.

## ALEUTS

The traditional winter residence of the sedentary fishing population of the Aleutian Islands, off southwestern Alaska, is a large underground collective house, rectangular in shape (occasionally, though rarely, round), entered through the roof. The supporting structure of beams filled in with logs creates an interior trapezoidal in section, as two of the walls are steeply inclined and all four are truncated by the flat roof over the central part. The sleeping pallets of the family groups are placed on continuous raised platforms along the walls, and there are accommodations for hundreds of individuals. In summer, these collective houses are abandoned for family tents covered in skins.

## ESKIMOS

These groups of hunters and fishermen in the subarctic regions of North America from the Bering Strait to Greenland have different architectural traditions, though they generally maintain separate residences in winter and summer. The winter settlements are made up of small clusters of dwellings along the seacoasts, each habitation separate but often communicating with the others. In summer the population is dispersed over vast areas and lives in tents. The traditional winter house is semiunderground, accommodating two or three families (in Greenland, as many as ten or more). It often (particularly in Alaska along the Bering Strait) has two entrances, one from above, the other from one side through a corridor. Building materials vary according to the resources available in the particular area. The supporting structure may be composed of the ribs and jawbones of the whale (not in Greenland), stones and driftwood (in Alaska and Greenland), or even turf. The kashim, a semi-interred dwelling found in the western regions, may be round, oval, or quadrangular, with a roof in the shape of a truncated pyramid (notably in Alaska along the Bering Strait). Sometimes it is entirely of stone, with a false vault covered by earth and lichen as well as flagged flooring with a hollow space beneath it, a central fireplace, and platforms along the sides.

The Eskimos at the mouth of the Mackenzie River in far northwestern Canada in the past had a type of cross-shaped dwelling with two entrances and two entrance corridors leading to a square central area; three trapezoidal chambers were connected with it at the sides and on a somewhat high level, which served as sleeping quarters for three families. The entire structure, supported in the center by forked posts, was completely covered with planks and given an outer revet-ment of earth. In the vicinity of the habitations there were often raised stone or wooden platforms on which provisions could be stored.

Special houses for ceremonies, much like the kashim of the western regions, are utilized only in the winter season, remaining shut up from March to November; they are found at Cape Prince of Wales, the western-most point of land on the North American continent. Also in use in northern Alaska is a domelike tent of skins that is covered with snow during the winter. Among the Eskimos of the central regions and Labrador one finds the igluak or igloo, a dome-shaped winter house built from blocks of hard-packed snow cut with knives and piled up edgewise following a spiral line, with the chinks filled in by loose snow. The top is closed with a keystone inserted from outside, and the entire construction is based on the principles used in building stone cupolas.

An igloo can be built in very few hours. While it is used in smaller form by the Polar Eskimos of Alaska and Greenland only as temporary quarters during migrations and hunts, among the Central Eskimos it assumes complex forms with dimensions of as much as sixteen feet in diameter and thirteen feet in height and with room for more than one family for the entire duration of the winter. Above the entrance, which usually faces south, there is a window closed with seals' intestines or a sheet of ice, and a hole at the summit of the dome draws off the smoke. Often there is a corridor in front of the entrance also made of snow blocks (among the Iglulik, notably), and it consists of a continuous row of low dome-shaped chambers used as storage places and as shelter for the dogs. The interior of the igloo itself may be lined with reindeer skins and is normally heated by oil lamps made out of soapstone; temperatures within reach as high as fifty-nine degrees Fahrenheit, thanks to the perfect insulation system and the body heat of the inhabitants. Often the igloos are grouped to intercommunicate, in which case a larger chamber serves as "parlor."

The most widespread type of summer tent is made up of a conical section plus a shedlike extension over the entrance, which gives the construction a horseshoe shape, the rounded back having a radial framework, the slightly trapezoidal front being double-pitched. Especially in Greenland, the tent is markedly inclined to leeward to offer less resistance to the wind.
*Plates 68–70, 161*

# NORTH AMERICA

## IROQUOIS

These woodland Indians of central New York State and the easternmost Great Lakes area of the United States and Canada organized as early as the 16th century in a League of Five Nations (expanded to six in 1722), the *Ongwano Sionni,* "those who all belong to the big tent," a complex economic, political, and ceremonial system. The territory of the Five Nations, stretching from the Hudson River on the east (Mohawk tribal territory) to the Genese River in western New York State (Seneca tribal territory), was interpreted symbolically as a great house in whose interior five fires burned; the pillars supportng the house were the tribal chiefs, the *sachems*.

An Iroquois village is composed of collective houses gathered around the council house used for assemblies, feasts, and religious rites, Every tribe has its own special fortified settlements to which to retreat when necessary, and the sites of villages are subject to change every fifteen years or so, when the farmland soil becomes exhausted. The multifamily "longhouse" can shelter from two to twenty-four families and, among the Huron tribe, may measure as much as 165 by 40 feet. The roof is either peaked or barrel-vaulted, and the supporting structure of crisscrossed poles is covered with elm or ash bark sealed on the exterior by a network of branches. The interior, entered through doors at either end, consists of two entrance chambers and a large central area, a common room flanked by continuous raised ledges, each family occupying its own sector. In the center of the common room is a row of hearths, one for every two or four families, and the smoke is drawn off by rectangular openings in the roof above each hearth, which can be opened or closed. The connection of the habitation with cosmic space is expressed by the east-west orientation of the principal axis. The division of the society into two groups, Wolves and Turtles, becomes especially evident during the ceremonies, when they gather at opposite ends of the longhouse.
*Plate 187*

## YUCHI

This chiefly agricultural population belongs to the Macro-Siouan linguistic group and lives in the Savannah River region in Georgia and South Carolina. The traditional dwelling is a multifamily vaulted cabin of pointed-arch section, the transverse arches being linked by longitudinal beams. The roof is covered with cypress bark and has a vent above the hearth.

## SEMINOLE

This hunting population of Muskogean lingustic stock in Florida lives in stockaded villages, which often contain a large number of cabins, generally rectangular with peaked roof, sometimes set up on piles because of the swampy terrain. Common, too, is a cylindrical hut with conical roof.

## CREEK

The Creek are agricultural Indians of the Muskogean linguistic group whose home is in the southeastern United States—specifically, most of Alabama and Georgia and parts of northern Florida. When the European colonizers came, the Creek were still living in large permanent centers, of which nothing survives except some archaeological evidence and old descriptions. The Creek "city" was organized around a central rectangular plaza surrounded by small hills on which were erected the principal public edifices. From a description of one of these settlements, Cussetah, we know that a broad plaza with a stele in its center was bounded along the major axis by two mounds. The first of these was rectangular, and on it were four edifices around a courtyard; the second was circular, marked by a round assembly building. The latter was unroofed in the center, and along the walls there were individual cells, as among the Yamassee and Cherokee Indians. An 18th-century description, by William Bartram, of Kulum indicates that that city, too, had such a plaza; Bartram also remarks that Creek cities were made up of numerous groups of four dwellings around a square courtyard entered at the corners, and that these multifamily houses had plastered wooden walls and a roof of cypress bark or wooden shingles.

## WINNEBAGO, KICKAPOO

These populations, speaking Siouan and Algonquin languages, engage in agriculture and live in the middle and upper Mississippi Basin. Their traditional dwelling is the wickiup, widely diffused throughout the Algonquin area, a rectangular or oval hut with a domical frame of curved wood. The oval wickiup, roughly twenty by fourteen feet with a maximum height of nine feet, has a solid transverse and longitudinal frame of branches, reinforced by a beam at the top supported by two forked poles, which does double duty as a support from which to hang the cooking pots over the fire below. There is a smoke vent in the roof and an entrance on one long side, usually facing east. The walls and roof are covered either with mats of about $6^1/_2$ by 15 feet—among the Kickapoo—or sheets of bark, among the Winnebago. The fireplace occupies the center of the interior, and there are pallets along the walls.

## MANDAN

The Mandan are a Siouan-speaking group in the Missouri basin. Their semipermanent villages and traditional dwelling, a kind of earth-lodge, are evidence of an agricultural past. The settlement is often protected by a stockade and may contain several dozen round, dome-shaped huts with a vent at the top and an entrance protected by a short corridor. Four poles in the interior support the roof and mark off a central area containing the round fireplace flanked by four seats. On the side facing the entrance, an elevated platform serves as common sleeping place. Two partitions, one behind the entrance and the other at a side, act as screens, the latter delimiting the part of the cabin where the horses are stabled.
*Plate 185*

## PAWNEE

These farmers and hunters of the Great Plains belonging to the Caddo linguistic group and living between the Platte and the Arkansas rivers build an earth-lodge dwelling with a kind of vestibule consisting of a semi- underground corridor. The central part of the floor is hollowed out, and along the walls a solid ledge is left to be used for sleeping places. In use also is a round, domed hut, set shallowly into the ground and partially covered with earth.

## CHEYENNE

Farmers and hunters living between the Arkansas and Missouri rivers, the Cheyenne completely transformed their economy in the 18th century, when horses were introduced. Becoming exclusively buffalo hunters, they adopted the tepee (*tipi*), the easily assembled conical tent of the Prairie Indians, which they set up according to a rigid ritual order in roughly circular summer encampments that might include a thousand tents and reach a diameter of two-thirds of a mile or more. The entrance to the camp faced east, and each sector was assigned to a different band. The center was sometimes marked by a large assembly tent.

The tepee, in use among all the nomadic tribes of the Great Plains, is round or slightly oval. Its dimensions vary considerably as does the number of tent poles and of buffalo skins used for the tent cloth. The frame is made up of a pyramid of poles. The first of these, near the entrance, is the most important, symbolizing the sky, while four others represent the four parts of the world, a significance likewise attributed to four stars cut out of skin and attached to the exterior of the tent. The tent cloth is left open at the entrance, which can be closed by a loose flap, and a smoke vent at the top can be closed by two small ear-shaped flaps ingeniously manipulated from below by a long pole. Inside, a lining the height of a man serves as additional protection against wind and rain. The hearth is in the center, the sleeping pallets along the walls. Tanning the skins, sewing and decorating the tent cloth, and putting up and taking down the tepee are all women's tasks, and the tent is transported on a *travois* (a platform on two trailing poles) dragged by a horse.
*Plate 103*

## WICHITA

This agricultural tribe of the Caddo linguistic group lives north of the Red River, in Oklahoma. The traditional dwelling is a hut with round ground plan and ogival section. The framework is made of bent poles tied by horizontal hoops that meet in the center and are reinforced, in the interior, by a circle of forked stakes connected by crosspieces. The two entrances, one at the east used in the morning and one at the west used in the afternoon, along with the four poles projecting above the top of the roof, which is covered with bundles of dried grass, all testify to the symbolic link between the dwelling and the four parts of the world, a recurrent motif in the cosmology of the North American Indian agricultural populations.

## PAIUTE

Seed gathering in the great basin east of the Sierra

Nevada, between the Columbia and Colorado rivers, in southwestern Utah and California, the Paiute bands, consisting of no more than a few dozen individuals, spend the winter together in a single camp but in summer disperse in small groups. The winter dwelling is a conical wickiup with hearth and smoke vent and a framework of juniper poles covered by branches and grass. An indispensable feature of every camp is the sweathouse for the men, located near a watercourse. In summer, semicircular windbreaks or shed roofs supported by four poles shelter the fire and the sleeping places.

## POMO

The Pomo are sedentary hunters and gatherers of California, whose traditional dwelling is either round with conical roof covered by bark or planks, or else hemispherical; in the latter case, it is covered with earth and entered from above and sometimes has exterior steps leading to the top of the dome. There are numerous public edifices such as houses for menstruating women, ceremonial huts for dances, and sweathouses also used by the men as assembly places.

## YUROK

These sedentary hunters and gatherers of California live in rectangular houses covered by a peaked roof reaching the ground. Among their special buildings are huts for menstruating women and a complex type of sweathouse.

## ZUNI, HOPI

The sedentary populations of maize growers in the southwestern states of Arizona, New Mexico, and Colorado belong to the group known as Pueblos, from the Spanish name for their compact villages, a type of settlement mostly found in the valleys of the Little Colorado River and the upper Rio Grande. The high point in the development of these settlements was reached in the 12th and 13th centuries and was followed by a marked reduction in their number and size as well as by numerous innovations in building techniques. The villages were located in valleys ("valley pueblos"), on plateaus rising steeply from the plains ("mesa pueblos"), or else inside enormous natural cavities or clinging to almost inaccessible rock walls ("cliff dwellings").

A pueblo is a single, unified, many-storied structure made up of numerous flat-roofed rectangular units with walls of flat stones held together with small chips, or clay. In the oldest pueblos, a cement of lime and gravel was used. It was poured and pressed between basketwork to make solid blocks of walls as much as $6^{1}/_{2}$ feet thick, which were then smoothed down, plastered over, and whitewashed on the inside. This, however, was supplanted by adobe, a technique involving unburnt, sun-dried bricks.

To the simple initial cell, rooms are connected for different purposes, and together they form a complete apartment. These separate dwellings are arranged in continuous rows in several-storied blocks staggered one above the other five to seven rows high and deep. The roof is built up in layers: log beams projecting beyond the walls, a network of joists, a layer of dead branches, another of stubble and leafy branches, and finally one of pressed earth. The flooring is made of stone slabs or adobe. Traditionally, there were no windows, and entrance was generally made from above through trapdoors on the roof-terraces reached by removable ladders or steps cut in the wall. In the cliff dwellings in particular, a need for defense is shown by the development of towers several stories high. The villages on the plains, for example Aztec and Bonito pueblos, are rectangular or semicircular in plan with high outer walls and with the dwellings terracing downward to the center of the settlement, a vast inside plaza designed for community and ceremonial use. In the mesa pueblos and cliff dwellings as well as the plains villages, semiunderground sacred chambers, the kivas, which are round in plan and covered with beams, are grouped in the plaza. These are entered from above by stairs. In the center of each is a fireplace, and a small hole in the pavement (sipapu) represents the entrance into the subterranean world. The significance of the kiva is clearly cosmological: It is a place of passage between the separate worlds of the underground spirits, men, and sky. The Zuni celebrated complex religious ceremonies in their kivas, and their altars are certainly models of the cosmic order.
Plates 5, 188–200

## NAVAHO

An agricultural and sheepherding population of Athapaskan origin, the Navaho emigrated into the semidesert areas of Arizona, New Mexico, and Utah, and live in settlements of a few huts. The traditional dwelling is the hogan, an earth-lodge, which in winter is buried in a mound of earth and stones. The supporting structure is composed of three forked posts from 10 to $11^{1}/_{2}$ feet high, which are joined at the top and set slantwise into the ground. These are arranged to make a circle—a pole at the west, north, and south—with another two at the east, where the entrance is, that converge slightly to form the frame of the door. The trapezoidal opening is fronted by a corridorlike flat-roofed vestibule only four feet high, and above the entrance is a window that admits light and acts as vent. The lodge is covered with bark, over which is spread a layer of earth. A more recent type of dwelling is a log cabin on a hexagonal or octagonal ground plan with roof covered by earth; it is clearly a variant of the earth-lodge, though the entire structure stands free above the ground. A hole in the center draws off the smoke. The cult house is simply a large hogan with a diameter of about twenty feet; there ceremonies are held—among others, the sandpainting ritual in which designs are made that cover the entire floor.
Plates 101, 201, 202

## SALISH

These fishermen and hunters live in the state of Washington and in British Columbia. The groups along the coast are sedentary and engage in fishing. Their village houses are made of cedar logs and beams and are much like those of the Nootka, though the cabins near the mouth of the Fraser River have a single-pitched shed roof. The Salish of the interior, in the basins of the Fraser and Columbia rivers, have a semiunderground winter dwelling of the earth-lodge type, with an entrance in the center of the roof by way of a log notched into steps. In summer they use a conical tent-hut.

## NOOTKA

Both the summer and winter villages of this chiefly sedentary fishing population in the southwestern part of Vancouver Island in British Columbia are made up of houses whose supporting structure is left permanently in place while the boards of the walls and roof are taken down and transported to another location where an identical house is put up to serve during the alternate season. The summer houses are lined up along the shore, and in winter the community retreats to the interior. The structure of the house, which may be as much as a hundred feet long by forty feet wide, is based on two large cedar posts at the sides of the front door that are connected by a crossbeam on which rests a ridgepole whose other end rests on a single pillar in the interior carved in anthropomorphic form. Two beams, parallel to the ridgepole, connect the posts at each of the four corners of the cabin. The cabin houses at least four family units, one in each corner, with the head of the group in the right rear corner; if there are more, they take their places along the side walls. Besides individual hearths for each family, there is a common fireplace in the center.
Plate 341

## KWAKIUTL

This by and large sedentary group of fishermen on the coast of British Columbia builds villages of houses aligned along the shore that are changed with the season, and even in the bad season they are often abandoned for better fishing sites. A broad street runs in front of the houses and is often raised on wooden foundations and extended by platforms projecting over the shore, giving open-air assembly places. Besides the totem poles that are a feature of Northwest Coast Indian culture, the Kwakiutl have their own highly refined architectural art—paintings often covering the entire facade of the house and depicting mythic forms of the whale, raven, thunderbird, and other creatures. The house, of logs and boards, has an inner structure based on two pairs of uprights, front and rear, connected at the top by a crossbeam and interconnected by two longitudinal beams.
Plates 342–344, 346, 354, 355

## HAIDA

These sedentary fishermen of Queen Charlotte Islands, British Columbia, and the southern end of the Alexan-

der Archipelago of Alaska live in villages strung out along the shore. A population census of Ninstints, on Anthony Island, taken in the first half of the 19th century, listed more than three hundred individuals distributed among twenty houses. The houses belonged to the different lineages, which were divided into two exogamous groups, Eagles and Ravens. Haida cabins are built from logs and planks and have slightly sloping peaked roofs. A totem pole is often incorporated into the center of the house front, which also has other decoration, and in such cases entrance is made through an opening in the pole itself. The interior has a single room occupied by a number of families in separate sectors partitioned off by mats hanging from the roof. The fireplace is in the center of a rectangular area hollowed out below floor level, and seats and couches are aligned on a step around it. These houses may be inhabited permanently or only during the winter.
Plates 329–333, 336, 338–340, 345, 352, 353

*For North America see also plates 97–100, 102, 182–184, 186, 334, 335, 337, 347–351, 356–358.*

## SOUTH AMERICA

### MOTILON

The Motilon are a hunting and farming people who live to the west of Lake Maracaibo in Venezuela and in Colombia. Their dwelling is a large collective hut with an apse at either end, about 165 feet long and accommodating up to three hundred persons. The roof extends to the ground and serves also as wall. It is supported by two parallel lengths of poles connected by crossbeams, and these divide the interior into the equivalent of three naves; the central one is reserved for the coamunity hearths and the side ones are occupied by the individual family units.

### TUKANO

Hunters and farmers in the Uapés River region of eastern Colombia, the Tukano live in large collective huts of rectangular ground plan (about ninety-five by sixty-nine feet, and about thirty-three feet high) with a peaked thatched roof. The supporting structure is composed of six rows of poles parallel to the short side and joined by longitudinal beams; the ridgepole rests on trusswork, as there are no poles down the center. The front gable is covered with matting, and below, where the door opens, the facade is faced with boards, which are often decorated. In the interior, the family units are placed along the walls in rectangular compartments separated by low partitions.
Plate 168

### DESANA

Farming, fishing, and hunting, the Desana live in the basins of the Rio Papuri and Rio Tiquié in Colombia and Brazil. Every patrilinear clan generally occupies a single large collective *maloca,* known here as *wi'i,* isolated in a clearing in the forest and facing a watercourse.

Each *maloca* can shelter a few dozen people. It is rectangular in plan with a double-pitched roof, though the end opposite the principal entrance is sometimes rounded. Each family has its own place along the walls. The symbolic significance of the interior architecture is made clear in the ceremonies and dances held there, which make precise reference to the cosmogonic myths. The interior is divided into two parts, male to the front, female to the rear, with the hearths located in the center. The three wooden frames that hold up the roof are painted red with black spots and are called "jaguars," and these symbolize the link between the clan and the fecundizing force of the sun and of nature.
Plate 166

### PIAROA

The Piaroa, hunters and farmers of the forests of the middle Orinoco River, in Venezuela, are scattered in groups over vast territory, and each occupies its own collective house, the *churuata,* built in the center of a small space cleared and used also for planting. The *churuata* is a large circular hut (diameter about 60 feet, height about 40) with a continuous convex-concave surface that comes to a point at the top. Inside is a central framework of four posts marking out a square space about 20 feet on a side, and at about $6^{1}/_{2}$ feet from the ground they are connected by crosspieces supporting, at their ends, the framework of the wall-roof made of crisscrossed, flexible branches. The pinnacle is supported by a complex lattice, and the entire wall-roof is covered with palm branches and fronds. The only entrance is protected by a double door. For windows, temporary openings can be made from the interior by pushing aside the leaves of the wall-covering with a long pole, and these can be changed with the movement of the sun. The family units occupy specific sectors along the walls, each having its own hammocks and hearth. In the center, besides a receptacle containing maize beer, there are two community hearths. The head of the group has his place in axial position facing the door.

At the edge of the forest is the "men's house," a roofed shed virtually closed over by palm fronds with a small opening that can be entered only on all fours.
Plate 173

### YANOAMA

Hunters and gatherers who recently have turned to agriculture, the Yanoama live in the region of the sources of the Orinoco River, between the Rio Casiquiare and the Rio Branco in Venezuela and Brazil. The traditional settlement takes the form of the *chapuno,* a circular or elliptical ring of huts around an open space. The individual huts, each no more than a large lean-to, may be separated or else closely juxtaposed; in the latter case, they form a single continuous truncated cone open in the center. The diameter of the *chapuno* depends on the number of lean-tos and may vary anywhere from a hundred to three hundred feet, housing up to a hundred or so individuals. The central open space is raised so that water will run off during the rainy season. Often the entire complex is protected by a palisade and the entrances are closed off at night by heaps of branches. During hunting expeditions and group migrations, small temporary family lean-tos, *tapiri,* are put up in a circle and inhabited for only a few days at a time.
Plates 79–96

### BORO

Farmers and hunters in the Amazon region between the Japurá and Putumayo rivers at the borders between Peru, Colombia, and Brazil, the Boro live in groups ranging from fifty to two hundred individuals in isolated clearings in the forest in a single large collective house, a square building with rounded corners covered by a roof pitched on four sides reaching almost to the ground and terminating in a ridgepole and two gables. The covering is of palm fronds. In the interior, the central space is used by all the inhabitants, although each family has its own place along the walls for its hammocks and hearth.

### JÍVARO

These hunters in the region of the Rio Santiago in Peru and Ecuador live in a large collective hut, the *jivaría,* with a rectangular ground plan usually curved at one end and a double-pitched roof. There are separate entrances for the men and the women, and a large signal drum is hung on the men's door. Along the walls inside there is a platform that does duty as sleeping place, each family having its own sector, and this is raised above the ground and inclined toward the center where the hearth is set up.
Plate 169

### WAPISIANA

This hunting and farming population of Arawakan linguistic stock inhabits the Rio Branco region in northern Brazil. Their villages include both single- and multi-family dwellings and a community house and are situated at the edge of the forest, in whose interior they have their farming plots in cleared-off areas. The dwelling may be rectangular, round, or oval, and house from one to four families. The interior is divided, and each sex has its own group of hammocks and even uses different doors located opposite each other. During hunting expeditions, they build a temporary triangular shelter of poles resting against a tree trunk and covered with palm fronds.

### TUPINAMBA

The Tupinamba are agricultural, speak a Tupi-Guarani

language, and live in the Brazilian coastlands. While their traditional villages are now a thing of the past, their organization in the 16th century is known from an account of the German explorer Hans von Staden. They lived in barrel-vaulted, rectangular collective cabins several dozen yards long with an entrance on a main side. The framework of beams and rafters was covered by leaves and straw. Three to seven of these large houses, each sheltering numerous family units, were grouped around a clearing used in common. The most frequent plan of the clearing was square, with four huts in each of the cardinal directions. The village was often protected by a fortified circular wall of logs piled in one or more tiers and having defensive devices to protect the gate.
*Plates 163–165*

## TIMBIRA

Gatherers and hunters belonging to the Ges linguistic group, the Timbira live on the upland plains of east central Brazil. The village, centralized in plan, is in theory divided into east and west halves as well as into two concentric groups, the *Kamakra* ("those of the central plaza") and the *Atukmakra* ("those of the periphery"). The ceremonial hut is located in the central plaza along with the hearths reserved for the men. The hearths are divided into six groups, three on either side, east and west. From this sacred zone of the men, paths radiating out in all directions lead to the huts of the women, which are disposed in a circle and fronted by a broad ringlike street where all the everyday nonreligious activities take place, including cooking.

## CHERENTE, CHAVANTE

These hunting and gathering peoples belong to the Ges linguistic group and are found on the upland plains of east central Brazil. Both the plan of the village and the architectural structure of the men's house, in the center, correspond to the division into six social groups, four plus two. The men's house is circular and dome-shaped, with a diameter of about thirty-three feet and a height of about twelve feet. The entrance door faces west, and the building has eight openings to mirror the radial partitioning of the interior. There the four principal groups have places around the center that correspond to the four cardinal directions, with the two additional groups placed respectively at east and west. The two moieties of the village, each made up of two classes plus one additional, are associated with the north and the south, and the general plan is horseshoe-shaped because of the two peripheral groups. During the rainy season, the habitation is a circular hut with a framework of semicircular arches linked by horizontal hoops and a central upright.

## BORORO

Hunters, gatherers, and farmers of the Mato Grosso plateau of southwestern Brazil in the vicinity of the sources of the Rio Paraguay, the Bororo construct

villages that consist of a circular plaza surrounded by family dwellings, which, in times past, used to fall into a number of concentric rings. In the center is the men's house, the *beitemmannageo*, a rectangular peaked-roofed building of about twenty-six by sixty-six feet with an adjacent plaza for dancing. Even in temporary camps inhabited for a single night, men are located in the center, women and children on the periphery. According to C. Lévi-Strauss, an east-west axis runs even through the men's house, which is itself oriented, and divides the village in two, with the eight clans separated into the *Escerae* ("the strong and superior") to the north and the *Tugarege* ("the weak and inferior") to the south. A secondary north-south axis divides the settlement into "upper" and "lower" halves. Each of the eight clans is divided into three classes whose members occupy a precise and symmetrical position in the theoretical schema of the village. The dwelling is female property and takes different forms according to the seasons: in the dry months, a simple conical shelter made of poles leaning against a central support and covered with palm leaves; in the rainy season, a rectangular peaked-roofed hut, sometimes elevated above the ground, with a ridgepole resting on two forked uprights.
*Plate 78*

## CARAJÁ, CHAMBISA, JAVAHÉ

These fishing and farming populations of the Mato Grosso plateau in western Brazil belong to the eastern Tupi linguistic group. The villages, which always have a very large men's house that is used also for storing the masks and for festivities, are of notable dimensions: thirty to ninety dwellings among the Chambisa, more than twenty among the Carajá and the Javahé of Banana Island. In the dry season, the Javahé inhabit huts lined up in one or two parallel rows along the riverbanks and, when the rains come, transport them bodily to the escarpments above.

The huts of the Chambisa, who live in the northern zone of the Rio Araquaia, are rectangular but rounded off at the ends and are covered with a convex double-pitched roof. They are covered with straw over a framework of three parallel rows of forked poles connected by longitudinal beams. These beams support the roof of bent branches, while other branches bent into arches but with a lesser radius are set up perpendicular to these and support the round ends.

The Carajá and the Javahé of Santa Anna Island and of Bananal Island in the Araquaia River have two types of dwelling, both rectangular with a framework of logs covered by palm thatch and easily disassembled and transported elsewhere. The first type, about five feet high, has a roof extending all the way to the ground, and it houses a single family. The second type can house about twenty persons and has a roof as much as thirteen feet high set on the lateral walls.

## CHIPAYA

The Chipaya are farmers and fishermen in the region of Lake Titicaca in Bolivia living in villages with a cen-

tralized plan that preserves the traditional division into two parts, *Mahah-Saya* and *Arah-Saya*, even in recent times when the school and the church have supplanted the community house on the principal plaza. The traditional habitation is circular in plan, tending toward a slightly truncated cone in elevation and with a diameter of ten to sixteen feet. It is built of loaves of sundried clay and has a flat or somewhat curved roof with an inner framework of branches. Other types of building with a false cupola or parabolic section are made of similar loaves of clay jutting into the interior, but these are now used only for storage; the recent type of dwelling is rectangular with a peaked roof covered with rushes.

## TOBA

The traditional dwelling of these gatherers and hunters of the central Chaco region in northern Argentina is a domelike round or oval hut made of bent branches, and their villages consist of no more than a few such huts around a central clearing. The Pilagà group has a type of settlement in which the ovoid huts are curved in such a way that the longitudinal axis makes an arc of a circle, the huts thus fitting neatly into the rounded perimeter of the central plaza.

## ARAUCANO

The Araucano are an agricultural population of the Andean areas of north central Chile and neighboring regions of Argentina whose dwelling is a large collective hut, the *ruka*, sheltering thirty to forty persons. The plan varies from one group to another and may be rectangular, rectangular with curved short ends, or polygonal, and the structure may be of beams, cane, or planks, with a thatched peaked roof usually sloping down to the ground and concealing the walls. In the absence of windows, ventilation is obtained by the open doorless entrances, and an opening at the top serves as smoke vent.
*Plate 170*

## TEHUELCE

Hunters and gatherers, the Tehuelce are located in the south Patagonian region of Argentina. Before adopting, at the same time, the *toldo* and the horse, the Tehuelce lived in huts of circular ground plan and arched section with a frame of bent branches tied at the top. For covering the hut in winter, there were furs; in the summer, bark, branches, and grass. Also used was a kind of windscreen covered with rush matting. The *toldo*, on the other hand, has a framework of forked poles in parallel rows (usually four of them), with the middle ones of different height, connected by crosspieces. Skins sewed together cover the tent on three sides with one flank left open; the interior is divided transversely into separate compartments by means of hanging skins.
*Plate 53*

## ALAKALUF

Fishermen at the extreme southern tip of Chile, the Alakaluf camp along the watercourses in dome-shaped huts built on a skeleton of branches or rushes bent into parallel arches and interlaced with half-circles that converge on the ground in two opposite points like meridian lines. The plan is circular or, more often, elliptical; in the latter case, the dimensions are roughly thirteen by eight feet, the height six feet, and the covering is of ferns, grasses, bark, or the skin of sea lions. There are two low openings, which are entered on all fours, opposite each other between two arches along the axis perpendicular to the meridians. The hearth, also elliptical in shape, is in the center.
*Plates 56, 57*

## ONA

As shelter, these hunters and gatherers of the eastern part of Tierra del Fuego, in Chile, use a screen with framework of two inclined branches tied at the top and covered with guancao skins sewed together. It serves mainly to protect the fire; for sleeping, the open space in front of the shelter is simply strewn with boughs. Another type of shelter is semicircular and truncated, and its skeleton of poles is covered with skins.

## YAMANA

These fishermen and gatherers of the southern part of Tierra del Fuego and the islands off Cape Horn (Chile and Argentina) have settlements that include at the most a few huts lined up on the seashore or along streams. Their transportable conical hut is a structure of poles tied at the top and covered with branches. For additional protection from cold, earth is heaped up on the outside. The hut for the initiation of the youths is elliptical in plan and domical in profile with a framework of two series of curved branches of various dimensions that intersect at right angles.
*Plate 55*

*For Central and South America, see also plates 14, 52, 71–77, 167, 171, 172, 174–178.*

# NORTH AFRICA

## BERBERS

The Berbers are herding and agricultural populations of the Mediterranean and Atlantic regions of North Africa, from Morocco to Libya. Among the sedentary groups, the dwellings are usually organized around courtyards, whereas the nomadic and seminomadic groups have various types of tents and tent-huts, which they inhabit seasonally. The *gurbi*, used in summer in Algeria, in winter in Tunisia, is built of dry masonry or logs with posts supporting a roof covered in *diss*, a layer of foliage and straw. In section, it is a conical cylinder or pointed arch. Often it is surrounded by an enclosure

in stonework. Very frequent in Libya is an underground dwelling accommodating several family units around an uncovered courtyard with a well. In the Garian region south of Tripoli, a large, enclosed, quadrangular court, about twenty to twenty-six feet high, is reached by a steep corridor and gives on rooms hollowed out of the rock, which have trapezoidal or oval ground plans and barrel-vaulted ceilings. Usually such a complex shelters four families, one at each side of the square court. Similar habitations are also found in the Cyrenaic and Fezzan regions of Libya. Frequent in central southern Tunisia is a type of settlement made up of *ghorfa*, rectangular constructions in stone built one above the other and—in Medenin and Metameur especially—gathered around quadrangular courtyards. The individual units are superimposed to a height of as many as five stories and are also set back to back. The lower ones are lived in and have flat beamed ceilings; the upper ones, reached by wooden or stone stairs jutting out from the front wall, are storerooms. The highest *ghorfa* is covered by a barrel vault.

The fortified settlement, in which the most important building is the storehouse for food, is widely diffused throughout the western regions and has various names: *gast* in Tripolitania, *ksar* in Tunisia and Algeria, *ksur* in Morocco. In the Atlantic areas of Morocco there is a castlelike type in clay-and-straw bricks with high tapering towers and only a few slits for air on the exterior. Here, the interior is laid out around a courtyard, the *fonduk*, which serves also as stables. The men live in the lower story, the women in the upper. Throughout this territory, the types of settlement, religious edifices, and decoration can be considered more or less popular expressions of Islamic style.
*Plates 8, 9, 39, 144, 436*

## TEKNA

The large tent of these nomadic or seminomadic herders in southwestern Morocco has a trapezoidal covering made of strips of cloth of camel's and goat's hair. Two main poles, often of unequal length (between seven and fourteen feet) cross almost at the top and support the tip of the tent by means of a wooden block with two notches. The interior space is very low in the slightly wider front part and toward the exterior, whereas the central area, beneath the inverted **V** of the two supports, rises much higher and assumes a conical profile.
*Plates 127–130*

## TUAREG

Nomadic and seminomadic herders of the central and western Sahara, the Tuareg live in tents or collapsible tent-huts in encampments that also include enclosures for the animals during long sojourns. The tent, whose sides are stretched irregularly by drawstrings and pegs, is roughly thirteen by sixteen feet, and in its center is the main supporting pole, which ends in a curved block of wood. Other minor poles, linked by crosspieces, support the cloth along the perimeter. Various materials are used for the tent cloth—skins of wild sheep in the

western regions; skins of sheep or goat (colored red) in the central regions; and a mixture of camel's hair and sheep's wool in the east—and sometimes the side walls are made of matting. The tent cloth may be held up by parallel wooden arches (as among the Aju-n-Tahlè); when raised in the center to give a domelike profile (as among the Tenghereghif), it is supported by a skeleton of reeds and sticks inserted between the horizontal crosspieces and the arches. In the Air region, a portable hut of branches and matting with circular ground plan and a depressed dome with a slight central prominence is frequently used. The supporting structure consists of a central pole with stakes around the perimeter supporting radial crosspieces. The roof is held up by a network of flexible branches and is of palm matting covered outside with a layer of firmly tied vegetable fibers.

## TEBU

Nomadic or seminomadic herders of the eastern Sahara (Libya, Niger, Chad), the Tebu usually employ a tent-hut of stakes and mats that can be disassembled and transported on camelback. In the few permanent centers near oases there are dwellings with a base of dry masonry about three feet high and with an upper trusswork of branches covered with grasses. Generally, the tent-hut is oval or rectangular with a framework of bent branches held up by forced st  and w th a co ering of straw matting or palm fronds fixed in place by wooden pins; much more rarely, the covering is made of s ns decorated with geometrical motifs. Just inside the door, which is at a corner, a cur ed m t forms a short entrance corridor. In the opposite corner, an area for the women is screened off with mats, and in the center is the hearth, made of four stones.

## KABABISH

This nomadic Bedouin population of camel breeders in the semidesert regions of central northern Sudan has encampments that vary in dimensions. The head of a tribe, the *sheik*, has double-pitched tents with the ridge oriented north-south and the entrance facing east, the direction of Mecca. The rectangular tent cloth (*bayt shugga*) s made of strips of camel's-hair cloth and is held up by a row of four forked poles, which mar the course of the ridge and by lower poles along the perimeter (*tarig* and *arfaf*). Between the two inner poles runs a beam, while the outer ones, the *kimn*, support the tent by means of curved wooden prop (*tawia*). The lateral walls of the tent can be closed by mo ble strips of goat's-hair cloth (*khaysha*), which, when raised outward, serve as awnings. In the interior, across from the entrance is the bed, and next to it, toward the north, is the *ufta*, a palanquin for the women on camelback. At the south a space is left free for food supplies and cooking.
*Plate 126*

*For North Africa, see also plates 34, 131, 132, 435, 462, 463.*

346

## WEST AFRICA

### DOGON

This agricultural population in the mountainous regions of the upper basin of the Niger in Mali lives in villages that are a highly organized aggregate of family houses (*ginna*), granaries, and sacred places. Studies pioneered by M. Griaule have exposed the correspondence between cosmogonic myths and the symbolic structure of reality in the thought and building activity of this people, and their architecture is now an obligatory point of reference in any discussion of the relationships between anthropomorphism and geometry and between myth and architecture. Thus, the center of the territory inhabited by the tribe is also held to be the origin of the spiral movement initiated by the ancestors that has given form to fields and homes alike. The village is, ideally, laid out in anthropomorphic form, with the plaza, assembly house, and blacksmith's forge as head, the family houses as chest, the altars as genitals as well as feet, and the houses for the menstruating women as hands and all these are disposed in such a way as to link social reality with the myth of origin. In the center of the village, in a circular open plaza (*Lébé dala*), the celestial world with the stars may be represented. The decorative details carved on the doors and walls of the granaries, the paintings in the sanctuaries and on the rock faces, and the assemblage of masks used in the ceremonies are all related to an interpretation of physical reality as "copy" of the diverse aspects of mythic reality. Even the family house (*ginna*), an ample terraced building of posts and mud, repeats a structure based on the human figure that has come down, through all the generations, from the time of the creation of the ancestors. On its front are niches representing those generations, and in its general plan can be distinguished the head (the round kitchen at the north), the torso (the central uncovered space), and the arms (the utility rooms to either side). The whole *ginna* represents the union of the man and the woman in the act of procreation. Important elements of the village include the granaries which, in the mountainous Bandiagara region, are built of stone or mud on the rocky slopes. Numerous also are sanctuaries in grottoes that serve as storage places for masks, and there are also open-air sacrificial altars.
*Plates 22, 33, 43, 44, 403–430*

### BAMBARA

A farming population of the upper Niger in Mali, the Bambara live in villages consisting of family enclosures, *sukala*, of brick cylindrical huts with conical roofs. The granary is a round construction in clay built with meticulous care, which functions as a gnomon to determine with precision the crucial dates for performing various agricultural activities.

*For Mali, see also plates 45, 464–470, 479–484, 486; for Niger, see plate 10; for Senegal and Guinea, see plates 11, 12, 29–31.*

### NABDAM

The Nabdam are a predominantly agricultural population located in northern Ghana between the Red Volta, White Volta, and Sissile rivers. An enclosure shelters all the members of an extended family. The traditional compound is in two parts. The front part, reached through an entrance marked by two rounded posts, which can be closed by laying beams across it, serves as shelter for the animals at night. A low bafflelike partition gives access to the courtyard surrounded by cylindrical huts with conical roofs. More complex compounds, like that of Azuri, the chief (*naba*) of Nangodi, reflect the modern evolution of Nabdam culture under colonial pressure, as it grew from a segmentary society to become a concentration of power in the hands of a hereditary chief. The *chefferie* of Nangodi is a very considerable aggregate of enclosures belonging to various members of the dynasty of Langyil. Rectangular huts house the heads of the various family groups; the residence of Azuri is of larger dimensions. The spirit of the ancestor Langyil is identified with a baobab tree that grows near his tomb inside the complex; its trunk represents his chest, its branches his arms. The traditional hut in which the women live is a round construction built up in successive rings of mud and covered with a thin and resistant coat of plaster. The arched entrance with its conspicuous cornice is protected inside by a semicircular wall of varying height which, without blocking the ventilation, prevents the animals from entering. Often there is exterior decoration, painted and incised with such geometrical motifs as circles, bands, crossed lines, and zigzags.

### DAGORTI, GONJA, LOBI

These agricultural populations on the east bank of the middle Black Volta River in northwestern Ghana dwell in compounds or villages of clay houses, whose ground plan is rectangular with rounded corners (among the Gonja and Dagorti) or curved, or a mixture of both (among the Lobi). The flat roof is also a terrace and rests on beams covered with palm fronds and supported by forked posts set away from the walls. The compound of the Lobi is entirely roofed over and has among its principal components granaries of clay, which are built elsewhere and then incorporated. The granaries jut out from the house terraces and are protected by a conical straw roof. They are reached from the terrace, which serves also as a drying place for food and has a continuous parapet that is simply the upward extension of the house walls. The bedrooms are grouped around a large living room. The houses of the Gonja and Dagorti have an open courtyard, with the rooms disposed around it.

The village of Seripe, dating from the end of the 19th century, is inhabited by the members of a clan of the Gonja tribe and is divided into five sectors, each with family houses of various sizes. The houses are entered either directly from outside or from the terrace-roof. The walls are plastered over with a mixture of clay, dung, and an adhesive liquid of vegetable origin that ensures impermeability and are decorated with geometrical motifs either impressed with the fingers or incised into the fresh plaster.

### BANDA, MO

The traditional settlement of these farmers of central western Ghana in the region of the Black Volta is a village, often populated by different tribal groups. The houses are built around courtyards, and the basic type is oblong with peaked thatched roof. A Banda village is an ensemble of isolated rectangular houses and courtyards, sometimes disposed with notable regularity along the sides of a main thoroughfare running from north to south. The courtyards are the scene of all domestic activities. The low houses have a wooden framework and walls of clay blocks. Outside verandas are frequent, made by extending the sloped house roof and supporting it with a number of posts. Among the Mo, courtyards are more open, and their dwellings, often isolated, are decorated with a wide band of black around the base that continues around the doorways.

### ASHANTI

A predominantly agricultural population in the forest regions of central southern Ghana, the Ashanti had already organized in the 19th century into a federative state with a king (*Asantahene*). Some centers, among them Kumasi, were of truly urban dimensions before 1850. Ashanti villages are made up of the characteristic family houses, the residences of the chief (*ahenfie*), a cemetery, and a sanctuary (*abosomfie*). The family house consists of a rectangular courtyard (*gyaase*), three sides of which are taken up by somewhat elevated, rectangular, clay buildings with steeply sloping peaked roofs covered by palm thatch. Known as *pato*, these lack inner dividing walls and are used as relaxation rooms, storage places, and kitchens. The fourth side is taken up by the sleeping room, whose entrance can be blocked by a mat. The same plan is found in the temple-sanctuary, where the *pato* serve both as kitchen and as shelter for the cult objects, including musical instruments, for which reason they are known as *atwenedan* (rooms of the drum). The extremely rich traditional decoration of the walls is chiefly geometrical, in low relief and filigree, and testifies to the centuries of commercial relations that the Ashanti have had with the states of the Sahara and Upper Volta and with such Nigerian cities as Kano and Zaria.
*Plates 440–444*

*For Ghana, see also plates 393, 431, 432; for Ivory Coast, see plates 18, 28, 32, 476–478, 485; for Upper Volta, see plates 19, 23–27, 394–397, 433, 434, 473–475.*

### KONKOMBA

These farmers of northern Togo live in castlelike mud constructions accommodating an entire extended family. Each of these "castles" (*ledechal*) is composed of a fortified courtyard surrounded by dwellings as well as kitchens, chicken coops, pigsties, and granaries—about fifteen structures in all. Entry is through the "house of access," which has two doors and serves as stables. It is larger than the other buildings, some sixteen to nineteen feet in diameter, with supporting posts in the center and along the walls.

Several of these *ledechal*, with patches of farmed land between them, make up a village. The individual units are round, with walls built of spherical or cylindrical clay bricks placed in a spiral. When the wall is built, a circular entrance is cut out of it about twenty inches above the ground and with a diameter of twenty-four to twenty-eight inches. As support, the conical roof has a tripod of forked poles, with their bifurcation at ground level, propped against the edge of the wall. To these are added secondary stakes, and the entire roof is covered with thatch also laid in spirals, with an inverted jug at the peak for protection from rain. Inner and outer walls alike are plastered over with a layer of clay and dung smoothed down by hand, and the interior is decorated with designs in black and white.

## KEMENU, TOFFINU

The Kemenu and Toffinu farm, fish, and breed stock in the lower valley of the Weme River and the lakelike swamp of Nokwe in Dahomey (now the People's Republic of Benin). The villages on solid ground are built up on piles because of the annual flooding, which lasts four months and enables the population to fish as well as farm. The groups living in the Nokwe swamp live by fishing alone. Among the numerous villages on piles accessible only by water the most important is Ganvye with about ten thousand inhabitants. The family dwelling is a very large rectangular hut of poles with walls closed by trellises and mats that are often colored. The roof, pitched on four sides and covered with grass, has a complex framework that makes the profile of its summit particularly conspicuous. On the exterior, a platform also raised on piles is used for social activities and daily tasks. Often a single one of these platforms may belong to three dwellings and function as a kind of courtyard open only at the entrance.

*For Dahomey and Nigeria, see plates 17, 360, 398–402, 437, 438, 454–461.*

## MUSGUM, MASSA

These agricultural and herding populations south of Lake Chad live in settlements based on the extended family. The individual dwellings are built at regular intervals into a wall enclosing the common courtyard. The dome-shaped huts, of pointed-arch section, are built of bricks of clay amalgamated with straw or pebbles to make an impasto known as *torchis* in French, "mud brick" in English. The hut is entered through an archway in a broad, porchlike frame. The plastic treatment of the exterior surfaces is particularly noteworthy. The curve of the dome is enlivened by continuous series of clay crests in the form of inverted **V**s, which make handy steps to climb during building and repairing, or by separate projections disposed alternately in horizontal rows across the entire surface. Notable, too, are the clay granaries, which are raised above the ground level.
*Plates 384–388*

*For Chad, see also plates 141–143, 162, 372, 389–392, 445–449; for Niger, see plates 15, 450–453, 471, 472.*

## MATAKAM

Farmers in the mountainous area of the northern Cameroons region, the Matakam live in settlements of dwellings set at some distance from each other, each housing an extended family. They are made up of a series of intercommunicating, conical-roofed, circular rooms, often without a central courtyard. The walls are of stone or clay, and the thatched roof is built elsewhere and simply fitted on—a practical measure since the thatch requires frequent renewal. The interior of the hut is clay and, especially among the Gudé, offers an interesting example of unified articulation of the space, as everything from the ledges for sleeping to the receptacles for storing food are molded of a single block of clay and carefully smoothed down.
*Plate 371*

## FALI

The territory of these farmers of the mountains of the northern Cameroons region is divided among four groups—from north to south, the Bossum, Bori-Peské, Kangu, and Tingelin—residing in villages housing several hundred persons. Generally, the basic unit is an enclosure occupied by an extended patrilinear family, each containing several conical-roofed cylindrical huts used as living quarters for the family head and his wives, or as kitchens, storerooms, guest huts, and so on. There are numerous and complex granaries of various types, which, like the huts, are built of *torchis* or *pisé*. A study by J.-P. Lebeuf has made the architecture of the Fali the best known, in all its aspects, of that of all the African populations practicing agriculture by hoeing and digging with mattocks. From the territory to household furnishings, the relationship between mythic world and spatial reality is manifested through correspondences that affect every aspect of the life and culture of this people. For this reason, it is possible to comprehend, in all its nuances, the significance of their constructions (not in themselves particularly original as compared with those of such neighbors as the Mandara), for architecture here is an integral part of the ritual repetition of the myth of origin.
*Plates 40–42, 373–383*

## BAMUM

The Bamum are an agricultural population in the Cameroons region, whose village dwellings have a specific alignment and assume distinctly different forms for men and for women. In the first decade of the 20th century, the architectural style of the Bamum was utilized in building the royal palace at Fumban. The common dwelling is cubical with a roof whose slopes flow smoothly into each other (it is either domed or has a ridgepole), a form intermediate between cupola and roof. The appearance is enriched by different kinds of vegetable material and, in the chiefs' houses especially, by a generous display of wooden sculpture.
*Plates 361–363*

## BAMILEKE

This agricultural population of the Cameroons region lives in complex villages based on a symmetrical plan. In the most widespread type, the habitations are lined up in parallel rows around the sides of a central plaza reserved for ceremonies and assemblies, at the edge of which is the large community house. The family hut has a square plan and is topped by a conical thatched roof. Materials and dimensions vary according to the purpose of the hut. The women's houses, some ten to thirteen feet on a side, are like the assembly houses and granaries in that they have a supporting structure of four corner poles with double walls of bamboo in crisscross latticework. On the exterior of the family hut, the gaps between the bamboo canes are plugged with clay, making a lively decorative effect. The conical roof is set on a circle of posts surrounding the rectangular walls. The doorway, raised above ground level, is closed with a sliding panel of bamboo, and often another entrance higher up the wall gives access to the granary in an attic just under the roof. In the huge public buildings that require the labor of hundreds of men, the roof is either conical or pyramidal with curved profile and rounded corners. An exterior colonnade has primarily a decorative function, accentuated by the carvings that ornament the door. The interior is often divided by cross-partitioning into four rooms.
*Plates 364–370*

## BAKOSI

A farming population of the Cameroons region, the Bakosi make their home in the forest zone between the Manenguba Mountains and Mount Kupa. The traditional settlement is either a village of family compounds or else an isolated enclosure in a clearing. The usual dwelling is a cylindrical hut with high conical roof and walls of interwoven branches supported by poles around the exterior. Every enclosure includes a special house, the *njeb*, for the head of the family; when the latter is particularly affluent and prestigious, the *njeb* has two doors and is also used for social and ritual functions. The *njeb* of the most influential man in the clan becomes the locale for important political and religious meetings and is known as the *esam*. The external poles between the two doors are frequently carved with totemic images, and a series of five, seven, or nine stones serves as seats during the outdoor assemblies and is symbolic of the ancestors. The family hut, one for each wife, is called *ndab* and contains the sleeping pallets and hearth plus a kind of lumberroom for the supply of firewood.

## EAST AFRICA

## SHILLUK

Farmers and herders of the southern Sudan, the Shilluk live in villages of a few family complexes around a central space used for dances and ceremonies. There are also small temples dedicated to the ancestors as well as community stables. Monogamous families live in two huts (dwelling and kitchen) with facing entrances, in an open space surrounded by a hedge. Polygamous families occupy an enclosure with a number of huts, one for each wife, around a courtyard. The dwelling unit, in each case, is a cylindrical hut about twenty-six feet across, with walls of superimposed, foot-high rings of clay, the height of a man. The tall roof, ogival in section, is supported on a frame of branches bent by heat and covered with reeds and rushes laid over a layer of grass. Often, especially in the animal shelters, the roof extends to the ground to protect the walls from the heat of the sun. The oval entrance, roughly forty by fifteen inches, can be closed with a mat. The flooring is made of a compact paste of black dirt applied to a pavement of clay over a base of straw and sand. Large clay jars are used for storing food.

## DINKA

These farmers and stockbreeders of the southern Sudan live in large villages either on the heights or in the flat plains that are subject to flooding so that the huts there must be raised on large platforms resting on piles. The cylindrical hut has a conical roof covered with successive layers of straw, which often jut out over the entrance. In the interior, used also as kitchen, a platform serves as storage place.

## MARIA

Stockbreeders of northern Eritrea (Ethiopia), their encampment is composed of tent-huts whose framework is in the shape of an inverted keel and covered by hides. The Red Maria put up, within a large tent, two facing huts separated by the hearth, one for the goats and a hemiellipsoidal one for the women.

## SAHO

Seminomadic herders of Eritrea (Ethiopia), the Saho build conical huts of branches and brushwood partially plastered with dung called *dasa*, which lack a central vertical support but are fixed at the base by a circle of stones. Also widespread is a cylindrical construction with conical roof, the *are*, that can be considered akin to the *byet* of the Amhara (see below). Its wall, about eighteen inches thick, is built of clay and dirt masonry, and the roof is supported by a central pole. The interior is divided in two—the front area for the men, the rear for the women—and an exterior loggia serves as shelter for the animals.

Among the Saho there are also groups settled in palisaded villages of four-sided huts similar to the *hedmo* of the Amhara. During the summer, they also occupy natural grottoes, partitioning the interior.

## KUNAMA

An agricultural population of Eritrea (Ethiopia), the Kunama inhabit multifamily enclosures often as large as entire villages. Their settlements are generally on upland slopes or on terraces connected with their plantations. The extended family comprises from five to perhaps thirty family nuclei and occupies a number of different types of hut grouped around a courtyard that does duty as a threshing floor and is surrounded by stakes linked by reeds or thorny branches. Among the specific kinds of hut are the sleeping room for the chief and his family, the kitchen, assembly house, storeroom-larder, guest hut, boys' hut, and stables. The habitation is normally cylindrical with a conical roof that does not jut out beyond the walls. Rarely, the structure is reinforced by a central pole with a wooden disk at its summit. The roof is covered with clumps of straw laid on in successive layers, and decorations in woven straw cover the frame of the door. Only the granaries, raised above ground, are plastered over with mud.

## MAO

The Mao are a predominantly agricultural population of Ethiopia, whose dwelling is a round hut, sixteen to twenty feet in diameter. The wall is made up of a ring of poles set at intervals of roughly eighteen inches and reaching a height of sixteen to twenty feet. These are fixed in a narrow pit, which is then packed hard with mud. The stakes are then bent and tied with double hoops of rushes to make pointed arches. The roofing is composed of bundles of straw. The chiefs' huts are larger, as much as thirty-two feet across and twenty-six feet high, and these also have a central pole. Among the southern Mao, cylindrical huts with conical roofs and walls of densely woven bamboo are built.

## AMHARA

Farmers of northern Ethiopia, this group lives in permanent settlements. Excluding the urban centers (*katamah*) composed by and large of rectangular, terraced houses, the traditional types of dwelling are the *hedmo* and the *tucul*. The former, widespread in the Eritrean uplands, has a rectangular ground plan with walls of clay and stones often over eighteen inches thick. Two or three rows of poles fixed inside the walls hold up crossbeams supporting a flat roof of branches. The interior is divided into two rooms by a row of jars holding grain. The front part (*medribèt*) is larger and is used as living area, animal shelter, and guest room; the inner part (*ushatè*) contains the hearth and the beds, which are permanent fixtures in masonry. Normally two *hedmo* are paired and share the same roof, front porch, and outdoor animal shelter. They are often built with their backs against a slope.

The *tucul* (an Arabic word; *byet* in Amharic) has a cylindrical body with a conical roof but occurs in a considerable diversity of dimensions and materials. The walls are usually of dry masonry, and the more complex types have more than one story and an interior laid out in concentric rings around a central area, forming ring-like corridors, which are used variously as dwelling space, storerooms, or stables. The central area, divided in two, is always circular and covered by a conical roof

of vegetable matter, though the outer walls are often quadrangular. A variant form, the *sagalah*, has two apses, or is oval, and its roof has a continuous pitch and is held up by a ridgepole resting on two main poles. Here, too, the interior is divided, but the separate halves are occupied by two families. The *sakero* of the Cafficho group is similar, with the central area (rectangular) used for sleeping and the lateral semicircular chambers for living quarters and kitchen.

The traditional habitation of the seminomadic groups, the *gwojò*, is a dismountable hemispherical hut, thirteen feet in diameter, between six and seven feet high, with a framework of bent branches and a grass roof. A conical type, about ten feet high, has a framework of poles supported by a central upright and is covered by bundles of grass laid over each other or tied to make a series of shelflike bands.

## GURAGE

This agricultural population of central Ethiopia lives in villages composed of cylindrical huts with conical roofs. A family unit may occupy one or more huts: the *xarar* for sleeping, the *zagar* for living, the *gwea* for cooking as well as keeping the animals. The supporting structure is a central pole, which holds the upper part of the roof by means of rafters (*wakas*) opening out like a fan. The wall is composed of wooden elements held together by thick horizontal ligatures of bamboo (*gerkaha*). Inside, any gaps are plugged with a coating of clay. The hearth is situated between the door and the central pole. Behind the bed (*angereb*), a platform raised on piles (*kot*) serves as larder.

## GALLA

The Galla are a predominantly farming population of southern Ethiopia, whose villages are organized around a central plaza used for the market and for community activities. Often a lean-to of poles covered by straw is set up on the plaza and used for the administration of justice. The traditional dwelling of the sedentary groups is a cylindrical hut with conical roof related to the *tucul* (see *Amhara*). Among the Arussi group in central Ethiopia, there survives a type of hemiellipsoidal hut of large dimensions with entrance on the long side and framework composed of two series of parallel arches of bamboo intersecting at right angles in the central area and inclined toward the sides, following the curvature of the hut as a whole. The Arussi in the vicinity of Harrar have a cylindrical dwelling with conical roof called *maná* that is divided internally into three areas: a shelf of stone covered with mats that serves as couch (*bohru*), a cooking place (*sunsumma*), and a space reserved for gatherings and family activities (*hushah*).

Particularly interesting are the funerary monuments of the Galla. Their tombs are covered by cylindrical tumuli in stone or bamboo or by domes of earth (for the heads of tribes among the western Galla) surmounted by a wooden statue, and the whole structure is surrounded by a moat.

349

## CHENCHA

The family dwelling of the Chencha, who farm in is southern Ethiopia in the region west of Lake Abaya, an elegant construction of interwoven fillets of bamboo, circular in plan (height and diameter about twenty-six feet) with a pointed-arch profile, and covered by layers of bamboo leaves. The door is adorned with a high semicircular protuberance ending above in a lunette, and this serves to shade the entrance and is elegantly linked to the dome. The same dormerlike structure protects the small smoke vents on the sides of the house. The interior is divided in two by a bamboo wall, the front part sheltering the family and livestock and containing the hearth, the rear serving as larder.

## SIDAMA

The settlement of this predominantly agricultural population of southern Ethiopia is either a village or a family enclosure. Among the Konso group, large villages are protected by a double ring of walls with two gates, inside which are the family enclosures. Between the enclosures, broad streets lead to the assembly house with its stone walls and domed roof and to the clearing for dances, which has in the center either a monolith or a sacred tree. The Konso dwelling is cylindrical with a conical roof, though in the southwest there are also semi-underground houses with terraces and with walls of dry masonry. The former type prevails in the western region; in the eastern region, however, the Sidama groups have round huts of continuous curvilinear section. The hut of the Gamò, ogival in section, is covered with straw laid on in strips and has a semiconical protuberance that contains the entrance. The hut of the Sidama, broad and low, of densely interwoven reeds, has a profile swelling outward near the bottom and then curving back inward at ground level.
*Plate 13*

*For Ethiopia, see also plates 13, 21, 58, 59, 133–136, 145–149.*

## SOMALI

The Somali, who occupy the interior of Somalia, are herders and farmers; the former live in the *agal* and the latter in the *mondull*. The *agal* is a hemispherical hut four to ten feet in diameter and five to eight feet in height, which is easily disassembled. The skeleton is a parallel series of branches bent into arches connected by horizontal hoops of gradually decreasing diameter. The covering is of matting or hides. Alongside the entrance, and protected by a hedge, is the hearth. Inside, in front of the door is a sack for conserving the *dura*, and to the sides are the sleeping pallets.

The *mondull* is a conical-roofed cylindrical hut like the *tucul* of the Ethiopian Amhara. Its diameter varies from eight to sixteen feet, its height from over six to ten feet.

The wall is composed of stakes linked by horizontal branches, and the resulting trellis is filled in with clumps of turf and plastered over with a mixture of earth and dung. The central supporting upright, the *tir*, is reinforced at the base by a ring of lime and sand and at the top by a wooden disk, the *cabar*. The roofing is of leaves, grass, or straw. A partition divides the interior to make an inner rear chamber reserved, according to Islamic custom, for the women.

In Mirjirtein, houses of masonry are numerous, among them the *garese*, which is in the form of a truncated cone with two stories and topped by a terrace. The coastal settlements, on the other hand, are made up of dwellings with rectangular ground plan and peaked roof, often supported by poles inside, and with walls of stakes and earth, mud, or dung, which often are plastered over. The interior is divided by partitions of vegetable fibers into various chambers; the one in the center belongs to the head of the family, those to the sides to his wives. A scaffolding in the central chamber serves to hold provisions.
*Plates 137–139*

## BON

Hunters in southern Somalia, the Bon use an alcove-like shelter of bent branches with a bed of twigs and grass. They also build domed huts with a framework of interwoven branches, only half of which is covered over.

## TURKANA

Herders and hunters in the region southwest of Lake Rudolf, in Uganda, the Turkana live in small villages composed of a few huts and enclosures for the livestock. A hedge of branches and boughs surrounds each village. The dwelling is the property of the woman and is made up of two parts, a hemispherical hut, the *akai*, for the night and a daytime shelter, the *ekal*, in the form of a quarter-sphere.

## ACHOLI

Herders and farmers in Uganda, the Acholi live in villages that, in the past, were of notable dimensions and were sited in commanding positions. The village was surrounded by a palisade, and the houses clustered around a central plaza containing a temple-hut and the sacred tree, the theoretical hub of the territory. The Acholi habitation is a cylindrical hut with conical roof about sixteen feet across, with walls of stakes and reeds plastered over with clay. The straw-thatched roof, either smooth or with staggered layers of thatching, culminates in a kind of tassel and is slightly inclined, sometimes projecting to make an outside porch. Special huts, called *otogo*, are set aside for the youths and maidens.

## GANDA

These farmers of the Bantu linguistic group in Uganda live in villages made up of large conical dwellings thirty-three to thirty-nine feet in diameter and twenty-six feet in height. The roof functions also as wall and is constructed on a wooden trellis and covered with straw. In the interior, it rests on two concentric rings of poles and opens in a semielliptical lunette, which protects a small porch at the entrance.

## CHAGA

The Chaga, farmers of Bantu linguistic stock, live in Kenya, near Mount Kilimanjaro. Their habitation is a hut of dome-shaped structure concealed under a roof descending to the ground. In earlier times, their dwellings were entirely underground; a steep corridor led down to rooms of different dimensions and functions (living quarters, sleeping rooms, storage places) connected with each other by subterranean passageways and with ceilings in the form of vaults or cupolas, complete with conduits for ventilation.

## MASAI

The Masai are herders in central Kenya and northwestern Tanzania. Their temporary settlement is a kraal, put up in a commanding site and containing family dwellings and a bachelors' hut. Surrounded by a hedge-wall with two entrances at opposite sides, it has a space in the center for the livestock enclosures. In a kraal described by Merker (*Die Masai*, Berlin, 1910), sixteen dwellings, in two semicircles with their entrances facing the center, were aligned mirror-fashion with respect to the transverse axis and therefore subdivided into four groups. The dwelling, the *tembe*, has a rectangular ground plan and rounded corners, is about 10 by 13 to 16 feet, with flat roof and walls that are about $5^1/_2$ feet high, and with an entrance at a corner. The roof is held up by a longitudinal beam and a series of posts, and the continuous wall-roof consists of a web of curved branches connected by a layer of straw, clay, and dung. To protect the entrance, the wall doubles backward in a spiral, and the resulting small vestibule serves to cut down the intense sunlight and to keep out flies.
*Plate 151*

## NYAMWEZI

The encampment of these stockbreeders of Tanzania takes the form of a small quadrangular kraal composed of a number of family dwellings (*tembe*) often surrounded by a thorny hedge. Frequently half-underground and with a tunnellike entrance, the *tembe* is rectangular in plan and has a flat or arched roof with rounded corners. Its framework of poles and branches is plastered over with mud. The entrance is usually at a corner, and the huts are lined up with their short sides adjoining.
*Plate 152*

# CENTRAL AND SOUTHERN AFRICA

## BAYA

The Baya are farmers at the eastern borders of Cameroon and in Ubangi (Central African Republic). A village comprises a few dozen structures around a central community plaza. The dwelling is cylindrical with very high conical roof descending almost to the ground, and with either rectilinear or concave-convex profile. A central supporting pole is frequent. The interior furnishings include large decorated terra-cotta jars for provisions, set up on clay stands. As temporary shelter, a more archaic type of habitation is used, with a hemispherical dome and an entrance preceded by a barrel-vaulted corridor.

## PYGMIES

This hunting population of the equatorial forest in certain specific localities between Cameroon and Zaire lives in small hunting camps, inhabited for brief periods only and consisting of no more than a few family huts around a roughly circular central space. Building the small huts (six to ten feet in diameter, five feet high) is entirely the work of the women. The framework is hemispherical and is made of branches bent into skewed arches. Among the Mbuti Pygmies, a fairly common type is a quarter-sphere with parallel arches. The covering is of large leaves of the *Phrinium*, which make the huts remarkably waterproof even in heavy rains.
*Plate 60*

## MANGBETU

Farmers and hunters of the northeastern Congo region, in Zaire, whose villages are sited along main roads or watercourses, the Mangbetu occupy single-family enclosures isolated from others by a stand of palm trees. There are two traditional types of dwelling: rectangular with peaked roof, which is used by the men, and cylindrical with very high conical roof, used by the women. Recently, the latter has become common for men and women. Still in use among the Popoie and Ngelima groups are extremely tall and slender round or square huts with conical or pyramidal roofs rising as high as twenty feet from a base no more than six-to-ten feet across.
*Plate 46*

## BAKUBA

This population of Bantu farmers in the southeastern Congo region (Zaire) lives in villages organized around an oblong clearing in the center of which are small huts where poisons and fetishes are stored; at the sides are the rectangular, peaked-roofed, bark-covered family dwellings.

## ROTSE

Farmers and stockbreeders of the upper Zambesi in Rhodesia, the Rotse belong to the Bantu linguistic group. In the 19th century, they were organized in a kingdom that dominated a vast area between Angola and Mozambique. The traditional habitation of the Rotse kingdom was an oblong hut with barrel-vault, covered with ferns and grass and with the entrance in a short wall. Sometimes the roof had four convex slopes, and the interior was divided into two compartments.

## MBUNDU

Farmers of the Bantu linguistic group in Angola, the Mbundu live in villages with a central plaza containing a large assembly hut and surrounded by oblong or square family dwellings with roof pitched in two or four directions and walls plastered over with clay and richly decorated.

## BUSHMEN

The Bushmen are a hunting and gathering population in the wasteland of the Kalahari Desert in Angola, Namibia (South West Africa), the Republic of South Africa, and Botswana. The hunting groups set up their shelters in a circle around a fire. Among the Heikum Bushmen, the shelters encircle a round clearing with the sacred tree at the center, at whose foot the assemblies are held. The shelter is either a windscreen in the shape of a quarter-sphere or a small dome-shaped hut with framework of branches covered by grass and leaves.
*Plate 62*

## HOTTENTOTS

Nomadic hunters and herders of South West Africa (Namibia), the Hottentots live in camps consisting of a ring of huts around a roughly circular clearing. The hemispherical huts, about thirteen feet in diameter, are easily taken apart. They have a supporting skeleton of flexible branches fixed vertically, tied together at the top, and connected by parallel horizontal loops. When hunting, the men use a simple semicircular windscreen of branches covered by twigs or grasses.
*Plates 159, 160*

## DAMARA

The Damara are hunters and gatherers of South West Africa (Namibia). The camp of the hunting group is no more than a ring of shelters around a clearing in whose center is the fire or a sacred tree. Besides windscreens, the Damara build broad hemispherical huts with a framework of bent branches covered with grass, though the traditional covering was a layer of mud.

## HERERO

These nomadic hunters of South West Africa (Namibia)

of Bantu tongue live in roughly circular encampments with a plaza (*khoro*) in the center for the fire and sacred tree. The chief's hut is set apart from the ordinary family huts (*pontok*) of domelike shape covered with earth or a plaster of clay and dung.

## CHWANA

These farmers and herders of Bantu tongue in the semi-desert central regions of South Africa (Republic of South Africa, Botswana) build large villages, which may hold twenty-five thousand inhabitants or more and are made up of cylindrical huts with conical roofs, which often have an outside veranda of poles.

## SOTHO

The traditional settlement of these stockbreeders of Bantu tongue in the eastern regions of the Republic of South Africa is a kraal with the family huts around an enclosure for livestock and with the chief's hut on the side facing the entrance. The huts are hemispherical, with oval ground plan and a frame of plant stalks covered with clay.

## ZULU

The Zulu are Bantu stockbreeders at the extreme southeastern tip of Africa, in the Republic of South Africa. Their kraals have a central enclosure for animals and provisions that is surrounded by the huts (*indlu*) in a ring. These are domelike with a slightly depressed profile and, as they are made of interwoven branches and reeds covered with stubble and straw, they are so light that they can be moved from place to place without being taken apart. Because of the thickly woven dome, the dwelling is referred to as *ukwakha umduzo* (knitwork). The internal structure is a frame made of two forked poles (*insika*) and a crosspiece (*umjanjato*) on which rest the rafterlike supports of the upper part of the roof, which has, as supporting framework, rushes bent into a parabola (*izi thungo*) over which is laid straw held down from outside by a net with radial segments and rectangular meshes (*umtwazi*). The hearth lies between the poles in the center of the hut, and the right side of the interior is reserved for the men, the left side for the women. Other types of roofing are also used: the dome may be covered by layers of straw disposed in layers (*ukwakha umdeko*) or its central part may be covered by a longitudinal mat (*indlu esikutulo*).
*Plates 156–158*

## TSONGA

These farmers of southern Mozambique traditionally live in villages of rounded contours surrounded by a palisade. Their cylindrical huts with conical roofs have walls of logs. The granaries, plastered outside, have roofs supported externally by a ring of poles. The plan of the village reflects the hierarchical structure of Tsonga

society. At the sides of the gate are the huts of the unmarried young men and young women; beyond, to the right and left, those for the brothers of the chief; in axial position facing the entrance, that of the chief and those of his wives.
*Plate 150*

*For Central and South Africa, see also plates 20, 47–50, 153–155, 359, 439.*

## WESTERN AND CENTRAL ASIA AND ADJOINING REGIONS

### RUWALA BEDOUINS

Nomad camel breeders roaming in a vast semidesert region of Syria, Jordan, Saudi Arabia, and Iraq, the Ruwala Bedouins follow fixed seasonal itineraries, so that year after year they make camp for weeks at a time always in the same localities. Three or four pairs of poles suffice for the framework of their tent, over which is stretched a cloth made of numerous strips of goat's wool in various lengths. The chief's tent is usually larger than the others, and its interior is divided into a smaller area for the chief and his guests and a larger one for the women and children and the receptacles for the provisions.

### KURDS

These farmers and herders in Kurdistan, a mountainous region at the borders between Iran, Iraq, the Aleppo zone of Syria, Turkey, and the Soviet Union, live in settlements that are stable or semipermanent depending upon whether agricultural or pastoral activities predominate. Particularly widespread is a type of dwelling, with circular ground plan and parabolic cupolalike roof, entire villages often being made up of this one type of hut, the *guba'd*. In the mountains, the *guba'd* is built of dry masonry; in the plains (for example, around Aleppo), of sun-dried loaves or bricks of clay. The individual structures, whose only aperture is a door, are combined into multifamily complexes and are often fronted by a circular open space delimited by a low wall.

### ARMENIANS

The Armenians are farmers and stockbreeders in northern Iran and the republic named for them in the Soviet Union. Their villages are large and compact, with the dwellings all oriented in the same direction. The traditional house, the *glkhatun*, is square, single-storied, topped by a complex cupola (*azarashenk*), and provided with an underground cellar. Inside the enclosure for the livestock there is often a second construction reserved for the men, the *odah*. More common, however, is the oblong house in stone and clay with roof-terrace used for sleeping outdoors on built-in platforms during the summer.

### AZERBAIDZHANS

These people live to the southwest of the Caspian Sea in Soviet Russia. They are chiefly occupied with agriculture and stockbreeding. A type of dome-shaped tent, the *kibitka*, used by nomadic groups has a simple structure of poles driven into the ground, tied together at the top, and then covered with felt.

### GEORGIANS

The traditional social structure of this agricultural population of Transcaucasian Soviet Russia was based on the extended family. In the western regions, the houses are mostly of wood, in the east of stone. Among the Kartli group, the house is semiunderground and set against a mountain wall; it has a flat roof and a central hearth. The most interesting traditional type is topped by a complex wooden steplike structure supported by poles (*darbazi*) with an opening in the center as smoke vent. The post closest to the hearth was thought of as the sacred support for the entire construction and was decorated with intaglio carving. In the mountainous zones of Georgia, especially in the Suanetia, the settlements are for the most part sparse or contain only a few family nuclei. They are dominated by very high stone tower-houses; in the lower of the two or three stories is the hearth in the center, and it is used as winter quarters and shelter for the animals; the middle story is used in the summer, and the top story serves as refuge and lookout post.

### OSSETS

Farmers and stockbreeders in the Soviet Caucasus, the Ossets live in compact villages on the hill slopes or in more dispersed complexes in the plains. In the high mountain valleys, the villages, comprising a single extended family residing in a number of habitations, used to be surrounded by a stone wall. As in Daghestan (see below), lookout towers are frequent. The traditional house has a single room with central fireplace and is divided into separate areas for the men and the women.

### CIRCASSIANS

Stockbreeders and farmers in the plains of the northwestern Caucasus and along the shores of the Black Sea in the Soviet Union, the Circassians have a traditional residence that consists of an enclosure divided into three parts: house, open yard, and enclosure for the livestock. The house is quadrangular, windowless, with a roof pitched in two or four directions, and has a wooden frame filled in with rushes and interwoven branches and plastered over with clay. A round hut near the main house serves as kitchen, and a type of easily disassembled tent-hut is often used as summer quarters; both of these are vestiges of a nomadism no longer practiced. The house is often divided into separate areas for the men and the women, though sometimes there are even separate houses for the sexes. Guests are lodged in special build-ings. The storehouse for grain is made of interwoven branches, is set up on poles, and has a round or cylindrical container for grain, and the roof is removable.

### ABKHAZIANS

This primarily agricultural population of the Caucasian coast of the Black Sea in the Soviet Union builds a rectangular house with a roof pitched in four directions, open in the center to give an air vent, and often with a chimney above the central fireplace to improve the draft. A more archaic type, round and plastered with clay, is used as cooking place.

### DAGHESTANS

This name comprises various populations in the Soviet republic of Daghestan in the Caucasus with a predominantly agricultural and pastoral economy, who inhabit villages normally situated on the mountain slopes. The traditional dwelling is in part carved out of the sloping terrain so that the rear wall is rock. It has a quadrangular ground plan and a terrace-roof. The extreme ethnic diversity of these peoples has resulted in unremitting conflicts between the various groups, which have necessitated building numerous lookout towers that either belong to the community as a whole or to the principal families.

The ordinary house has a single room, but more complex types reflect family divisions (men and women separated according to Islamic custom) as well as the owners' status, the houses of wealthier families having more than one story. Sometimes each house is separated from the others and surrounded by its own rectangular fortified enclosure.

### KIRGHIZES, UZBEKS, TURKMEN, KAZAKHS, KARA-KALPAKS

These populations of farmers and stockbreeders live in Soviet republics that bear their names in Central Asian Russia. The sedentary groups build rectangular houses that often form part of large agglomerations, whereas the nomads use the *kibitka*, a type of *yurta* based on a trellis frame (see *Mongols, Turks*). Very frequently now two types of dwelling are used, and there are numerous local variations in materials (unbaked bricks, earth mixed with straw, trelliswork plastered over with clay) as well as in types of *yurtas*. These assume a diversity of form (as, for example, among the various Turkmen groups). Among the sedentary groups, the *yurta* is nowadays often no more than a household accessory or a shelter for the animals. Thus, among the Kara-Kalpaks it is used as a summer house set up in the courtyard and, in the winter, as a shelter erected inside the house itself.
*Plate 122*

### MONGOLS, TURKS

Nomadic and seminomadic herders in the vast semidesert regions of Central Asia from Mongolia to the Caspian Sea in both Mongolia and the Soviet Union, the Mongols and Turks traditionally live in extended-family encampments of cylindrical tents capped by domes of varying degrees of shallowness. This type of habitation, in virtually identical forms, called variously *yurta*, *kibitka*, or *ger*, was documented in the 13th century, in the history of the Mongols by Joannes de Plano Carpini and in Marco Polo's *Travels*. The groups involved to some extent in agriculture also build flat-roofed clay houses and live in villages that often are fortified.

The *yurta* is made up of two parts: a cylindrical base-wall to the height of a man, and the upper covering, which among the Mongols takes the shape of a truncated cone and among the Turkish groups that of a very shallow dome. The diameter may be from sixteen to thirty-two feet, the height between ten and eighteen feet, and the cylindrical wall is composed of four to twelve sections, each consisting of a network of branches or wooden slats crisscrossed so as to form, when opened, a trellis of squares set on edge, diamond-fashion. The separate sections of the trellis as well as the frame of the door are tied together with strips of leather, wool, or silk. The rods that form the framework for the cloth covering (among the Turkish groups) are fixed at the upper part of the base, often reinforced by a ring of cloth, at every intersection of the trellis. These rods are inserted, at the top of the tent, into holes in the "crown," a wooden wheel whose spokes are either strictly horizontal or rise saucerlike to the top; a round hole is left open in the center of the crown to act as air vent. Sometimes the crown is also held in place by two inlaid and painted props. The door, too, is decorated, and during the day the entrance is protected by a felt hanging or a mat that can be rolled up. The *yurta* is covered with a number of layers of felt, often in different colors to indicate the social position of the owner, and these are cinched in place by thick ties. Other materials may also be used, among them bark, fronds, and matting. The interior, entered from the southwest, has a floor covered by furs or wool carpets. The disposition of the furnishings is regulated by a strict ritual and hierarchical order: in the center, the stove or fireplace; on the side opposite the door, the bed and small table for a guest along with the sacred images; to the right (toward the southeast), the pallets used for the head of the family and his wife together with the chests for clothing; to the left (toward the northwest), the beds of the children. *Plates 115–116*

## BASHKIRS

This population of Turco-Tatar language lives in the southern Ural Mountains of the Soviet Union. Their economic activity varies according to the region: in the west and north, agriculture; in the east and south, stock-breeding. In central Bashkiria the usual habitation was, in the past, a conical tent covered with bark. Among nomadic or seminomadic groups, much use is still made of the *yurta*, which occurs in the various types found in the Central Asian steppes, often divided into two parts, with the right half reserved for the women.

A recent product of the influence of the Russian *izba* is a windowless log cabin, much favored in the mountainous zones of the Urals; in the arid zones the farmers' houses are semiunderground and built of turf, which is also used to cover the roof. A type of house of unbaked bricks resembles the winter dwelling of the Kazakhs, and many houses are now built with mixed materials such as osiers and clay or stones and clay, and these are quadrangular in plan with a flat roof.

## ALTAIS

The Altais are seminomadic stockbreeders of Turkish language in the Altai territory, the upper part of the Ob basin in the Soviet Union, Asia. Among the southern Altais, the dwelling used to be a *yurta* of Mongol type, covered in felt, whereas in the northwestern zones it was, instead, a conical tent covered with bark. In some northeastern areas, a hexagonal log cabin became widespread in the 19th century in association with the introduction of agriculture by the expanding Russian Empire.

## BURYATS

Stockbreeders in the area of Lake Baikal and the Mongolian regions of the Soviet Union, the Buryats were predominantly nomadic before the spread of the Russian Empire induced them to settle down to farming in the 17th century. Until then, they had lived in *yurtas* of Mongol type, but these were gradually replaced by wooden houses, which might have as many as eight, ten, or twelve sides and were always built on a centralized ground plan. More recently, a rectangular cabin with peaked roof has gained favor, and the first examples described in the 18th century were windowless but had a central opening at the top to siphon off the smoke.

## LURS

The Lurs are nomad stockbreeders of Luristan in Iran. In western Luristan, the tent has a barrel-shaped frame and is covered with matting. Among the Bakhtyars, the tent covering is laid over a simple series of stakes around three sides of a rectangle, in whose center is the fireplace, while the fourth side remains open. In other groups, the woolen tent cloth is made up of a number of separate strips and is laid over three poles connected by a horizontal beam. To the top of each pole is affixed a curved piece, which gives the tent its characteristic profile. The Papi have a flat-roofed summer hut, the *kula*, in which a series of forked poles in parallel staggered rows support a web of interwoven branches covered by successive layers of fronds. The hut is closed on three sides with movable walls of mats and branches, and the fourth side remains open here, too. A partition of matting divides the interior into separate quarters for the men and the women. A rectangular annex at the rear shelters the animals. *Plates 123–125*

## BALUCHIS

Nomad stockbreeders of Baluchistan in Iran and Pakistan, the Baluchis have a barrel-vaulted tent with a skeleton of parallel wooden arches over which a woolen covering is stretched by cords attached to the short sides. In summer, the tent cloth remains lifted up to make a simple shelter against the sun. In winter, the tent is completed by lengths of cloth on the sides and rear, with a mat covering the entrance and other mats, stiffened by clay, reinforcing the walls. The animals are sheltered in tents or in enclosures of poles and matting.

## KAFIRS, TADZHIKS

These agricultural populations live in Soviet central Asia, Afghanistan, and northern Pakistan, and their villages are composed of complex, many-storied buildings. For basic structure, these have alternate layers of wood and stone with balconies on trestles of poles. For defensive reasons, often there are no outside windows, and towers, too, are quite common, with access to the upper stories only by ladders set against the outside of the building. What are to all intents and purposes small fortresses are built with the same technique and usually have rectangular ground plans with square towers at the corners and no openings other then small slits for ventilation hollowed out of the layers of wood.

## AFGHANS

Stockbreeders and farmers of Afghanistan, these nomad groups set up a winter camp of a few dozen tents, *kizhdi*, in one or two rows, with the chief's tent in the center and, at the west, an open sacred area delimited by stones and set aside for prayers. The most common kind of tent has the form of a barrel vault with arches held up in the center by forked poles, which, in some cases, also support a horizontal **T**-shaped crossbar. The sedentary herders have stone houses with domed roofs covered with mud, with a chimney in the center. The farmers generally live in two-storied rectangular houses built of bricks of sun-baked clay and straw. The houses are topped by a terrace, and the ground floor serves as shelter for the animals, the upper floor as living quarters, with separate rooms for men and women.

## TIBETANS

The traditional settlement of the farming populations of Tibet consists of villages or hamlets usually perched on mountain slopes. The family dwelling is rectangular, with walls made of stone cemented with mud or of bricks of raw clay, and there is a terrace-roof supported by posts in the interior. The windowless ground floor serves as stables or storeroom; the second floor as winter living quarters; the third, directly under the terrace-roof, as summer quarters. The seminomadic breeders of livestock often have separate dwellings for winter and summer. The former is a simple single-roomed structure of masonry, the latter a tent (*rebò*) covered with cloth of goat or yak wool dyed black and known as the "black tent." The tent frame is made up of two poles supporting a crosspiece and held upright by guy ropes attached to a series of stakes on the outside. The tent cloth is stretched tight with ropes and pegs. The entrance is at a side, and there is a smoke vent at the top. The tent is erected on a platform of earth or brushwood and is often surrounded by a wall of unmortared stones or of mud.

For Western and Central Asia and adjoining regions, see also plates 1–4, 6, 7, 16, 117–121.

# SOUTH ASIA AND MADAGASCAR

## VEZO

Fishermen of the southwest tip of Madagascar, the Vezo build their settlements on the seashore. They consist of conical tents built of masts and sails from their boats.

## BETSILEO

Farmers and stockbreeders of the west central uplands of Madagascar, the Betsileo site their villages in the center of their terraced rice fields. The huts are rectangular and peak-roofed. A characteristic decoration, evidence of cultural connections with Southeast Asia, is the long upper extension of the edges of the roofs carved to resemble horns.
*Plate 263*

## BEZANOZANO

These farmers of eastern Madagascar as recently as the last century lived in fortified villages on the heights, though now they occupy the valley bottoms. The old defensive palisades were notable for their gates, in some cases large roundish stones engaged between two posts. The traditional dwelling is rectangular with double-pitched roof, laid out on a north-south axis and with the entrance on the west side. It clearly reflects the cosmological beliefs the Bezanozano share with many other Madagascan populations. The center of the house, and of cosmic space, is represented by the central supporting upright. The northwest corner is sacred to the ancestors and guests and is known as the *zoro firarazana*, the ancestors' corner, while the east side of the house contains the beds of the parents and children.

The spatial directions are associated with the twelve zodiacal signs and therefore with the months. The signs and months are in turn associated with the house walls, two for each side and one for each of the four corners. Thus, beginning at the northeast corner, we have *alahamady* (Aries); on the east wall, *adaoro* (Taurus) and *adizaoza* (Gemini); in the southeast corner, *asorotany* (Cancer); on the south wall, *alahasaty* (Leo) and *asom-*

*bola* (Virgo); in the southwest corner, *adimizana* (Libra); on the west wall, *alakarobo* (Scorpio) and *alakaosy* (Sagittarius); in the northwest corner, *adijady* (Capricorn); on the north wall, *adalo* (Aquarius) and *alohotsy* (Pisces). The four principal months correspond to the corners, the eight secondary ones to the sides. The house itself is thought of as corresponding to the lunar month of twenty-eight days, so that three days are associated with each corner and four with each wall.
*Plates 140, 256, 259*

For Madagascar, see also plates 254, 255, 257, 258, 260–262.

## VEDDA

Hunters and gatherers of the southern region of the island of Ceylon (Sri Lanka), the Vedda often live in shelters beneath rocks or in caves. In widespread use are an elementary type of screen, merely a single-pitched windbreak held up by two props, and small huts of brush and bark.

## TODA

The villages (*mand*) of these herders in the Nilgiri Mountains of the southern Deccan area of India may consist of as few as two or three single-family habitations. Special sacred villages (*tirieri mand*) have two dwellings for the priests and a conical temple of wood and bamboo. Every village has a stone enclosure (*tuer*) for the buffaloes and a storage place (*palthci*) for the milk of the sacred buffaloes, a cylinder set into the ground and topped by a spindle-shaped roof made of increasingly smaller rings of rushes and covered with straw, about thirteen feet high. The habitation is rectangular in plan, with a supporting framework consisting of two to five slightly depressed pointed arches made of bundles of rushes tied tightly; the horizontal elements are also made of rushes. The roofing is composed of strips of straw laid horizontally like tiles. At both the front and the back of the house there is a freestanding board wall. The front one is set back about three feet to leave a covered area in front of the entrance, to either side of which a mound of earth serves as a seat. The interior may have a single room or be divided into two or three noncommunicating rooms accessible only through doors opened in the lower part of the vault. In the simplest type of interior there is a ledge of earth on one side on which the sleeping pallets are laid; on the other side are the hearths and the mortar, which is simply a hollow in the ground. The hut may be either half-underground or elevated, but in either case it is surrounded by an unmortared stone wall.
*Plate 35*

## KURUMBA, URALI

The Kurumba are hunters and gatherers, in part also farmers, in the mountains of the southwestern Deccan area of India. The dwelling of the agricultural groups is a rectangular one-room bamboo hut with the roof

pitched in two or four directions and covered by grass. At most a dozen of these huts make up a village.

Among the Urali, at the extreme southern tip of the Indian subcontinent, there is a tree hut beside every habitation, in part supported on poles and reached by long ladders, where the inhabitants take refuge from elephants during the night. The village food storehouses are also on platforms in the trees and are covered by a peaked roof.

## CHENCHU

Hunters and gatherers in the Hyderabad region of India, Chenchu build camps that consist of a dozen or so conical or conical-cylindrical bamboo huts (*koya*) disposed around a circular clearing. During the dry season, they simply shelter under screens of branches and leaves.

## MURIA

The Muria are farmers in central India, southeast of Nagpur, living in villages made up of numerous dwellings. A family occupies two or three wooden or bamboo huts around a small courtyard, with the stalls for the animals set well apart. A larger and richly decorated hut, the *gotul*, serves as collective dwelling for the young people of both sexes.

## NAGA

This agricultural population of the mountainous zones of Assam (India) and northern Burma lives in villages often of considerable dimensions with as many as a few hundred huts all aligned along a single street. Frequently, the village is composed of a number of semi-autonomous communities, each with its own house for the bachelors. Frequent, too, are fortifications made of poles, hedges, and earth embankments. The villages of the Naga-Lhota, with gates at either end, are usually sited on a crest that dominates a length of road and along this hilltop the dwellings are aligned. In the center of the village grows a ficus tree sacred to the tribal community; at its foot, ritual sacrifices are made and sacred stones piled up.

The dwellings of the Naga groups are often set up on piles, except among the Angami. The Lhota have a bamboo multifamily hut with slightly raised floor, a convex semicircular front facing the street, and a platform at the rear. Inside, each family has its own hearth. The huts of the Ao have the roof projecting markedly either at the sides or at the front, where it is held up by a central pole and lateral poles inclined out fanwise to make a kind of covered veranda.

The collective buildings, such as houses for the men, warriors, and assemblies, are carefully constructed and of particular interest. Those of the Lhota, measuring about thirteen by forty feet, have a markedly elevated roof supported by carved pillars to form an upper veranda-terrace. The warriors' house of the Ao has a semicircular projecting facade, whose upper part is covered with straw to form a semiconical roof, while

the lower part, with the door in its center, is of bamboo. The houses of the chiefs are often very large and built with much care. The houses of the Tankhul chiefs have slightly convex front walls made of boards, and the projecting gable beams intersect at the top to make a motif resembling two huge horns that is widely diffused among the Naga groups.
*Plates 36–38*

## KACHIN

Farmers of northern Burma, the Kachin live in villages made up of collective houses. The structure of the settlement apparently lacks any precise plan because of the use of geomancy (divination by figures or lines) to select the position of every new house. The habitation is a longhouse with a corridor, and in it each of the family units has its own place along the walls. Special places are reserved for the head of the extended family and for the cult altar, while covered verandas serve as recreation areas, storage places, and stalls for the animals.

## VA

These farmers and stockbreeders in the Kengtung region of central eastern Burma live in villages of houses strung out along a central thoroughfare, where, in the past, the headhunters' trophies, now replaced by anthropomorphic pillars, were displayed. Every house was surrounded by a stockade of bamboo, and the villages, clinging to mountainsides, were defended by an earthwork wall and a camouflaged moat. The dwelling is of wood, raised above the ground, and has a low double-pitched roof.

## LOLO

The Lolo farming villages are located in a mountainous zone of the Yunnan province of southern China, bordering on Indochina, at an altitude of five thousand to sixty-five hundred feet (the valleys are occupied by the Chinese). Their dwelling is rectangular with wooden floor and walls of bamboo and clay and a roof covered with boards. The interior is divided into three rooms: one to the left serving as sleeping quarters; one in the center, where the fireplace is used as living area; and one to the right occupied by the servants and livestock. Beside the house there is a lookout tower two or three stories high, and around it a quadrangular earthwork wall often rises higher than the house itself.

## RADE

The villages of this agricultural population of South Vietnam were formerly fortified with palisades. Their dwelling is a very large, rectangular collective house as much as 165 feet long, set on piles and oriented on a north-south axis. The peaked roof is covered with leaves; the walls are made of tightly woven bamboo. The entrance, on a long side, is protected by a veranda.

Inside, the front part is used for receiving guests and for festivities, and the central part is reserved as residence, consisting of a central corridor with family quarters along the sides, each with its own cooking area. At the very back lives the chief. The area under the house, between the piles, is used as shelter for the animals.

*For Vietnam, see also plates 266–271; for Khmer Republic, see plates 264, 265.*

## ANDAMANESE

These hunters and gatherers live in the Andaman Islands in the Bay of Bengal, an Indian possession. The most common dwelling is a lean-to with single-pitched roof held up by four poles and covered with brushwood, with or without a platform. An encampment comprises about fifteen of such shelters (separate ones for bachelors, maidens, and married women) around an oval dancing plaza, at one end of which the fire is kept perpetually burning. The Onghi of Little Andaman, however, live in large circular huts of shallow dome-shape twenty-six feet in diameter, sixteen feet high, with an upper vent for smoke and ventilation. Every hut houses the entire group of up to about a dozen families.
*Plate 54*

## SEMANG

The temporary camps of these hunters and gatherers of the Malay Peninsula (Thailand, Malaysia) are generally oval or circular with the fire in the center, and the family shelters around it. Among the Jehai group, the shelters, either single or double, are disposed around a central clearing, but each has its own hearth and a shelf or platform inside for sleeping, with special shelters reserved for the youths and for married couples. Normally the habitation has a simpler structure: a kind of screen is made of three lengths of bamboo fixed vertically in the ground and reinforced with forked stakes, and these bamboo poles are connected at the top by a horizontal rod, which is pulled forward and over by lianas of *rotang*, providing a narrow roof. Sometimes the bamboo poles are tied together directly and bent to form a more pronounced curve, then covered with palm leaves. Often these shelters are coupled, in which case they assume the shape of a barrel vault or dome. Still others have a structure of vertical poles and flat roof, marking out a semicylindrical space. Frequent, too, is the double-pitched shed raised above the ground either entirely open or with a single wall, set against a tree, among whose branches is often built a bamboo platform.
*Plate 61*

## KUBU

The Kubu are seminomadic farmers in the interior of Sumatra (Indonesia). They live in a rectangular shelter without walls and with a peaked roof supported by a

pole at each corner and by two others on which the ridgepole rests. Two long beams rest on natural forks in the corner poles, about twenty inches above the ground, and support a platform of narrow planks that fills half of the roofed-over space and holds the sleeping pallets.

## NIAS ISLANDERS

These agricultural people of the Indonesian island of Nias live in rectangular villages with a central axis dominated by the house of the chief. A correspondence between the plan of the settlement and the mythic and cosmological beliefs of these people is expressed in a series of hierarchical principles and symmetries. To the sides of the central plaza, in rectangular sectors often preceded by a kind of piazza, are aligned the common dwellings that comprise the "halves" of the village. The chief's house, which is much larger and more painstakingly built, sometimes coupled with the village's "temple of origins," occupies a dominant position, situated, both symbolically and in reality, at the most elevated point of the terrain. More numerous here than in other Indonesian centers are megalithic constructions such as pavements, staircases, altars, and sculptures. The common dwelling is a rectangular hut with a roof pitched in two or four directions. The walls are extremely complex, projecting markedly at the front beneath the eaves with horizontal bands emphasized rhythmically by apertures. A typical structural element is a vertical support in trident or **V**-shape found in the front portico of the common houses as well as on the facades of the more monumental residences of the chiefs and the assembly houses.
*Plates 274–276*

## MINANGKABAU

An agricultural population of the west central zone of Sumatra (Indonesia), the Minangkabau live in rectangularly laid-out villages that have a complex network of territorial associations. The house for assemblies is considered the center of the territory (*negari*), presided over traditionally by four clans (*suku*). In the village, whose main thoroughfare runs from north to south, the built-up area (*kampung*) is counterbalanced by the concentric periphery (*bukit*). The east and west halves of the villages, separated by the rectangular central plaza, are recognized to be different. The principal building of the village is the assembly house (*balai*) where the various kinship groups are represented and which serves also as dormitory for the youths.

The traditional habitation is collective, a wooden edifice built with extreme care and refinement, often entirely covered with decoration. The most complex type has a central rectangular nucleus with an entrance on a long side. To the sides are annexes, seemingly telescoped into each other, that become progressively smaller and higher toward the ends, as they are elevated on piles. A lateral double gable at the lowest point of the complex saddleback roof emphasizes the transverse axis of symmetry. The lines of the eaves along the length of the

building are slightly curved to follow the upward movement of the lines of the structure toward the ends. The ridge lines of the roof accentuate that movement and swoop up to form sharply pointed tympanums at the ends of two (or even three) saddleback roofs of different lengths interpenetrating one into the other. In the interior, each family occupies a room (*bilik*) with its own hearth, and an area is set aside for the women to work in.
*Plates 284–288.*

## BATAK

These farmers in north central Sumatra (Indonesia) have villages with a complex and highly organized social and architectonic structure. Usually the settlement is more or less oblong in shape, with a central plaza along whose sides are aligned the family houses, special buildings, storehouses for rice, and the communal houses. Systems of fortification with palisades, earthworks, and a single entrance gate have fallen into disuse now. The rectangular dwelling (*baga*), elevated above the ground, is an elegant wooden construction, often richly decorated with carvings and paintings with geometrical and floral motifs, its walls flaring outward to form an inverted truncated pyramid. The thatched roof is double-pitched, with a marked saddlelike depression in the middle. At the short ends, it is cut off obliquely to make a steeply peaked gable projecting over the end walls. A few stairs lead up to the elevated front entrance that gives on an axial corridor, off which are places for the individual families, each with its own hearth and separated from each other by partitions of matting. Each *baga* houses from four families (among the Toba-Batak) to eight (among the Karo-Batak). There are numerous collective buildings, most notably the square men's house used also for assemblies (*sopo*) and the houses for the unmarried youths and girls. A special house is also set aside for the village smith. The square storehouses for rice are built with great care. Many different types of roof are used for these various buildings; a common one has four pitches complicated by pyramidal secondary pitches, extremely high, sharp gables, and a characteristic "lantern" with four triangular double pitches, a small version of the storehouse that frequently crowns the buildings.
*Plates 277, 279–283*

## DAYAK

A farming population in Borneo (Malaysia, Indonesia), the Dayak have as traditional settlement the large collective house sheltering the entire extended family. Some populations use the longhouse only occasionally, for assemblies and festivities, living in smaller huts built on piles in the cultivated fields, accommodating no more than two or three families. The large collective house is almost always isolated and may shelter as many as three hundred individuals. In some rather rare cases, a number of such houses may be grouped together or aligned in parallel rows and are then connected by a front veranda. The peaked-roofed longhouse is built

of wood and bamboo and is normally set up on piles. It may be from six hundred fifty to almost a thousand feet long and only about thirty-two feet wide. The central part of the interior is taken up by a corridor that may or may not be roofed, and off this lie the apartments of the individual families. This central area is also used for domestic work. Construction is always carried out with great care, especially in the interior, and the roof beams and entrance stairs are often carved. Quite often there is a veranda along a long side. The first section of the corridor is a ceremonial area where the sacred fire is kept perpetually burning; at the extreme rear are the sleeping quarters for the men.
*Plates 179–181*

## TORADJA

These farmers in the interior of the island of Celebes (Indonesia) build villages that consist of large houses set up on piles. Particular care is taken in building the house used for male assemblies and for festivities and ceremonies (*lobo*). The traditional dwelling of the Saadang Toradja is a long collective house with saddleback roof rising steeply and projecting so markedly at the ends as often to require extra support by poles on the exterior. All the visible parts are often richly decorated with geometrical motifs and the ritual buffalo horns.
*Plate 289*

*For Indonesia, see also plates 273, 278; for the Philippine Islands, see plate 272.*

# AUSTRALIA AND OCEANIA

## TASMANIANS

These nomadic gatherers and hunters of the Australian island of Tasmania became extinct in the 19th century. Rarely were their habitations grouped to form small settlements. In the three villages of which traces have been found and which were inhabited only on festive occasions, small huts of bark and grasses, about 6$\frac{1}{2}$ feet high, were disposed in two concentric rings around a clearing with a sacred tree. A simple arched screen of branches and leaves held up by poles served to protect the fire, while the usual dwelling was a quarter-sphere of branches covered by bark or a hemisphere with the hearth in the center and the opening toward the east. On the east coast, large conical huts of interwoven branches covered with bundles of grass have been found, and these were collective dwellings capable of housing perhaps thirty persons.

## ARANDA

As for other Australian tribes, the territory of these hunters and gatherers of the Northern Territory of central Australia is a highly meaningful aggregate of

places believed to have been created in mythic times by the ancestors who shaped the world.

On their periodic moves, the Achilpa group carry with them, as means of orientation, the sacred pole (*kauwaauwa*), symbol of the center of the world, which is fixed into the ground pointing in the direction of the march at each resting place. It constitutes a visible link between the tribe and the mythic creation of the world by the legendary heroes of the "dream-time." The encampment is made up of small family shelters around a fire, though during the dry season a framework of two forked poles holding a crosspiece on which rests a large piece of bark bent into half-barrel shape is set up.

*For Australia, see also plates 63–67.*

## TOR

Farmers and hunters of western New Guinea, whose villages are usually sited along watercourses, the entire Tor population moves into temporary quarters periodically, for agricultural activities or hunting. Fortified villages in places affording natural protection are occupied only intermittently. The settlement is made up of rectangular peak-roofed dwellings elevated on piles, and in its center is the house for assemblies and religious ceremonies, the *faareh*, a large circular construction with conical roof. The framework of the frond-covered roof is made of beams disposed radially, and it rests on the walls and on an outside ring of poles forming a circular veranda. Inside the house, two parallel rows of upright supports create a long corridor connecting the entrances at either end. This space is occupied by the men during the ceremonies, while the two lateral semicircular areas are reserved for the women. Above the latter are two atticlike places for storing food and two dormers as depository for human skulls. In the center of the *faareh* rises a pole that does not have a supportive function but, during the ceremony inaugurating the house, is cut at about three-quarters of its height and connected by a crosspiece with the two storage places, an operation intended to reproduce the castration of the primordial hero who constructed the world. The *faareh* as a whole symbolizes the union of the male and female principles, which is repeated ritually during the course of ceremonies reproducing the first event in the era of creation.

## MBOWAMB

This agricultural population of New Guinea lives in villages composed of characteristic round-ended, rectangular dwellings whose flooring is about a foot below ground level. They are divided internally by two walls of interwoven laths delimiting a central area (entrance and living quarters with kitchen and hearth) and two semicircular lateral rooms reserved, respectively, for the men and the women and children.

## GOGODARA

These farmers of southern New Guinea live in a large

longhouse, the *genama,* accommodating the entire tribal group. The building is rectangular and raised on piles, up to two hundred feet long and fifty to sixty feet wide. The interior is made up of a central corridor reserved for the heads of families and two lateral series of small rectangular compartments (*kiate*) for the women and children. One end of the house is assigned to the unmarried young men, the other to the aged.

## MAILU

The settlements of these farmers and fishermen in southeastern New Guinea and a few islands along the coast are strung out along the seashore. On the island of Mailu, the village consists of two rows of multifamily houses facing each other, with the space between them given over to the *dubu,* the houses for the assemblies of the men belonging to the four clans (Morau, Maradubu, Urumoga, Bodeabo). Each clan controls a length of the "street" and a group of habitations housing the subclans which, in their turn, are made up of numerous families. The dwelling of the large extended family is a rectangular building on high piles with entrance at the front and a roof-wall of slightly concave profile and pointed-arch section.
*Plate 221*

## GHENDE

Farmers and hunters, the Ghende belong to the group of mountain Papuans in northeastern New Guinea. Besides the family huts for women and children (*taga*), there are a considerable number of buildings for different social functions in their settlements, and they belong to a good many distinct architectural types. The dormitory-hut for the men (*tauya*) is cylindrical with a conical roof, while that for daytime use and men's ceremonies, the *bandia,* is elliptical in plan, and the women's hut, the *angaingo,* is rectangular and has a peaked roof.

## MONO

Farmers of the Trobriand Islands off New Guinea, the Mono lay out their villages on a generally round plan. The village of Omarakana is made up, as are some others, of two irregular rings of buildings disposed concentrically around a sacred clearing used for dances and also containing the community burial ground and the chief's house, the *lisiga.* The inner ring is composed of painstakingly built storehouses for the yam crop and of houses for the bachelors; the outer ring contains the rectangular family huts with roofs in the form of a pointed arched vault. The open space between the two rings is used for the ordinary everyday activities of the village, chiefly the women's domestic tasks.
*Plate 237*

*For New Guinea, see also plates 210–220, 222–236.*

## KANAKA

Predominantly agricultural, the Kanaka of New Cale-

donia, a French possession in southern Melanesia, live in villages composed of houses that are either rectangular and peak-roofed or else cylindrical with conical roof. The village is laid out along a carefully cleared large thoroughfare used for ceremonies, which is flanked by palms and araucarias, between sixteen and forty feet wide and perhaps thirty-two to two hundred feet long. The thoroughfare belongs to the "male" clan. One or more straight secondary streets leave it at right angles, and these are flanked by poplar trees (which correspond to the "female" clan) and lead to the small rectangular family huts, which are the property of the women. During the period when the population must work steadily in the somewhat distant fields, they take shelter there in temporary huts with bays at two ends.

In axial and elevated position with respect to the main thoroughfare is the large cylindrical house with conical roof belonging to the men and occupied by the chief. This building, the *pilù,* sits on a base of stones in Polynesian fashion and is about thirty-two feet across and about forty feet high. On an exterior ring of poles rests the radial framework of the roof, supported in the center by a tall pole, the *rhea,* at the top of which is a totemic sculpture. The roof covering is made of three layers of matting, fronds, and straw laid in strips like tiles. The low walls are covered with bark. The sill, jambs, and lintel of the door are sculpted, and the hearth lies between the door and the central pole. *Plates 249–252*

## MAORI

The Maori of New Zealand live chiefly by agriculture, particularly in the northern island, Tkana Maui. Their fortified villages (*pa*), sited in easily defensible positions, are for the most part occupied only temporarily. They are surrounded by moats sometimes filled with water and by several rows of roughly circular palisades on which carved posts are raised. One type of terraced village has in its center, at its highest point, a clearing for the houses of the chief and nobles with those of the commonalty around them, thereby reflecting the society stratified by class. The entrance to the village, defended by high platforms at the sides, is a wooden arch often richly carved.

The dwelling (*whare*) is rectangular with peaked roof and a front veranda demarcated by the projecting roof and side walls. The simplest type is a hut of logs and thatch, whereas the residences of the chief and nobles are solid structures of wooden planks, with rows of supporting posts in the interior, walls of woven rushes alternating with decorated wooden panels, and an elaborately ornamented facade. Large carved and painted panels cover the slopes of the roof, the corners of the house, and the jambs and lintel of the door. The front wall often has a small window as well as a door. A ritual order determines the use of the various types of architectural decoration applied to the carved panels of the walls (*pou-pou*), the gables (*maihi*), the doors (*pare*), and the thresholds (*paepae*). The peak of the roof is crowned by a carved figure, the *teko-teko.* The storehouses for provisions take the form of miniature replicas of the dwellings set up on one or four decorated posts, and the same model serves for the large assembly

houses (*whare runanga*) and the priests' colleges (*whare kura*). Traditionally, the architects were members of a corporation that also presided over building the extremely elegant boats. Precise rules had to be followed, especially for the assembly houses, from the initial choice of the wood to the consecration of the building, a rite involving the sacrifice of the young son of a chief.
*Plates 318–328*

## TIKOPIA

This Polynesian population of farmers and fishermen of the island of Tikopia, north of the New Hebrides, lives in villages along the shores. At the water's edge are the sheds for the canoes; toward the interior there are the dwellings, kitchens, and cultivated fields in parallel rows.

This arrangement reflects a radial conception of space, with the center in the interior of the island, the result being a characteristic asymmetry in the structure of the dwellings. The rectangular houses with peaked roofs reaching almost to the ground and covered with palm leaves are aligned with the long sides parallel to the shore. The main axis of the house divides the interior into two parts: the right half (*mata-paito*), toward the sea, is considered sacred and has walls without openings; the left half, toward the interior of the island, is profane, and the five doors of the house open into it, two at the front (one for the men exclusively, the other for general use), one at the rear reserved for the head of the family, and two toward the interior of the island for guests, women, and men who must enter the kitchen.

## FIJIANS

The farming population of the Melanesian archipelago of Fiji lives in villages that conserve vestiges of the ancient megalithic type of construction. The annual rites for the dead used to take place in a rectangular clearing, which was surrounded by slabs (*mara*) fixed upright into the ground, and which contained stone altars (*nanga*). In the center of the settlement was a plaza with the cult house (*mbure*), and in the past there were defensive palisades and moats around the villages. The traditional house is rectangular with markedly sloping roof of two or four sides and a log framework covered with bamboo, cane, and rushes. The ridgepole, projecting at either end, often rests on vertical beams that make a kind of trusswork with the guy ropes binding them. The interior, entered from the narrow side, is divided into a front area used as living quarters and dormitory and a higher portion in the rear where the domestic activities take place.
*Plates 295–298*

## SAMOANS

The native population of the Samoan archipelago (the eastern part a dependency of the United States, the western part independent but protected by New Zealand) traditionally engages chiefly in agriculture and

fishing, living in villages either oblong in plan or organized around a circular or oval central plaza, the *malae,* which was once the site of religious ceremonies and continues to be the political and social center of tribal life centering about the assembly house. Thanks to the social stratification into five classes, there are numerous small *malae* belonging to the leading families and serving for their private religious activities. The traditional dwelling, the *fale,* may be circular, rectangular, or rectangular with rounded ends (provisional annexes). The cooking area is outdoors. The house is set up on a platform paved in a mosaic of coral rock. The walls are simply an open colonnade of posts that can be closed off with palm-leaf mats during the night or for protection against wind and weather. Particularly in the large buildings to be used for assemblies and ceremonies, the high roof has a carefully constructed framework of inclined, parallel wooden arches and a crosswise, denser minor network. The covering is of leaves of the sugar cane and palm thatch.
*Plates 304–308*

## TAHITIANS

This predominantly agricultural population lives in the archipelago of the Society Islands, a French possession. There are numerous vestiges of megalithic constructions, including semicircular platforms for archers (*vahi-tè-a*), rectangular platforms for assemblies and feasts (*tahua-umu-puaa*), and sacred enclosures (*marae*), which are broad plazas for ceremonies and assemblies. The latter are rectangular or, more rarely, square in shape and are delimited by a wall of dry masonry which, on Tahiti, may reach a height of ten to thirteen feet. Inside these walled plazas there are altars, carved stones, or a sacred edifice, usually a rectangular stone step-pyramid set against a narrow side of the enclosure, while smaller pyramids are often found outside the walls.

The village is made up of scattered houses separated by gardens and small plantings, often connected by paved streets. The traditional house is rectangular, sometimes very elongated, with a double-pitched roof rounded off into a semicone at the narrow, curved ends. The entrance is on a long side. The walls are covered with a trelliswork of cane outside, with matting inside, and the interior is partitioned off by hanging mats.
*Plates 299–301*

## HAWAIIANS

In the small villages of this predominantly agricultural population of the Hawaiian Islands (USA), the traditional dwelling is rectangular with either a double-pitched roof or a roof with four pitches and an entrance on a long side. The covering is of layers of grasses, and verandas are frequent. The ridgepole makes a kind of trusswork, as in Samoa and Fiji.

## MARQUESANS

The inhabitants of the archipelago of the Marquesas Islands, a French possession, are agricultural. There are imposing vestiges of megalithic constructions on the islands such as platforms (notably on the island of Nukuhiva), large irrigation basins, monolithic statues (*tiki*), and sacred enclosures (*meae*) that served for religious and social ceremonies and as burial ground for the chiefs. In the center of each village is a plaza with a large hut for feasts and assemblies, which contains an altar and is supported on a stone terrace and raised on piles. Other special edifices include huts for tattooing the men. The traditional dwelling is a rectangular hut of poles covered with matting that rests on a stone platform as much as ten feet high and is reached by stairs. On the front part of the platform there are carved stones, seats, and inclined slabs used as backrests. The hut is divided into two parts; the front, the veranda, is protected by a short sloped roof held up by four carved poles and is about fifteen inches lower than the rear part, which is covered by a steeper roof that serves also as wall.
*Plate 299*

## EASTER ISLANDERS

The ancient population of farmers and fishermen of Easter Island (a possession of Chile) left impressive megalithic stone platforms and colossal statues as well as traces of villages and habitations. Ceremonial platforms (*ahu*) for funerary purposes were erected along the coasts. On each of these vast platforms of hewn stones, as large as 295 by 100 feet, fifteen or so statues were aligned with their backs to the ocean. About 460 of these trachyte statues (*moai*) survive, human busts ranging from 10 to as much as 52 feet in height. Some 250 were erected on the coastal *ahu*, the others have been found on mountain slopes, unfinished and not entirely hewn clear of the rock wall.

The dwelling of these islanders was normally a hut of elliptical ground plan (sometimes rectangular and half-underground) covered with rushes, matting, or grasses and standing either isolated or in a small group. Collective houses with extremely elongated spindle-shaped ground plans as long as 328 feet, with barrel vaulting of wooden arches supported by a central beam on posts, may perhaps have been intended to imitate the form of the underside of a boat. The sanctuary of Orongo at the southwest end of the island, inhabited only during the annual festivity, was built entirely of stone, with oval rooms backing on the rock and covered with false vaults, and these are accessible only through a narrow passageway. Petroglyphs and small ritual sculptures, which were protected in sacred caves, are plentiful.
*Plates 309–317*

*For Oceania, see also plates 51, 203–209, 238–248, 290–294, 302, 303.*

# SELECTED BIBLIOGRAPHY

*Revised and edited by Ronald Forsyth Millen*

*Publications appearing in more than one section of the bibliography are referred to in condensed form after the first entry, with only the author's name and the date of publication followed by a capital letter in parentheses indicating the section of the bibliography where the work first appears and, where relevant, also by a small letter indicating the subsection.*

## (A) GENERAL

*Archaeology and Ethnography. World Archaeology* 3, special number (1971).

BALANDIER, G *Anthropologie politique*. Paris: Presses Universitaires Françaises, 1967.

BELMONT, N., ed. *L'Art et les sociétés primitives à travers le monde*. Paris: Hachette, 1964.

BIEBUYCK, D. P., ed. *Tradition and Creativity in Tribal Art*. Berkeley: University of California Press, 1969.

BOAS, F. *Primitive Art*. Cambridge, Mass.: Harvard University Press, 1927. Reprint. New York: Dover, 1955.

CHANG, K. C., ed. *Settlement Archaeology*. Palo Alto: Stanford University Press, 1968.

CHOMBART DE LAUWE, P. "Les Rapports entre le milieu social et la famille en relation avec l'organisation de l'espace." In *Transactions of the 3rd World Congress of Sociology, Amsterdam, 1956*. London: International Sociological Association, 1956.

COON, C. S. *The Hunting Peoples*. Boston: Little, Brown with Atlantic Monthly Press, 1971.

COPANS, J. et. al. *L'Anthropologie: Science des sociétés primitives?* Paris: De Noël, 1971.

CRANSTONE, B. A. L. "Environment and Choice in Dwelling and Settlement: An Ethnographical Survey." In Ucko, P. J., Tringham, R., and Dimbleby, G. W., eds. *Man, Settlement and Urbanism*. London: Duckworth, 1972.

DAVEY, N. *History of Building Materials*. New York: Drake Publishers, 1970.

DEFFONTAINES, P. *Géographie et religions*. Paris: Gallimard, 1948.

DOLLFUS, J. *Les Aspects de l'architecture populaire dans le monde*. Paris: A. Morancé, 1954.

DOUGLAS, M. "Symbolic Orders in the Use of Domestic Space." In Ucko, P. J., Tringham, R., and Dimbleby, G. W., eds. *Man, Settlement and Urbanism*. London: Duckworth, 1972.

DRÖBER, W. *Die Kartographie bei den Naturvölkern*. Erlangen: Junge & Sohn, 1903.

*Ethnologie régionale*. Vol. 1: *Afrique-Océanie. Encyclopédie de la Pléiade*. Paris: Gallimard, 1972.

FORDE, C. D. *Habitat, Economy and Society: A Geographical Introduction to Ethnology*. London: Methuen, 1934. Reprint. New York: Dutton-Everyman.

FORGE, A., ed. *Primitive Art and Society*. London and New York: Oxford University Press, 1973.

FRASER D. *Village Planning in the Primitive World*. New York: Braziller, 1968.

FRASER, D., ed. *The Many Faces of Primitive Art: A Critical Anthology*. Englewood Cliffs, N. J.: Prentice-Hall, 1966.

GUIDONI, E. "Antropomorfismo e zoomorfismo nell' architettura 'primitiva'." *L'Architettura: Cronache e Storia* (Milan) 19, 1974.

———. "Etnologiche Culture." In *Dizionario Enciclopedico di Architettura e Urbanistica*. Vol. 3. Rome: Istituto Editoriale Romano, 1968.

*L'Habitation indigène dans les possessions françaises*. Paris: Société des éditions géographiques, maritimes et coloniales, 1931.

HALL, E. T. *The Hidden Dimension*. New York: Doubleday, 1966.

LABAT, P. "L'Habitation et la famille dans diverses civilisations: Aspects ethnologiques." In Chombart de Lauwe, P., ed. *Famille et habitation, et conception de l'habitation*. Travaux du Groupe d'Ethnologie Sociale, vol. 1. Paris, 1959.

LANTERNARI, V. "L'Abitazione." In Grottanelli, V. L., ed. *Ethnologica*. Vol. 2. Milan: Labor, 1965.

LEE, R. B., ed. *Man the Hunter*. Chicago: Aldine, 1969.

LÉVI-STRAUSS, C. *Anthropologie structurale*. Paris: Plon, 1958. Translation. *Structural Anthropology*. New York: Basic Books, 1963.

MARTIN, R. D. "Concepts of Human Territoriality." In Ucko, P. J., Tringham, R., and Dimbleby, G. W., eds. *Man, Settlement and Urbanism*. London: Duckworth, 1972.

MOHOLY-NAGY, S. *Native Genius in Anonymous Architecture*. New York: Horizon Press, 1957.

NORBERG-SCHULZ, C. *Existence, Space and Architecture*. New York: Praeger, 1971.

OLIVER, P., ed. *Shelter and Society: Studies in Vernacular Architecture*. New York: Praeger, 1969.

PETTAZZONI, R. *Miti e leggende*. 4 vols. Turin: UTET, 1948–63.

———. *L'omniscienza di Dio*. Turin: Einaudi, 1950.

RAPOPORT, A. *House Form and Culture*. Englewood Cliffs, N. J.: Prentice-Hall, 1969.

ROWLANDS, M. J. "Defence: A Factor in the Organization of Settlements." In Ucko, P. J., Tringham, R., and Dimbleby, G. W., eds. *Man, Settlement and Urbanism*. London: Duckworth, 1972.

RUDOFSKY, B. *Architecture Without Architects: A Short Introduction to Non-Pedigree Architecture*. New York: Doubleday, 1969.

RYKWERT, J. *On Adam's House in Paradise: The Idea of the Primitive Hut in Architectural History*. New York: Museum of Modern Art, 1973.

SEVERIN, T. *Vanishing Primitive Man*. New York: American Heritage Press (McGraw-Hill), 1973.

*Shelter*. Bolinas, Calif.: Shelter Publications (distrib. New York: Random House), 1973.

SUTTON, F. X. "Representation and Nature of Political Systems." *Comparative Studies in Society and History* 2 (1959).

*Le Symbolisme cosmique des monuments religieux*. Papers delivered at a congress sponsored by Istituto Italiano per il Medio e Estremo Oriente, Rome, April–May, 1955. Rome: Edizioni Ismeo, 1957.

TERRAY, E. *Le Marxisme devant les sociétés "primitives."* Paris: Maspero, 1968. Translation. *Marxism and "Primitive" Societies: Two Studies*. New York: Monthly Review Press, 1972.

THOMAS, W. L., JR., ed. *Man's Role in Changing the Face of Earth*. Chicago: University of Chicago Press, 1956.

UCKO, P. J., TRINGHAM, R., and DIMBLEBY, G. W., eds. *Man, Settlement and Urbanism*. London: Duckworth; Cambridge, Mass.: Schenkman (distrib. General Learning Press), 1972.

## (B) ARCTIC AND SUBARCTIC REGIONS

BOSI, R. *I Lapponi*. Milan: Einaudi, 1959. Translation *The Lapps*. London: Thames & Hudson; New York: Praeger Publishers, 1960.

FORDE, C. D. "The Yukaghir: Reindeer Hunters in the Siberian Tundra." In FORDE 1934 (A).

LEVINA, M. G., and POTAPOVA, L. P. *Istoriko-etnografichesky Atlas Sibiri*. Moscow and Leningrad, 1961.

MANKER, E. "Lapsk Kultur vid Stora Lule alvs källsjöar." *Acta Lapponica*, 1944.

MONTANDON, G. *La Civilisation ainou*. Paris: Payot, 1937.

POPOV, A. A. *The Nganasan: The Material Culture of the Tavgi Samoyeds*. Bloomington: Indiana University Press, 1966.

SIMONSEN, P. "The Transition from Food-gathering to Pastoralism in North Scandinavia and Its Impact on Settlement Patterns." In UCKO, TRINGHAM, DIMBLEBY 1972 (A).

TOKAREV, S. A. *Etnografiya narodov SSSR*. Moscow, 1958.

VORREN, O., and MANKER, E. *Lapp Life and Customs*. London: Oxford University Press, 1962.

### (a) Eskimos

BANDI, H. G. *Eskimo Prehistory*. College: University of Alaska Press, 1969.

BOAS, F. "The Central Eskimo." In *Bureau of American Ethnology, Annual Report No. 6*. Washington, D. C., 1888.

———. *The Eskimo of Baffin Land and Hudson Bay*. Bulletin of the American Museum of Natural History 15 (1907).

COLLINS, H. B. "The Origin and Antiquity of the Eskimo." In *Annual Report of the Smithsonian Institution, 1950*. Washington, D.C., 1951.

FORDE, C. D. "The Eskimo: Seal and Caribou Hunters in Arctic America." In FORDE 1934 (A).

HOFFMAN, W. J. "The Graphic Art of the Eskimos." In *U.S. National Museum, Annual Report, 1895*. Washington, D.C., 1897.

HUGHES, C. C. *An Eskimo Village in the Modern World*. Ithaca, N. Y.: Cornell University Press, 1960.

LAUGHLIN, W. S. "The Aleut-Eskimo Community." *Anthropological Papers of the University of Alaska* 1 (1952).

MATHIASSEN, T. *Archaeology of the Central Eskimos*. Report of the Fifth Thule Expedition, 1921–24. Copenhagen: Gyldendalske Boghandel Nordisk Forlag, 1927.

## (C) WESTERN AND CENTRAL ASIA AND ADJOINING REGIONS

BARTH, F. *Le Nomadisme dans les montagnes et sur les*

hauts-plateaux de l'Asie du Sud-Ouest: les problèmes de la zone aride. Paris, 1963.

————. Nomads of South Persia: The Basseri Tribes of the Khamseh Confederacy. New York: Humanities Press, 1961.

FAYEIN, C. "La vie pastorale au Dhofar." Objets et Mondes 11 (1971).

FEILBERG, C. La Tente noire: Contribution ethnographique à l'histoire culturelle des nomades. Copenhagen: National-museets Skrifter, Ethografisk raekke, 1944.

FORDE, C. D. "The Kazak, Kirghiz and Kalmuck: Horse and Sheep Herders of Central Asia." In FORDE 1934 (A).

————. "The Ruwala Badawin: Camel Breeders of Northern Arabia." In FORDE 1934 (A).

HUDSON, A. Kazak Social Structure. Yale University Publications in Anthropology, vol. 20. New Haven: Yale University Press, 1964.

MOWSESJANZ, P. TER. "Das Armenische Bauernhaus." Mitteilungen der Anthropologischen Gesellschaft 20 (1922).

MUSIL, A. Manners and Customs of the Rwala Bedouins. Oriental Explorations and Studies, no. 6. New York: American Geographical Society, 1928.

TOKAREV, S. A. See (B), above.


## (D) SOUTH ASIA

BOULBET, J. "Modes et techniques du pays Moa." Bulletin de l'Ecole Française d'Extrême-Orient 52 (1965).

DOURNES, J. "Aspects de l'habitat et techniques de construction des Sre aux Jörai." Objets et Mondes 11 (1971).

————. Coordonnées: Structures jörai familiales et sociales. Paris: Institut d'Ethnologie, 1972.

ELWIN, V. Nagaland. Shillong, India: P. Dutta, 1961.

FORDE, C. D. "The Semang and Sakai: Collectors in the Malayan Forests." In FORDE 1934 (A).

GLOVER, I. C. "Settlements and Mobility Among the Hunter-Gatherers of South-east Asia." In UCKO, TRINGHAM, DIMBLEBY 1972 (A).

GOUROU, P. Esquisse d'une étude de l'habitation annamite dans l'Annam septentrional et central du Thanh Hoa au Binh Dinh. Paris: Editions d'art et d'histoire, 1936.

IZIKOWITZ, K. G. "The Community House of the Lamet." Ethnos (Stockholm) 1–2 (1943).

MARRIOT, MCK., ed. Village India: Studies in the Little Community. Chicago: University of Chicago Press, 1955.

PARIS, P. "Décor et construction des maisons Kha entre Lao-Bao et Saravane." Bulletin de l'Ecole Française d'Extrême-Orient 45 (1952).

PARMENTIER, H. "La maison commune du village Bahnar de Kombraih." Bulletin de l'Ecole Française d'Extrême-Orient 45 (1951).

ROBEQUAIN, C. "L'Indochine." In L'Habitation indigène 1931 (A).

SKEAT, W. W., and BLAGDEN, C. O. Pagan Races of the Malay Peninsula. London: Macmillan, 1906. Reprint (2 vols.). New York: Barnes & Noble.

VELDER, C. "A Description of the Mrabri Camp." Journal of the Siam Society 51 (1963).


### (a) Madagascar

ARNAUD, R. "Quelques portes fortifiées des anciens villages du chaînon d'Ambohimarina au nord d'Ivato." Bulletin de Madagascar 20 (1970).

BATTISTINI, R., VÉRIN, P., and RASON, R. "Le Site archéologique de Talaky." Annales de l'Université de Madagascar 1 (1963).

BLOCH, M. Placing the Dead: Tombs, Ancestral Villages and Kinship Organization in Madagascar. New York: Seminar Press, 1971.

DECARY, R. "La Protection des plantations et la conservation des récoltes à Madagascar." Journal de la Société des Africanistes 29 (1959).

DUBOIS, H. M. Monographie des Betsileo (Madagascar). Paris: Institut d'Ethnologie, 1938.

JULIEN, G. "Madagascar." In L'Habitation indigène 1931 (A).

LINTON, R. The Tanala: A Hill Tribe of Madagascar. Field Museum of Natural History, Anthropological Series, no. 22. Chicago, 1933. Reprint. New York: Kraus-Thomson, n.d.

MILLE, A., and VÉRIN, P. "Premières observations sur l'habitat ancien en Imerina." Bulletin de l'Académie Malgache (Tananarive) 45 (1967).

POIRIER, J. Les Bezanozano. Paris, 1970.

————. "Données écologiques et démographiques de la mise en place des Proto-Malgaches." Annales de la Faculté des Lettres et Sciences Humaines (Tananarive), 1965.

————. "Les Origines du peuple et de la civilisation malgaches: Madagascar avant l'histoire." Bulletin de Madagascar 16–17 (1966–67).

RIBARD, M. E. "Contribution à l'étude des aloalo malgaches." L'Anthropologie 34 (1924).


## (E) INDONESIA AND THE PHILIPPINES

FIRTH, R. Housekeeping Among Malay Peasants. 2d ed. New York: Humanities Press, 1966.

GULLICK, J. M. Indigenous Political Systems of Western Malaya. London: Athlone Press; New York: Humanities Press, 1958.

JOSSELIN DE JONG, P. E. DE. "An Interpretation of Agricultural Rites in Southeast Asia." Journal of Asian Studies 24 (1965).

KOENTJARANINGRAT, R. M., ed. Villages in Indonesia. Ithaca, N. Y.: Cornell University Press, 1967.

NGUYEN VAN HUYEN, Introduction à l'étude de l'habitation sur pilotis dans l'Asie du sud-est. Paris: P. Geuthner, 1934.

SPENCER, J. E. Land and People in the Philippines. Berkeley: University of California Press, 1952.

VAN WOUDEN, F. A. E. Types of Social Structure in Eastern Indonesia. The Hague: Martinus Nijhoff, 1968.

WINSTEDT, R. The Malays: A Cultural History. Singapore: Kelly & Walsh, 1947. Rev. ed. London: Routledge & Kegan Paul, 1950.

WINSTEDT, R., and JOSSELIN DE JONG, P. E. DE, The Indonesian Town. The Hague and Bandung, Java, 1958.


### (a) Sumatra

BACHTIAR, H. W. "Negeri Taram." In KOENTJARANIN-GRAT 1967 (E).

BARTLETT, H. H. "The Sacred Edifices of the Batak of Sumatra." Occasional Contributions from the Museum of Anthropology, University of Michigan 4 (1934).

DE BOER, D. W. N. "Het Toba-Bataksche huis." Mededeelingen van het Bureau voor de Bestuurzaken 23 (1920).

JOSSELIN DE JONG, P. E. DE. Minangkabau and Negri Sembilan: Socio-Political Structure in Indonesia. The Hague: Martinus Nijhoff, 1952.

SCHNITGER, F. M. Forgotten Kingdoms in Sumatra. New York: Humanities Press, 1964.

————. "Megalithen von Batakland und Nias." Jahrbuch für prähistorische und ethnographische Kunst 15–16 (1941–42).

SINGARIMBUN, M. "Kutagamber: Village of the Karo." In KOENTJARANINGRAT 1967 (E).

VERGOUWEN, J. C. The Social Organization and Customary Law of Toba-Batak of Northern Sumatra. The Hague: Martinus Nijhoff, 1964.

WESTENENK, L. C. "De Minangkabausche nagari." Mededeelingen van het Bureau voor de Bestuurzaken 17 (1918).


### (b) Other Islands and Archipelagoes

BARTON, R. F. The Kalingas: Their Institutions and Custom Law. Chicago: University of Chicago Press, 1949.

CHABOT, H. T. "Bontoranba: A Village of Goa, South Celebes." In KOENTJARANINGRAT 1967 (E)

COOLEY, F. L. "Allang: A Village on Ambon Island." In KOENTJARANINGRAT 1967 (E).

CUNNINGHAM, C. E. "Order in the Atoni House." Bijdragen tot de Taal-, Land- en Volkenkunde 120 (1964).

————. "Soba: An Atoni Village of West Timor." In KOENTJARANINGRAT 1967 (E).

DE BOER, D. W. N. "Het Niassche huis." Mededeelingen van het Bureau voor de Bestuurzaken 25 (1920).

FRASER, D. "South Nias Islanders, Indonesia." In FRASER 1968 (A).

FREEMAN, J. D. Iban Agriculture. Colonial Research Studies, no. 18. London: Her Majesty's Stationery Office, 1955.

GEDDES, W. R. The Land-Dayaks of Sarawak. Colonial Research Studies, no. 14. London: Her Majesty's Stationery Office, 1954.

GEERTZ, C. "Form and Variation in Balinese Village Structure." American Anthropologist 61 (1959).

GOETHALS, P. R. "Rarak: A Swidden Village of West Sumbawa." In KOENTJARANINGRAT 1967 (E).

Institute of Pacific Relations: Bali: Studies in Life, Thought and Ritual. The Hague: W. van Hoeve; and Bandung, Java: Djanal Raya Timur, 1960–.

JAY, R. R. *Javanese Villagers*. Cambridge, Mass.: Harvard University Press, 1969.

KAUDERN, W. A. "Structures and Settlements in Central Celebes." In *Ethnographical Studies in Celebes, 1917–20*. Vol. 1. Göteborg: Elanders, 1925.

MILES, D. "The Ngadju Longhouse." *Oceania* 35 (1964).

MORRIS, H. S. *Report on a Melanau Sago Producing Community in Sarawak*. Colonial Research Studies, no. 9. London: Her Majesty's Stationery Office, 1953.

SCHÄRER, H. *Ngadju Religion: The Concept of God Among a South Borneo People*. The Hague: Martinus Nijhoff, 1963.

SUZUKI, H. *The Religious System and Culture of Nias, Indonesia*. The Hague: Excelsior, 1959.

YONG DJIET TAN, R. "The Domestic Architecture of Bali." *Bijdragen tot de Taal-, Land- en Volkenkunde* 123 (1967).

## (F) OCEANIA (GENERAL).

ARCHEY, G. *South Sea Folk: Handbook of Maori and Oceanic Ethnology*. Auckland: War Memorial Museum, 1937. 2d ed., 1949.

BODROGI, T. *Oceanian Art*. Budapest: Corvina, 1959.

BOUGE, L. G. *Contribution à l'étude des pilons océaniens*. Paris: Librairie Larose, 1931.

BÜHLER, A., BARROW, T., and MOUNTFORD, C. P. *Oceania and Australia: The Art of the South Seas*. New York: Crown, 1962.

GOLSON, J. "Archéologie du Pacific Sud: résultat et perspectives." *Journal de la Société des Océanistes* 15 (1959).

GREEN, R. C., and KELLY, M., eds. *Studies in Oceanic Culture History*. Vol. 1. Honolulu: Bernice Pauahi Bishop Museum, 1970.

GUIART, J. *Océanie*. Paris: Gallimard, 1963. Translation. *The Arts of the South Pacific*. New York: Braziller, 1963.

HIGHAM, C. F. W. "The Role of Economic Prehistory in the Interpretation of the Settlement of Oceania." In GREEN, KELLY 1970 (F).

LANTERNARI, V. *Oceania*. Vol. 2 (1959) of PETTAZZONI 1948–63 (A).

LEENHARDT, M. *Folk Arts of Oceania*. New York: Tudor, 1950.

———. "L'Océanie." In *L'Habitation indigène* 1931 (A).

MAHLER, R. *Siedlungsgebiet und Siedlungsplätze in Ozeanien*. Supplement to *Internationales Archiv für Ethnographie* 11 (1898).

SCHMITZ, C. A. *Oceanic Art: Myth, Man, and Image in the South Seas*. New York: Harry N. Abrams, 1972.

TISCHNER, H. *Die Verbreitung der Hausformen in Ozeanien*. Leipzig: Verlag der Werkgemeinschaft, 1934.

TOUMARKINE. D. D. "L'Ethnologie océanienne en URSS (Situation actuelle et état des recherches)." *Journal de la Société des Océanistes* 18 (1962).

YAWATA, I. and SINOTO, Y. H., eds. *Prehistoric Culture in Oceania: A Symposium*. Honolulu: Bernice Pauahi Bishop Museum, 1968.

## (G) AUSTRALIA

BERNDT, R. M. and C. H. *The World of the First Australians*. Chicago: University of Chicago Press, 1964.

BERNDT, R. M. and C. H., eds. *Aboriginal Man in Australia*. Sydney: Angus & Robertson, 1965.

CAPELL, A. "Myths and Tales of the Nunggubuyu, South-east Arnhem Land." *Oceania* 31 (1960).

DAVIDSON, D. S. "Hunting Territory in Australia." *American Anthropologist* 30 (1928).

ELIADE, M. *Religions australiennes*. Paris: Payot, 1972. Translation. *Australian Religions: An Introduction*. Edited by V. Turner. Ithaca, N. Y.: Cornell University Press, 1973.

ELKIN, A. P. *The Australian Aborigines*. 4th ed. Sydney: Angus & Robertson; New York, Doubleday, 1964.

———. *Kinship in South Australia*. Sydney: Australasian Medical Publishing Co., 1940.

GOULD, R. A. "The Archaeologist as Ethnographer: A Case from the Western Desert of Australia." *World Archaeology* 3 (1971).

HIATT, L. R. "Local Organisation Among the Australian Aborigines." *Oceania* 32 (1962).

HOWITT, A. W. *The Native Tribes of South-east Australia*. London and New York: Macmillan, 1904.

MASSOLA, A. *Aboriginal Place Names of South-east Australia and Their Meanings*. Melbourne: Landsdowne, 1968.

MOUNTFORD, C. P. *Art, Myth and Symbolism of Arnhemland*. Cambridge: Cambridge University Press, 1956.

MUNN, N. D. "The Spatial Presentation of Cosmic Order in Walbiri Iconography." In FORGE 1973 (A).

RAPOPORT, A. *Australian Aborigines and the Definition of Place*. Sydney: University of Sydney Press, n.d.

ROTH, H. L. *The Aborigines of Tasmania*. Halifax: F. King & Sons, 1899.

SPENCER, B. *Native Tribes of the Northern Territory of Australia*. London: Macmillan, 1914. Reprint. New York: Humanities Press, 1972.

SPENCER, B., and GILLEN, F. J. *The Native Tribes of Central Australia*. London: Macmillan, 1899. Reprint. New York: Dover, n.d., and Humanities Press, 1968.

———. *The Northern Tribes of Central Australia*. London: Macmillan, 1904. Reprint. New York: Humanities Press, 1969.

STANNER, W. E. H. "Aboriginal Territorial Organisation: Estate, Range, Domain and Regime." *Oceania* 36 (1965).

———. "On Aboriginal Religion." *Oceania* 30, no. 2 (1959); 30, no. 4 (1960); 31, no. 2 (1960); 31, no. 4 (1961); 32, no. 2 (1961); 33, no. 4 (1963). Published as *On Aboriginal Religion*. Sydney: University of Sydney, 1964.

STREHLOW, T. G. H. *Aranda Traditions*. Melbourne, 1947. Reprint. New York: Johnson Reprint Corp. (Harcourt Brace Jovanovich), 1968.

TINDALE, N. B. "Ecology of the Aboriginal Man in Australia." In A. Keast, ed. *Biogeography and Ecology in Australia*. New York: Humanities Press, 1959.

WARNER, W. L. *A Black Civilization: A Social Study of an Australian Tribe*. New York: Harper, 1937. Reprint. New York: Harper Torchbooks.

WARSON, T. *The Prehistoric Arts: Manufactures, Works, Weapons, etc. of the Aborigines of Australia*. Adelaide, 1897.

## (H) MELANESIA AND MICRONESIA

BÜHLER, A. "Der Platz als bestimmender Faktor von Siedlungsformen in Ostindien und Melanesien." *Regio Basiliensis* 1–2 (1959–60).

GUIART, J. *Structure de la chefferie en Mélanésie du Sud*. Paris: Institut d'Ethnologie, 1963.

KRÄMER, A. "Der Haus- und Bootbau der Marshallinseln." *Archiv für Anthropologie* (Brunswick) 3 (1905).

LYONS, H. "The Sailing Charts of the Marshall Islanders." *Geographical Journal* (London) 72 (1928).

MALINOWSKI, B. *Argonauts of the Western Pacific*. New York: Dutton, 1922. Reprint. 1953.

———. *Coral Gardens and Their Magic*. New York: American Books, 1935.

MARGOT-DUCLOT, J., and VERNANT, J. "La Terre et la catégorie du sexe en Mélanésie." *Journal de la Société des Océanistes* 2 (1946).

RIESENFELD, A. *The Megalithic Culture of Melanesia*. Leiden: E. J. Brill, 1950.

SCHLESIER, E. *Die Erscheinungsformen des Männerhauses und das Klubwesen in Mikronesien: eine ethnosoziologische Untersuchung*. The Hague: Mouton, 1953.

SCHMITZ, C. "Balam: der Tanz- und Kultplatz in Melanesien als Versammlungsort und mimischer Schauplatz." *Die Schaubühne* (Emsdetten) 46 (1955).

SCHÜCK, A. *Die Stabkarten der Marshallinsulaner*. Hamburg: H. O. Persiehl, 1902.

SPOEHR, A. *Marianas Prehistory: Archaeological Survey and Excavations on Saipan, Tinian and Rota*. Chicago: Field Museum of Natural History, 1957.

THILENIUS, G., ed. *Ergebnisse der Südsee-Expedition der Hamburgischen Wissenschaftlichen Stiftung 1908–1910, 1914–1938*. Hamburg: Hamburgische Wissenschaftliche Stiftung, 1913–.

### (a) New Guinea

AUFINGER, A. P. "Siedlungsform und Häuserbau an der Ray-küste Neuguinea." *Anthropos* 35–36 (1940–41).

BATESON, G. "Social Structure of the Iatmiil People." *Oceania* 2 (1932).

BEHRMANN, W. "Die Wohlstätten der Eingeborenen im Innern von Neu-Guinea." In F. Ratzel, ed. *Festband Albrecht Penck*. Stuttgart: J. Engelhorn, 1918.

BELSHAW, C. S. *The Great Village: The Economic and Social Welfare of Hanuabada, an Urban Community in Papua*. London: Routledge & Kegan Paul, 1957.

BODROGI, T. *Art in North-East New Guinea*. Budapest: Hungarian Academy of Sciences; New York: International Publications Series, 1961.

BÜHLER, A. *Heilige Bildwerke aus Neu-Guinea*. Basel: Museum für Völkerkunde, 1957.

CRANSTONE, B. A. L. "The Tifalmin: A 'Neolithic' People in New Guinea." *World Archaeology* 3 (1971).

FIRTH, R. "Notes on the Social Structure of Some South-Eastern New Guinea Communities," *Man* 52 (1952).

FORGE, A. "Normative Factors in the Settlement Size of Neolithic Cultivators (New Guinea)." In UCKO, TRINGHAM, DIMBLEBY 1972 (A).

———. "Style and Meaning in Sepik Art." In FORGE 1973 (A).

FRASER, D. "Mailu, New Guinea." In FRASER 1968 (A).

HATANAKA, S., and BRAGGE, L. W. "Habitat, Isolation and Subsistence Economy in the Central Range of New Guinea." *Oceania* 44 (1973).

KOOIJMAN, S. *The Art of Lake Sentani.* New York: Museum of Primitive Art, 1959.

LEWIS, A. B. *Carved and Painted Designs from New Guinea.* Anthropological Design Series. Chicago: Field Museum of Natural History, 1931.

MEGGITT, M. J. "House Building Among the Mae-Enga, Western Highlands Territory of New Guinea." *Oceania* 27 (1956–57).

VILLEMINOT, J. and P. *La Nouvelle-Guinée.* Paris, 1966.

WHITEMAN, J. "Change and Tradition in an Abelam Village." *Oceania* 36 (1965).

WILLIAMS, F. E. *The Natives of the Purari Delta.* Territory of Papua, Anthropology Report No. 5. Port Moresby, New Guinea, 1924.

*(b) New Caledonia*

AVIAS, J. "Contribution à la préhistoire de l'Océanie: les tumuli des plateaux de fer en Nouvelle-Calédonie." *Journal de la Société des Océanistes* 6 (1949).

———. "L'évolution de l'habitat indigène en Nouvelle-Calédonie de 1843 à nos jours." *Journal de la Société des Océanistes* 10 (1953).

GIFFORD, E. W., and SHUTLER, D., JR. *Archaeological Excavations in New Caledonia.* University of California, Anthropological Records 18. Berkeley and Los Angeles, 1956.

GIRARD, F. "Acquisitions nouvelles du Département d'Océanie." *Objets et Mondes* 1 (1961).

GUIART, J. *L'Art autochtone de Nouvelle-Calédonie.* Nouméa, New Caledonia: Editions de la Société des Océanistes, 1953.

LEENHARDT, M. "La féte du pilou en Nouvelle-Calédonie." *L'Anthropologie* 32 (1922).

———. *Gens de la Grande Terre.* Paris: Gallimard, 1937.

———. *La Grande Case,* Paris, 1965.

———. *Notes d'ethnologie néo-calédonienne.* Paris: Institut d'Ethnologie, 1930.

LOBSIGER-DELLENBACH, M. and G. "Dix bambous gravés néo-calédoniens du Musée des Arts Africains et Océaniens (Paris)." *Journal de la Société des Océanistes* 23 (1967).

*(c) Other Archipelagoes*

CLAY, R. B. "The Persistence of Traditional Settlement Pattern: An Example from Central New Ireland." *Oceania* 43 (1972).

DEACON, A. B. "Geometrical Drawings from Malekula and Other Islands of the New Hebrides." *Journal of the Royal Anthropological Institute of Great Britain and Ireland* 64 (1934).

EPSTEIN, A. L. "Variation and Social Structure: Local Organisation on the Island of Matupit." *Oceania* 35 (1964–65).

FORDE, C. D. "The Eastern Solomons." In FORDE 1934 (A).

FRASER, D. "Trobriand Islanders, New Guinea." In FRASER 1968 (A).

GIFFORD, E. W. *Archaeological Excavations in Fiji.* University of California, Anthropological Records 13. Berkeley and Los Angeles, 1951.

GILL, S. "Bwayma: The Trobriand Yam House." Term paper, Columbia University, 1963. Cited in FRASER 1968 (A).

GIRARD, F. "L'importance sociale et religieuse des cérémonies exécutées pour les malanggan sculptés de Nouvelle-Irlande." *L'Anthropologie* 58 (1954).

GUIART, J. "Les Nouvelles-Hébrides." In *Ethnologie régionale* 1972 (A).

———. "L'Organisation sociale et politique du Nord-Malekula." *Journal de la Société des Océanistes* 8 (1952).

———. "Sociétés, rituels et mythes du Nord Ambrym (Nouvelles-Hébrides)." *Journal de la Société des Océanistes* 7 (1951).

IVENS, W. G. *Melanesians of the Southeast Solomon Islands.* New York: Benjamin Blom, n.d.

MONTAUBAN, P., and O'REILLY, P. "Mythes de Buka, Iles Salomon." *Journal de la Société des Océanistes* 14 (1958).

NEYRET, J. M. "Notes sur la navigation indigène aux îles Fidji." *Journal de la Société des Océanistes* 6 (1950).

O'REILLY, P. "Deux sites fortifiés du district de la Roche dans l'Ile de Maré (Iles Loyalty)." *Journal de la Société des Océanistes* 6 (1950).

———. "Mégalithes Hébridais: une sépulture du chef et deux autres tombes à Nagire, Ile d'Aoba." *Journal de la Société des Océanistes* 7 (1951).

———. "Nouvelles-Hébrides: Mallicolo. Sculpture de faîtage en racine de fougère." *Journal de la Société des Océanistes* 8 (1952).

QUAIN, B. *Fijian Village.* Chicago: University of Chicago Press, 1948.

ROCH, G. *Materielle Kultur der Santa Cruz Inseln.* Berlin, 1971.

ROTH, G. K. "Housebuilding in Fiji." *Journal of the Royal Anthropological Institute of Great Britain and Ireland* 84 (1954).

ROWE, W. P. "A Study of the Geometrical Drawings from the New Hebrides." *Journal of the Royal Anthropological Institute of Great Britain and Ireland* 66 (1936).

TISCHNER, H. "Bemerkungen zur Konstruktion und Terminologie der Hausformen auf Neu-Irland und Nebeninseln." In Schmitz., C. A., and Wildhaber, R., eds. *Festschrift A. Bühler.* Basel: Pharus Verlag, 1965.

*(I) POLYNESIA*

BUCK, P. H. *Vikings of the Sunrise.* New York: F. A. Stokes, 1938.

EMORY, K. "A Re-examination of East Polynesian Marae." *Pacific Anthropological Records* 11, 1970.

GATHERCOLE, P. "The Study of Settlement Patterns in Polynesia." In UCKO, TRINGHAM, DIMBLEBY 1972 (A).

GOLDMAN, I. *Ancient Polynesian Society.* Chicago: University of Chicago Press, 1970.

GOLSON, J., ed. *Polynesian Navigation: A Symposium on Andrew Sharp's Theory of Accidental Voyages.* Wellington, 1962.

GREEN, R. C. "Settlement Pattern Archaeology in Polynesia." In GREEN, KELLY 1970 (F).

———. *Settlement Patterns: Four Case Studies from Polynesia.* Asian and Pacific Archaeology Series, vol. 1. 1967.

GROUBE, L. M. "The Origin and Development of Earthwork Fortifications in the Pacific." In GREEN, KELLY 1970 (F).

NEVERMANN, H. "Pyramiden in Polynesien." *Baessler-Archiv* (Berlin) 28 (1955).

SAHLINS, M. D. *Social Stratification in Polynesia.* Seattle: University of Washington Press, 1958.

WILLIAMSON, R. W. *Religious and Cosmic Beliefs of Central Polynesia.* 2 vols. Cambridge: Cambridge University Press, 1933.

*(a) New Zealand*

BEST, E. *Maori Agriculture: The Cultivated Food Plants of the Natives of New Zealand.* Dominion Museum Bulletin, no. 9. Wellington, 1925.

———. *Maori Storehouses and Kindred Structures.* Dominion Museum Bulletin, no. 5. Wellington, 1916.

———. *The Pa Maori: An Account of the Fortified Village of the Maori in Pre-European and Modern Times.* Dominion Museum Bulletin, no. 6. Wellington, 1927.

BUCK, P. H. *The Coming of the Maori.* Nelson, N. Z.: Cawthorn Institute of Scientific Research, 1925. 2d ed., 1929. Reprint. Wellington: Whitcombe and Tombs, 1949.

———. "Maori Decorative Art: House Panels." *New Zealand Institute Transactions* 53 (1921).

COWAN, J. "The Art Craftsmanship of the Maori." In *Art in New Zealand.* Vol. 2. Wellington: H. H. Tombs, 1928.

FIRTH, R. "The Maori Carver." *Journal of the Polynesian Society* 34 (1925).

———. "Maori Hillforts." *Antiquity* 1 (1927).

———. *Primitive Economics of the New Zealand Maori.* New York: Dutton, 1929. 2d ed., as *Economics of the New Zealand Maoris.* New York: Humanities Press, 1959. Reprint. Mystic, Conn.: Lawrence Verry, 1973.

GROUBE, L. M. *Settlement Patterns in New Zealand Prehistory.* University of Otago, Occasional Papers in Archaeology, no. 1. Dunedin, N. Z., 1965.

HAMILTON, A. *The Art Workmanship of the Maori Race in New Zealand.* Dunedin, N. Z.: For the Royal Society of New Zealand, 1896–1901.

HOCKEN, T. M. *Contributions to the Early History of New Zealand (Settlement of Otago).* London: Sampson Low & Co., 1898.

KENNEDY, J. *Settlement in the South East Bay of Islands, 1772: A Study in Text-aided Field Archaeology.* University of Otago, Studies in Prehistoric Anthropology, no. 3. Dunedin, N. Z., 1969.

MEAD, S. M. *The Art of Maori Carving.* Wellington: A. H. & A. W. Reed, 1961. 2d ed., 1967.

PHILLIPS, W. J. *Carved Maori Houses of Western and Northern Areas of New Zealand.* Dominion Museum Monographs, no. 9. Wellington, 1955.

———. *Carved Pieces of the Eastern Maori House Districts of the North Island (New Zealand).* Records of the Dominion Museum, no. 1. Wellington, 1942–44.

———. "Historical Notes on the Carved House Nuku Te Apiaki." *Journal of the Polynesian Society* 79 (1970).

———. *Maori Houses and Food Stores.* Dominion Museum Monographs, no. 8. Wellington, 1952.

PHILLIPS, W. J., and MacEWEN, J. M. "Carved Houses of Te Arawa (New Zealand)." *Dominion Museum Records in Ethnology* (Wellington) 1 (1946); 2 (1948).

SKINNER, H. D. *The Maori Hei-Tiki.* Otago Museum Booklet, no. 1. Dunedin, 1946.

### (b) Society Islands

BAESSLER, A. "Marae und Abu auf den Gesellschaft-Inseln." *Internationales Archiv für Ethnographie* 10 (1897).

EMORY, K. "Stone Remains in the Society Islands." *Bulletin of the Bernice Pauahi Bishop Museum* (Honolulu), no. 116, 1933.

GARANGER, J. "Recherches archéologiques dans le district de Tautira (Tahiti, Polynésie Française)." *Journal de la Société des Océanistes* 20 (1964).

GREEN, R. C. et al. "Archaeology on the Island of Mo'orea, French Polynesia." *Anthropological Papers of the American Museum of Natural History* 51, pt. 2 (1967).

HANDY, E. S. C. "History and Culture in the Society Islands." *Bulletin of the Bernice Pauahi Bishop Museum* (Honolulu), no. 79, 1930.

HANDY, W. C. "Handicrafts of the Society Islands." *Bulletin of the Bernice Pauahi Bishop Museum* (Honolulu), no. 42, 1927.

HENRY, T. "Ancient Tahiti." *Bulletin of the Bernice Pauahi Bishop Museum* (Honolulu), no. 48, 1928.

*Tahiti et la Polynésie Française. Journal de la Société des Océanistes* 15, special number (1959).

### (c) Marquesas Islands

KELLUM-OTTINO, M. *Archéologie d'une vallée des îles Marquises: Sites anciens et histoire de Hane à Va-Huka.* Paris: Editions de la Société des Océanistes, 1971.

LINTON, R. "Archaeology of the Marquesas Islands." *Bulletin of the Bernice Pauahi Bishop Museum* (Honolulu), no. 23, 1925.

———. *The Material Culture of the Marquesas Islands.* Memoirs of the Bernice Pauahi Bishop Museum, no. 8. Honolulu, 1923. Reprint. New York: Kraus Thompson Organization.

SINOTO, Y. H. "An Archaeologically Based Assessment of the Marquesas Islands as a Dispersal Center in East Polynesia." In GREEN, KELLY 1970 (F).

———. "A Tentative Prehistoric Cultural Sequence in the Northern Marquesas Islands, French Polynesia." *Journal of the Polynesian Society* 75 (1966).

SUGGS, R. C. "The Archaeology of Nuku Hiva, Marquesas Islands, French Polynesia." *Anthropological Papers of the American Museum of Natural History* 49, pt. 1 (1961).

### (d) Easter Island

HEYERDAHL, T., and FERDON, E. N., JR. *Archaeology of Easter Island.* Reports of the Norwegian Archaeological Expedition to Easter Island and the East Pacific. Albuquerque: University of New Mexico, 1961. Rev. ed. (2 vols.). Chicago: Rand McNally, 1962–66.

LAVACHERY, H. "Archéologie de l'île de Pâques: le site d'Auakena." *Journal de la Société des Océanistes* 10 (1954).

METRAUX, A. "Easter Island Sanctuaries: Analytic and Comparative Study." *Etnologiska Studier*, no. 5, 1937.

ROUTLEDGE, S. "Survey of the Village and Carved Rocks of Orongo, Easter Island." *Journal of the Royal Anthropological Institute of Great Britain and Ireland* 50 (1920).

### (e) Other Archipelagoes

BELLWOOD, P. "Archaeology on Rarotonga and Aitutaki, Cook Islands: A Preliminary Report." *Journal of the Polynesian Society* 78 (1969).

BUCK, P. H. "Arts and Crafts of the Cook Islands." *Bulletin of the Bernice Pauahi Bishop Museum* (Honolulu), no. 179, 1944.

———. *Arts and Crafts of Hawaii.* Bernice Pauahi Bishop Museum, Special Publications, no. 45. Honolulu, 1957.

———. "Samoan Material Culture." *Bulletin of the Bernice Pauahi Bishop Museum* (Honolulu), no. 75, 1930.

DAVIDSON, J. M. "Settlement Patterns in Samoa Before 1840." *Journal of the Polynesian Society* 78 (1969).

EMORY, K. P., and SINOTO, Y. H. "Eastern Polynesian Burials at Maupiti." *Journal of the Polynesian Society* 73, (1964).

EYDE, D. B. "On Tikopia Social Space." *Bijdragen tot de Taal-, Land- en Volkenkunde* 125, (1969).

FIRTH, R. *We the Tikopia.* London: George Allen and Unwin, 1936. 2d ed., 1957.

GARANGER, J. "Recherches archéologiques à Rangiroa, archipel des Tuamotu." *Journal de la Société des Océanistes* 22 (1966).

GIFFORD, E. W. "Tongan Society." *Bulletin of the Bernice Pauahi Bishop Museum* (Honolulu), no. 61, 1929.

KRÄMER, A. *Die Samoa Inseln.* 2 vols. Stuttgart: E. Schweizerbart (E. Nägele), 1902–3.

MEAD, M. "Social Organization of Manua (Samoa)." *Bulletin of the Bernice Pauahi Bishop Museum* (Honolulu), no. 76, 1930.

PARK, J. "A Consideration of the Tikopia 'Sacred Tale'." *Journal of the Polynesian Society* 82 (1973).

SEURAT, L. G. "Les Marae des îles orientales de l'archipel des Tuamotu." *Anthropologie* 16 (1905).

VERIN, P. "Les Vestiges archéologiques de Rurutu (Iles Australes, Polynésie Française)." *Journal de la Société des Océanistes* 20 (1964).

*Wallis et Futuna. Journal de la Société des Océanistes* 19, special number (1963).

## (J)  NORTH AMERICA

BUSHNELL, G. H. S. *The First Americans: The Pre-Columbian Civilizations.* New York: McGraw-Hill, 1968.

CATLIN, G. *Illustrations of the Manners, Customs and Condition of the North Indians.* 5th ed. 2 vols. London: H. G. Bohn, 1845.

CERAM, C. W. *Der erste Amerikaner: Das Rätsel des vor-Kolumbischen Indianers.* Reinbeck: Rowohlt, 1971. Translation. *The First American: A Study of North American Archaeology.* New York: Harcourt Brace Jovanovich, 1971.

DOCKSTADER, F. J. *Indian Art in America: The Arts and Crafts of the North American Indian.* Greenwich, Conn.: New York Graphic Society, 1968.

EWERS, J. C. *Artists of the Old West.* New York: Doubleday, 1973.

FEDER, N. *American Indian Art.* New York: Harry N. Abrams, 1971.

HODGE, F. W., ed. *Handbook of American Indians North of Mexico.* 2 vols. Bureau of American Ethnology, Bulletin no. 30. Washington, D. C., 1907–10.

MORGAN, L. H. *Houses and House-Life of the American Aborigines.* U.S. Geographical and Geological Survey of the Rocky Mountain Region: Contributions to North American Ethnology, vol. 4. Washington, D.C., 1881.

MÜLLER, W. *Die Blaue Hütte: Zum Sinnbild der Perle bei nordamerikanischen Indianer.* Wiesbaden: F. Steiner, 1954.

OWEN, R. C., DEETZ, J. J. F., and FISCHER, A. D. *The North American Indians: A Sourcebook.* New York: Macmillan, 1967.

SARFERT, E. "Haus und Dorf bei den Eingeborenen Nordamerikas." *Archiv für Anthropologie* (Brunswick) 35 (1909).

WATERMAN, T. T. "The Architecture of the American Indians." In Kroeber, A. L., and Waterman, T. T. *Sourcebook in Anthropology.* New York, 1931. Rev. ed. New York: Johnson Reprint Corp. (Harcourt Brace Jovanovich).

———. "North American Indian Dwellings." In *Annual Report of the Smithsonian Institution.* Washington, D. C., 1925.

WILLEY, G. R., ed. *Prehistoric Settlement Patterns in the New World*. New York: Wenner-Gren Foundation for Anthropological Research, 1956.

*(a) Pueblo and Navaho Indians*

BUNZEL, R. L. "Introduction to Zuñi Ceremonialism." In *Bureau of American Ethnology, Annual Report No. 47*. Washington, D. C., 1929/30.

DIXON, K. A. *Hidden House: A Cliff Ruin in Sycamore Canyon, Central Arizona*. Flagstaff: Museum of Northern Arizona, 1956.

DUTTON, B. P., ed. *Indians of the Southwest*. Santa Fe: Museum of New Mexico, 1963.

EGGAN, F. *Social Organization of the Western Pueblos*. Chicago: University of Chicago Press, 1950.

ERDOES, R. *The Pueblo Indians*. New York: Funk & Wagnalls, 1968.

FEWKES, J. W. "The Cave Dwellings of the Old and New Worlds." In *Annual Report of the Smithsonian Institution*. Washington, D. C., 1910.

FORDE, C. D. "Ethnography of the Yuma Indians." *University of California Publications in American Archaeology and Ethnology* 28 (1931).

———. "Hopi Agriculture and Land Ownership." *Journal of the Royal Anthropological Institute of Great Britain and Ireland* 61 (1931).

———. "The Hopi and Yuma: Flood Farmers in the North American Desert." In FORDE 1934 (A).

LANGE, C. H. *Cochiti: A New Mexico Pueblo*. Austin: University of Texas Press, 1959.

LOWIE, R. H. "Notes on Hopi Clans." *Anthropological Papers of the American Museum of Natural History* 33, pt. 6 (1929).

MILLS, G. *Navaho Art and Culture*. Colorado Springs, Colo.: Taylor Museum, 1959.

MINDELEFF, C. "Navaho Houses." In *Bureau of American Ethnology, Annual Report No. 17*. Washington, D. C., 1900/1901.

MINDELEFF, V. "A Study of Pueblo Architecture: Tusayan and Cibola." In *Bureau of American Ethnology, Annual Report No. 8*. Washington, D.C., 1891.

PEPPER, G. H. "Pueblo Bonito." *Anthropological Papers of the American Museum of Natural History* 27 (1920).

RAPOPORT, A. "The Pueblo and the Hogan: A Cross-Cultural Comparison of Two Responses to an Environment." In OLIVER 1969 (A).

REED, E. K. "Types of Village-Plan Layouts in the Southwest." In WILLEY 1956 (J).

SEBAG, L. *L'Invention du monde chez les Indiens pueblos*. Paris: Maspero, 1971.

SEDGWICK, W. T. *Acoma, the Sky City: A Study in Pueblo History and Civilization*. Cambridge, Mass.: Harvard University Press, 1926.

STUBBS, S. A. *A Bird's-Eye View of the Pueblos: Ground Plans of the Indian Villages of New Mexico and Arizona with Aerial Photographs and Scale Drawings*. Norman: University of Oklahoma Press, 1950.

TALAYESVA, C. *Sun Chief: The Autobiography of a Hopi Indian*. New Haven: Yale University Press, 1942.

WATSON, D. *Cliff Palace: The Story of an Ancient City*. Ann Arbor: n. pub., 1940.

WHITE, L. A. *The Pueblo of Sia (The Sia Indians, New Mexico)*. Washington, D. C.: US Government Printing Office, 1962.

WHORF, B. L. "Linguistic Factors in the Terminology of Hopi Architecture." *International Journal of American Linguistics* 19 (1953).

*(b) Northwest Indians*

ANDREWS, R. W. *Indian Primitive*. Seattle: Superior Publishing Co., 1960.

BARBEAU, M. "Totem Pole: A Recent Native Art of the Northwest Coast of America." In *Annual Report of the Smithsonian Institution*. Washington, D. C., 1931.

BARNETT, H. G. "The Nature of the Potlatch." *American Anthropologist* 40 (1938).

BOAS, F. "The Decorative Art of the Indians of the North Pacific Coast of America." *Bulletin of the American Museum of Natural History* 9 (1897). Reprinted in BOAS 1955 (A).

DRUCKER, P. *Indians of the Northwest Coast*. New York: McGraw-Hill, 1955. Reprint. New York: Doubleday, Natural History Press, 1963.

———. *The Northern and Central Nootkan Tribes*. Bureau of American Ethnology, Bulletin no. 144. Washington, D. C., 1951.

DRUCKER, P., and HEIZER, R. F. *To Make My Name Good: A Re-examination of the Southern Kwakiutl Potlatch*. Berkeley: University of California Press, 1967.

EMMONS, G. "The Whale House of the Chilkat." *Anthropological Papers of the American Museum of Natural History* 19, pt. 1 (1916).

FORDE, C. D. "The Nootka, Kwakiutl and Other Peoples of British Columbia." In FORDE 1934 (A).

FRASER, D. "Haida of the Pacific Northwest." In FRASER 1968 (A).

HOLM, B. *Northwest Coast Indian Art: An Analysis of Form*. Seattle: University of Washington Press, 1965.

INVERARITY, R. B. *Art of the Northwest Coast Indians*. Berkeley and Los Angeles: University of California Press, 1950.

KRIEGER, H. W. "Indian Villages of Southeast Alaska." In *Annual Report of the Smithsonian Institution*. Washington, D. C., 1927.

WATERMAN, T. T. *Native Houses of Western North America*. Museum of the American Indian, Heye Foundation, Indian Notes and Monographs, Misc. 11. New York, 1921.

*(c) Other Populations*

BUSHNELL, D. I. *Native Villages and Village Sites East of the Mississippi*. Bureau of American Ethnology, Bulletin no. 69. Washington, D. C., 1919.

———. "The Origin and Various Types of Mounds in Eastern United States." *Proceedings of the 19th International Congress of Americanists*. Washington, D. C., 1917.

———. *Villages of the Algonquian, Siouan and Caddoan Tribes West of the Mississippi*." Bureau of American Ethnology, Bulletin no. 77. Washington, D.C., 1922.

DORSEY, G. A. *The Arapaho Sun Dance: The Ceremony of the Offering Lodge*. Field Museum of Natural History, Anthropological Series, no. 4. Chicago, 1903. Reprint. New York: Kraus-Thomson, n.d.

———. *The Cheyenne*. Field Museum of Natural History, Anthropological Series, no. 9. Chicago, 1905.

DORSEY, J. O. "Camp Circles of the Siouan Tribes." *American Anthropologist*, 1889.

FORDE, C. D. "The Blackfoot: Buffalo Hunters of the North American Plains." In FORDE 1934 (A).

———. "The Paiute: Collectors in the Great Basin." In FORDE 1934 (A).

FRASER, D. "Cheyenne Indians." In FRASER 1968 (A).

GRIFFIN, J. B., ed. *Archaeology of the Eastern United States*. Chicago: University of Chicago Press, 1952.

GRINNELL, G. B. *The Cheyenne Indians: Their History and Ways of Life*. 2 vols. New Haven: Yale University Press, 1923.

HEWITT, J. N. B. "Iroquoian Cosmology." In *Bureau of American Ethnology, Annual Report No. 21*. Washington, D.C., 1903.

KROEBER, A. L. *Handbook of the Indians of California*. Bureau of American Ethnology, Bulletin no. 78. Washington, D.C., 1925.

LAUBIN, R. and G. *The Indian Tipi*. Norman: University of Oklahoma Press, 1957.

LONGACRE, W. A., and AYRES, J. E. "Archaeological Lessons from an Apache Wickiup." In Binford, S. R. and L. R., eds. *New Perspectives in Archaeology*. Chicago: Aldine, 1968.

MÜLLER, W. *Glauben und Denken der Sioux: zur Gestalt archäischer Weltbilder*. Berlin: D. Reiner, 1970.

———. *Die Religionen der Waldlandindianer Nordamerikas*. Berlin: D. Reiner, 1956.

ROSE, F. G. *The Indian and the Horse*. Norman: University of Oklahoma Press, 1955.

SHETRONE, H. C. *The Mound Builders*. New York: Appleton, 1930.

SILVERBERG, R. *Mound Builders of Ancient America: The Archaeology of a Myth*. Greenwich, Conn.: New York Graphic Society, 1970.

SPECK, F. G. *A Study of the Delaware Indian Big House Ceremony*. Publications of the Pennsylvania Historical Commission, no. 2. Harrisburg, 1931.

SQUIER, E. G., and DAVIS, E. H. *Ancient Monuments of the Mississippi Valley: Comprising the Results of Extensive Original Survey and Explorations*. Washington, D.C., 1848.

SWANTON, J. R. *The Indians of the Southeastern United States*. Bureau of American Ethnology, Bulletin no. 137. Washington, D.C., 1946. Reprint. Westport, Conn.: Greenwood Press, n.d.

(K) CENTRAL AND SOUTH AMERICA

BANNER, H. "O Indio Kayapó em seu acampamento." *Boletim do Museu Paraense Emilio Goeldi* (Belem), n.s., Antropologia, no. 13, 1961.

Biocca, E. *Mondo Yanoama*. Bari: De Donato, 1969.

———. *Viaggi tra gli Indi*. 4 vols. Rome: Consiglio Nazionale delle Ricerche, 1965.

Dietschy, H. "Männerhäuser, heilige Pfahl und Männerplatz bei den Karaja-Indianern Zentral-brasiliens." *Anthropos* 55 (1962).

Fernandes, F. "A análise funcionalista da guerra: possibilitades de apliçao á sociedade tupinamba." *Revista do Museu Paulista* (São Paulo) 3 (1949).

Forde, C. D. "The Boro of the Western Amazon Forest." In Forde 1934 (A).

Guyot, M. *Les Mythes chez les Selk'nam et les Yamana de la Terre de Feu*. Paris: Institut d'Ethnologie, 1968.

James, A. G. "Village Arrangement and Social Organization Among Some Amazon Tribes." Ph. D. dissertation, Columbia University, New York, 1949.

Lévi-Strauss, C. *Tristes Tropiques*. Paris, 1955. Translation. *Tristes Tropiques: A Study of Tribal Society on the Amazon*. New York: Atheneum, 1964.

———. "La Vie familiale et sociale des Indiens Nambikwara." *Journal de la Société des Américanistes* 37 (1948).

Lizot, J. "Les Yanomami: économie ou société?" *Journal de la Société des Américanistes* 60 (1971).

Palavecino, E. "Tipos de tienda usados por los aborigenes sudamericanos." In *Proceedings of the 23rd International Congress of Americanists (New York, 1928)*. New York, 1930.

———. "Von der Pilagá-Indianern im Norden Argentiniens." *Anthropos* 28 (1933).

Reichel-Dolmatoff, G. *Desana: Simbolismo de los Indios Tukano de Vaupés*. Bogotá: Universidad de los Andes, 1968.

Rodríguez-Lamus, L. R. *Arquitectura indigena: los Tukano*. Bogotá, 1966.

———. "La arquitectura de los Tukano." *Revista Colombiana de Antropologia* 7 (1958).

Serrano, A. *Los aborigines argentinos*. Buenos Aires: Editorial Nova. 1947.

Soustelle, G. *Tequila: un village nahuatl du Mexique oriental*. Paris: Institut d'Ethnologie, 1958.

Steward, J. H., ed. *Handbook of South American Indians*. 7 vols. Bureau of American Ethnology, Bulletin no. 143. Washington, D.C., 1946–59.

## (L) AFRICA (GENERAL)

*Africa. Edilizia Moderna*, nos. 89, 90, special numbers (1967).

Bascom, W. R. "Urbanism As a Traditional African Pattern." *Sociological Review* (University of Keele) 7 (1959).

Davidson, B. *The Africans: An Entry to Cultural History*. London: Longmans, 1969. Also as *The African Genius: An Introduction to African Cultural and Social History*. Boston: Atlantic Monthly Press, 1970.

Frobenius, L. *Das unbekannte Afrika*. Munich: C. H. Beck, 1923.

Glück, J. F. "Afrikanische Architektur." *Tribus*, n.f., 6 (1956).

Goody, J. *Technology: Tradition and the State in Africa*. London: Oxford University Press, 1971.

Labouret, H. "Afrique occidentale et équatoriale." In *L'Habitation indigène* 1931 (A).

Leiris, M., and Delange, J. *Afrique noire: la création plastique*. Paris: Gallimard, 1967. Translation. *African Art*. New York: Golden Press, 1968.

Leuzinger, E. *Afrika: Kunst der Negervölker*. Baden-Baden: Holle Verlag, 1959. Translation. *Africa: The Art of the Negro Peoples*. 2d ed. New York: Crown, 1967.

Mallows, E. W. "Gli schemi di insediamento pre-europei a sud del Sahara." In *Africa* 1967 (L).

Oliver, P. *Shelter in Africa*. New York: Praeger, 1971.

Prussin, L. "An Introduction to Indigenous African Architecture." *Journal of the Society of Architectural Historians* 33 (1974).

Randles, W. G. L. "Pre-colonial Urbanization in Africa South of the Equator." In Ucko, Tringham, Dimbleby 1972 (A).

Schachtzabel, A. *Die Siedlungsverhältnisse der Bantu-Neger*. Leiden: E. J. Brill, 1911.

Tempels, P. *La Philosophie bantoue*. Paris: Présence Africaine, 1969.

*Villes africaines*. Cahiers d'Etudes Africaines 13, special number (1973).

Walton, J. *African Village*. Pretoria: J. L. Van Schaik, 1956.

———. "Patterned Walling in African Folk Building." *Journal of African History* 1 (1960).

Wieschhoff, A. "Afrikanische Architekturen." *Mitteilungen des Forschung-Instituts für Kulturmorphologie* 7 (1935).

## (M) NORTH AFRICA

Andrews, P. A. "Tents of the Tekna, Southwest Morocco." In Oliver 1971 (L).

Bataillon, C. et al. *Nomades et nomadisme au Sahara*. Paris: UNESCO, 1963.

Bernard, A. *Enquête sur l'habitation rurale des indigènes de l'Algérie*. Algiers: Imprimerie Orientale Fontana Frères, 1921.

———. *Enquête sur l'habitation rurale des indigènes de la Tunisie*. Tunis: J. Barlier, 1924.

Bernard, A., and Lacroix, N. *L'Evolution du nomadisme en Algérie*. Algiers: A. Jourdan; Paris: A. Challamel, 1906.

Borg, A. "L'Habitat à Tozeur." *Cahiers des Arts et Techniques d'Afrique du Nord* 5 (1959).

Claver, M. "Fabrication de toiles de tentes." *Bulletin de Liaison Saharienne* 4 (1953).

Despois, J. *Le Djébel Nefousa (Tripolitaine)*. Paris: Larose, 1935.

Etherton, D. "Algerian Oases." In Oliver 1971 (L).

Faulée Urban, M. "Sceaux de Magasins Collectifs." *Journal de la Société des Africanistes* 25 (1955).

Hicks, D. "The Architecture of the High Atlas Mountains." *Arena* (London) 82 (1966).

Jacques-Meunié, D. *Architectures et habitats du Dadès, Maroc présaharien*. Paris: C. Klincksieck, 1962.

———. *Greniers-Citadelles au Maroc*. Paris: Arts et Métiers Graphiques, 1951.

———. "Les Oasis des Lektaoua et des Mehamid." *Hespéris*, 1947.

Jacques-Meunié, D., and Meunié, J. "Abbar, Cité royale du Tafilalt (Maroc présaharien)." *Hespéris*, 1959.

Laoust, E. *L'Habitation chez les transhumants du Maroc central*. Institut des Hautes Etudes Marocaines, Collection Hespéris, 6. Paris: Librairie Larose, 1935.

———. "L'Habitation chez les transhumants du Maroc central: L'irherm." *Hespéris*, 1934.

Lozach, J. and Hug, G. *L'Habitat rurale en Egypte*. Cairo: Institut Français d'Archéologie Orientale, 1930.

Martin, A. G. P. *A la frontière du Maroc: les Oasis sahariennes (Gourara, Touat, Tidikelt)*. Algiers: Edition de l'Imprimerie Algérienne, 1908.

Maunier, R. *La Construction collective de la maison en Kabylie*. Paris: Institut d'Ethnologie, 1926.

Meunié, D. J. See Jacques-Meunié, D., above.

Montagne, R. *Villages et kasbas berbères; Tableau de la vie sociale des Berbères sédentaires dans le sud du Maroc*. Paris: F. Alcan, 1930.

Mosseri, V. M., and Audebeau Bey, C. *Les Constructions rurales en Egypte*. Cairo: Institut Français d'Archéologie Orientale, 1921.

Pâques, V. *L'Arbre cosmique dans la pensée populaire et dans la vie quotidienne du nord-ouest africain*. Paris: Institut d'Ethnologie, 1964.

———. "Le Belier cosmique: son rôle dans les structures humaines et territoriales du Fezzan." *Journal de la Société des Africanistes* 26 (1956).

Paris, A. *Documents d'architecture berbère, Sud de Marrakech*. Paris: Larose, 1925.

Peltier, F. and Arin, F. "Les Modes d'habitation chez les 'Djabaliya' du Sud tunisien." *Revue du Monde Musulman* 16 (1909).

Scarin, E. "Insediamenti e tipi di dimore." In *Il Sahara italiano, Fezzàn e oasi di Gat*. Rome: Società Geografica Italiana, 1937.

———. *L'insediamento umano nella Libia occidentale*. Verona: Mondadori, 1940.

———. *Le oasi del Fezzàn*. Bologna: Zanichelli, 1934.

———. "Tipi indigeni di insediamento umano e loro distribuzione nella Tripolitania settentrionale." In *Atti del I Congresso di Studi Coloniali*. Florence: L. S. Olschki, 1931.

Terrasse, H. *Kasbas berbères de l'Atlas et des oasis; Les grandes Architectures du sud-marocain*. Paris: Horizons de France, 1938.

Verity, P. "Kababish Nomads of Northern Sudan." In Oliver 1971 (L).

Wenzel, M. *House Decoration in Nubia*. London: Duckworth, 1972.

365

## (N) EAST AFRICA

BROOKE, C. "The Rural Village in the Ethiopian Highlands." *Geographical Review* (New York) 49 (1959).

CALCIATI, C. and BRACCIANI, L. *Nel paese dei Cunama.* Milano: Società Editrice "Unitas," 1927.

CERBELLA, G. *Aspetti etnografici della casa in Etiopia.* Rome: Istituto Italiano per l'Africa, 1963.

CIPRIANI, L. *Abitazioni indigene dell'Africa Orientale Italiana.* Naples: Edizioni della Mostra Missione Napoli, 1940.

EVANS-PRITCHARD, E. E. *The Nuer.* London: Oxford University Press, 1940.

FORDE, C. D. "The Masai: Cattle Herders on the East African Plateau." In FORDE 1934 (A).

GEBREMEDHIN, N. "Some Traditional Types of Housing in Ethiopia." In OLIVER 1971 (L).

LEBEL, P. "On Guragé Architecture." *Journal of Ethiopian Studies* 7 (1969).

LEWIS, I. M. *A Pastoral Democracy: A Study of Pastoralism and Politics Among the Northern Somali.* London: Oxford University Press, 1961.

ROBBINS, L. H. "Turkana Material Culture Viewed from an Archaeological Perspective." *World Archaeology* 5 (1973).

TROWELL, M., and WACHSMAN, K. P. *Tribal Crafts of Uganda.* London: Oxford University Press, 1953.

WOODBURN, J. C.: Ecology, Nomadic Movement and the Composition of the Local Group Among Hunters and Gatherers: An East African Example and Its Implications." In UCKO, TRINGHAM, DIMBLEBY 1972 (A).

## (O) WEST AFRICA

BAKARI, K. "L'Afrique occidentale pré-coloniale et le fait urbain." *Présence Africaine* 22 (1958).

CLARK, J. D. "Mobility and Settlement Patterns in Sub-Saharan Africa: A Comparison of Late Prehistoric Hunter-Gatherers and Early Agricultural Occupation Units." In UCKO, TRINGHAM, DIMBLEBY 1972 (A).

DAVID, N. "The Fulani Compound and the Archaeologist." *World Archaeology* 3 (1971).

DIETERLEN, C. "Mythe et organisation sociale au Sudan Français." *Journal de la Société des Africanistes* 25 (1955).

———. "Mythe et organisation sociale en Afrique Occidentale." *Journal de la Société des Africanistes* 29 (1959).

FORDE, C. D., and KABERRY, P. *West African Kingdoms in the Nineteenth Century.* London: Oxford University Press, 1967.

FROELICH, J. C. "The Architecture of Islam in West Africa." *African Arts* 1 (1968).

GARDI, R. *Auch im Lehmhaus lässt sich's leben.* Berne: René Gardi, 1973. Also as *Architecture sans architectes.* Berne: René Gardi, 1974.

HASELBERGER, H. *Bautraditionen der Westafrikanischen Negerkulturen.* Vienna: Herder, 1964.

LE MOAL, G. "Les Habitations semi-souterraines en Afrique de l'Ouest." *Journal de la Société des Africanistes* 30 (1960).

MORTON-WILLIAMS, P. "Some Factors in the Location, Growth and Survival of Towns in West Africa." In UCKO, TRINGHAM, DIMBLEBY 1972 (A).

POSNANSKY, M. "Aspects of Early West African Trade." *World Archaeology* 5 (1973).

PRUSSIN, L. "Contribution à l'étude du cadre historique de la technologie de la construction dans l'ouest africain." *Journal de la Société des Africanistes* 40 (1970).

———. "Sudanese Architecture and the Manding." *African Arts* 3 (1970).

### (a) Mauretania and Mali

BRASSEUR, G. *Les Etablissements humains au Mali.* Mémoires de l'Institut Français de l'Afrique Noire, no. 83. Dakar, 1968.

CALAME-GRIAULE, G. "Notes sur l'habitation du plateau central nigérien (région de Bandiagara)." *Bulletin de l'Institut Français de l'Afrique Noire,* ser. B, vol. 17 (1955).

DIETERLEN, G. "La Serrure et sa clé (Dogon, Mali)." *Echanges et Communications* 1 (1970).

DUCHEMIN, G. J. "A propos des décorations murales de Oualata." *Bulletin de l'Institut Français de l'Afrique Noire,* ser. B, vol. 12 (1950).

DU PUIGAUDEAU, O. "Contribution à l'étude du symbolisme dans le décor mural et l'artisanat de Walata." *Bulletin de l'Institut Français de l'Afrique Noire,* ser. B, vol. 19 (1957).

ENGESTROM, T. "Wall Decorations of the Oualata Type at Bamako." *Ethnos* (Stockholm) 20 (1956).

FROELICH, J. C. "Niani, ancienne capitale de l'Empire du Mali." *Recherches Africaines* (Conakry), n. s., 1, 1969.

GRIAULE, M. *Dieu d'eau.* Paris: Editions du Chêne, 1949. Reprint. Paris: Fayard, 1966. Translation. *Conversations with Ogotemmêli: An Introduction to Dogon Ideas.* London: Oxford University Press, 1965.

———. *Masques Dogons.* Paris: Institut d'Ethnologie, 1938. 2d ed., 1963.

GRIAULE, M., and DIETERLEN, G. *Le Renard pâle.* Paris: Institut d'Ethnologie, 1965.

HAMET, I. "Villes sahariennes." *Revue du Monde Musulman* 19 (1912).

JACQUES-MEUNIÉ, D. *Cités anciennes de Mauritanie, provinces du Tagant et du Hodh.* Paris: C. Klincksieck, 1961.

———. "Cités caravannières de Mauritanie: Tichite et Oualata." *Journal de la Société des Africanistes* 27 (1957).

MINER, H. *The Primitive City of Timbuctoo.* Princeton, N. J.: Princeton University Press, 1953.

LEIRIS, M. "Faîtes de case des rives du Bani, bassin du Niger." *Minotaure* 2 (1933).

MEILLASSOUX, C., with contributions by M. P. Ferry and G. Dieterlen. "Les cérémonies septennales du Kamablò de Kaaba (Mali), 5–10 avril 1968." *Journal de la Société des Africanistes* 38 (1968).

MEUNIÉ, D. J. See JACQUES-MEUNIÉ, D., above.

MONTEIL, C. *Une cité soudanaise: Djenné, métropole du delta central du Niger.* Paris: Société des éditions géographiques, maritimes et coloniales, 1932.

N'DIAYE, F. "Contribution à l'étude de l'architecture du pays dogon." *Objets et Mondes* 12 (1972).

PALAU MARTI, M. *Les Dogon.* Paris: Presses Universitaires Françaises, 1957.

PÂQUES 1964 (M).

### (b) Upper Volta, Niger, and Chad

BERNUS, S. *Particularismes ethniques en milieu urbain: l'exemple de Niamey.* Paris: Institut d'Ethnologie, 1969.

CAPRON, J. "Univers religieux et cohésion interne dans les communautés villageoises Bwa traditionnelles." *Africa* 32 (1962).

DUPUIS, A., and ECHARD, N. "La poterie traditionnelle hausa de l'Ader." *Journal de la Société des Africanistes* 41 (1971).

GRIAULE, M., and LEBEUF, J.-P. "Fouilles dans la région du Tchad." *Journal de la Société des Africanistes* 18 (1948); 20 (1950); 21 (1951).

IZARD, M. "La Formation de Ouahigouya." *Journal de la Société des Africanistes* 41 (1971).

———. "Introduction à l'histoire des royaumes Mossi. 2 vols. Recherches Voltaiques. Paris: Centre National de la Recherche Scientifique, 1970.

———. *Traditions historiques des villages du Yaténga, I. Cercle de Gourcy.* Recherches Voltaiques. Paris: Centre National de la Recherche Scientifique, 1965.

LEBEUF, A. "Boum Massénia, capitale de l'ancien royaume du Baguirmi." *Journal de la Société des Africanistes* 37 (1967).

———. *Les Principautés Kotoko: Essai sur le caractère sacré de l'autorité.* Etudes et Documents de l'Institut d'Ethnologie. Paris: Centre National de la Recherche Scientifique, 1969.

NICOLAS, G. "Fondements magico-religieux du pouvoir politique au sein de la principauté hausa du Gobir." *Journal de la Société des Africanistes* 39 (1969).

PÂQUES, V. "Origines et caractères du pouvoir royal au Baguirmi." *Journal de la Société des Africanistes* 37 (1967).

SCHWEEGER-HEFEL, A. and M. "L'Art Nioniosi." *Journal de la Société des Africanistes* 36 (1966).

URVOY, Y. "L'Art dans le territoire du Niger: Niamey." *Etudes Nigériennes* 2 (1955).

### (c) Ivory Coast, Guinea, Sierra Leone, and Senegal

APPIA, B. "Les forgerons de Fouta-Djallon." *Journal de la Société des Africanistes* 35 (1965).

CREAC'H, P. "Notes sur l'art décoratif architectural foula du Haut Fouta-Djallon." In *Comptes Rendus de la 1ère Conférence Internationale des Africanistes de l'Ouest (Dakar, 1945).* Paris, 1951.

GESSAIN, M. "Note sur les Badyaranké (Guinée, Guinée Portugaise et Sénégal)." *Journal de la Société des Africanistes* 28 (1958).

HOLAS, B. *L'Image du monde Bete.* Paris: Presses Universitaires Françaises, 1968.

KANE, E. R. "La Disposition des cases de femmes dans le carré du mari commun." *Bulletin de l'Institut Français de l'Afrique Noire* 26 (1945).

LITTLE, K. L. "The Mende Farming Household." *Sociological Review* (University of Keele) 40 (1948).
———. *The Mende of Sierra Leone: A West African People in Transition.* New York: Humanities Press, 1967.
MEILLASSOUX, C. *Anthropologie économique des Gouro du Côte d'Ivoire.* Paris: Mouton, 1964.
———. "Plans d'anciennes fortifications (*Tata*) en pays Malinké." *Journal de la Société des Africanistes* 36 (1966).
PELISSIER, P. *Les Paysans du Sénégal.* St.-Yrieix (Haute-Vienne): Imprimerie Fabrèque, 1966.
POUJADE, J. *Les Cases décorées d'un chef du Fouta-Djallon.* Paris: Gautier-Villars, 1948.
SIDDLE, D. J. "War-Towns in Sierra Leone: A Study in Social Change." *Africa* 38 (1968).
TEXEIRA DE MOTA, A., and VENTIM NEVES, M. G. *A Habitacão indígena na Guiné portuguésa.* Bissau: Centro de Estudos da Guiné Portuguesa, 1948.
THOMAS, L. V. "Pour une systématique de l'habitat Diola." *Bulletin de l'Institut Français de l'Afrique Noire* ser. B, vol. 26 (1964).

*(d) Ghana*

ABRAMS, C., BODIANSKY, V., and KOENIGSBERGER, O. *Report on Housing in the Gold Coast.* United Nations, 1956.
ARCHER, I. "Nabdam Compounds, Northern Ghana." In OLIVER 1971 (L).
BENNETH, G. "Small-scale Farming Systems in Ghana." *Africa* 43 (1973).
HUNTER, J. M. "The Clans of Nangodi: A Geographical Study of the Territorial Basis of Authority in a Traditional State of the West African Savanna (Northern Ghana)." *Africa* 38 (1968).
MUMTAZ, B. "Villages on the Black Volta." In OLIVER 1969 (A).
PRUSSIN, L. *Architecture in Northern Ghana: A Study in Forms and Functions.* Berkeley and Los Angeles: University of California Press, 1969.
———. *Villages in Northern Ghana.* New York, 1966.
RUTTER, A. F. "Ashanti Vernacular Architecture." In OLIVER 1971 (L).
SWITHENBANK, M. *Ashanti Fetish Houses.* Accra: Ghana University Press, 1969.
WILLS, J. B., ed. *Agriculture and Land Use in Ghana.* London: Oxford University Press, 1962.

*(e) Togo, Dahomey, and Nigeria*

BASCOM, W. R. "Some Aspects of Yoruba Urbanism." *American Anthropologist* 64 (1962).
———. "Urbanization Among the Yoruba." *American Journal of Sociology* 60 (1955).
BEIER, H. U. "Sacred Yoruba Architecture." *Nigeria Magazine*, no. 64, 1960.
———. *The Story of Sacred Wood Carvings from a Small Yoruba Town. Nigeria Magazine*, special number (1957).
BOHANNAN, L. and P. *The Tiv of Central Nigeria.* International African Institute Ethnographic Survey of Africa: West Africa 8. London, 1953.

CAMPBELL, M. J. "The Walls of a City." *Nigeria Magazine*, no. 60, 1959.
CHADWICK, E. R. "Wall Decorations of Ibo Houses." *The Nigerian Field* 6 (1931).
CROWDER, M. "Decorative Architecture of Nigeria." *West African Review* (Liverpool) 25 (1954).
———. "The Decorative Architecture of Northern Nigeria: Indigenous Culture Expressed in Hausa Craftsmanship." *African World*, February, 1956.
DALDY, A. F. *Temporary Buildings in Northern Nigeria.* Lagos, 1945.
DANBY, M. "Ganvié, Dahomey." In OLIVER 1971 (L).
FEILBERG, C. G. "Remarks on Some Nigerian House Types." *Folk* 1 (1959).
FORDE, C. D. "The Yoruba and Boloki: Hoc Cultivators in the African Forests." In FORDE 1934 (A).
FOYLE, A. M. "House in Benin." *Nigeria Magazine*, no. 42, 1953.
———. "Some Aspects of Nigerian Architecture." *Man* 53 (1953).
FRASER, D. "Yoruba, Nigeria." In FRASER 1968 (A).
GOODWIN, A. J. H. "Archaeology and Benin Architecture." *Journal of the Historical Society of Nigeria* 1 (1957).
GREEN, M. M. *Ibo Village Affairs: Chiefly with Reference to the Village of Umueke Agbaja.* New York: Frank Case, 1964.
KIRK-GREENE, A. "Decorated Houses in Zaria." *Nigeria Magazine*, no. 68, 1961.
LALLEMAND, D., and ISSIFOU, A. H. "Un rite agraire chez les Kotokoli du Nord Togo: la Fête Suwa." *Journal de la Société des Africanistes* 37 (1967).
MABOGUNJE, A. L. *Urbanization in Nigeria.* London: London University Press, 1968.
———. *Yoruba Towns.* Ibadan: Ibadan University Press, 1962.
MERCIER, P. "L'Habitation à l'étage de l'Atakora." *Etudes Dahoméennes* 11 (1954).
MOORE, G. and BEIER, U. "Mbari Houses." *Nigeria Magazine*, no. 49, 1956.
MORGAN, W. B. "The Grassland Towns of the Eastern Region of Nigeria." *Transactions and Papers of the Institute of British Geographers* 23 (1957).
MOUCHTIN, J. C. "The Traditional Settlements of the Hausa People." *Town Planning Review* (Liverpool), 1964.
MURRAY, K. C. "Arts and Crafts of Nigeria: Their Past and Future." *Africa* 14 (1943).
NADEL, S. F. *A Black Byzantium: The Kingdom of Nupe in Nigeria.* London: University of London Press, 1942.
NICOLAS, G. "Essai sur les structures fondamentales de l'espace dans la cosmologie hausa." *Journal de la Société des Africanistes* 36 (1966).
OJO, G. J. *Yoruba Culture: A Geographical Analysis.* London: University of London Press, 1966.
———. *Yoruba Palaces.* London: University of London Press, 1966.
PALAU MARTI, M. "Notes sur les rois de Dasa (Daho-

mey, A. O. F.)." *Journal de la Société des Africanistes* 27 (1957).
———. *Le Roi-Dieu au Bénin, Sud Togo, Dahomey, Nigéria Occidentale.* Paris: Berger-Levrault, 1964.
SCHWERDTFEGER, F. W. "Housing in Zaria." In OLIVER 1971 (L).
———. "Urban Settlement Patterns in Northern Nigeria (Hausaland)." In UCKO, TRINGHAM, DIMBLEBY 1972 (A).
THOMAS, N. W. "Decorative Arts Among the Edo-speaking Peoples of Nigeria: Pt. 1, Decoration of Buildings." *Man* 10 (1910).
WATERLOT, E. G. *Les Bas-Reliefs des bâtiments royaux d'Abomey (Dahomey).* Paris: Institut d'Ethnologie, 1926.

*(f) Cameroon*

BÉGUIN, J.-P. *L'Habitat au Cameroun: Présentation des principaux types d'habitat.* Paris: Office de la recherche scientifique d'Outre-mer, 1952.
BINET, J., "L'Habitation dans la subdivision de Foumbot." *Etudes Camerounaises* 3 (1950).
DUGAST, I. "L'Habitation chez les Ndiki du Cameroun." *Journal de la Société des Africanistes* 10 (1940).
FROELICH, J. C. "Le Commandement et l'organisation sociale chez les Fali du Nord-Cameroun." *Etudes Camerounaises* 9 (1956).
HURAULT, J. "Essai de synthèse du système social des Bamiléké." *Africa* 40 (1970).
ITTMAN, J., "Das Haus der Kosi in Kamerun." *Afrika und Übersee* 44 (1960).
LEBEUF, A. and J.-P. "Monuments symboliques du palais royal de Logone-Birni (Nord-Cameroun)." *Journal de la Société des Africanistes* 25 (1955).
LEBEUF, J.-P. *L'Habitation des Fali, montagnards du Cameroun septentrional: Technologie, sociologie, mythologie, symbolisme.* Paris: Hachette, 1961.
LEVIN, M. D. "House Form and Social Structure in Bakosi." In OLIVER 1971 (L).
MALZY, P. "Quelques villages fali du Tinguelin, Nord-Cameroun, région de la Bénoué." *Etudes Camerounaises* 9 (1956).
TARDITS, C. "Panneaux sculptés bamoun." *Objets et Mondes* 2 (1962).


(P) CENTRAL AFRICA

BALANDIER, G. "Problèmes économiques et problèmes politiques au niveau du village Fang." *Bulletin de l'Institut d'Etudes Centrafricaines* 1 (1950).
BALANDIER, G., and PAUVERT, J.-C. *Les villages gabonais: aspects démographiques, économiques, sociologiques; projets de modernisation.* Mémoires de l'Institut d'Etudes Centrafricaines, no. 5. Brazzaville, 1952.
BAUMANN, H. *Steinbauten und Steingräber in Angola.* Beiträge zur Kolonial-Forschung, Tagungsband 1. Berlin, 1943.
BIEBUYCK, D. "Fondements de l'organisation politique des Lunda du Mwaantayaav en territoire de Kapanga." *Zaire* 11 (1957).

DECORSE, J. "L'Habitation et le village au Congo et au Chari." *Anthropologie* 16 (1905).

FRASER, D. "Mbuti Pygmies." In FRASER 1968 (A).

LEBEUF, A. M.-D., "Aspects de la royauté Batéké (Moyen-Congo)." In *Selected Papers of the Fifth International Congress of Anthropological and Ethnological Sciences* (*Philadelphia, 1956*). Philadelphia: University of Pennsylvania, 1960.

MARGARIDO, A. "La Capitale de l'Empire Lunda: un urbanisme politique." *Annales des Economies, Sociétés, Civilisations* 25 (1970).

MCKENNEY, M. G. "The Social Structure of the Nyakyusa: A Reevaluation." *Africa* 40 (1973).

MOLET, L. "Aspects de l'organisation du monde des Ngbandi (Afrique Centrale)." *Journal de la Société des Africanistes* 41 (1971).

RAPONDA-WALKER, A., and SILLANS, R. *Rites et croyances des peuples du Gabon: Essai sur les pratiques religieuses d'autrefois et d'aujourd'hui*. Paris: Présence Africaine, 1962. Also as RAPONDA, A. *Rites et croyances des peuples du Gabon*. New York: Panther House Ltd., n.d.

REYNOLDS, B. "Kwandu Settlement: Isolation, Integration and Mobility Among a South-Central African People." In UCKO, TRINGHAM, DIMBLEBY 1972 (A).

RICHARDS, A. I. "Huts and Hut-building Among the Bemba." *Man* 50 (1950).

TURNER, H. W. "The Spatial Separation of Generations in Ndembu Village Structure." *Africa* 25 (1955).

WOODBURN, J. *Hunters and Gatherers: The Material Culture of the Nomadic Hadza*. London: British Museum Publications, 1970.

## (Q) SOUTH AFRICA

BIERMANN, B. "Indlu: The Domed Dwelling of the Zulu." In OLIVER 1971 (L).

BRUWER, J. "The Composition of a Cewa Village (Mudzi)," *African Studies* (Johannesburg) 8 (1949).

FORDE, C. D. "The Bushmen: Hunters in the Kalahari Desert." In FORDE 1934 (A).

FRASER, D. "Bushmen." In FRASER 1968 (A).

KUPER, H. "The Architecture of Swaziland." *Architectural Review* 100 (1946).

MARSHALL, L. "!Kung Bushman Bands." *Africa* 30 (1960).

MITCHELL, J. C. *The Yalo Village*. Manchester: Manchester University Press, 1956.

MTHAWANJI, R. "Urbanization in Malawi." In OLIVER 1971 (L).

SCHEBESTA, P. "Die Zimbabwe-Kultur in Afrika." *Anthropos* 21 (1925).

VAN VELSEN, J. *The Politics of Kinship: A Study in Social Manipulation Among the Lakeside Tonga of Nyasaland*. Manchester: Manchester University Press, 1964.

WALTON, J. "South African Peasant Architecture: Nguni Folk Building." *African Studies* (Johannesburg) 8 (1949).

# LIST OF PLATES

376

# PHOTOGRAPH CREDITS

*Numbers refer to plates. Sources for some illustrations taken from books and articles are given in the List of Plates.*

Basel, Museum für Völkerkunde: 235, 236, 247, 248, 285

Bergamo, Tito and Sandro Spini: 369–371, 425, 427, 430, 484

Copenhagen, Nationalmuseet: 289

Hamburg, Museum für Völkerkunde: 323, 324, 327

Honolulu, Bernice P. Bishop Museum: 295–297, 300, 305–308

Marseille en Beauvaisis (Oise), Frank Christol, Fontaine-Lavaganne: 365, 368

Milan, Alessandro Gogna: 210–218

New York, American Museum of Natural History: 5, 101, 197, 199, 333, 335–337

New York, New York Public Library, Picture Collection: 102

Paris, Phototèque, Musée de l'Homme: 1–4, 6–12, 14–32, 34–38, 45–51, 53–55, 57–59, 69–73, 75, 76, 100, 104–106, 108, 110–112, 116–125, 131–133, 139–149, 152, 153, 159, 160, 169–172, 174–179, 181, 190, 193, 205–209, 219, 222–230, 233, 238, 240–244, 246, 251–258, 260–262, 264, 265, 267–273, 277–279, 280, 281, 283, 284, 286–288, 290, 298, 301–303, 309–317, 319–321, 326, 328, 340, 346, 348, 350, 361–363, 367, 372, 385–387, 389–392, 394–402, 406–421, 423, 424, 426, 428, 429, 433, 435–438, 450, 453, 457–461, 464, 467, 468, 470–480, 482, 483, 485, 486

Paris, Collection Roger Viollet: 33, 282, 481

Pretoria, Department of Information: 157

Rome, Ettore Biocca: 83–85, 87–96

Vatican City, Archivio Fotografico, Gallerie e Musei Vaticani: 200, 231, 232, 245, 263

Victoria, B.C., Provincial Archives: 330–332, 334, 339, 343, 344, 347, 349, 351, 356–358